The New York
CO-OP BIBLE

Also by Sylvia Shapiro

The Co-op Bible

The New York CO-OP BIBLE

Everything You Need to Know
About Co-ops and Condos:
Getting In, Staying In,
Surviving, Thriving

REVISED EDITION

Sylvia Shapiro

Thomas Dunne Books ⁂ St. Martin's Griffin
New York

THOMAS DUNNE BOOKS.
An imprint of St. Martin's Press.

www.stmartins.com

Library of Congress Cataloging-in-Publication Data

Shapiro, Sylvia.
The New York co-op bible : everything you need to know about co-ops and condos: getting in, staying in, surviving, thriving / Sylvia Shapiro.
p. cm.
Rev., enl. ed. of: The co-op and condo bible. 1st St. Martin's Griffin ed. New York: St. Martin's Griffin, 1998.
ISBN 0-312-34075-3
EAN 978-0312-34075-9
1. Apartment houses, Cooperative. 2. Condominiums. 3. Apartment houses, Cooperative—New York (State)—New York. 4. Condominiums—New York (State)—New York. I. Title: Co-op bible. II. Title: Everything you need to know about co-ops and condos. III. Shapiro, Sylvia. Co-op bible. IV. Title.

HD7287.72.U6S49 2005
643'.27—dc22

2004066058

D 12 11 10 9 8 7 6 5 4

In memory of my father,
whose sense of humor inspired this book,
and for my mother, whose spirit guided it to completion

Contents

Introduction to the Revised Edition

It's amazing what unexpected consequences an unintended book can have. As I explained in the introduction to the first edition, this wasn't a book I ever planned to write. I became an "expert" in co-ops and condos by chance and necessity when my own building converted and someone had to take the reins. No sooner did *The Co-op Bible* appear than my phone started to ring: Do I have to let the board onto my terrace to fix the roof? Can I get the phone numbers of fellow shareholders to mount a proxy contest? How can we get the sponsor to give up control? What can I do if the board refuses to add me to the proprietary lease even though I've been living here for twenty years? How do I get the board to give me information about the money it's spending? What can I do about my dog?

Board members also weighed in. Is it okay to approve sublets based on the shareholders we like? How much can we charge in renovation fees? Can we circulate our board minutes directly to owners instead of preparing a newsletter? Do we have to provide election results to unsuccessful candidates for office? Can I use the information I get as a director to buy apartments on the cheap? Should we exercise our right of first refusal?

When real emergencies threatened, I made house calls. In one building where the board had replaced the lobby decor more often than J. Lo has switched husbands, shareholders wanted to know what they could do to stop the redecorating—and the assessments. In another building, directors were tainted by the real estate assessors' scandal, and a new slate wanted advice on how to take control of the situation.

I met with prospective purchasers, shareholders, and board members at seminars and lectures; I listened to what they had to say and heard what they wanted to know, and have incorporated their suggestions. Many of you asked, How can I find that case mentioned about illegal sublets or flip taxes (or whatever topic was dear to your heart), so I have included a list of the decisions referred to throughout the book in endnotes at the back of this revised edition, though I caution all you civilians not to play lawyer.

A lot has happened since the first edition of this book came out. Co-op boards have accumulated more power than ever. Condo boards are trying to usurp some of the powers traditionally reserved for their co-op cousins. Sponsors have had their comeuppance and may not be able to stick around so long. Shareholders have gotten some relief from boards that tax them to death. Apartment prices have shot up and building finances have been hard hit. The new, improved *New York Co-op Bible* incorporates all the latest developments that you need to know in order to answer the most important questions:

- How do I prepare my application so the board says yes?
- What are the rules if the building has only a right of first refusal?
- If I don't go through with that condo contract, can the seller keep my deposit? What if the building is a co-op?
- Is that renovation fee the board charges a reasonable fine or an unenforceable penalty?
- Can I keep my dog even if the co-op has a "No Pet" policy? What if I live in a condo?
- Can my condo board impose a flip tax? Prohibit subletting?
- Can the sponsor continue to hold on to apartments (and control), or does it have to sell apartments as they become vacant and cede power to shareholders?
- Are the sublet fees the board charges legal?
- Can I be held personally liable if someone gets injured in the common area of my condo? What about in a co-op?
- Can the board evict me if they don't like the way I behave?

You will find the updated answers to these and all the other questions you need resolved so you can buy and live smart in the regime of your choice. *The New York Co-op Bible* gives you the straight talk on every aspect of co-op and condo living, from conception to departure—and in between.

Many of you used this book to help you through your apartment quest and ameliorate the angst of your encounter with the board, figuring once you passed the gauntlet, you'd done your duty and had all the information you needed. I urge you to reconsider that short-sighted strategy—and to get your money's worth from this volume. For most of us, our apartment represents the biggest single amount of money we'll ever plunk down, and the bundle of cash it takes to become an owner has only gotten fatter in the time since the first edition came out. In my own building, prices have nearly doubled. You wouldn't relegate the fate of your investments even to a professional money manager without paying attention to what she's doing, and you should do no less in assuring proper oversight of your co-op or condo after you're in, especially given their unique management structure.

As you probably know, this sui generis system puts unpaid volunteers in charge of multimillion-dollar enterprises and grants them the legal power to carry out that role, but it neither requires them to have the requisite expertise nor provides them with the depth of management necessary to fulfill their mandate. Based on all I've heard from you, and on my own extended tenure, I'm convinced the time has come to do something about it. To that end, chapter 19 proposes a revised model of co-op and condo governance. Since this book first appeared, courts have granted boards ever greater authority: chapter 10 addresses the growing power divide. And in case you decide to really take control of your residential destiny, chapter 17 tells you what you need to know to join the ruling ranks.

I remain at the helm of my building's board, which I guess qualifies me for sainthood—or a sanitarium. I can report that board members and shareholders continue to coexist in relative peace and harmony, which is not to say that we haven't had an occasional controversy. Not long ago, we almost came to a clash of wills when someone decided it was time to redecorate the corridors; unfortunately, rather than present the suggestion to the board via a letter or phone call, which is standard operating procedure in my building, he embarked on a preemptive strike. In the stealth of night, the secret campaigner slipped petitions under every shareholder's door (save those of the directors), allowing the mastermind to retain his anonymity while requiring all those he had incited to identify themselves in the name of his cause. We communicated directly with our constituents, even tried to arrange a meeting by leaving a memo on the bulletin board to "Deep Throat." (This response elicited criticism from one shareholder who, more familiar with Linda Lovelace than with Watergate, took us to task for our pornographic posting!) The whole episode died down as quickly as it had been stirred up, without the instigator ever having been unmasked. Clearly, he hadn't read *The Co-op Bible*, because he violated two central tenets for successful shareholder action: Don't up the ante if you don't have to, and don't act anonymously.

We've also had our share of boardroom drama over the past year, occasioned by the change in our managing agent. After what you might call a healthy airing of our philosophical differences, things seem to have returned to relative normalcy. Even so, now that I've experienced up close and personal some of the problems inherent in the present system of governance, I'm more convinced than ever that change is in order.

I know the common wisdom is that being board president is a thankless task, but I think it's more like participating in a real-life novel: you never know what's going to happen next. Certainly I didn't expect that call from the doorman at 7 A.M. on New Year's Day.

"Peter, do you know what time it is?" I asked as I stumbled out of bed and toward the buzzer.

"I'm sorry," the voice came back, "but I didn't know what to do."

"About what?" I demanded.

"The lady from apartment X—she came down in the elevator to the lobby with nothing on."

"Nothing at all?"

"Not a stitch."

"Well, what did you do?" I asked, now that I'd been shocked to attention.

"I gave her my coat."

Good to know that there are still a few gentlemen left, I thought as I made my way down to the lobby to help devise a more permanent solution to our resident nude.

I hope this new edition of *The New York Co-op Bible* will impart to you the lessons I have learned in my continuing education so that whether you choose to be a member of the rank and file or part of the ruling elite, you will live wisely and well.

1

Which Regime Is Right for You?

EVERY CLOUD HAS A SILVER LINING

I know what you're thinking: You should have bought five years ago; ten would have been even better. Then for a couple of hundred thousand dollars (which almost anywhere else on earth would buy baronial splendor), you could have gotten more than a closet (otherwise known as a studio). When this book first appeared, the bull market in apartments was in the early stages of a relentless rise. Everywhere I went, people asked, "Should I buy now—or wait?" I took out my crystal ball, but alas it was cloudy. Coulda, shoulda, woulda—I say, forget about it and focus on the here and now. Market timing in co-ops and condos is no more reliable than the stock market.

So look on the bright side, and at all the catastrophes averted in the interim. You missed the opportunity to join Gwyneth Paltrow, Calvin Klein, and all those other A-list celebs who stampeded to buy into Richard Meier's downtown architectural wonder before it broke ground, and who, now that it's above ground, are all warring with each other. You didn't have to pay the stratospheric real estate taxes that we owners have been hit with over the past few years. And hopefully, you've had a chance to save a bundle while waiting on the sidelines.

Over the long haul, knowing what to look for (and the pitfalls to avoid) makes the difference. If you follow *The Co-op Bible*'s lessons, you will learn how to buy smart. Then, if a downturn comes, your apartment will retain its value while others slump—and perhaps more important, you will have found your residential soul mate. But first you need to know which way to go.

PHILOSOPHICAL DIVIDE

No apartment is an island unto itself. Whether co-op or condo, you're not just buying a place to call home, you're joining a political regime. Before you start pounding the pavement, you ought to do some serious soul-searching. Do you subscribe to the Three Musketeers School of Government—all for one, one for all, prepared to link your fortune (and fate) with your fellow apartment mates? Then co-op may be the way to go. Or are you cut from the Marlboro Man mold—determined to go your own way, free from the ties that bind to communal ownerkind? Then condo may be right for you. Although the apartments you view may be deceptively similar in appearance (whether cavernous lofts or pristine penthouses), they can mask fundamentally different worldviews. That's why buying an apartment is a mind and (out of) body experience. In preparation for the task you need a little philosophical tutoring to be sure that both your inner and outer selves make the right choice. This chapter gives you straight talk on the great co-op/condo debate—what does each offer and which way of life is best for you—and why "condop" may be the way to go for the philosophically confused.

Unmasking the Truth

So what are you really buying—or, more accurately, buying into? In the case of co-ops, you may be getting that Classic Six (with Riv Vu), but what you are buying (in a legal sense) is not a home, not even a piece of property, but shares in a corporation. The co-op corporation owns the building and (usually) the property outright (what lawyers call *fee simple*). It sells shares to you representing your proportionate ownership in the corporation (the tangible manifestation of which is your apartment). The number of shares you get is a function of the total number outstanding in the corporation and the percent of that total your apartment represents. I am the proud owner of 404 shares in my co-op representing my duplex two-bedroom penthouse with terrace. In another building that same apartment may entitle me to a totally different number of shares. It's not the number but the proportion that counts. Together with those shares, you get a long-term lease (called a *proprietary lease*) from the corporation that entitles you exclusively to occupy those digs you may have thought you were buying outright.

As a result of this arrangement, you have a schizophrenic status. Even though you may have emptied every last piggy bank—and then some—to buy a place of your own, you're still a tenant under the proprietary lease from the co-op corporation, your new landlord. But you're also an owner—of a part interest in the corporation—which gives you a right to a say in the management of the property (through election of directors and exercise of your vote).

In a condo, you're more directly realizing that American dream of having a home of one's own. Although the apartment of your eye may be stacked high in the sky, it's real property—and if you buy it, you'll own it outright (in fee, as they say). In addition to individually owning your own unit, you also get an undivided proportionate interest, together with your fellow dweller-owners, in those common areas that you all traverse (but don't live in)—halls, corridors, lobbies, basement, and the like (they are called *common elements*). As proof of your ownership you get a deed (though not a white picket fence) like your suburban home-owning friends.

The deed describes the unit and your share of the common elements—the better for the taxing authorities to find you out.

And since you own outright you are your own residential lord and master—those days as a lowly tenant forever gone. No need to worry about the confusion caused by divided selves, so you can save some shrink bills and rest assured that your residential sanity will remain intact.

From these different worldviews flow numerous consequences for the institution, and for you, as one of its members.

External Law

Co-ops and condos come into being—and exist—under different legal systems. The basic system of condo life and law in New York State is set out in what is creatively called the Condominium Act.[1] It tells the requirements for establishment of the condo state, the system of taxation, and how and by whom it shall be governed. The act decrees that each condo shall be administered according to its own bylaws and presided over by a board of managers elected by the owners.[2] We'll revisit the act and see what it says in specific contexts later, but for now you can give yourself a pat on the back that you know of its existence. The Constitution serves as the cornerstone of our government and our way of life; if you're planning to buy a condo you should remember that the act will be fundamental to its governance and your existence.

Co-ops don't have a Rule of Law they can call their own. Their form of government is based on a legal pastiche. Because they're corporations, they're formed under New York State's Business Corporation Law and have to abide by its provisions. These include a requirement that the affairs of the corporation shall be run by a board of directors, as well as specific rules for the election and removal of board members and for shareholder participation.[3] But since these provisions, specific though they may be, were passed to suit the needs of Wall Street corporations, not Main Street co-ops, they're not always a perfect fit. So, as we'll see, sometimes we have to look beyond the strictly corporate to real estate or landlord-tenant concepts to get the answers to our questions.

Internal Governance

Taking their lead from the requirements imposed by the law, co-ops and condos set up their own internal form of government. In co-ops the basic system that you'll live under is spelled out in a documentary triumvirate. First, there's what's called the *certificate of incorporation*, which brings the co-op into existence. It sets out the bare essentials for legal life: the name of the co-op; the purpose for its formation; the total number of shares—and since with life comes lawsuits, the name of the agent to be served when (not if) the co-op gets sued (preferably not during your watch). Now that you know what this document is, you can (for most purposes) forget about it (unless you want to sound like a lawyer when co-op small talk comes up at the next cocktail party). What really count in co-op operations are the other two: the *bylaws* and the *proprietary lease*.

The bylaws set out the structure of government: the size and power of the board of directors; the powers and responsibilities of the corporate officers; procedures for the election and removal of corporate officers; procedures for shareholder and board meetings; voting rights and requirements—even procedures for bylaw amendments, which often can be accomplished by shareholder vote or unilateral board action.

If the bylaws establish the form of government, the proprietary lease puts government into everyday action. It is the compact that defines the rights and obligations of shareholders as tenants and the co-op corporation (acting through the board) as landlord. Most of the things you care about (before and after buying) are here for the looking. Want to know what restrictions there are on selling or subleasing? What control the board has over alterations? Who's responsible for repairing what? What limits exist on the use of your apartment? How cash requirements (and your maintenance) are to be determined? What your respective rights are in case you default? The nuts and bolts of the co-op regime are in the lease.

But the nitty-gritty, quality-of-life details (on matters mundane but essential) are in the *House Rules*, which are made part of the lease. Unlike the lease, which in most co-ops takes two-thirds of you shareholders to change, the board can amend the rules on its own—leaving open the possibility of power grabs if you shareholders are not mindful.

Condos have a duo of governing manifestos: the *declaration* and the *bylaws* together establish the entity and set up and activate its government. The declaration delivers the condo into the world as a legal entity. It announces its creation: describing the building and the land on which it sits; the common elements that you'll share; and the individual units that you'll buy, as well as their respective uses—whether residential or professional or commercial. It names the obligatory contact person if anyone wants to sue and sets out the method of amendment, which usually requires a two-thirds vote by owners. But from your perspective, what matters most is that the declaration assigns each apartment a percentage interest in the common elements. While you can forget about the other legal mumbo jumbo, this designation is important because it determines your relative voting rights and financial obligations for common charges and assessments.

As with co-ops, bylaws in condos establish the governmental framework: the size and power of the board of managers; the designation and duties of condo officers; procedures for the selection and removal of condo officers; unit owner voting rights; and procedures for board and unit owner meetings. But unlike co-ops, condo bylaws don't just set up the government, they also regulate its actions and the relationship between you owners and the board of managers. Think of condo bylaws as combining the governmental functions separately served in co-ops by the bylaws *and* the proprietary lease. (Remember, though, a co-op board is your landlord, a condo board is not.) All the fundamental rights and obligations of unit owners are set out in the bylaws. Want to find out the policies of your condo on use restrictions, sales, subleasing, alterations, common charges? Here's the place to go for answers (as we will when we get to these and other specific questions).

Since any change in condo bylaws would alter the essential nature of government, the law says that at least two-thirds of owners have to approve.[4] Because co-op bylaws are more restricted, many co-ops let the board change them on its own. This is an important difference. As you'll see, this means that in order to be valid, fundamental board powers have to be set out in a condo's bylaws, but usually they appear in a co-op's proprietary lease (which can only be amended by shareholders). So as we go forward, don't get confused by the term *bylaws*. It means one thing in co-ops, but something different in condos.

As in co-ops, it's the House Rules that prescribe the regimen of daily living. The Condo Act specifically authorizes their promulgation.[5] Initially put in place by the plan's creator, called the *sponsor*; they can be changed by the board.

Agents or Authoritarians

Given the different legal systems that bring condo and co-op boards into being, it's only natural that they have different foundations for their powers (which we'll explore in chapter 9). But you should have a basic idea of what you're getting into *before* you commit your cash and yourself to the cause. Their names give you a hint. In co-ops, board members take on the directorial mantle—and title—of those bigwigs who sit in corporate boardrooms. In condos, they're more familiarly denominated as managers, descriptively (and, it is hoped, functionally) closer to the people they serve.

It's no accident. Co-op boards get their broad power to manage from the Corporation Law. They don't have to come to the shareholders for most of it. The concept in condos is different. Their boards don't have any law that independently energizes (and empowers) them. Instead, they act as agents for the owners. It's from you, the people, that they ultimately derive their power—a fact that should (but doesn't necessarily) instill some humility. Not only the theories but (as we'll see) the scope of co-op and condo board power differs on such key issues as borrowing and spending, sales and sublets—and more.

United or Independent

It's not just the relationship between you and the board that differs from co-op to condo; so do the ties that bind you and your fellow owners. As a shareholder in a co-op your economic destiny is inextricably intertwined with that of the other owners. Even though you each have individual apartments, you are all co-venturers and part owners in the corporation (in proportion to your respective interests). Each of you is responsible for paying your share of the total co-op expenses (through your monthly maintenance). Together you sink or swim—a scary thought, and one that should color the conduct of your affairs as a shareholder.

The interdependence is great because the communal expenses are mighty. Most co-ops have mega-sized underlying mortgages secured by the property. They also get hit with heavy-duty real estate tax bills covering the entire property. Together these two items (which often amount to millions) can make up significantly more than half of the co-op's expenses. You pay your fair share when you send in those monthly checks. But if someone doesn't pay, the co-op is still responsible, which means all of the remaining shareholders may have to pay more.

In condos, you're a relative financial maverick. It's your credit rating that counts more than your fellow owners'. There is no underlying mortgage because the Condo Act says there can't be one.[6] Any mortgage or lien that may have existed has to be paid before the sponsor sells that first apartment. And while you do pay real estate tax, you go it alone. As owner of your individual piece of property, with its own tax and lot number, your tax bills are sent directly to you, not to the board included in one lump sum for the whole building. In co-ops, if the neighbor down the hall decides to stiff the taxing authorities, his problem may become your problem. But in condos the stiffer's headache stays his own.

Even in condos, you're not entirely free from the masses that surround you. Though you are spared the major shared responsibility of taxes and mortgage debt service, you're still linked with your fellow owners in shouldering the burden of the other (not inconsiderable) expenses of the enterprise—from labor to repairs to maintenance to management. (See chapter 3 for more.)

First or Last

Although the finances of co-op shareholders may be more intertwined than those of condo owners, ultimately it's the latter who may have to pick up the shortfall. In the event of a default and foreclosure by a fellow owner, the co-op takes priority over the lending bank. It's the reverse in condos, where the bank takes priority over the building.[7] This means that the bank would have to pay the co-op any maintenance charges due *before* it could apply sales proceeds to its outstanding loan. In contrast, in these circumstances, condos get only what's left over *after* the bank has been made whole, which more often than not is nothing.

As a buyer, you may find the relative lack of financial scrutiny in condos appealing, but as an owner, it may come back to haunt you if you and your fellow owners (not the bank) end up footing the bill for the defaulter.

Individual or Collective

Depending on whether you buy a co-op or condo, you may be exposing yourself to big-time potential liability. Let's say a visitor slips and falls on the newly polished lobby floor, or a chunk of the roof parapet falls off and injures someone. Now, these are not the kinds of things you're thinking about as you begin your search—and until recently they were not something that had to be on your radar screen, because any damage to an injured party most likely would have come from the building's insurance. That's all changed with a decision that said *individual* condo owners may be held *personally* liable.[8]

A passerby seriously hurt by a piece of fence that fell off the roof of a condo sued, but its $2 million in liability insurance wasn't enough to cover potential damages. A condo itself has no assets, because as we've just seen, owners each own their own apartments and a proportionate share in the common elements. In this case, *you*, not the building, are the would-be deep pockets, along with your fellow owners, and each of you could be liable for a part or *all* of the damages (jointly or severally liable, as lawyers like to say). Shareholders don't face the same risk, because a co-op owns the building, so any uninsured damages could come out of its assets.

All this is the first, not the last, word on the subject, but nonetheless it's a risk you should be aware of going in.

Real or Personal

The nature of what you own is different, depending upon whether you buy in a co-op or condo. To the uninitiated, an apartment is just an apartment. But for those in the know, an apartment can be real or personal—property, that is. Not something you want to lie awake thinking about as visions of fireplaces and French doors dance in your head after a hard day at the hunt. But it is an issue you ought to take notice of (when you are conscious) because it can affect your rights as a buyer and an owner (and, when the time comes, as a seller).

If you buy in a condo, you're getting the real thing. How do you know?

The Condo Act tells you so. It says that each apartment, together with its common interest, constitutes real property for all purposes.[9] Why should you care? Because the law says that sale of real property can't be restrained. This means that condo boards can't control apartment transfers. In most condos, the board has no right to approve or reject purchasers; it has only what's called a right of first refusal. (See chapter 4.) This power vacuum translates to freedom of exchange for you—whether coming in or going out.

But in personal property there is board power. The transfer of a co-op is considered a transaction in personal property, which the law says can be restrained. That's a key reason why co-op boards can (and do) exercise such an iron grip over transfers (and shareholders). But that's not the end of the story. As a co-op owner you get shares in the corporation (which are personal property) and a proprietary lease (which is closer to real property). This indivisible combination of two irreconcilable interests in the co-op raises questions of whether the interest you own in the apartment is personal for all purposes or just some. Not anything you should lose sleep over while in hot pursuit, but something you should tuck away in that gray matter for future use.

The truth is that co-ops are like chameleons. Their characterization as real or personal property changes depending upon which aspect predominates in a particular transaction—a situation that can lead to trouble. Say you're having a will drafted to pass on your place to someone near and dear when you leave these earthly bounds. Better not rely on some general bequest of real or personal property to do the trick, but be sure that will specifically spells out your intent to convey your co-op or those lawyers (and your relatives) could be battling for years after your demise.

Landlord or Tenant

Your own status also is a function of your residential choice. Since you own your apartment outright in a condo, you're your own landlord. In a co-op, even though you're an owner, you're also a tenant (under that proprietary lease) with the co-op (through the board) acting as landlord. Maintaining that underdog status is not without benefits. Lots of laws passed to protect renters from overreaching landlords have come to the rescue of top-dog shareholders because they live under a landlord-tenant relationship. Renters' rights have been applied to protect shareholders' pets from eviction,[10] their roommates from removal,[11] and their premises from uninhabitable conditions.[12] Of course, every silver lining has its cloud, which in this context means that co-op boards get landlords' legal weapons to make shareholders pay pronto.

Though condo owners may live in a similar state of multidwelling madness, they don't rate the same protections because, as the law sees it, they're the bad-guy landlords. This separate and unequal treatment under the law probably is not enough to make you choose one form over another, but you ought to know that different rights come with the respective co-op and condo territories.

Natural or Unnatural

The status of those around you may also differ. Like them or not, in co-ops your fellow shareholders are real people (at least in the biological, if not the sociological, sense). But in condos owners may be legal (though not necessarily natural) persons. The Condo Act permits unit ownership not only by breathing beings but also by bloodless entities such as corporations, partnerships, trusts, and estates.[13] So if that Fortune 500 firm wants a luxury pad back East for its up-and-comer CEO to crash in or if that South American republic needs a home away from home for the head of its diplomatic corps, it usually has no choice but to buy in a condo.

In fact, the tax laws that once defined shareholders so as to limit ownership only to "individuals" now allow ownership by any "person"—which includes legal beings (trusts, estates, partnerships, corporations).[14] While some co-ops (including my own) allow shareholders to transfer their apartments to trusts for estate-planning purposes, many can (and do) close their doors to all but members of the human species. Presumably that's what you are, since you're reading this book. But know that if you buy a condo you could be sharing your space and casting your ownership lot with unnatural beings. Not the sort that almost visited us in *A.I.*, but corporate owners whose occupants are passing through on business, giving the building more a transient than homey feel.

Perception or Reality

Neither co-op nor condo comes cheap (at least not in these parts), but co-ops may appear to purchasers to have the price advantage. To some extent the difference is more illusory than real. Each apartment in a co-op is burdened by its share of the underlying mortgage that covers the whole building. Condos do not have such mortgages. They have to be paid off before apartments are sold. So the price you pay for your apartment includes within it whatever debt there may have been.

If you buy an apartment for $500,000 in a condo, that's the total price for now and forever. If you buy an apartment for $500,000 in a co-op, that's the price you'll pay at closing (and the price your down payment is based on), but it's not really the total price. To figure that out you have to include your share of the building's mortgage debt. So, for example, when I bought as an insider (I'm not saying for how much), our building had a $5.5 million mortgage. My share on a percentage basis is almost $50,000 (not pocket change by any means). This cost is reflected in my monthly maintenance charges, which include my share of the building's mortgage debt service.

The real difference is that in condos you pay the total price up front, while in co-ops you pay most of it up front and the remaining part over time (plus interest) through your maintenance. All of which goes a long way to explain why co-op maintenance charges are usually higher than condo common charges.

More or Less

The flip side of this is that you get bigger tax breaks in co-ops than in condos. In order to put co-op owners on the same tax footing as their home-owning fellow citizens (and voters), those IRS softies allow shareholders to deduct against federal, state, and local income taxes their proportionate share of mortgage payments and real estate taxes incurred by the co-op. (Not to worry: you'll get a year-end statement from the co-op telling you how much this is.) Together, these two items can make 50 percent (or more) of your maintenance payments tax-deductible.

But you can't deduct what you don't pay (unless you want to do a stint in some less-than-comfortable federal lodgings). Since condos have no underlying mortgage, there are no interest payments to deduct. All you can deduct are those real estate taxes you pay directly on your own apartment. Of course, in both co-ops and condos you can deduct the interest you pay on your own apartment's mortgage.

MIXED BREED

Although you may think you're ready for the apartment hunt, you are not yet Master of the Universe. To achieve that singular status, you need to get a grasp of a third, more exotic residential breed called a *condop*—a cross between a condominium and a co-op. Conceived by real estate developers in the laboratory of riches, it has survived (if not multiplied) in the New York apartment jungle. What is this residential mutant? A mixed-use building subdivided into two (or more) condominium units, one of which is owned by a co-op.

Here's how it works. A fifteen-story high-rise has valuable stores and a garage on the ground floor that bring in gushers of money in rental fees—and residential apartments on the remaining fourteen floors. A condo is established for the entire property. Then a co-op corporation is formed and becomes the owner of the residential space (which exists within the condo) and, in turn, sells the apartments to you. Rather than let shareholders share in the wealth generated by the stream of dollars coming from the stores and garage, the sponsor skims the income-producing cream off the top and keeps the commercial condo unit—or sells it to some third party for a mint.

There can be legitimate reasons for this (legal) skimming, most of which benefit the sponsor, not the shareholders. Not only does this arrangement give the sponsor certain tax advantages, it also allows it to cash in on the commercial space without having to fight off claims of "sweetheart" leases. (In converting rentals to co-ops and condos, some sponsors entered into long-term leases for commercial spaces that were way below market rate, an abuse that finally led to the passage of protective legislation.[15] Shareholders got smart about these sweetheart leases and, with the help of the law, challenged these deals as unconscionable—and won.)[16] To get around the law (and still get the benefits), sponsors created the condop. Rather than take back a lease (which deprived shareholders of their fair share of profits on the commercial space), they just take back the whole unit and keep the stores (and cash flow) for themselves (thereby denying shareholders *any* benefit).

In the interests of full disclosure, there can be a shareholder-friendly reason for going the condop route. You have the folks at the IRS to thank for not wanting you to get spoiled by having too much of good thing. You'll remember they said you could deduct your share of the mortgage interest and real estate taxes. As a condition for letting you do that, 80 percent or more of the co-op's income each year has to come from the shareholders (what's called the "80/20 test"). Normally that's no problem; where else is the money coming from? But if the building has ritzy stores that throw off lots of rent, that rent could exceed 20 percent of the co-op's annual income, thereby jeopardizing shareholder tax deductions. Rescuing shareholders from the grip of the IRS is one supposed reason for using a crossbreed, but there are other methods short of mutation that achieve the same result.

Nothing in the building's physical self lets you know that you're dealing with one of these hybrids. (Though if I were you, I'd ask if the building has any stores or other commercial or professional spaces.) Either the broker will tell you, or you'll figure it out as soon as you see the offering plan. It is a breed not to be feared but understood.

Daily existence in a condop is no different from life in a co-op. I know; I live in one. And I'll warrant you that if you asked, most of my fellow shareholders would say they live in a co-op (which they and I do, only it's also part of a condo). Since the two types of units coexist in one building's body, they share common elements (land, foundations, supports) and systems (water, fuel, electricity, labor) and divide the cost, though not always equitably (see the next section). But since they are two distinct legal entities, they have separate boards (I sit on both the co-op's board of directors and the condo's board of managers), separate governments (and governing documents), separate budgets, even separate lot numbers (so those tax bills know where to go).

That's the legal angle—which shouldn't affect you much as a shareholder. (You probably won't even notice the difference.) What you should focus on (before you buy) are the practical consequences of living in a crossbreed.

Share and Share Unalike

In a condop, co-op and condo exist as two selves within one body, and they have to draw life and breath from the same sources. Whether it's electricity to get that AC going, fuel to keep the heat toasty warm, or water to flow where it has to go, in a condop both commercial and residential spaces need life support. The critical question: Does each pay for its fair share of nourishment, or is the commercial unit sucking the co-op dry and taking dollars from shareholders? To find out you should ask to see the condo budget, which breaks out the allocation between the two. Even when you see the numbers, you may not be able to answer this one by yourself. You may need (and it's worth getting) a financial professional to help. The cost allocation between co-op and condo is fixed when the building comes into existence. If the sponsor keeps the commercial space, it may also set its expense share disproportionately low, which means shareholders (including you) will pay more maintenance than they should.

Once the cost split is set, it's hard to change—though not impossible, especially if the board is on the case. We tried without success during our negotiations for an across-the-board rollback in the co-op's allocation. Afterward, we figured (and meter readings confirmed) that those restaurants in the commercial space were using more than their fair share of water. Although we couldn't control the flow, we did reach an agreement with the sponsor to turn the dollar tide back by resetting the numbers. Recently we got a further reduction when it turned out that another water-guzzling commercial tenant wasn't paying its proportionate share. But, as you look for an apartment, don't count on changes in the numbers you see. Whatever the split is now, assume it will be the same in the future. And if it turns out you'll be paying too much more than your fair share, you may want to pass on the deal.

Out of Control

If you're a control freak and care not only who dwells within the building but also who shops there, then buying into a condop may pose a potential problem. It's not the board but the sponsor that decides who should fill the spaces, and its prime interest is finding tenants with cash, not class. This often can mean high rent–paying restaurants. We got some protection by coming to an agreement with our sponsor during the conversion of our building that prohibited certain kinds of operators from making our home theirs. Even more worrisome is when an unknown entity (unconnected with the rest of the building) gobbles up all the commercial space for fun and profit (its, not yours). Its priority may be dollars per square foot, not value to shareholders—which means you could wind up waking to the aroma of Big Macs wafting from the street, braving crowds of OTB junkies out front, or (trying to) sleep to the beat of an all-night club.

Liberal to a Fault

Lots of condops take not only their name but their mind-set from condos. Even though they have the corporate structure of a co-op, they have the laws of a condo: no board approval for sales, no restrictions on sublets, and no minimum financing requirements. Such antiauthoritarian provisions may help the sponsor sell out quick, but they also can leave problems in their wake.

What makes sense for condos doesn't necessarily work for co-ops. Since condo owners are more financially independent, it may be okay for the board to have less control over who joins the body politic and how much they have to contribute (via down payment) to join. But in co-ops you can't disassociate yourself (at least financially) from your fellow shareholders. So, even though you want to be sure they can pay their own way, if the board has no control, it can't.

I tell you this from hard experience. Mine is a condop with condo-style rules on sales and sublets. On more than one occasion the board has been faced with applicants whose finances may not permit them to rent in one of the sponsor's buildings but may allow them to buy because the board can't reject (though it can delay; see chapter 4). And although my condop has been lucky (and hasn't had any mishaps thus far)—as a purchaser you should know that these provisions are a potential problem.

ONLY YOU KNOW FOR SURE

So what's the right way to go? There's not an either/or answer; it's a mixed bag. If ease of getting in and out is a top priority, then condos beat out co-ops. But remember, no matter how much of a hassle (and humiliation) moving in or out may be, most of your time is spent staying put. And if you care who you're surrounded with all the while, the balance shifts back to co-ops.

Lest you reply that co-ops are residential country clubs that keep out any but their own kind, let me assure you that there are sound financial reasons for saying no to many applicants. I see them on a regular basis in reviewing applications. While there are overreaching boards that seek to clone themselves and seem to reject anyone else, most condo boards can reject no one.

So while the social milieu in condos may be more democratic, the proportion of deadbeats also may be higher. Since you have fewer expenses in common with fellow owners in condos than in co-ops, this fact may not be so troubling, but it sure is a trade-off worth thinking about before you buy.

If control of the purse strings is high on your list, condos seem to win. In co-ops, boards usually can spend (and borrow) without limits (and without asking you). In condos, they have to get your permission beyond certain preset limits that vary from building to building. The result: unit owners not only can curtail the cash flow, they can forestall the work. No matter that the roof collapses while they debate and wait—something that almost happened in a condo where the board had a $50,000 spending limit but needed $100,000 to fix the roof and had to get owner approval for the rest.

The way I see it, it's not so much one system of government that's superior to another, but who's doing the governing that matters most. (That response, no doubt you'll say, is the board president in me talking.) As an outsider, getting the true scoop on the board is probably one of the most difficult assignments you'll face. If you ask the board, you'll get the candor of a political incumbent running for re-election. If you ask the seller, don't expect much more. Best to go directly to the hustings and get the unvarnished (but, hopefully, not unpopular) truth from their constituents. To do this, get a few names of insiders (from the broker, seller, doorman). Be creative in your investigative techniques—here's your chance to start honing your sleuthing skills, which I assure you will serve you in good stead once you're on the other side.

THE CHOICE MAY NOT BE YOURS

Just because you know what you want doesn't mean you'll get it. In New York, co-op supply outstrips condo stock by a mile. So even if you decide you're a philosophical freedom fighter—and want to encamp in a condo—you may have to hang up your fatigues or move to practically anywhere else in these United States, where condos abound and co-ops are scarce. Or at least sacrifice your ideal apartment vision for your ideals.

But that's all changing. Lots of people figure that if they can come and go as they please, condos are the place to be (which, as we've seen, ain't necessarily so). To meet that demand, practically every new building for sale since this book first appeared has been a condo. So if you're patient you are more likely to find that apartment of your dreams under a condo roof. But beware! At the same time that buyers are running to win a spot in one of those let-freedom-reign regimes, lots of condo boards are reining in freedoms and following the more authoritarian lead of co-op boards. In one condo I know, the bylaws allowed (and the board imposed) flip taxes, those tithes co-ops often charge when you go to sell (see chapter 18) and sublease rules (chapter 15). So don't assume that the condo you've found is as freedom-loving as you think without first reading its governing manifesto.

Your decision may not be dictated by the laws of supply and demand but by your employer's decree. Many companies condition relocation benefits on your buying a condo so you (meaning they) can get out quick and easy. If you have to move in the future at the company's request, then it assumes the responsibility for selling your place and assures you a certain minimum price. A friend of mine who moved for work from Atlanta to New York had no choice but to buy a condo if she wanted to keep her relocation protection. Since the company will be left holding the bag when the time to sell comes, it doesn't want to get caught up in board battles. It just wants cash on the line, the sooner the better.

Or it may just be you. Not too many co-ops will welcome you with open arms if you're a *People* magazine starlet who brings paparazzi in her wake, or a politico who doesn't travel without scads of bodyguards, or a foreign diplomat here in these United States with immunity and without cash, or even a regular Joe whose credit could use a little platinum luster. If that's the case, better cut to the chase and think condo from the start.

NEW CONDO RISKS

Over the past several years, lots of new condos, many with designer labels and price tags to match, have been invading the skyline. If you're into the next new thing, they may hold allure, but they also come with special risks.

Older buildings that have had years, or decades, to age are like fine (or not so fine) wine: basically, you know what you're getting. But with new buildings it's impossible to tell in advance what kind of vintage they'll be. That's the problem. If you're a risk taker, or a fan of Richard Meier or Frank Gehry or some other trophy architect, you may be tempted to buy from a floor plan while the apartment of your dreams is only a twinkle in the eye. The price of bragging rights for being first on the block (or in the building) is usually a 20 to 25 percent deposit, part paid when you sign the contract, the rest by set dates along the way to completion. The rationale for hefty payments from preconstruction buyers is to protect the developer, who's keeping the apartments off the market for so long. What about you? Suppose your life (or the world) changes in the two or more years between contract and completion: you get married, or divorced, or change jobs, or have to move. Can you get all, or any, of your money back?

Thanks to The Donald, the answer is no. Two billionaire Turkish brothers bought a bundle of penthouses on the top floors at Trump World Tower, so many that they got a $7 million bulk discount and paid only $32 million, for which they put down a deposit of $8 million, 10 percent at signing, the rest over time. Then came September 11, 2001. Tall was scary, not chic. And the name Trump, they said, was now a terrorist target. We want our deposit back, the brothers clamored. The first court said, The Donald gets to keep the 10 percent—that's standard for a default in real estate contracts, but I don't know about the remaining 15 percent. That $4.8 million is a lot of money even for a billionaire. On appeal a higher court said, It may be a lot of money, but the billionaire boys knew what they were getting into, and besides, that's the standard amount for new construction, high-end condos. The Donald got to keep it all.[17] So buy, if you must, from a piece of paper, but not before you seriously consider the risk of loss if you have to pull out. (Also consider that when buying a newly built condo you'll likely have to pay some of the costs normally shouldered by the seller. See chapter 5.)

Even if the building is already standing, you don't know if it will set like a cheesecake that was slowly cooled to smooth perfection or one that has cracks to show from its abrupt trip out of the oven. It could have lousy ventilation or faulty electrical systems or poor waterproofing or structural defects that you don't find out about till after you move in. What's your remedy? Can your new condo board go after the architect or engineer or the construction firm that screwed up? Not necessarily. Although they're the ones that caused the mess, the sponsor—not the condo—is the one that has a contract with them. To you that may not matter, but to the law it does. The answer depends on what that document says or, more accurate, how a court interprets the agreement. There have been lots of fights of late with differing results. Basically, it comes down to this: If the contract makes the condo (or you owners) *intended beneficiaries* of the deal, you may be able to get relief.[18] If it doesn't say anything on the subject—or worse—says the benefits are not assignable to third parties, you're probably out of luck, especially if the sponsor (the only other potential deep pocket) is insolvent.[19]

What all of this means is that if you buy into a new building and there are construction or design defects, your board may have an uphill battle in getting the money back to fix them, and in the interim at least, owners may be assessed to make necessary repairs—not something you ordinarily bargain for when you sign on the dotted line to buy for a set price. A friend of mine bought into a new condo loft in Brooklyn: four years and two sets of attorneys later, the board is still fighting over who's going to fix the leaking brickwork.

The bright spot in this mess is that justice sometimes works in reverse. When a subcontractor who had worked on the common elements of a Tribeca warehouse that was converted to a condo wasn't paid by the developer, he tried to get his money by foreclosing on a mechanic's lien. And when that didn't work because he made a mistake in filing, he tried to recover the balance from the board (and sponsor) of the new building, but the court said no. The owners had already paid for their apartments when they bought them, and shouldn't have to pay any more.[20]

REGIME GUIDE

Don't get nervous if you haven't committed to memory all that you've just learned. To prepare you for what lies ahead here's a travel-size chart to refer to on the road (or the streets) that reduces what you have to know to its bare essentials—enough to prevent you from making any mistakes of consequence. Should you find yourself suffering a memory lapse or in need of a quick philosophical refresher, flip to it for easy reference (and reassurance).

Condo	**Co-op**
1. Getting in is a relative snap	1. May have to hassle with the board
2. Board only has right of first refusal	2. Board (usually) can reject for no (or any) reason
3. Price usually higher since you pay mortgage debt up front	3. Price appears lower but you're taking on a share of building's underlying mortgage
4. Common charges usually lower since they don't include real estate taxes or mortgage payments	4. Maintenance higher because it includes your share of real estate taxes and mortgage payments
5. Get your own homeowner's deed and tax lot	5. Get shares in a corporation and a proprietary lease
6. You're your own lord and master	6. You're a tenant and an owner
7. Property you own is real	7. Property you own is real and personal
8. No underlying mortgage to drag the building (and you) down	8. Underlying mortgage—watch out for its terms
9. Harder to borrow to meet capital needs	9. Easier to get money if building is financially fit
10. Pay your own property taxes	10. Pay your share of building's real estate taxes as part of maintenance

	Condo	Co-op
11.	Comparatively financially independent because shared expenses are fewer	Financially interdependent with your fellow shareholders
12.	Owns the land it sits on (and you own your proportionate undivided share)	Usually owns, but may lease the land it sits on
13.	Board can't spend (or borrow) above set limits without owner approval	Board can spend (and borrow) now and tell shareholders later
14.	Bylaws govern	Bylaws and proprietary lease govern
15.	Board can pass or amend House Rules	Board can pass or amend House Rules
16.	Board often distributes budget in advance	Board usually doesn't hand out budget in advance
17.	Board has to provide annual financial statement	Board has to provide annual financial statement
18.	No renovation without board approval	No renovation without board approval
19.	Generally rent your place out as you please	Board tells you how and when to rent out
20.	Usually sublease without a fee	Subleasing can cost you
21.	Takes second position to bank in collecting arrears	Gets outstanding arrears before bank gets paid back
22.	Potential personal liability for injuries in common areas	No personal liability for injuries in common areas
23.	You can sell without sharing the wealth (flip taxes are rare)	If you sell you may have to share the wealth (if flip tax in place)
24.	Getting out is relatively easy	No exit without approval of your buyer by the board

2

Preparing for the Hunt

GET READY

Once you find your philosophical center, you're ready to proceed in earnest with the search. You can choose the traditional path or opt for more unconventional hunting techniques that may not only yield apartment results but also prepare you to take on the establishment once you become a member of the owner rank and file. This chapter tells you how to winnow through the co-ops and condos out there till you find the one that's right and what questions you need answered to be sure your selection is politically (and emotionally) correct.

For some the hunt is a necessary means to an end—to be endured, not savored. For others, it is an entertaining end in itself, a form of urban archaeology—or sociology—or a little of both. When else do you get to peer into people's private lives and see whether they prefer Louis-Philippe or Philippe Starck, English country or formal French, or their own idiosyncratic eclecticism?

I count myself among the apartment voyeurs. I take walks down brownstone-lined Greenwich Village streets after dark when their brightly illuminated windows offer up interior vistas invisible by day. When my building was in the process of converting to condop, I got the chance to pursue my design affliction in earnest and indoors. We brought in an engineer to take stock of its physical condition, including all of the two-hundred-plus apartments (in the company of a negotiating committee member). While my comrades shunned inspection duty, I saw opportunity and agreed to go on the rounds (all two-hundred-plus). Not only did I gain insight into the people I'd been living among for more than a decade, but that's how I found the penthouse that ultimately became mine.

For those of you who prefer more conventional means of entry to those locked apartment doors, you can link up with one of the Keepers of the Lists (a.k.a. real estate brokers). Within the confines of those pounds of computer printouts they carry lie the vital statistics: address, apartment number, and price for all the apartments in their stock. Now that multiple listings have come to the big city, and brokers have to share new listings within three days, they—and you—should have more apartment inventory instantly at their fingertips.

As you probably know, the broker works for, and gets paid by, the seller.

Six percent of the purchase price is still the normal broker's commission, but like everything else, that amount may be negotiable depending upon the state of the market or how attractive the listing is, especially now that discount (online) brokers have entered the fray. Though the check handed over at the closing is signed by the seller, it is funded by the cash *you* forked over. Let's say you're buying a prime Village one-bedroom for $500,000 or a Soho loft for $1 million. That translates to a $30,000 or $60,000 commission respectively. Just remember, nothing is binding until there's a signed contract. Although you may have shaken hands or even committed your offer to writing, the seller can—and in overheated markets many do—enter into higher-priced deals with someone else, leaving you jilted at the real estate altar.

BEATING THE SYSTEM

Is there a way to beat the system and buy directly from the seller—thereby getting a little advance training in counterestablishment techniques that will help prepare you for life in the co-op and condo trenches? The truth is that these days, the vast majority of transactions are handled by brokers, as I can tell you from having reviewed countless sales packages over more than a decade. Although it's harder than before, depending on your level of risk tolerance and sense of adventure there may still be several alternative paths.

Luck Scouts You Out

The best deal, bar none, requires you to do nothing but be in the right place at the right time. The owner of the building you've been renting in for decades finally decides to cash out, and you can cash in by buying your place for a bargain-basement price. In order to get enough renters to buy to push its plan through, the sponsor usually cuts a deal to sell tenants their apartments at a uniform price per share way below market. That's how I got my penthouse. I never won a bingo game, or even got so much as two numbers right on a lottery ticket, but when Lady Luck finally arrived at my doorstep, I hit the jackpot. The apartment I bought as an insider at conversion, more than a decade ago, is now worth *six times* what I paid for it. (Of course, before I could claim my prize, the tenants' committee—of which I was a member—had to give luck a hand and negotiate for *everyone* in the building the ability to trade rights, not just buy the apartments they lived in. But that's a story for another book.)

Unfortunately, those days are a thing of the past. Most buildings coming to market are newly built condos, not converted rentals. And the handful of conversions out there do not offer the deep 50 percent off-market discounts that used to make insiders salivate.

Self-Help Scouting

It used to be all you needed were some entrepreneurial instincts and a finite universe to succeed on your own. When my building was converting, it appeared at first that there was nothing bigger to be had than my one-bedroom. I figured I'd flip and use the proceeds to buy a larger apartment on the outside.

Since I knew the Village buildings like the back of my hand, I went straight to the source—those standard-bearers who stand guard—and began dispensing good tidings in the name of Andrew Jackson in exchange for a little inside information. The flow unleashed by a few well-placed presidents was amazing. I had doormen waking me with hot tips at seven A.M., calling after me in the street, or cornering me discreetly with informational paybacks. The whole thing got out of hand. When I went to visit a friend at a nearby Fifth Avenue building, I was greeted by the doorman with such effusiveness that I had to do some explaining.

And when that same friend—a creative type, uncomfortable with such crass commercialism—was in the market for a new place, he deputized me to do his dispensing. Alas, by that time the informational well had run dry.

FSBO is the newspaper advertising lingo that lets you know an apartment is For Sale By Owner. Most sellers, though, sign written contracts with brokers giving them an *exclusive right* or an *exclusive agency* to sell their place. Under an exclusive right, which is how most apartments are sold, the seller agrees to act only through the broker he retained for a specified period of time, usually three to six months. (Although that broker can solicit others to help and they may get a cut of the commission.) But if, as a prospective purchaser, you come to the seller on your own (you heard through a friend or someone you met on a date—stranger things have happened) and you want to work out a deal to buy the apartment, he still has to refer your inquiry or offer to the broker. And he has to pay the full (usually) 6 percent commission.

With an exclusive agency, the seller can deal directly with potential buyers not introduced by the original broker—but not with other brokers. Usually the listing broker cobrokes the transaction with the army of agents out there and splits the fee with whomever makes the sale. If the seller finds you on his own (he heard you're looking, he knows you've getting divorced) legally he can sell to you without paying the broker a commission.

But the reality is that most sellers who sign up with the List Keepers don't want to be bothered with unvetted strangers invading their private domains. Whether it's because they believe the pros will get them a better price, lack the entrepreneurial instincts to engage in self-help scouting, or fear some crazy will turn up at their door, the result is the same. Brokers control the stock of most good apartments.

So long as the seller has signed up with a broker he'll probably let his agent do the legwork and pay a commission, which ultimately comes out of the cash you hand over. Unless you can cut a private deal with the seller *before* he's enlisted a broker or answer one of those few "direct from owner" ads, your chances of skirting the system and buying direct from a resident owner are slim.

Direct Hit

Of course you can try buying directly from the sponsor, a route that may not only save you money but allow you entry without board approval (see chapter 5). If the building is newly built or just converted to co-op or condo status, it's easy. Just step up to the sales office and buy from the marketing outfit chosen by the sponsor to promote the plan. There's more flexibility in how they're compensated, and thus potentially more room for price negotiation. Anyway, if you're one of the first in line to buy, the sponsor may give you a break to get the ball rolling.

Even longtime co-ops typically have sponsor-owned apartments—often some of the best. Stories of perpetually young octogenarians living in the poshest apartments on pennies a day as rent-stabilized tenants have achieved the status of New York lore. (In my own building, some of the choicest penthouses are occupied by ninety-five-year-old renters whose health is a constant source of concern.) When the fountain of youth runs dry, these apartments revert to the sponsor, who can offer them on the open market.

An enterprising buyer will not wait for the information to hit the street, but will get an edge over the crowd by directly contacting the sponsor's in-house sales or transfer agent. This way you can kill three birds with one call: get the first crack at a hot apartment, avoid paying a fee, and cut out the need for board approval. The easiest way to find out the identity of the building's sponsor is to ask the doorman. If he doesn't know, he can direct you to the managing agent, who will have the answer. If you prefer library research to street talk, there are plenty of readily available resources in print that match up sponsors with their buildings.[1]

My mother bought direct from the sponsor several years after our building had converted. And when in true New York fashion the unsuccessful competing bidders were so determined to have the apartment that they threatened to sue, I knew she had made a good deal.

Treasure Hunting

If you're a true bargain hunter you may want to try the foreclosure route, though I warn you, this can be a dicey proposition and is not recommended for the uninitiated or faint of heart. Foreclosures take place when a shareholder (or owner) defaults on mortgage payments and the bank can't collect. In order to get its money back, the bank sells the collateral (the apartment) at auction. Basically, the bank wants to be made whole, and to protect itself against a shortfall it bids the total amount it's owed (including expenses). If you outbid the bank (or any other bidders who show up) by a dollar the apartment can be yours—sometimes for a price way below market.

How do you get wind of these deals? Don't expect any high-priced ads (or color brochures) enticing you to visit with Riv Vus, WBFs or triple mint conditions. The only tip you'll get is a bare-bones legally required notice (usually in the trusty *New York Times*) telling you the apartment number, location, and number of shares (or percent interest), and where and when the sale will be held.

There are real risks in going this route, which is why it's mostly real estate pros (cum speculators), not newlyweds, doing the bidding. You buy "as is"—sight unseen and condition unknown—unless you can find out, which is why even for those in the know some advance scouting is necessary. Even though you won't be invited into the apartment, make a visit to the building. (If you know of its reputation because you or a friend already owns an apartment there, you're way ahead of the game.) Pry loose what information you can from the doorman; call the agent; contact the bank doing the selling. Get a judgment and lien search so you can tell if you are not only buying the prior owner's apartment but also taking on his debts. Just as important as the apartment's condition is what—or worse, *who*—is in it. Whether animal, mineral, or vegetable—alive or dead—it's your responsibility (and cost) to get rid of it (or them). If the defaulter hasn't moved his stuff or himself, as the new owner you'll have to get him (and his possessions) out before you can get in—all of which can be an expensive legal exercise. The one and only time a bank foreclosed on an apartment in our building, the board bid and bought (then resold it at a tidy profit) for the co-op. But we knew the ex-owner was long gone. And he asked to remove all that he had left behind (thus saving us the time and trouble).

If your scouting has uncovered enough positive intelligence (or you're willing to take the gamble) and you decide to go for it—just be sure to bring a pile of cash or a certified check equal to 10 percent of the highest price you're willing to pay. No personal checks are accepted and no dispensations are given. When our board sent a representative to bid for the building at auction, the price went a tad above our pre-authorized limit and he had to empty his own wallet to make up the difference.

Assuming you have done your homework, the end result may be worth the headache. Not only can you land an apartment on the cheap, but you may also be exempt from the need for board approval. (See chapter 5.)

FINDING TRUE LOVE

Now that you know how to find it, the real question is: What are you looking for? As for the apartment itself, you're on your own. Some prefer blondes; others, brunettes. You may get turned on by a curvaceous silhouette; for me, it's a sensuous smile. Nothing I say can (or should) change your mind or alter the course of finding your idea of true love. With apartments, as in life, when you find the object of your affection you'll know. It may be luxuriant moldings or a rambling layout that makes your knees buckle. Maybe it's vast space or vaulted height that sends a shiver of delight down your spine. Whatever—only you can tell.

Problem is, even more than people, apartments come with baggage. There's the money issue. Is the building creditworthy or could you get socked with its debts? Only with co-ops and condos, finances are even more complicated (and potentially more harmful). Since your apartment is part of a larger whole, you have to consider the financial well-being of the entire entity and its constituent owners. This is a topic worthy of its own investigation, which we'll look at in the next chapter.

But before money comes affection. Does the building have the right karma? Is your personality in sync with its persona so that when you walk through that door each evening you feel at peace and at one with your fellow owners and your surroundings? I'm not preaching any touchy-feely sixties-style love fest. (I wasn't a hippie back then.) But you need to get enough hard facts to know whether you want to call that co-op or condo—as opposed to the particular apartment—home. This involves checking out the building's mind and body.

The best way to psych out the building's mind-set is to take a look at its policies on both life-defining issues (such a subleasing, flip taxes, and alterations) and more mundane matters (pets, repairs, guests). These will give you a sense of whether you're on the same wavelength, politically and philosophically, as the board—and how much it will cost to live (and leave) the building. We'll revisit each of these issues in detail—I'll even counsel you how to overcome unreasonable rules. But at this stage, if the differences are too great based on your initial investigation, then maybe it's better to break off the relationship before it gets started.

The Color of Money

Before you fall head over heels, better find out if you can afford the object of your desire. That depends not only on the price (which is surely the first question you've asked) but also on what other financial barriers to entry the board has erected. So long as they're uniform standards, uniformly applied, co-op boards can put you to the test.

Passage usually depends in part on how big a pot of money you can fill without going to the bank for a loan. Most co-ops set limits on how much you can borrow to finance the purchase of your place. The numbers vary from zero down and 100 percent financing (if the bank will oblige) to 100 percent down and zero financing. The norm is probably 20 to 25 percent cash—enough to ensure stability without stripping you bare. Still, the hauter the building, the higher the cash requirement. You know you have arrived when you have to tie up your assets and show up at the closing with a bag of money big enough to pay every last dollar in cash.

But for every action there is a reaction. In this case it's the so-called negative pledge loan, which lets you have your status apartment and keep (more of) your cash—to run with the bulls or recreate on the Riviera. The way these work: you go behind the board's back (and its rules) and borrow more from a willing bank than the co-op allows. You may (supposedly) be bound by the board's restrictions, but banks are not. So they lend you the extra money, you preclose and then present the cash at the closing as your savings. In return, you give the bank collateral: cash in a trading account, stock shares in the co-op, certificates of deposit—whatever you and they have agreed on. The board's none the wiser and the building's not been hurt—or so the theory goes. There's not a lot boards can do to prevent these backroom deals. They can ask outright on the purchase application if you're getting excess financing, figuring you won't want to lie outright or condition their consent on your agreeing not to enter into such a deal. But no one has thus far gone to jail and no co-op is known to have sued—yet. The choice is yours.

In addition to regulating how much you have to put down, some co-ops regulate how much you must have left—via net worth requirements. They want to be sure you've socked away enough for safety in case you (or the building) has an emergency. How much is enough? Whatever they say. The amount could be measured as a multiple of your purchase price, let's say two times. (You buy an apartment for $500,000; you need a cool million sitting in the bank.) It could be an absolute number or some other permutation.

Apart from what you already have stashed away, some buildings impose conditions on what you have coming in—via income tests of their own making. No matter that the bank is satisfied with your cash flow (and commits to the loan), the board can (and some do) demand more. It can require that your monthly payments (maintenance and mortgage) make up a lesser percentage of your gross income. The bank is ready to give you the money because your housing costs are just north of 30 percent of your income but the board says no entry unless they're south of 25 percent. It can establish its own income criteria (net or gross) using multipliers, percentages, some combination, or something else.

Since most condo boards have little control over sales, they don't impose such strict financial conditions. Assuming you're financing your purchase, if you pass inspection with the bank (many of which demand 20 percent down) and get a commitment, that's probably all you need (plus the cash to close). A few co-ops (including my own) have followed the free market path of condos and erect no monetary barriers, but they're in the vanguard—and the minority.

The Key to Borrowing

Unless you're so loaded that you're paying all cash, you'll want to be sure that the building makes it easy to borrow. Banks extend loans secured by a pledge of co-op shares and assignment of the proprietary lease. To protect their investment, financial institutions require the board to sign on to what's called a *recognition agreement*, by which the co-op agrees to notify the lender if the shareholder doesn't pay maintenance (so they can pick up the slack and protect their collateral), and recognizes in advance the lender's right in case of default to sell the apartment to a third party approved by the board. Most boards are willing to enter into a so-called "Aztech" recognition agreement that sets out the bank's rights, but a few will not, or will demand their own form, a problem you should know about before you proceed.

The Cost of Departure

Probably the last thing you're thinking about as you gather together those bushels full of money to pay for your apartment purchase is shelling out still more—when you go. But suppression of the true state of affairs, no matter how painful, can cause permanent emotional or economic scarring. That's why you want to know *before* you buy how much it will cost to sell—due to a flip tax or waiver fee. Rare in condos, but all too common in co-ops, their calculation and amount vary widely (as we'll see in chapter 18).

Many take a percent of the price at which you sell. They cut the co-op in right off the top whether or not you make a profit—and even if paying it means increasing your *loss*. I'd also be real nervous about buying into a building where the board has been given carte blanche authority (usually in the lease) to set the amount of any flip tax. A shortfall in revenues or a need for capital improvements could mean a heavy flip tax hit after you're in. While not without some of the same concerns, at least a modest (same) fee for all (which some buildings use) has the benefit of relative certainty. If you're philosophically opposed (as I am), then declare yourself a conscientious objector and move on to fee-liberated territory.

The Price of Admission

You may have to pay coming in by making a contribution of several months' charges to the cash reserve fund. In some buildings, it's not a contribution but a "deposit" that you get back when you leave. My friend had to deposit two months' maintenance when she moved into her co-op. The building gets the use of (and interest on) the money, which is returned when she departs—and replenished by whoever buys her place. Whether long-term loan or outright gift, if there's such a requirement you'll need to have the cash before you can close. So you'd better find out, and figure out, if you can handle these additional amounts. Likely, you'll also have to pay for the privilege of moving in—and out—and the wear and tear they engender, which can set you back $250 to $500 or more, each way.

Fee (or Free) for All

Watch out for other fees, not the sort that will break your bank but those that may dampen your spirit. And more important, there are fees that should warn you that you are about to enter a regimented society ruled by a heavy-handed board. There may be monetary discipline for dogs without a leash, guests without prior approval, bladers rolling through the lobby, baby carriages blocking the entryway. Look in the lease and/or House Rules for these civility enforcement measures and ask to be sure. The more of these fines there are, the more I'd worry. Either the populace needs to be controlled or the board is out of control—neither of which augurs well.

Remaining or Renting Out

Unless you are a couch potato and never stray far from home, I urge you to read the building's sublet rules with care. I can tell you from the requests our board gets that not all the building's shareholders read (or believed) them. Some co-ops have official policies against investors (those who buy to lease, not live) and will reject them right off the bat. If complete sublease freedom is what you're after, you'd better go condo (or those few condo-style co-ops) at the outset—where the regulations are few and the leasing is easy—though, as we'll see, this is changing.

Many co-ops (though fewer than before the crashlet of the late eighties) ban subleasing of any sort, which means if you decide to stray you still have to pay for maintaining that vacant apartment. The majority allow for regulated renting out—usually for one or more years within a set time. (See chapter 15 for the full sublet story.) The questions to ask now are these: How often can you rent out? How long (or short) can your sublease be? And how much will it cost you?

And finally, even if you really never budge from that TV, you still want to know the sublet rules; they'll tell you if your fellow shareholders are like-minded homebodies at heart or globe-trotting hotshots who'll rent out, leaving you surrounded by strangers like a fish out of water.

Alone or Together

If you plan to share your space with a warm and cuddly (but nonhuman) companion, you'd better find out (first) if they're allowed and (second) if they'll be welcome. The answer should be in the lease (co-ops) or bylaws (condos) or House Rules. You may even be asked to identify your pets in your purchase application or get permission for their presence. Although New York is animal-friendly territory, there are lots of buildings that have declared themselves off-limits to pets of any stripe and pursue their prohibition with a doggedness that tells you plenty about the masters of solitude who dwell within.

Should you successfully sneak your poodle past the censors, there may be ways thereafter to avoid the prohibition (see chapter 14), but can you and your pooch find true happiness among such antifriendly constituents? And assuming you are an advocate of equality before the law, you'd better check out those House Rules to see what limits they impose on your pet's liberties—from physical restraint to separate and unequal building transportation. If your investigation turns up anything less than full and fair integration for your four-legged friend, maybe you should look elsewhere.

Occupational Therapy

As we'll see (chapter 15), most co-op leases have provisions limiting who, besides the owner (and his or her immediate family), can live in the apartment. You need to pay attention up front to what they have to say, lest you wind up in need of occupational assistance. Say your hip, rich uncle wants to buy a downtown pad to swing in sometimes and let you live in all the time. Better find out first if the lease says you can. Or perhaps you plan to buy a studio so your toddler's nanny can have a place to stay nearby. Best to know now that you may have to live *with* her, rather than find out after you've purchased and paid (as did one unhappy couple).[2]

Live or Work

It's not only who can live with (or without) you, but what you can do in your apartment that matters. Most of us buy co-ops or condos to call home, but with work only a computer screen away, the line between the two is becoming ever more fluid. If all you want to do is log on to the Internet or let your fingers do the walking on the keyboard, no problem—and no need to think any more about it. On the other hand, if you plan to use your apartment for some more substantial enterprise—an artist's studio, a doctor's office, a babysitting service—you'd better focus up front on the lease (or bylaws). Does it say your apartment may be used for *residential purposes only* or allow you to conduct a *home occupation*, and if the latter, what can (and can't) you do? (For the answer, see chapter 16.)

Succession (Automatic or Problematic)

For most married couples this is a nonissue. The vast majority of co-ops exempt spouse-to-spouse transfers from board approval (whether through death or divorce). The trend of legal developments is to extend these same rights to domestic (but unmarried) life partners. But that doesn't mean all co-ops have done so (whether through oversight or for some other reason, you'll have to decide). My only point is that if this is an issue affecting you, it's best to know before you buy what the lease (and the board) have to say on this so you won't be confronted with trouble down the line.

(Not So) Trivial Pursuits

There are a host of lesser issues—from repairs to appliances to guests—none of which by themselves (or probably even in combination) is a deal breaker for most of us. But these restrictions are good indicators of the moral and political code you'll be living under. The official documents rarely tell the whole story about these kinds of things, so you need to ask. Take repairs. By the letter of their law, in both co-ops and condos *you* are responsible for most repairs inside your apartment, including most electrical work (though the wires are inside the walls)—even for plenty of plumbing problems (if the affected pipe is attached to the sink, not in the wall). (See chapter 8 for the complete lowdown.) And some buildings, including my friend's, interpret this literally, nickeling and diming owners and charging for everything—even replacing a washer. Legal? Absolutely. But it's also a sign of an uptight and mean-spirited authority that likely extends to matters more fundamental. I'd prefer to live in a building where the board is disposed (and the building has the cash) to cut shareholders some slack and engender goodwill in the process.

Aesthetic Aura

You may think I'm nuts (though you've heard nothing yet of my design fetishes), but I decided against buying one apartment because the chandelier in the building's lobby was too hideous to behold. If aesthetics aren't high on your list, you probably won't notice if the lobby decor is Bauhaus or Biedermeier and will care even less. But if these things assume mood-altering proportions for you, you'd better decide before you buy whether you can learn to live with (if not love) the lobby (and hallway) decor—and what they say about the personalities of your fellow owners-to-be. Are they innocent inheritors of the decor disaster? In which case, you may become fast friends united in the common redecoration cause. Or are they the active creators of the design debacle, determined to uphold their aesthetic viewpoint against any would-be deconstructivists? Not a promising indicator.

Personal Makeover

Although you (usually) can't control the look of the public spaces, you can decorate as you will in your private domain. But, as we'll see in chapter 7, whether in co-ops or condos, you can't renovate without board consent. So if you're the type who plans to remake the apartment you buy—or combine and control several units—you need to get an indication of board approval for your plans beforehand. Otherwise, you could find yourself in the position of those prospective purchasers at an Upper East Side co-op who said the seller and broker had given assurances that the board would allow them to build an enclosed terrace to their apartment. After they had signed the contract, they found out that the building was overbuilt and the board wouldn't approve their plans, so they sued, claiming they'd been fraudulently induced to enter the contract. Although the court let stand their complaint, that determination only marked the beginning of the battle.[3] To avoid such an inauspicious beginning, go directly to the source to get written approval for your plans, at least, in concept. Also take a look at the alteration agreement you'll be operating under to be sure there are no insurmountable surprises. That's where you'll find out how much the building may charge for each day of renovation, and how much more it will cost if your project goes overtime. (See chapter 7 for details.)

Just as important, you should find out if the apartment you're buying previously underwent significant alterations. Unless they were done right, you could inherit a headache. One purchaser of a $3 million Park Avenue co-op found out after she signed the contract that the seller had engaged in major renovations without getting all the necessary approvals, a discovery that led to a dispute between the two with return of her $300,000 deposit hanging in the balance.[4]

Clean Bill of Health

Every building is supposed to comply with building and zoning codes, and the Certificate of Occupancy certifies that it does (though plenty of co-ops have less than accurate C of Os). This problem is often overlooked, but especially if you're buying an apartment that was originally designated as a doctor's apartment and office, or one that was previously combined, you or your lawyer had better see what the C of O says or, in the worst-case scenario, you could be confronted with the nightmare of having to change the certificate for the whole co-op (if possible) in order to do work on your own apartment.

Get Physical

Of course, the apartment should grab you, preferably with a gutwrenching intensity that says "Be mine." But it would be a mistake to get so caught up with its singular (apparent) perfection that you ignore the physical aspect of the rest of the entity of which it is but a part. Such examination will either confirm the appearance of the overall robust condition of the building or reveal internal decay that could eventually infect your apartment, diminishing its beauty and value. How do you find out?

Go underground—to the basement, that is. You expect the residential corridors of power to be spit-and-polish clean (if not, make a note), but if the bowels of the building, where the real work gets done, are equally impressive, that's one of the best signs that the building is well kept. Ignore at your own peril signs of Mickey's friends. The problem could be a temporary aberration due to construction outside. But you'd better ask—unless you *want* uninvited cheese-eating visitors. (Trust me, they know how to get from the basement to the penthouse.)

Walk the stairwells, where (in most buildings) few residents (but many other creatures may) tread. Ride the elevators. Not only will they take you where you want to go, they'll also tell you if the building's vertical transport is in need of overhaul (which could cost you big) or expose other unwanted truths. I was hooked on a classy apartment in a lower Fifth Avenue building until I took a trip in the elevator, where I found an extermination list so thick that my interest was terminated.

Walk the halls. Not just the floor where your intended is located but a few others picked at random. I did this in one building only to flee in terror at the number and variety of locks that warned against some unknown danger threatening from beyond (turned out it was a roof-jumping cat burglar).

Visit the laundry room, the compactor room. These will give you a reading on the level of civility and cleanliness of your would-be fellow owners.

Do Your Homework

Apartments don't come with the Good Housekeeping seal of approval. Basically, what you see is what you get in the apartment you're about to buy—and in the building. That's why there's no substitute for due diligence. If you could have found out the true state of affairs on your own, you won't be able to complain later that you didn't know—whether the issue is a faulty certificate of occupancy (publicly on file), an assessment coming down the pike,[5] or a noisy upstairs neighbor. Purchasers of a Soho co-op that was zoned for joint living/work space learned their lesson the hard way, finding out after the fact that their upstairs neighbor used his place as a furniture factory. A lightbulb should have gone off when the board told them at the interview that the owner above was a carpenter who used heavy machines. They figured it couldn't be true and didn't bother to inspect his loft or to read the co-op's minutes (which disclosed that his hammering and chiseling had killed prior deals), and then were stuck with an unlivable apartment.[6]

If there's a whiff of trouble, especially about something that could make or break the deal for you, do your homework *before* you sign the contract. As added protection, your lawyer should try to get as broad as possible a representation from the seller—though, of course, his hired gun will try to narrow it down.

Having done your homework (both on paper and on-site), if you are convinced that mind and body are sound (and compatible with yours), it's time to get down to money. But before you go that next step, better take the tests that follow to see whether you and your residential partner are really made for each other.

ARE YOU COMPATIBLE WITH YOUR CHOSEN?

Is the building an advocate of open enrollment or limited admissions?

- Does the board have discretion to approve or reject your application?
- Is it liberal (or restrictive) in passing on purchase applications—and how long does it make you wait for an answer?
- Or is the board limited to only a right of first refusal? (See chapter 4.)

Does it subscribe to the jet-setter or couch potato theory of subletting?

- How often can you lease out your place?
- What's the maximum (and minimum) length of each lease?
- Do you have to pay to rent?
- How is the sublet fee calculated?

Does it have an open-door (or closed-door) guest policy?

- Who can stay in your apartment with (or without) you?
- For how long?
- Do your sleepovers need board approval?
- Are your extended family members free to come and go as you (and they) please?
- What is the price of noncompliance?

Is it a believer in sharing or keeping your wealth?

- Is there a flip tax (or a waiver fee) when you sell?

- How is it calculated?
- Will you have to pay whether or not you make a profit?

Does it allow (or ban) occupational pursuits?

- Is your apartment limited to residential use?
- Or can you use it for a home occupation?

Is it pet-friendly or pet-phobic?

- Does the building allow pets?
- How many?
- Do they need board approval for entry?
- Are there any size/weight restrictions (for your pets, not you)?
- Are there any rules restricting their freedom once accepted?

Is it an autocratic or a democratic society?

- Can you order in without getting into trouble?
- Can you wash and dry without descending to the lower depths?
- Can you park your perambulator outside your door without getting ticketed?
- What other aspects of your daily existence are regulated by board rules?
- What punishments or fines are inflicted for flouting the law?

Does the building encourage or discourage personal empire building?

- Are there any restrictions on the kinds of apartment renovations allowed?
- Must work be completed within specified time (or seasonal) limits?
- Are there any violations against the building from overzealous renovators that may limit your grand design?
- Will the board approve your plans?
- How much will you have to pay to renovate?

Is it physically fit or out of shape?

- Has the major body conditioning already been done (elevators, windows, roof, repointing)?
- Is the building structurally sound and are its systems (plumbing, electric, gas) A-OK? (You may need outside help for this one.)
- Are there any telltale signs of unwanted visitors?

Is it aesthetically acceptable or intolerable?

- Can you abide the lobby (and corridor) decor?
- If not, are there any plans for change?
- Will they make things better or worse?

SHOULD YOU TIE THE KNOT?

32–38 Points:	You've found your residential soul mate! Get thee to a closing as soon as possible.
26–32 Points:	It may not be true love, but it's a comfortable fit. (Anyway, passion fades, friendship endures.)
20–26 Points:	Maybe you should do some more dating before you decide.
Below 20 Points:	Better go back to the co-op (or condo) meat market.

Tallying the Results

Score one point for each of the above compatibility factors on which you and your chosen see eye to eye.

CAN YOU AFFORD YOUR TRUE LOVE?

Step 1

How much is the apartment?

- What's the asking price? ________
- Are there any seller-motivating factors?
  - Is it a messy divorce?
  - Is it an estate anxious to sell?
  - Is it a relocation company that wants out?
  - Has it been on the market a long time?
  - Is the owner (and his furniture) already out?
  - How much were you able to knock off? (–) ________
- Are there any buyer-motivating factors?
  - Are they contiguous apartments?
  - Are there any unique features (terrace, layout, duplex)?
  - Are there others already bidding?
  - How much will all this cost you? (+) ________

What's the bottom line? ________

Step 2

Is it a good deal?

- What did the last apartment in the line sell for? ________
- Was its condition as good as or better than yours? ________
- What are other comparables in the area going for? ________
- All signals are "Go" if your bottom line is lower.

- What's the monthly maintenance? ________

- What's the maintenance for comparable apartments in neighboring buildings? ______
- How much is the maintenance per square foot (divide maintenance by total square feet)? ______
- Things look great if your maintenance (or, in condos, common charges plus real estate taxes) is lower and not more than $1.25 per square foot. ______

If the answer is "Yes," go for it.
If "No," you decide if love wins out over money.

Step 3

Do you have the cash?

- How much is the down payment? ______
- Does the building impose any cash requirement? ______
- What's the contract balance due at closing? ______
- How much is your lawyer's fee? ______
- What are the bank's closing costs? ______
- Are any fees due your mortgage broker? ______
- For condos, how much mortgage recording tax is due (see chapter 5)? ______
- What (if any) amount of maintenance do you have to prepay? ______
- How much of a cash reserve contribution is there? ______
- How much of an escrow deposit? ______
- What more does the building want (move-in fees, etc.)?
- What's the total hit? ______
- How much cash do you have left? ______
    - Is it enough to buy a Big Mac? ______
    - Is it enough to live in your usual style? ______
    - Is it enough to meet the building's net worth requirements? ______

If "Yes," proceed to Step 4.
If "No," return to Step 1.

Step 4

Can you manage the upkeep?

- What are the monthly charges (condo buyers, include $\frac{1}{12}$ of annual real estate tax)? ______
- How much in assessments per month? ______

- What are your monthly mortgage payments? __________
- What does it all add up to? __________
- Multiply that number by 12. __________
- Is the result less than 33 percent of your yearly gross income? __________

If "Yes," you probably have a green light.
If "No," you may be in trouble.

Step 5

Can you keep up with your other obligations?

- How much do you pay monthly in student loans? __________
- In credit card balances? __________
- In car or other loans? __________
- In alimony to your ex? __________
- What does it all add up to? __________
- Multiply this other debt by 12 and add the total from Step 4 (line 5). __________
- Is the result less than 40 percent of your annual gross income? __________

If "Yes," love and money likely are a match.
If "No," your true love may be too rich for your blood (or at least your pocketbook).

3

Arming Yourself with the Financial Facts

TAKING AIM

Given the difficulty of the hunt and the nature of the human psyche, no sooner does our gaze fix on that perfect pad than we fall in love and become blind to reason. Watch out. Apartments can be as deceptive as mates—good to look at but rotten to the core. Don't get caught up in the beauty-is-skin-deep syndrome. You can dump that guy or gal, but once your apartment illusion is shattered you are left to bear the brunt of the economic fallout, sometimes paying the ultimate price—loss of your dream digs.

For years I coveted a prewar beauty with Juliet balconies and double-height windows and promised myself that when I had piled up enough greenbacks I would call it home. As the time approached, I found out that those already there were fleeing like lemmings because the lease for the land it sat on was running out—threatening to leave the building with no ground under it. I switched my focus to a Gothic treasure with tracery windows and climbing ivy, but with maintenance so high (due to out-of-whack finances) that nobody could sell even with prices slashed. I considered buying into another visual jewel with fireplaces and views of lower Fifth—and, it turned out, a mortgage that could choke the building and its shareholders (and already had done in the sponsor, who defaulted).

By now you get the drift. Resist the siren call of those soaring ceilings and lash yourself to the mast if you must to avoid buying into the cult of beauty without first checking out the financial flesh and bones that lie beneath the surface. This chapter will give you the facts you need to carry out that investigation. How to decide if the building has enough cash in the bank for comfort (or will be calling on you for maintenance or assessment hikes). How to figure out if the board has over-leveraged the building or is fiscally conservative. What consequences can befall you if your co-op leases rather than owns its own land. How to tell if the sponsor is friend or foe, rich or poor, or just plain hanging around too long. Where you can look for answers to everything you always wanted to know but were afraid to ask about finances (from budgets to annual statements to board minutes), and what they should say to make you proceed with—or pass—on the deal.

READY, SET, GO

Staking out that ideal place may require making some fashion sacrifices, forsaking those Manolo Blahnik spikes for the cushy comfort of a pair of Nikes as you chalk up miles in your residential quest. (Personally, I'd rather suffer.) But when it comes to financial due diligence you can let your fingers do the walking (bejeweled, manicured, or au naturel—it's up to you). Once you've tracked down the offering plan, financial statements, budgets (if available), and minutes, you should have most of the evidence you need to make a rational financial judgment.

The offering plan contains the original deal (and documents) for selling apartments when the building was converted or constructed. Here's where you'll find the original bylaws and proprietary lease (co-ops) or bylaws (condos), together with any amendments and identification of any special risk factors present at the creation (a balloon mortgage with rising interest rates; a building that rents, not owns, its land). If the sponsor still has a 10 percent interest, it has to file annual plan amendments disclosing and updating its financial status. Although you may turn green with envy when you see what insiders paid, just shield your eyes and read the rest.

The law requires both co-ops and condos to prepare (and distribute) annual financial statements setting out the condition of the building for the past year.[1] You should compare their actual numbers with the projected expenses given in the previous years' budgets. So ask to see three to five years of each. When you tire of numbers, make a request for board minutes (one to three years' worth), the closest you'll get to a running narrative of what's going on in the building. If there are problems, physical or financial, they'll show up here. And you can determine if your dollars will be the solution. Your reading may even reveal secrets about your own planned acquisition that could change the target of your affections. (Turns out, for example, your seller combined without board or Buildings Department consent and you may inherit his feud.)

Once you have the documents in hand you're ready to begin. Here's what to look for.

RESERVING YOUR DOLLARS

As a board member, one of the first things I check out in purchase applications is how much cash the buyer has in the bank. It always gives me a safe, warm feeling to know she or he has more than the minimum to squeeze by standard financial measures. So, too, if you want peace of mind, you should try buying into a building that not only has comfy surroundings but a cash cushion.

Show Me the Money

If you're lucky, a nice fat stash will still be sitting (and swelling) in the building's bank account when you arrive on the spot. How did it get there? Most likely from past and present shareholders. The initial infusion probably came from the sponsor, who under law has to contribute 3 percent of the total price.[2] In co-ops this means the *aggregate insiders' price* (the total number of shares times the insider price per share, without regard to any underlying mortgage). So if 44,000 shares were offered under the plan at the last insider price of $400 per share, the total price would be $17.6 million and the sponsor would have to fork over $528,000 to the reserve fund after the closing.

In condos, the total price is also the aggregate insider price for all units, but given the way condos are structured this price includes amounts that would be part of a co-op's mortgage. Still, the result is that the total price and the minimum reserve fund in a condo are more than if the same building were converted to a co-op. Since condo owners usually pay more for their places (because they pay the mortgage debt up front), it all comes out a relative wash. And to the extent shareholders have taken up the cause, claiming unequal justice, the courts have said it's equal enough given the differences between co-ops and condos.[3]

Newly constructed buildings that (supposedly) start out in tip-top shape don't get the benefit of any legally required sponsor aid, though many offering plans for newly built condos require each unit owner to kick in several months' common charges to the communal kitty at closing.

Odds are that by the time you're buying into the building the money the sponsor has poured in already has flowed out. The silver lining in this cloud is that unlike string-tied sponsor cash, which by law can be used only for capital improvements, shareholders can spend the money they've plowed in themselves however they want, so long as the board hasn't earmarked it for some special purpose.

If the building's vaults are overflowing, you probably don't care about the source of such largesse. Most often they're not. Some boards subscribe to the slow and steady school of saving, and replenish funds through a budget line item that shareholders pay for as part of maintenance rather than waiting for a crisis and imposing an assessment. Others are more entrepreneurial and creative. In one building where the roof space was underutilized, the board built a penthouse, sold it for a bundle, and poured the profit into its reserve fund. In my building, years back, we bought an apartment at a foreclosure sale, flipped it, and put the profit away for a rainy day.

Is It Enough?

Now that you know how much is in the reserve account (and how it got there), you should ask, Is it enough to keep the building in relatively mint condition for the foreseeable future without the board's coming to shareholders for a refill? There's no pat answer. Assuming no emergencies lurk on the horizon and the issue is maintenance, usually $5,000 to $6,000 per apartment should be adequate to give you cold comfort (though in most buildings the number is significantly less). In my building, with 229 apartments (at $5,000 each), that comes out to $1.145 million. Others want to see an amount equal to three to six months' operating expenses. Of course, if the roof is about to collapse, the elevators are past their prime, and the windows are beyond replacement age, I'd want to see more.

How does a buyer uninitiated in the ways of building high finance and low maintenance know what's enough? It's not easy. In order to show owners how much it would cost to keep their building physically fit, some years back those accountants adopted guidelines requiring buildings to disclose the useful life of their common elements, the cost to replace them, and where the money would come from to do the job.[4] Caught between divining the future and getting hit with a lawsuit if their prognostications were wrong, most boards (including my own) figured silence is the safer course. What they usually tell you (hidden in a footnote in the financials) is they think they have enough (from current reserves and borrowing power) to meet capital replacement needs. All this, of course, leaves you back at ground zero, trying to figure out what needs doing and whether there's sufficient money to do it.

How to Find Out

Don't be bashful. Ask the seller and the broker what projects are in the works and how they're being funded. The board minutes may give you a more reliable picture because they reflect what is actually on the board's agenda. The problem is that some major plans may be inchoate—known by the board (though not necessarily the owners) to need doing but not yet calendared for action in the minutes. To head off fallout from this information gap you can try one of two options. Though it may be unorthodox given the power politics of the admissions process, as far as I'm concerned there's nothing wrong with calling the people with the most current information—the board members—and asking. In my years as a board president, only one prospective buyer called to inquire—and she earned my respect, not annoyance. If the conversion is relatively recent, ask to see the engineer's report that the Tenants' Association commissioned or any subsequent reports that exist. It should tell you the major work ahead.

If the cash on hand is way below the comfort line, you want to know if the main reason is no money or no work. Try a little reverse psychology to find out. Sellers may be mum about divulging prospective projects that will cost you money (and scare you away), but they'll talk till they drop about retrospective work (which is paid for and proof of increasing apartment values). And if it turns out from their report and your inspection that everything already has been overhauled and is in triple-mint condition (as those ads say), it may be okay that there are fewer dollars.

The truer story may be lots of work but little cash, or not so much work and even less cash. That's probably the case because most buildings subscribe to the here and now savings philosophy. The idea is to leave the cost of improvements for those in residence when the building needs improving rather than to have today's owners foot the bill for tomorrow's expenses. (A philosophy that, as you'll see, extends to mortgages, too.) What this means is that if you're there when the roof's about to cave or the elevators collapse, you'll probably be assessed.

But if the coffers are at dangerously low levels, you'd better find out how the board plans to fill the cash (and credibility) gap for such things (assessments, maintenance hikes, flip taxes, and tax rebates). Sometimes the building has available a line of credit negotiated as part of a refinancing deal. This should be evident from looking at the financials (see below), in which case fewer on-hand cash reserve dollars may be okay. Remember, though, you'll be paying (not getting) interest on that money. If the need is great and the dollars are few, the board's method of choice may determine whether you should buy or pass on the deal.

PAYING YOUR FAIR SHARE

It's good to know that the building has money socked away for a rainy day, but you and your fellow owners are the ones who are going to be paying the day-to-day freight via monthly charges and, if need be, special assessments. Their amount can be a surrogate for the building's financial (and physical) health, and it can impact your own fiscal well-being. So you want to know what's in store. Just as important, make sure that those already there are keeping up their end of the bargain—otherwise you could wind up paying more than your fair share.

Clockwork Dollars

Apart from the dent you've left in your bank account by paying the purchase price (and assuming a mortgage), your biggest financial bite comes from the monthly checks you'll be sending in like clockwork to keep the enterprise (co-op or condo) running. The maintenance fee is one of the first bits of information the broker imparts to you. Most brokers will tell you as a (very) rough rule of thumb that maintenance (co-ops) or common charges plus real estate taxes (condos) shouldn't be more than $1.25 per square foot. If the number is totally off the wall, you may start worrying (or at least asking questions), but if it's higher because of a terrace or some other unique feature, don't get uptight.

The absolute number is only the first step in the investigation. You also want to know whether that number is in line with the maintenance fees charged by other buildings and not too steeply on an incline within the building. To get the answer you need an internal and external reality check. On the outside, how do the monthly charges for your palace in the sky stack up against those of like size and distinction in high rises of comparable lineage? If they're on the low end, that's good news. Mediocrity is fine for these purposes, too. But an overachieving score that wrecks the maintenance curve is not. It means trouble on at least two fronts. Since monthly charges are a direct function of building expenses, a high number indicates some cost may be out of control—could be real estate taxes or mortgage interest (two of the big three in co-ops; see below). To get the answer you'll need to examine the financials or the budget. Then there's what I'll call the reverse fiscal psychology problem. Beyond certain acceptable limits, the higher the maintenance, the lower the purchase price. Most people will stay away even if the maintenance is high because there's a large mortgage at under-market rates. Logical or not, the maintenance is perceived as being "too much." As a purchaser, you may think you're getting the better end of the deal by paying a high maintenance fee in exchange for a low purchase price, but just wait till you want to sell—and nobody's biting. Watch out.

As an inside indicator, you want to take a retrospective look and compare the present maintenance with the numbers past (three to five years). In this context, relative flatliners signify robust financial health. They show that the board has a good-enough handle on key expenses so they don't have to keep coming to owners for more. On the other hand, if the maintenance trend resembles the volatility of the Dow—or worse, the trajectory of a NASA launch—you need a diagnosis, which you should be able to get by looking at the financials.

Prospectively, the question to ask is whether (and by how much) the maintenance will rise in the coming year. If the board has prepared the budget and announced the maintenance levels, you should have no problem getting the answer. In most buildings (including my own), numbers are announced at the same time each year, so you should be able to tell if hard information is at the ready. If the seller represents a level of increase that turns out to be way off, you may have a claim. One New York co-op buyer sued the seller for misrepresenting that maintenance charges would go up only 5 percent when he knew they'd rise by more than 25 percent—and the court said he had a case.[5] But, believe me, you don't want to go that route. Better do your homework—and let past history be your guide.

Once (and Future?) Payments

High or low, you know going in what monthly charges are. But if you're not careful you could get hit by those (sometimes) silent killers—assessments. Both condo and co-op boards can impose them on owners, usually to pay for some capital improvement for which there's not enough cash on hand. These can be major ticket items. Below the surface of that prewar beauty, the pipes are corroding and need to be replaced so the water keeps flowing. The glazed brick skin, considered the height of 1960s chic, needs a total face-lift—unfortunately, not an uncommon occurrence. I've watched in disbelief as several downtown buildings replaced their facades brick by crumbling brick, which shareholders paid for dollar by assessed dollar. A building nearby sprung a gas leak, forcing shareholders to turn off their stoves and open up their pocketbooks to pay hundreds of thousands in assessments to fix it.

Sometimes the assessment can be a stopgap measure because the co-op has too *much*, not too *little*, money. Sound crazy? It's done to prevent loss of the co-op's 80/20 status. (Remember, 80 percent of the co-op's income has to come from the building's shareholders so that they can keep their tax deductions.) That's exactly what one West Side co-op recently did when it couldn't reach a settlement over rent with its garage tenant and didn't want to jeopardize its status with the taxing folks. The garage demanded a refund, but the court said the board instead could assess shareholders to restore the balance.[6]

A relatively painless maneuver being used these days by co-op boards (including ours) to cushion the blow of soaring budgets is to assess shareholders the amount of real estate tax rebates they otherwise would have received under a law passed to equalize their tax status with that of homeowners. Before you enter their kingdom, you might want to ask if that's the building's policy.

If it's a done deal and the assessments are officially passed and imposed, they're usually considered additional rent (so if you don't pay you'll be just as much in default as if you don't pay those regular monthly charges). And there's a space for the amount on that sales contract, right below the maintenance fees, the better for you to see the total damages.

You'll also want to know not only how much the additional payment will be but how long it will be in place and what it will be for. It can be a flat sum payable all in one pop or monthly installments to fund some ongoing improvement program. If it's due in monthly payments, I'd want to know if they're of finite duration to pay for some project of fixed amount (an elevator modernization contract that's been signed, a window replacement program with set dollars), or are they based on an estimate (in which case those monthly assessments can go on ad infinitum and become stealth maintenance increases).

Sometimes the board comes to owners *after* it has already spent the money and needs the cash quick. To get out of that mess, the board in my friend's condo planned to borrow in bulk from a bank and collect (with interest) from owners over five years. That is, until my friend suggested the option of interest-free payments up front for those who had the cash. Let this be a lesson that you could get hit not only with assessments but interest to boot.

The real danger is if assessments are coming down the pike but not yet passed. As an insider you know (or can find out) the scoop. Even when prospective assessments haven't reached the gossip stage (so owners may not know), the board may have the inside information. As a prospective buyer, you're in a gray—and potentially more deadly—area.

So long as you're put on notice of potential liability (even if what you are told is not the whole story), you can't complain later. Take it from a buyer in a downtown landmark who tried. He was told before he bought his half-million-dollar digs that the building needed repairs. At the closing he signed a letter, prepared by the co-op, acknowledging that he'd been advised that imposition of a special assessment for roof repairs was likely imminent. A year later, when it turned out that the bill for all this was more than he had bargained for, he sued—but got nowhere. Since he had been notified of the work he could (and should) have dug deeper.[7]

The harder question is not *how much*, but *whether* the seller knew about the assessment and didn't tell. Worried about the possible cost of facade repairs, another prospective purchaser signed a contract in which the seller (whose wife was on the board) represented he didn't know of any proposed assessment under consideration by the board. When at the interview he found out that the board was considering a $750,000 assessment, he claimed he was duped and demanded his deposit back. It's not clear, the court said, sending the case back down to a lower judge to find out if at the time of the sale the assessment was a mere contemplated possibility or a fully ripened proposal—and leaving both buyer and seller in limbo.[8]

Most of the time you won't get much outside help, so you need to take self-help to protect against assessment shock. Of course, you should ask what's coming. But if there's nothing concrete and the seller doesn't know (or isn't talking) the steps I've set out for analyzing cash reserve adequacy should stand you in good stead on the assessment front.

One last tip that could save you thousands. Be sure to get lots of loss assessment coverage in your homeowner's policy. This will reimburse you for assessments imposed by the board resulting from some covered loss to property owned collectively by all unit owners (hurricane, explosion or other natural disaster or act of God) for which the building's insurance doesn't pay. Usually this is because there's a large deductible or the building's coverage isn't sufficient. (It won't help you out if the board assesses you just for cosmetic or capital improvements.) When the board passes the cost on to you, you can pass it on down the line to your insurer—that is, if you're covered. The tippee is my Florida friend who got hit with a $6,000 bill from Hurricane Andrew's destruction and got back only $1,000 because she had standard assessment coverage, when for a few dollars more she could have been home (and assessment) free. So be sure to ask and spring for the extra few bucks; they could save you thousands.

Negative Income

You want to buy into not only good, but also paying, company. That's why you should check the amount of arrears (which should be evident from the financial statement and budget). I wouldn't obsess about a couple of late-paying shareholders (say no more than 5 percent). But if the sponsor is significantly in arrears, that's a danger signal. Although the co-op may be able to collect rents directly in such case, that may not entirely resolve the problems and can create problems of its own.

Condos are more arrears prone than co-ops. They require less financial scrutiny to get in and often attract investors, who tend to be the first to get going when the going gets rough—leaving lots of unpaid charges behind. Since condos take second position behind the banks in collecting on amounts outstanding, this means they (and you) can wind up with substantial write-offs. It's not a big problem when the market is firm, but back after the Asian economy went bust, I was told of one building where seven foreign investors walked, leaving a pile of unpaid charges in their wake. Don't get caught buying into a sinking ship.

MORTGAGING YOUR FUTURE

After having been subjected to the third degree by your banker, you're probably so relieved to have a mortgage commitment in hand that you may not stop to think your loan is only part of the debt you're taking on when you buy into a co-op. Most co-ops have significant underlying mortgages. In its simplest terms, an *underlying mortgage* is a loan from a bank to a co-op with the property serving as collateral. Condos are mortgage free. (See below.) As a shareholder in the corporation you assume your proportionate share of the debt and pay interest over time as part of your maintenance fees.

Most often mortgage interest is one of the Big Three in co-op budgets, together with real estate taxes and labor. Although the present era of relatively cheap money has made borrowing less painful, still the loan terms are probably one of the most important items and potentially can make or break a building. So you'd better focus on them even before you go shopping for your own loan.

Formula for Success or Disaster

Now that you've mastered the terminology you need to look at the numbers. The place to start is the total amount of debt outstanding. Since buildings vary in size from micro to macro, the best way to look at debt is to break it down into an average amount per apartment. If it works out to somewhere between $30,000 and $50,000 per unit you're in the comfort zone. Obviously, larger apartments will bear a larger proportionate amount. Although my apartment's share of debt is about $50,000, the *average* debt per unit in my building is only about $23,000. Anything below that means the building (and you) has a built-in safety cushion. But beware of stratospheric debt levels. All you need do is recall the corporate collapses from the greed-is-good eighties to understand what a crushing debt load can do to a co-op. A spike in interest rates or a shortfall in revenue and your co-op could join the casualty list.

Assuming the amount of debt is reasonable, you want to see that its terms are also fair. Many of the issues are the same ones you would focus on for your own mortgage—only with bigger dollars. At the top of the list is the interest rate. If it's way out of line with current rates you should ask why. Don't look a gift horse in the mouth if the building has the benefit of below-market rates—but find out the reason. Is it because the board was lucky (or smart) in locking in when rates were low? Or is it the first leg of an adjustable mortgage that has nowhere to go but up? Or is it an introductory rate offered by the sponsor at conversion that is set to rise over time? The first is unvarnished good news. The other two could mean trouble.

On the flip side, what should you do if the rate is way over the top? First, I'd find out if a refinancing is in the works that will bring it (and possibly the maintenance fees) back down. And if not, why not. One possibility is that the loan has what's called a yield maintenance provision (demanded by many co-op lenders) that effectively requires the building to make up the spread in interest rates if it pays off the mortgage before maturity, and generally makes premature refinancing too costly. Another is that the mortgage doesn't allow for prepayment, so you're locked in for the long term. Even worse, maybe the building is in such bad financial shape that it can't go back to the moneylenders for a better deal. Or finally, the board simply may be asleep.

Just as important as rate is kind. Is it a balloon mortgage that can burst in your face? In this case, the building pays only interest and at maturity has to pay back the whole amount it borrowed. It's like treading financial water—except at the end of the day the building can sink like a stone if rates are way higher than when they began. Say you bought at conversion into a building with a $6 million, five-year balloon at 7 percent interest. Caught in an uptick when the balance comes due, the building has no choice but to pay more for the money—and you shareholders sure will feel the 10 percent pain. That's what happened to lots of buildings that were leveraged to the hilt during the 1980s wave of conversions only to get hit with a rush of rising rates that almost pushed some under. Now that rates are comparatively low this scenario is not a major concern. But like hemlines, interest rates rise and fall, and it could happen again.

The trend in co-ops is toward mortgages that pay down principal as they go (so-called self-amortizing loans). Instead of going nowhere, that $6 million mortgage gets paid away to oblivion or down to $4 million (or some other number) at maturity, depending on the amortization schedule. There's no doubt that less debt means a securer financial future. The issue is whether the shareholders in residence today should pay for the brighter tomorrow of those to come. If you're the day-trader type who focuses on the short-term bottom line, you'll probably say no. But if you're of the Warren Buffett value school you'd vote yes. Assuming you plan to stick around for even a while, you're sure to reap the benefits of the end result (well before they come due) through enhanced apartment prices that flow from reduced debt. (So you know which side of the philosophical debate I come out on.)

Finally, look at the duration of the loan, a factor I'd consider more important as a dependent than as an independent variable. Since good things don't last forever, the lower the rate the longer the building should go out. Conversely, the higher, the shorter—with the caveat that refinancings don't come cheap. Everyone wants a piece of the action, from mortgage brokers to title insurers. Their collective pie (including potential prepayment penalties) can run into the hundreds of thousands. So before you can figure if it makes sense to refinance you have to factor in the costs. That's the theory, but, in fact, most banks won't lend to co-ops beyond ten years, a few go to fifteen, and even fewer past that.

What's the Verdict?

Putting it all together spells the difference between stability or escalation (or, if you're lucky, reduction) in costs. Avoid buying into a building with a balloon imminently coming due and either no refinancing worked out or a refinance with skyrocketing rates. Everything else being equal, you're better off putting your dollars into a co-op that borrows directly from the lender rather than paying trumped-up interest to the sponsor in a wraparound mortgage. Look for a building with a decent mortgage in place for at least the next five years. The better the deal, the further out you should look for it to go—and the more secure you can be that your maintenance will stay in check.

When a window of opportunity opened in our existing mortgage, my building's board took advantage of relatively low rates to go out long term paying down principal along the way—so at the end, instead of having $5.8 million in debt the shareholders will have only a little over $3 million, a relative bite-sized loan for a building the size of ours. For those who've been paying close attention, our mortgage initially went from $5.5 to $5.8 million due to loan costs and extra cash we took out, but has since come down below the original amount as we pay down principal.

Is There Any More Leverage?

Lots of co-ops figure they may as well get while the getting's good. So when they refinance their mortgages, they try to get access to whatever other money they can—just in case. Usually this is by way of a line of credit for up to a certain amount made available (as needed) at a preset interest rate by the same lender. The building only pays for the money if, and when, it uses it. Some mortgage lenders won't give credit lines, in which case the board should negotiate a deal that allows the building to get secondary financing. As part of my building's refinancing, we can go out and borrow more money; the only limitation on the amount is that it can't exceed a 30 percent loan-to-value ratio. That means the total amount of debt against the property can't be more than 30 percent of its fair market value. Since we got a self-amortizing loan, the longer out we go the lower our principal balance—and the more we can borrow (if needed).

As a buyer, it's good to know that the building has taken present steps to assure possible future cash needs. But if the board is at the point where it's already drawing down on the credit line or has borrowed against the limit, that's more leverage and more interest. It's *total debt* that matters. So when figuring if your building falls within acceptable debt levels ($30,000 to $50,000 per unit) be sure to include both mortgage and any other financing amounts.

Mortgage (But Not Necessarily Debt) Free

It's a whole different story for condos: The Condo Act didn't specifically authorize condos to borrow, so lenders were gun-shy about lending, even if the building's bylaws said it could take on debt (and most do not). On the practical side, since condos themselves don't own either the individual apartments or the common elements, they can't mortgage them. Since they have no collateral, banks didn't want to lend. Since banks wouldn't lend, condo boards had to go directly to the source and get the money from cash reserves or assessment of unit owners. That might be okay for lobby renovations or elevator modernizations, but the cost of capital improvements that became necessary as buildings aged was too much to make owners pay up front out of their own pockets.

In order to help buildings fund capital needs without owners going broke, the Condo Act was amended to allow condos to join the indebted ranks.[9] There are two ways to go. If the condo's bylaws already allow borrowing, the law blesses that authority. If not, the law provides independent authority for condos to go to the well to fund major repairs, subject to certain conditions. The board has to wait until the building is in operation at least five years (by which time the sponsor should no longer be in control) before signing that IOU. Even then it can't hock the farm without getting the consent of a majority of unit owners, and if owners don't want to borrow you can say so in the bylaws, thereby nullifying the law. To assure lenders that buildings are good for the money, banks get security from unit owners' common charges. And they can order an increase in monthly charges, if necessary, to keep those payments rolling in on time, even foreclose liens against individual defaulting units.

On the plus side of the ledger, borrowing would spread out the pain on owners since the money can be paid back in smaller doses over time (as part of monthly charges) rather than in a lump sum assessment up front. On the minus side, the money would cost more since the condo (and you owners) have to pay interest to the bank. Worse, interest payments can't be deducted from taxable income because these loans aren't secured by real property. (Though creative accountant types have come up with possible ways to make the loans deductible.)

But so far the law hasn't helped that much. Owners don't want to commit the condo (and thus themselves) to taking on a pile of debt, and banks aren't knocking down the doors to lend, which means that for now most condos will continue to regard you unit owners as the bank and come to you for assessment dollars—a fact you should focus on if there's significant work that needs to be done. In the event the board already has used its borrowing power, is it to stabilize or strangle the building? In order to tell you need to take a look at the interest rate, loan amount, type, and duration to assess what impact the condo's debt will have on you.

SITTING ON A TIME BOMB

You probably figure since you're plunking down all that cash to own a home in the sky you also own the land under it. That's a safe assumption for condos. By law, condos in New York (with few exceptions) have to own the ground they sit on.[10] And you own your proportionate piece. But co-ops can lease their land and some do. It's not something most buyers focus on. You can find out easily enough if your chosen building is a real estate renter (in legalese, a leasehold) by perusing the offering plan. Though, truth is, for the uninitiated ground-lease talk is certain to make you skip the pages. I'm giving you fair warning that you should sit up and take notice, because the arrangement could be deadly to your co-op's health.

Pain Without Gain

Probably one of the main reasons you want to shed your renting ways is so you won't throw away money every month without getting something for it. If you buy into a leasehold building you will not break entirely free. These rent-a-plot deals are usually set up as part of the conversion. The sponsor sells the apartments represented by shares in the co-op corporation. At the end of the day the co-op owns the building but the sponsor (or some other entity) continues to hold title to the land on which the building sits—and rents it back to the shareholders—for a price.

If the sponsor gets a nice, fat annuity, what do the shareholders get? The privilege of paying that annuity in the form of rental charges, usually many hundreds of thousands of dollars a year. There are different methods of fixing ground rent. One way is to ascribe a dollar amount to each unit on a monthly basis. Another is to derive a number based on the landlord's desired return multiplied by the value of the land. Either way, you'll pay plenty. On top of that, even though the co-op doesn't own the land, under most lease arrangements it pays real estate taxes. Usually the amount is split between the co-op, which pays tax on the building (by far the lion's share), and the landowner, who pays taxes on the property. This means each shareholder pays a proportionate share (through maintenance charges) of an amount that can reach to seven figures. (Though that pain is partially eased by getting an income tax deduction at year-end.)

That's just the beginning of potential trouble.

Limited Lenders

Nothing makes banks more nervous than uncertainty. Since leases don't last forever (though many are for a very long time), some bankers just turn their backs on co-ops that rent their land. You're probably lucky if you find out when you apply for a mortgage as a prospective purchaser, expecting an easy yes, only to get a decisive no. Assuming there's a mortgage contingency clause, you're probably off the hook because the bank turned you down. And there's still time to change your mind and buy into a land-owning co-op.

My friend found out the hard way when he was nixed for a refinance by his original lender. The only thing that had changed since the lender first gave him the cash was its policy. No sooner did the market take a dive than the bank decided to dump land-leasing co-ops from its loan portfolio. Although the lender caved in my friend's case, beware that buying into a leasehold co-op may limit your lending options, at least in down markets.

Mortgage Money

Even though the co-op doesn't own the land outright it can have a mortgage on its leasehold interest. But the terms may not be as favorable as they would be if the co-op called the land its own. It all depends on the lease terms. If the lease goes out from here to almost eternity (ninety-nine years is common) with set reasonable periodic renewal rates along the way, the building may be able to deal with the banks on an almost equal mortgage footing. But if the lease's life has almost run out (or was short to begin with), or if there's any uncertainty about renewal, the co-op may pay increased mortgage costs.

Expiration Countdown

Usually these ground leases run for a relative infinity, with renewal provisions included. The rent may be fixed for the first ten to fifteen years, with a predetermined increase for the next ten to fifteen years and another preset increase for the period thereafter. This means that for an initial period of twenty-five to thirty years you can tell how much rent the co-op will have to pay. If the provisions for renegotiation are too frequent or not fixed at set percentages at specific intervals—or worst of all, if the expiration of the lease is near—watch out. If you're around when Father Time comes calling, you could be in for a rough and expensive ride. Unless the lease is renewed your building is a co-op without a country (or at least a plot of land). Given this Mayday scenario, it's not like the co-op holds all the negotiating chips. The closer the co-op's lease gets to the wire without a resolution, the higher the stakes.

In one building I know, insurrection was narrowly averted. Board and landlord stood at an impasse as the ground-lease clock ticked down. Both sides brought in their lawyers, who had a litigation ball. But lots of shareholders bolted, settling for certain lower prices rather than face the great unknown. A deal was finally inked, and prices have since come roaring back along with the market. But, personally, I'd prefer being able to sleep at night to wondering whether the land was going to be pulled out from under me.

Unchecked Maintenance

Even if these situations have a relatively happy ending, they usually come at a price. If it's a case of renewal within the initial period, the co-op knows how much it will have to pay, but it still has to come up with the cash. (Since we're not talking rent stabilization here, these raises can be heavy.) Beyond the known time zone, better be prepared for full-scale war and soaring costs (and maintenance).

Or the board may decide to buy the land, thereby converting the co-op from renter to owner status (as the lawyers would say, from leasehold to fee ownership). But land doesn't come cheap (especially in the Big Apple), and such a purchase usually means taking on a fairly giant-sized mortgage. Paying off the debt service also translates into big-time maintenance hikes for shareholders. My friend was living in his co-op for nearly twenty years when the sponsor finally decided to sell the land on which it sat—for a whopping $30 million. The deal was great for the owner, who cashed out at top dollar after having collected a fortune in rent while the value of the property headed skyward. Although the co-op wound up in greater control of its destiny, the building was saddled with a debt so large that shareholders will be shelling out lots more in maintenance for years before they make a dent in it.

Ultimate Price

Sometimes it's not just a question of paying more but of paying the ultimate price (co-operatively speaking). This can happen when the cost of land acquisition is simply too great for the populace to stomach. Don't think we're talking hypothetical hysteria. I know someone who bought into a co-op a number of years back not focusing on the fact that the building leased its land. Everything seemed hunky-dory until the board finally bit the bullet and bought the land—bringing financial ruin to at least some shareholders. Unable to meet the soaring costs, the individual I know was forced to bail out, cutting a deal with the bank that held his mortgage but losing his apartment in the process. That experience was enough to sour him on co-op life and send him back to the rental ranks.

There are some (currently) stable land-lease co-ops out there. But why take the chance? At some point either the co-op will turn acquisitive and target the land (taking on a mountain of debt) or it will be forced to renegotiate to rent for more (maybe lots more). Neither is good news. My advice: Stay away from any building that doesn't both worship *and* own the ground that it sits on.

BECOMING UNYOKED

It's not just leases that can have a long-lasting effect on buildings—so can their creators. The conversion craze, with sponsors turning rentals into co-op and condo gold, is a thing of the past. By far, most buildings that come to market for sale are newly built condos that may be all but sold by the time they're actually up. The sponsor takes the money and runs, and the new owners take charge and elect a resident board. There may be issues with the sponsor, but (as we saw in chapter 2) they usually deal with construction, not control.

The situation is different in co-ops and condos that came into being via conversion, where the influence of the sponsor may linger long after the creation. Even though the law says that the sponsor has to give up voting control the *sooner* of five years after the conversion or when its ownership interest drops below 50 percent, as we'll see (chapter 9), there are ways to effectively extend a sponsor's grip beyond that limit. Moreover, because rent-stabilized tenants are allowed to stick around (under noneviction plans), the sponsor's ultimate departure could be delayed a decade—or more—and if it chooses not to sell apartments that become vacant, even longer than that (though, as we'll see, the law may force it to sell).

Fact Finding Made Easy

Although the building you are considering may have been around for a while, the sponsor could still be a significant, if not controlling, presence. The larger the position it holds, the more it could impact operation of the building—and the more you want to know about its identity and how it operates. Under the law[11] so long as the sponsor (or its affiliate) still holds at least a 10 percent interest, it has to disclose certain financial facts in any offering plan and amendments that should give you a pretty fair notion of whether you want to live (or invest) under the same roof.

1. Ownership Tally

First, the sponsor has to tell you how many unsold units it still owns, as well as how much maintenance it pays out and how much rent it takes in every month. This way you can figure out at a glance whether the cash flow is positive or negative, an all-important indication of its (and the building's) financial health. This is especially important if the sponsor still owns lots of apartments.

2. IOUs

If the sponsor has any financial obligation to the building (other than sending in those monthly checks) or to lenders, it has to let you know. Say it's responsible for making periodic payments to the cash reserve fund—its status should be in there. Or suppose some of the apartments it owns are subject to mortgages or other financing commitments. That, too, has to be disclosed.

3. Dollar Source

Then the sponsor has to tell you how it's going to pay for what it'll owe. This is usually a rote recital that it will get the money from rent, proceeds of apartments it decides to sell, or its own resources. If it's paying everything on time you know it means what it says. If not, you may have to dig deeper.

4. Credit Rating

You'll want to know, and the sponsor has to report, whether (and for how long) it's been current or deadbeat in meeting the financial responsibilities it has to report. Is it sending in those monthly checks like clockwork or taking its time? Is it paying pronto what it owes to banks on mortgages it may hold on its own apartments? The answer is here.

5. Multiple Diversions

While your primary focus should be on how the sponsor is treating your co-op or condo, it helps to know if it has stakes in other buildings that may be a drain and could affect the cash flow in your building. The sponsor has to list any properties in the state where it holds more than 10 percent of the unsold apartments and tell you if it's making on-time payments there. Or if not, the amount of each delinquency.

Grading the Results

If the sponsor gets an A on its report card, you can rest relatively assured that it'll continue to pay its financial dues to the building. (Human nature doesn't change.) But if it's anything less than current in paying monthly maintenance or mortgage charges, you'd better find out why (and whether there's reason to believe things will change) before you proceed. Otherwise you could be in for trouble before you start.

Apart from the strictly financial, it's nice to know what kind of business partner you'll have. You can get some sense by doing a litigation check on the sponsor (an investigation many buildings will demand of you as a ticket to admission). Here the best news is no news; out of court means out of trouble. If the sponsor has been hauled into legal warfare by would-be shareholders as part of a conversion strategy, you can take it with a relative grain of salt. But look more seriously at complaints dealing with payment defaults, construction defects, or deficiencies in repair and maintenance obligations. These all presage potential problems.

No matter who the sponsor is and how good it is, if it holds too many shares for too long there can be trouble. Here are some reasons.

Numbers Don't Lie

If the sponsor still holds a large chunk of apartments years after the conversion, you want to know why. Some explanations are benign—maybe the geriatric set (who've been there since creation—the building's, that is) have decided not to go or buy until they're called by their Maker. Since they pay rents to die for and figure they won't be around long enough to reap the earthly rewards that come from amassing equity, most pass on buying for reasons that are personal (not sponsor or building related). If that's the case (and you really want in), bide your time, let nature take its course, and eventually the apartment could be yours. (Though it first reverts back to the sponsor, who is sure to charge today's, not yesteryear's, prices.)

Then there are forces beyond reason that may affect the number count. The same stampede mentality that affects the Wall Street gang grips the co-op (and condo) crowd, who rush to buy when the market's hot (and prices are high) and stay away when it's cold (and prices are cheap). I witnessed this phenomenon in my own building, which converted at a near-market bottom, with prices so low you couldn't lose money, yet saw only modest insider participation. Several years later, when the market (and prices) took off, those who had passed on the deal clamored to buy. Even though it's illogical (and counterintuitive), a high number of unsold apartments could just be the result of a dormant market.

On the other hand, lots of remaining unsold apartments may mean the sponsor has decided to dig in its heels and wait—till the market comes back, till its tax situation requires, or till hell freezes over. This could spell BIG trouble. (For why, read on.)

Admissions Anarchy

One of the main draws of buying into a co-op is strict community control. That power is lost if the sponsor owns a big block of shares. It can sell or rent to whomever it wants (ax murderer or angel) whenever it wants, unchecked by the need to get board approval. If your object is self-selection in fellow shareholders, beware when an outside authority controls the admissions process.

Free Ride

Not only is the sponsor above the approval fray, it is also beyond the reach of fees other shareholders may have to pay for the privilege of selling or subletting. Where the sponsor still has a big presence, this exemption can have a dual effect. Since the sponsor won't be paying, the amount of cash from flip taxes (and other fees) flowing into the building's coffers will be diminished—at least for the short term. Though it won't be paying, as an owner it'll get the benefit of all the money pouring in from shareholder sales—whether used to fatten the cash reserve account, fund capital improvements, or facilitate some other value-enhancing purpose.

Dried-Up Dollars

So long as the sponsor holds sway, the banks stay away. Whether they're being asked to refinance the building's underlying mortgage or to fund individual shareholder loans, most banks want to see more than 50 percent of the apartments in shareholder hands before they'll break open their checkbooks. They figure a stable building is a sold building, since individual owners who call their apartments home are less likely than the sponsor for whom it's only an investment to cut and run if the going gets tough. If banks won't lend to the building, you'll have a tough time getting a mortgage to buy—which makes it harder for existing owners to sell—which can decrease values in the building.

This downward spiral has been checked because a rising market has encouraged banks to let loose (or at least to let looser) in their lending requirements for both buildings and individuals. Some years back we refinanced our co-op's underlying multimillion-dollar mortgage with ease and without 50 percent (but close to it). Though now that our building is much closer to 100 percent sold, our shareholders get the best interest rate around.

Which Way Is the Flow

Just like you and me, the sponsor has to pay monthly charges for all the apartments it owns. Unlike the rest of us, the sponsor isn't living there. By law it has to continue to lease to rent-stabilized tenants for the rest of their lives (at relative pennies a month). Whether it can continue to rent out vacant apartments for whatever the market will bear is now less certain. If the total rent it collects is more than the monthly maintenance it pays the cash flow is positive, so it should have no problem paying what it owes. But if the flow goes the other way (which could happen if lots of those penny-wisers remain) it may not take in as much as it has to shell out. You'd better find out how the sponsor plans to make up the difference or risk serious problems down the line. The more apartments the sponsor holds, the deeper in the red it can go, taking you down with it.

Under the Thumb

Aside from dreams of escalating equity, one of the main reasons for buying is to throw off those renter's shackles and take charge of your residential destiny. That political and psychological goal can be defeated—or at least delayed—if the sponsor is still a major presence. So long as the sponsor controls the board, which it can do by naming designees and/or voting in sympathizers, it controls the building—and you. This means it can cut corners to avoid paying more maintenance, defer improvements so there won't be assessments, hire or fire who it will. And to be sure its mandate is followed, it can bring in its own handpicked henchmen of the legal, accounting, or other advisory variety.

Stratified Society

The more apartments the sponsor owns long term, the greater is the danger of a permanent underclass of renters and the potential for a two-tiered state. Renters want to have an equal say with owners in the society in which they live. Owners think renters have no right to such a say because they haven't put their money where their mouths are. This clash of wills can turn ugly, especially if it involves special perks that didn't previously exist and that smack of shareholder privilege—who gets first crack at emptying their clutter into the storage room, or buying a ticket to health at the gym, or turning into bronzed gods or goddesses on the roof deck—are all potential bones of contention. You may be lucky enough to find a building where the partisans and patricians are above the fray—but I wouldn't count on it.

Reverse Caveat

Having sounded the alarum bells, it's only fair to say that some sponsors bring peace and prosperity. Most of them have deeper pockets than those of us buying a mere apartment or two. Assuming the sponsor hasn't overleveraged itself (or the building) and is in for the long haul it can actually bring credibility and credit to the co-op or condo in addition to institutional knowledge.

Freed from Limbo

Now that you know the perils of purchasing into a top-heavy building, you can avoid them by just saying no. Maybe you found out only after the fact that the building you have your eye on has a lot of sponsor-owned apartments. Should you take the plunge anyway?

There's good news to report. Most plans say that the purpose of the offering is "*sale* of cooperative apartments for use as homes by purchasers." Even though that's what they said, nobody knew if that meant the sponsor had to sell *any*, let alone *all*, apartments after the plan became effective. Some sponsors used conversion as a means to escape the bonds of rent regulation and charge free-market rates when apartments became vacant, thereby getting a nice annuity for themselves but leaving owners stuck in legal limbo.

The sponsor has finally been shown the door, thanks to a band of shareholders (and their board) who remained stuck in their own building, prisoners of a sponsor who still held 62 percent of all the shares—and ceased to update its offering plan so that it *couldn't* sell any shares. As a result of the sponsor's intransigence, shareholders were unable to refinance the building's mortgage or get loans on individual apartments or resell. When the owners discovered that the sponsor had rejected offers to buy, they sued, claiming the sponsor had breached its contract in the offering plan to sell enough shares within a reasonable time to make their building a "viable" co-op. We can't say yet if you're right or wrong, the state's highest court told them, but you've told us enough to state a valid claim against the sponsor for its failure to sell.[12]

It remains to be seen *how many* shares the sponsor has to sell for a co-op to become "viable" and *how long* it has in which to sell them, but recognition of the shareholders' claim marks a major potential shift in the balance of power. Recently, another co-op tipped the scale still further in the shareholders' favor when it sued a sponsor that had stopped selling apartments several years after it converted the building in 1985, and still held 66 out of 125 units. You've got to stop renting—and start selling vacant apartments, the co-op demanded. You're right, is basically what the judges said.[13]

How will all this ultimately shake out? It's too soon to say. The Attorney General has proposed regulations that would require sponsors to disclose in their offering plans whether they intend to sell all the units, and if not, the percent and number of apartments they intend to withhold.[14]

You should be aware that there's a potential glitch in the good news. At the same time that courts are telling sponsors they have to sell apartments when renters move out, they're also telling renters they can stay more or less indefinitely (thereby precluding sponsors from selling). Here's what I mean: For years everyone thought the law[15] said that rent-stabilized tenants who lived in a building *before* it converted (and chose not to buy) could remain so long as they stayed alive, but that those who rented at market rate *after* the conversion had no such protection and could be told by the sponsor to go when their lease was up.

That was all changed when a court took the side of an enterprising renter whose lease was up and didn't want to leave. The judges said the law was meant to prevent dislocation of tenants who rent from sponsors, so market-rate renters are protected, too. They can't be ousted without cause and can't be charged unconscionable rent. (For you lawyers out there, the decision turns on the definition of "non-purchasing" tenants under the Martin Act.)[16] Obviously, the fact that these renters can remain puts a wrinkle in the sponsor's duty to sell. To make matters more complicated, other judges have said the first court was wrong, and that market renters have no protection so sponsors *can* (indeed *must*) sell vacant apartments.[17]

For your purposes, what's important is that if you're stuck in a building where the sponsor won't go, you shareholders now have a potentially significant remedy to break free of its clutches. If you're thinking of purchasing in such a co-op, I'd suggest you wait till the problem is resolved rather than buy into a lawsuit.

STAYING WITHIN LIMITS

You have to live within your means and so does your co-op or condo. To see if it is and how much it will cost you, take a look at the budget and financial statements. The budget sets out the building's annual projected income and expenses. In my building, the board prepares and distributes a budget before year-end to shareholders so they can see what's in store for the coming year. Although boards (co-op and condo) are required by law to hand out financial reports detailing the building's condition for the year past, they are not legally required to tell owners in advance what they have budgeted. As a matter of practice, many condo—but not co-op—boards distribute budgets. As a potential member of the body politic, I'd want to know if my financial leaders were going to be tight-lipped or open to question. And one way to find out is to ask if the board's policy—and practice—is to provide advance annual information.

The budget should be at break-even, meaning income levels are equal to expenses. It may be okay for countries to run at a deficit. They just keep on borrowing and taxing until the numbers work out right. It doesn't work that way for co-ops and condos. If the board continues to underestimate line item expenses (even though there's cash on hand at year-end to make up the difference), eventually things will catch up. Banks don't like that kind of deficit spending—and neither should you, because as an owner you'll be asked to help balance the budget. You want to focus not only on absolute numbers but on trends over time. (To do this, ask to see at least three—better, five—years' worth of numbers.) That way you can see if expenses, like inflation, have remained tame (an indication that maintenance increases will be subdued), or if they're on a steeper trajectory.

Source of Supply

Before the board can spend the cash it has to earn it, or at least collect it. That's where you come in. By far and away the bulk of revenue comes from those monthly charges you shareholders and unit owners pay over the year. In co-ops this amount is a function of the total number of shares outstanding times the annual charge per share. In condos the calculation is based on the percent interest in the common elements apportioned to each unit. In either case, the number is the income headliner.

Deadbeat Dollars Don't Count

The board can't spend dollars that it doesn't have. So first you should find out if there are any significant shareholder arrears. Assuming that any owner defaults are within acceptable limits, the budget still should reflect this reality by discounting the anticipated monthly income. Unless the board has reason to believe the situation will change (for better or worse), the percent of income lost during the prior year can serve as an estimate. I'm happy to say that my building has a faithful shareholder flock who keep their noses to the grindstone and pay on (and sometimes ahead of) time. So I have no experience in deriving discounted cash flows—and hope to remain blissfully ignorant.

Extra Dollars Do

On the other hand, if the board is enterprising and opportunity knocks, there may be real (and welcome) dollars coming from outside sources that could put a lid on what you'll have to lay out as an owner. The possibilities are many: the call of Hollywood (my building was approached by film location scouts); the cash of cellular antennae (another incipient but unrealized income stream); the rent of prosperous stores (our sponsor, as owner, gets it all); the dollars that flow into our coffers from renting out storage space; or the jingle of laundry room change (now cards), which we collect from our washer/dryer supplier. Whatever the origin, the dollar amount generated should be listed in the budget. Before you count on permanent maintenance relief, you'd better find out if these are expected to be ongoing revenues or one-shot deals, à la my building's movie shoot.

But too much of a good thing can be no good. Remember, the IRS requires that at least 80 percent of a co-op's annual income must come from shareholders to preserve and protect tax deductions for their proportionate share of the co-op's real estate tax and mortgage interest. If the building gets more than 20 percent from outsiders it has an "80-20" problem and you could have a tax problem. Better find out the board's solution before you buy and hope it doesn't have to go the assessing route.

Level of Demand

Whatever its source, the amount of revenue listed has to be sufficient to pay for the itemized expenses. Their numbers vary depending on whether you're looking at a walk-up or a towering colossus, but regardless of size the kinds of things needed to make a building tick are the same. Here are the highlights you should focus on:

The Big Three

In co-ops the killer triumvirate is taxes, mortgage, and labor. (Condos, as you know by now, have no mortgage and you pay your own real estate taxes.) These three items make up the bulk of the co-op's budget. Their relative magnitude is so great that they dwarf all else and can seal the building's financial destiny. So you'd better pay attention even if numbers aren't your thing.

1. Territorial Taxes

Assuming your co-op owns that postage-sized plot of land it sits on, it still pays taxes in perpetuity for the privilege. In the present climate real estate taxes can eat up more than a third of a co-op's budget.

Out of Control: The system used to determine how much your building (and thus you) pays is not for the fainthearted. In the past few years it has become even more irrational than usual for several reasons: First, as a result of the financial crisis that hit the city post–September 11, real estate taxes have followed a sharp upward trajectory (while the stock market went the other way), throwing all predictions out the window. Around the same time, a bribery scandal hit the tax assessors, casting doubt on the legitimacy of values they had previously fixed on many buildings and, with so many of them going to jail, raising questions about *how*—and *by whom*—the assessing of co-ops and condos would be done. Though the powers that be promised to reform the system so that *anyone* could understand it, they haven't yet delivered, so it remains more impenetrable than ever. You don't have to be an expert, but because the number is now so eye-popping that it could have significant consequences for your building, you need to know enough to tell if the figure for your co-op or condo makes "sense" in the context of a less-than-sensible system.

How It's Determined: As a co-op (or condo) owner you're at a disadvantage from the start. The way real estate taxes are calculated for high-rise homeowners you pay more than your stand-alone home-owning New Yorkers for a property having the same market value. My share of taxes for my two-bedroom is more than $8,000, probably close to what the taxes would be on a brownstone that's twice as big and twice as expensive. Although some political stabs at equalization have been made, the disparity remains. You know what they say about fighting City Hall.

The amount of real estate tax you pay is a function of two factors: the property's value and the tax rate. Each January the voice of God (speaking through government bureaucrats) announces what's called the "assessed value" of the property. In theory, co-ops and condos are assessed as if they were rental properties: by determining their "rental" income and then projecting a rate of return. This fiction makes it necessary to look at the income generated by supposedly comparable rental buildings—including stabilized, control, market-rate, and decontrolled tenants—to come up with a value that, by definition, is neither certain nor reliable. Moreover, although rental values have gone down over the past several years (and are now stabilizing) valuations for co-ops and condos have gone up, often dramatically. Given these confusing realities, in practice it's anyone's guess what number's going to roll off the press and into the boardroom. Although my building's lawyer has explained the origin of, and adjustments to, our assessed value, I confess that even after all this time I haven't fully mastered the supposed logic.

Anyway, that's only half the story. Once you know the value, you need to know the tax rate. While the value is specific to each building, the rate applies to all properties within a class. The city decides how much money it needs and then sets the rate to fill the shortfall (supposedly in July, but usually not till November). When the financial crisis hit at the end of 2002, the city hiked the rate a whopping 18.5 percent to $12.51 per 100 dollars of value. The combined effect of soaring values *and* rates has wreaked havoc on co-op budgets (and condo owners who pay direct) resulting in staggering annual maintenance increases of 20 percent or more. Our real estate taxes have gone from approximately $650,000 to more than $900,000 in about three years, although our valuation has finally begun to inch downward, and the tax rate has just been lowered slightly, both of which portend possible relief on the horizon. (To be sure the building doesn't get totally destroyed with increasing tax bills all at once, the co-op is assessed at a so-called transitional value that releases the pain in gradual doses. But that's for the advanced course, which you needn't worry about unless and until you get on the board—a deterrent if ever there was one.)

Is There Any Remedy? The board can't control what value is slapped on the property, but it can (and should) fight to stop any unwarranted upward spiral. There's an army of lawyers out there (a.k.a. the Certiorari Corps after the name of the proceeding) whose sole function is to do nothing but. (See chapter 13.) My building's board (as do those of most co-ops) signs up one of them every year to do battle with the bureaucracy in hopes of getting the assessed value reduced to a more rational amount. The way the game usually works—it's heads, the city wins; tails you lose—if the value goes down, the rate goes up. (In times of fiscal crisis, buildings get hit with a double whammy: both value *and* rate go up.) Let's say the assessed value of the building is $6 million at a current tax rate of $12.50 per 100 dollars. The following year the assessed value goes down to $5.8 million, a bit of good fortune that evaporates when you're told the tax rate is going up to $12.75. You should check to be sure the board is taking the taxing authorities to task—and with what results.

To get an accurate picture you need to look at the trend over time (say, five years). The past few years have been extraordinary and, hopefully, not a predictor of future trends. In more normal times, I'd want to see a nice even keel or a slow steady rise. I'd be nervous if those taxes were hurtling ahead full throttle. Either the board is not challenging the authorities, so they keep on increasing the property's value, or something's out of whack and a real dispute exists between board and bureaucrats over value—in which case the building could be in for a long legal battle. While your chosen co-op may ultimately win, you take a gamble. And in the interim, guess who pays? When it comes to taxes it's guilty until proven innocent.

Are You Getting a Refund? It's not always a one-way tax street. To encourage self-improvement, the city puts its money where its mouth is and allows buildings to take tax abatements based on a percentage of the total cost of capital improvements—spread out over approximately eleven years. (Of course, getting the money requires a cadre of counsel who cash in themselves on the deal. See chapter 13.) These rebates amount to a lot more than the refund checks you and I get in the mail. My building's new windows (which cost around $500,000) not only sealed the building against winter drafts but secured for us a $250,000 tax break (over about eleven years). Our elevator modernization yielded an additional $125,000 in breaks. New buildings sometimes get substantial tax rebates that go on for years.

These breaks are good while they last but have a finite life. Check to see whether there are any ongoing rebates in effect and if they show up (usually as a note to the financial statement) as a reduction in the co-op's real estate tax. (Some boards instead earmark the refund amounts to replenish the cash reserves.) If none are in sight, ask if any are in the offing. The truth is they're harder to come by now because rebate relief is unavailable once a building's average apartment value hits a certain level, and in the bull market of the past few years many have surpassed this threshold. But assuming such relief already is in place it can bring down taxes and take maintenance along with it. Conversely, if the building is getting a healthy dose of tax relief from refunds, how long do they last? When the party's over, your maintenance may rise to cover the (sometimes substantial) gap their absence creates.

2. Mortgage

By now you know (probably more than you want to) about co-op mortgages. The budget and financial statements give the facts and figures needed to determine if the mortgage you'll be proportionately assuming as a shareholder is one you (and the building) can tolerate. From it you should be able to see the size and terms of the loan and the annual payment amounts of interest and principal (if the mortgage is self-amortizing). While those interest payments are sure to be substantial, take heart. The greater the amount, the larger will be your share of the allowable tax deduction at year-end.

3. Labor

This is the single biggest item in most condo budgets (and way up there in co-ops). With labor, it's basically what you see is what you'll get—and pay for. Since most co-ops and condos are in the union grip, staff size, building class (A = luxury), and salary levels are predetermined; apart from curbing overtime, there's little the board can do to control costs. Every three years the union threatens to push costs out of control and life into chaos (no one to polish, sweep, mop, or greet) as we go through the cyclical renewal ritual. If past experience is any guide, the biggest hit is not wage hikes (which usually amount to about 3 percent annually) but benefits (which soared this year due to a shortfall in pension and health benefits that owners were contractually bound to fund). There's no point in blaming the board, because it can't do anything about this. Just be aware that if you're buying at the brink of expiration you're in for a period of transitional cost uncertainty until the new contract is negotiated.

Potential Troublemakers

A number of the remaining budget items make up a relatively small percentage of the total and are normally benign, but recent circumstances have conspired to make them financially toxic.

Protection Money

Until September 11, 2001, no one talked about insurance. A lawsuit against a building could increase its risk rating, and premiums, for several years; otherwise, they remained boringly constant. But when the World Trade Center came down, premiums went up and up—without looking back, and nobody knows where, or when, the meteoric rise will end. Overnight, buildings saw their premiums double, triple, and more. If the high-rise was high profile or near the UN or a tunnel or other terrorist target, it became practically uninsurable. Some larger buildings couldn't get terrorist coverage till the government stepped in. Even though as a percentage of total cost, insurance is still low on the totem pole, in absolute terms the numbers have been sobering. In the three years since September 11, my building's premiums have gone from $28,000 to almost $70,000; a larger nearby building has seen the price of coverage jump from $100,000 to close to $400,000. Although increases have moderated, they haven't yet reversed course.

On top of the staggering cost, most buildings have no real choice. There are only a few major players that write coverage. If one bids low, the others bid so high as to be uncompetitive. Hopefully, by the time you're reading this, insurance quotes will start coming down, but for now they're out of the ball park, and you'll be paying as never before.

Energy

Remember what happened to fuel prices during the Gulf War? With what's going on in Iraq and the whole Middle East, they're way higher now than they were then. Maybe what co-ops and condos are paying per gallon is a bargain compared with what you've been shelling out for gasoline, but this fuel hike has been the final straw for many budgets already straining from soaring real estate taxes and insurance premiums.

Free Flow (a.k.a. Water and Sewer)

For the price of water there should be Perrier flowing through the pipes. When the city switched from billing for water based on how much space buildings took (determined by frontage) to how much water they used (measured by meters) washing and drinking got more expensive. Only since nobody bothered to read the meters, nobody sent bills—leaving boards to go with the flow and without a clue as to how much they owed. My building waited a year and a half after the building converted till shareholders finally got soaked. After that, rather than risk a deluge (or a claim of default) we went begging for bills (not that we necessarily got them even then) and did our best in the interim to guess what the damage would be. You'll be happy to know that boards no longer need tea leaves to divine how much water they've used. Meter readings are fed directly into a computer system, allowing buildings to predict the flow with reasonable certainty. So if the numbers fluctuate more than minimally from year to year, I'd want to know why.

Rundown

A quick eyeballing of the remaining items should tell you the rest of the story. Burgeoning legal bills may mean the building is entrenched in legal warfare. (At the very least, I'd want to know what kind of lawsuit I was buying into and how long it was expected to last.) The management fee could go up—but if it rises by too much, there's always another agent out there. Amounts designated for repairs could go out the window if lightning strikes and the roof railing needs replacing. On the other hand, capital improvements, not usually a budget line item, could mean real money and substantial assessments.

The rest is relatively minor dollarwise. A uniform rise? Maybe a change in doorman look from button-down to bedecked hussar. We went the other way from overdone to minimal monochromatic. Or a costly shift in garden design from untended naturalism to manicured topiary. Neither will break the bank, but such items may tell you something about the board (that you may not want to know).

Safety Cushion (a.k.a. Contingency)

It's always nice to have a little something to spare—just in case. (The roof collapses, the boiler bursts, the price of snow removal skyrockets due to unnatural and prolonged arctic blasts.) Rather than ask owners for anything extra, most boards cut budgets close to the bone. So don't be surprised if your board leaves no margin for error (and no line for contingencies)—just hope it's gone the more politically expedient way and built some fat into the budget numbers themselves. If the board is brave enough to openly allow for a contingency, it suggests a cushy and stable-enough cash situation that insiders won't complain—a potentially good sign for an owner-to-be.

Prepaid Money

The human condition is such that we tend to spend what we have without thinking about tomorrow. This can be a dangerous tendency in co-ops and condos because when that day comes the board will go to you. To minimize the risk a little insurance in the form of separate accounts for big-budget items is a comforting thought. Sometimes the discipline is imposed from without by the mortgage lender, who demands (and controls) the escrow accounts into which the board must make monthly real estate tax deposits. That way, instead of having to come up with hundreds of thousands at the eleventh hour (each quarter), it knows when the building writes the check it'll have the cash to cover. (Just think what happens to your good intentions when temptation rears its head—a new Prada spring arrival, that Armani at half price—and you'll understand the necessity of enforced saving.)

All the better if the board is self-disciplined and on its own sets up (and regularly funds) separate accounts for killer expenses that come due periodically. When my building refinanced, the board took control of our real estate tax payments (which we deposit monthly in escrow accounts) so we not only have the cash but thousands extra in interest. Such advance planning shows that the building has a stable and sufficient cash flow and a board that knows how to harness it.

CRIB NOTES

In case all this financial talk has left you on edge, you should find comfort and confidence in the checklist that follows, which crams into a few pages the essentials of all that you've learned. It tells you exactly what questions to ask (and what answers to hope for) while out in the field.

FINANCIAL CHECKLIST

The Right Questions to Ask to Get the Answers You Need
(and Sound Like a Pro in the Process)

	What to Ask	Answer
Mortgage	• What is total amount of underlying debt (for co-ops)?	Building's financial statement/budget should tell you.
	• How much debt is there per unit? (Divide total by number of units.)	From $30,000 to $50,000 per unit, you're in the safety zone.
	• What is the interest rate?	The lower the better.
	• How long does the loan go out?	The lower the rate, the longer the better.
	• Is it an interest-only or self-amortizing loan?	Paying down principal brings financial stability.
	• Is maturity imminent?	Then what plans are there for refinancing?
Cash Reserves	• What is the total amount?	Building's financial statement/budget should tell you.
	• How much is this per unit? (Divide total by number of units.)	Hope for $5,000 or $6,000, though less is typical.
	• Has the major capital improvement work been done?	"Yes" means a reserve fund on the low side is less of a worry.
	• Are there any big-ticket projects outstanding?	Better ask if there's enough cash to pay or, if not, where it's coming from.
	• What plans does the board have for replenishing a reserve fund that's run low?	Bottom line: How much will it cost you?

	What to Ask	Answer
Sponsor	• What percent interest does the sponsor still own?	The less the better, but think twice if it still owns more than 50 percent.
	• Is its cash flow positive or negative?	Positive is always better, but the more it owns the more important this is.
	• Is it selling or renting apartments that become vacant?	Beware sponsors who don't sell. You may become a prisoner in your building.
	• Is it letting resident owners run the show or is it trying to keep control?	Better to be in control of your residential destiny. That's why you're buying.
	• Is it a sponsor who's credit-worthy and current in payments?	Then not necessarily a problem if it still owns a large interest.
Land	• Does the building own its land?	"Yes" is the best answer.
	• If not, how long does the lease run?	The longer the better, assuming the terms are favorable.
	• What are the renewal terms?	Look for predetermined rent increases at infrequent intervals.
	• Is expiration (or renewal without precalculated increases) imminent?	Danger! Warning! Maintenance could go sky-high.
	• Are there any plans to buy the land?	"Yes" may be good depending on cost. "No" means lease problems stay.
Your Share	• Has maintenance risen modestly over time or followed a steeper slope?	Flatliner is best. Expect inflationary increases. Steep spikes can mean problems.

	What to Ask	Answer
	• Is there a maintenance increase in the offing?	"No" is nice, but "Yes" is okay if the increase is reasonable.
	• Are there any significant arrears?	A sponsor in default could mean trouble, especially if it owns a large stake. If individual owners are in default, you usually don't have to worry in co-ops (lender usually pays). Could be more troublesome in condos.
	• Are there any assessments coming down the pike?	Hope the answer is "No." If "Yes," you need to know how much, how long, and for what.
Budget	• Are the budgets at break-even?	They should be. Watch out for deficit spending.
	• Is there adequate cash flow?	"Yes" is what you want. If not, where's the shortfall coming from?
	• What's the co-op's history of real estate taxes?	Look for stable payments over time, though *all* buildings have been hit with huge hikes in the past few years.
	• Is there any substantial line item that shows steep increases out of step with overall market trends?	Watch out, especially if the culprit is one of the Big Three or a looming lawsuit.

4

Penetrating the Front Lines: The Application Made Easy

KNOWING THE RULES—AND USING THEM TO GAIN ENTRY

So you've found that dream house in the sky, signed on the dotted line, and plunked down a hefty contract deposit. Its finances check out and its philosophical leanings comport with your own. Now all that stands between you and the keys to your new digs are the guardians of the fortress (a.k.a. the board of directors) and the ritual of approval—a procedure designed to turn even the most confident warrior into a weak-kneed supplicant. But if you know the rules of engagement before you start you can use your strategic advantage to beat the board at its own game.

This chapter provides you with a step-by-step game plan on how to approach the application process from a position of strength. It explains the different admissions standards (and how to leverage them), prepares you for the informational onslaught and invasion of privacy, and offers inside tips on the dos and don'ts of completing your own application.

UNDERSTANDING THE ADMISSIONS STANDARDS

One of the first things you'll want to know is what I'll call the standard of admission for the building you've targeted. No doubt having talked with friends who've been bloodied in entrance battles with co-op boards, you're convinced that no matter the building, the board reigns supreme. (Condo boards have less muscle but can still make life difficult.) In many buildings, especially the old-line bastions of conservatism, the board still has authority to approve or reject. But the silent majority of shareholders is speaking out—demanding the right to exercise its own free will when it comes to selling apartments. As a result, many boards have had their power checked so that some cannot act unreasonably and others cannot act at all.

How do you know what standard you're up against? The only sure way is to get a copy of the proprietary lease or bylaws (must reading before you sign any contract), where all this will be spelled out. Understanding where the balance of power lies will enable you to formulate an effective admissions strategy and help you to decide when to fight and when to retreat. (And even if it turns out that the board has the advantage, if you follow the plan laid out here you should wind up master of the approval process.)

The Old Guard

If you are dealing with a building where the Old Guard is still in control, chances are you'll be facing the traditional co-op provision. It gives the board broad discretion to accept or reject you for any reason or no reason so long as there is no illegal discrimination. If you read the proprietary lease (as instructed) it would say something like this:

> The Lessee [here, the selling shareholder] shall not assign this lease or transfer the shares to which it is appurtenant or any interest therein, and no such assignment or transfer shall take effect as against the Lessor [the co-op] for any purpose, until . . . consent to such assignment shall have been authorized by resolution of the Directors, or given in writing by a majority of the Directors. . . .

If these are the rules you are playing by, the board is legally despotized. It can turn you down because it doesn't like your financial credentials or your social connections, or just because you're having a bad hair day. Since the board doesn't have to give you a reason for rejection, it's hard to prove discrimination even if that's the real reason. (Of which, more in chapter 6.)

The Moderates

In many buildings, where enough shareholders have gotten shafted by the board in selling, they have put a lid on the power of the entrenched director forces. One way of doing this is by taking away the board's absolute authority to approve or reject and instead limiting it to not unreasonably withholding consent. This is how one building made the change:

> The Proprietary Lease will be amended to provide that the Board of Directors may not unreasonably withhold its consent to a proposed assignment of the Proprietary Lease and the shares allocated to an apartment by a Tenant-Shareholder.

Such a provision should give you a psychological and tactical edge over the traditional standard. Although the board can still reject, it cannot engage in wholesale slaughter of proposed purchasers. Under this standard it is unlawful for the board to turn you down for the kinds of subjective (non)reasons the Old Guard routinely gets away with. To say no the Moderates would have to come up with a reason that any third party would view as objectively rational. While a bad hair day may do it for the old-liners, if the Moderates tried such an excuse they'd be the ones done in. To turn you down, they would have to show that you were not financially qualified under accepted banking standards or would not be a fit neighbor by some objectively provable criteria.

Since the Moderates are under the gun from their constituent shareholders (and the courts, which ultimately enforce the rules) they use the veto with greater care—which means you are more likely to get in. But if, despite these limitations, they say no, you should have a leg up if you decide to go head-to-head with them. (For more on that, see chapter 6.)

The Libertarians

In some buildings, when it comes to buying and selling the free market reigns and the ruling class has been reduced to a relative figurehead. These buildings have jettisoned the notion of board approval altogether and replaced it with what's called a *right of first refusal.* This standard, long the norm in condos and making inroads into co-ops (including my own), allows shareholders to sell and outsiders to buy, unfettered by board restraints. If the building on which you have set your sights subscribes to the politics of free will, its proprietary lease would have a provision like this:

> Within thirty days of receipt of the notice and such other information as the board may reasonably require from the Contract Lessee [the selling shareholder], the board shall exercise its exclusive right to purchase the apartment (or designate another to purchase the apartment) on the same terms and conditions.

Under a right of first refusal, the board does not have *any* discretion to reject the purchaser outright. The Libertarians' only theoretical option, if they don't like you or your credentials, is to offer to buy the apartment on the same terms and conditions. But usually this is no option at all because co-ops are not in the business of buying real estate, do not have the money to make such a purchase, and may not have the authority to borrow for it even if they wanted to.

This all spells opportunity for you. Here's what I mean. From my experience as a board president reviewing applications for years, few involved in the purchase process fully understand how the right of first refusal works and take for granted that the traditional co-op standard governs. Nor have I disabused them of the notion of the power-clad board. This, I must confess, is due to the fact that I am a Libertarian by force, not free will. (When my building converted, the offering plan stuck us with a proprietary lease containing a right-of-first-refusal provision.)

While loath to admit it in my capacity as board president, the truth is that in buildings with a right of first refusal, the *buyer* has more leverage than the board. So long as you submit a completed application—even if it shows on its face that your financial credentials are wanting—the Libertarians can't just say no. They can make your life difficult, cause delay, claim your offer to buy is not bona fide, demand more information. (Indeed, I have tried all these tactics, and more, in an effort to keep out financial deadbeats.) But at the end of the day, the board's only (unrealistic) recourse if it doesn't want you is to buy the apartment.

So be patient, even friendly; try charm. There's no point in being belligerent when the end result is a foregone conclusion. Although the board may try to call your bluff, if you know your rights and just sit tight, it eventually will surrender.

Of course, there are ways to do these dicey deals so that neither the buyer nor the board comes away feeling vanquished. Take the case of the aspiring model whose father wanted to pay cash to buy his daughter an apartment. But she had no visible means of support to pay the maintenance. We asked for (and got) Dad to deposit a year's maintenance into escrow (which was about the time it took for the daughter to establish her own credit—and get her first photo shoot). The buyer got approval on the fast track and we got financial protection for the building—enabling both to claim victory.

A final caveat for those applying to buildings with Libertarian leanings: Do not relinquish your advantage by giving the board an out. Although it can't say no even if your qualifications are subpar, it can (and most definitely will) demand additional documents and maybe even an interview if your application is incomplete. If you hope to cover up some problem by omitting certain facts or supplying inconsistent information—don't try it. The board will likely unleash a war of attrition, requesting missing and backup documents to the beginning of time, hoping that you will go away rather than submit to its demands. So long as your application remains incomplete, the Libertarians do not have to make a decision and your application will sit there in legal limbo.

The Freedom Fighters

It's those freedom-loving condos where the right of first refusal came to be and is still the order of the day. That's because, as you know, condos are real property. Though we're living in the technological era, we're selling real estate in the dark ages. That's where the rule against perpetuities and the rule against unreasonable restraint of alienation got their start. I'm proud to say I slept through most of this in law school. I learned what I know from Kathleen Turner, who (if you recall) understood the rule well enough to get away with murder in *Body Heat*. For those who missed the flick or need a quick refresher, here's the deal:

The idea of the first rule is to prevent real property from being tied up by postponing to a remote time (defined in Shakespearean legal lingo as lives in being and children conceived) the vesting of some future interest. The second rule says that all (vested) property interests should be transferable without unreasonable restrictions. All you need to know is that these rules are the reason that condo boards have virtually no say over the sale of apartments. (Since the transfer of co-ops is considered personal property, the board, not the rules, controls.) Although the Condo Act says that condo bylaws can have provisions governing the sale of apartments,[1] lots of lawyers think that doesn't override the rules. And no court has been asked to decide. So for now (and probably a long time to come), if you buy in a condo, all you'll face is a right of first refusal similar to this one:

> Upon receipt of the notice from the Unit Owner . . . the Board of Managers may elect, by notice to such Unit Owner . . . to purchase such Residential Unit, together with the Appurtenant Interest . . . on the same terms and conditions as contained in the Outside Offer and as stated in the notice from the offering Unit Owner.

A little knowledge can be a dangerous thing. Lest you be thinking that even the right of refusal violates the rules, you're not alone. A couple of condo buyers who were thwarted in their effort to get that perfect pied-à-terre by a board that exercised its preemptive right gave it a good fight—and lost. The court said the right is okay under the rules.[2] Under the right of first refusal, condo boards can ask for information, and within reason you have to provide it,[3] but they can't impose conditions on the sale.[4] As ineffective as this right is in co-ops that have Libertarian leanings, it's even more emasculated in most condos. If co-op boards have the will (and can come up with the cash) they can buy an apartment on behalf of you shareholders. The co-op board doesn't have to ask for permission of the building's shareholders. But in democratically disposed condos, a majority of unit owners has to agree before the board can act.

Of course, what the bylaws giveth, the board taketh. It usually makes you agree in advance, as a condition of purchase, to sign a power of attorney giving it authority to exercise its right of refusal and buy the apartment. That device frees the board's hand, except when the bylaws specifically require that owners be present and vote on the issue at a meeting. When the board at one Queens condo that had such a provision tried to rely solely on its powers of attorney to take advantage of a good deal and buy, the court invalidated the deal for lack of proper owner approval.[5] Courts are on your side, allowing boards to exercise their right of refusal only if they have followed the bylaws to the letter—and number. One condo board whose managing agent had received but not transmitted a unit owner's offer to purchase within the twenty days it had to exercise the right of first refusal was told, It's too late to act. The clock starts ticking when your agent gets the word.[6] When another condo board took more than the forty-five days allowed under its bylaws to exercise its right, it got the same answer.[7]

As you can see, for the most part chances are (next to) nil that a condo board will exercise its right. So unless you're a modern-day Jack the Ripper or a descendant of Lizzie Borden, you're safe—and you're in.

TAKING THE ANGST OUT OF THE APPLICATION—KNOWLEDGE IS POWER

Now that you have contract in hand, and empowered with the knowledge that you may be able to approach the board more as equal than supplicant, you should be able to face the challenge of the application with a spirit of defiant confidence. And knowing in advance what you'll have to give to the board should help you psychologically prepare for the intrusion into your privacy—and get your financial house in order. The format in which you'll have to fork over your life's history varies from building to building, but the substance sought is pretty constant—and ever increasing. (Despite attempts by a broker task force to get buildings to sign onto a uniform five-page application, most boards still insist on going their own way.) So get those copy machines whirring and start churning out your own personal paper trail. Here is a rundown of what you can expect to produce.

Checking Out Your Financial and Personal Well-Being

Credit Check

The board will require (and you will pay for—at about $75 each) one or more credit reports so that it can scan your credit history in a nutshell. Apart from rating your payment of credit card, student loan, mortgage, and other debt, credit reports verify employment, landlord, and banking references. If you know you have disputed or delinquent amounts outstanding, you had better settle up pronto (well before you embark on your application process). If you act with dispatch you may be able to get the problem excised so the board is none the wiser. But even if you can't wipe the slate clean, your rehabilitation attempt may buy you some breathing room with the board.

Reports to Uncle Sam

Most buildings require you to submit tax returns for the past two to three years—the surest way, they figure, to get the truth about your income. Boards look for a pattern of consistent earnings—all the better if on the rise—sufficient to carry maintenance, mortgage, and possible assessment charges. Returns that show erratic income—huge compensation one year followed by none the next, common among the freelance and entrepreneurial set—are sure to produce board agita. Try calming their nerves by volunteering additional information that will show a steady stream of earnings (a long-term contract, or a pile of principal that produces loads of interest, or a letter from a client confirming your irreplaceability).

Boards examine your returns as much for what they don't show as for what they do. Suppose you are paying cash for your apartment but the income line says zero. The board may assume the money is laundered and force you (and the cash) to come clean with some legitimate explanation.

And it's always nice if the income you report on your tax return jibes with the number your employer gives. Otherwise the board may conclude that you're guilty of financial dirty tricks—and as a possible felon, not fit to live in their midst.

Financial Snapshot

It may not be painless to expose your financial life, but at least now it is standardized. In an effort to make the process more uniform for boards (and presumably, less burdensome for you) the Real Estate Board has come up with a standard financial statement that has become the industry norm. You'll have to set out all your worldly assets: stocks and bonds, cash and money market accounts, Keoghs and IRAs, contract deposit and everything that is (or could be spun into) gold, including personal property. If you think you'll bolster your financial standing by representing that you have belongings of many zeroed value, forget about it. Boards regularly discount such undocumented and illiquid assets, and if too much of your wealth is tied up in them, it could work against you. One couple I know who preferred Al Hirschfeld drawings to bank accounts got the cold shoulder from a co-op board that wanted to see piles of cash, only to be accepted by another board more aesthetically inclined. Ultimately, the art-loving shareholders proved themselves more financially savvy than the board of either building, as the prices of their drawings soared upon the artist's death, giving them a net worth well beyond what cash in the bank would have yielded—and way above the buildings' requirements. On the other side of the ledger, you'll have to identify any amounts you owe: from credit card loans to auto installments, mortgage to notes payable. Boards want to see that you have a healthy bottom line, netting out assets against liabilities, and that you have adequate cash flow from salary and other income to fund your total monthly expenses.

Proof Positive

Don't expect the board to take you on faith. It will usually ask for some (or all) of the backup documents substantiating the numbers you put on your statement, so make sure the information you provide represents reality, not wishful thinking.

- ***Real Money:*** For starters, you'll have to fork over bank and brokerage statements proving your dollars exist in the amount and name listed.
- ***Closing Cash:*** A special target is the cash you'll need to close the transaction. For some boards, it is not enough that you have the money; they want to see (as proof of your financial rock solidness) that it comes from your sweat—or at least your coffers (as opposed to those of some rich relative)—and, if suspicious, may ask for bank statements going back several months to be sure that it does.
- ***Gift Horse:*** Other boards take the opposite tack, allowing you the benefit of cash infusions from benevolent givers, but insisting that you produce a so called "Gift Letter" to be sure the money is yours free and clear, no strings (or note) attached.
- ***Tricky Assets:*** Some things can't be easily documented. Recently, we had a would-be purchaser whose main asset was stock in a private British company not traded on any exchange. Another buyer's money was in real estate, not cash. Don't get bent out of shape if the board asks for appraisals or other information when your assets are difficult to prove or document.

Sworn Dollars

Some buildings, including mine, figure if you and your accountant swear to the numbers underlying your financial fitness they will be closer to the truth. On that theory, they require you to submit a net worth affidavit that lists in abbreviated form your assets, liabilities, and current net income. (Having reviewed numerous applications with such affidavits, I have my doubts as to whether an accountant's signature is a guaranty of reliability—or even whether the signature itself is genuinely reliable.)

Bank Approval

Assuming the transaction is being financed, supplying a completed mortgage application and commitment is necessary, but rarely sufficient. For most boards, it is not enough that you have satisfied the bank that's lending you the stash of cash that you are financially fit. They want to know that you still have plenty left to pay the building and have socked enough into your apartment that you will not walk away if the market goes south. To be sure of this they impose building demands regarding the amount of cash you must have on hand, your total net worth, and the minimum amount of cash you must put down to purchase. (All this was spelled out in chapter 2.)

And remember, the numbers you supplied to the bank in your loan application had better be in sync with those you put on your financial statement.

Assorted Testimonials

It's standard practice in most buildings to require you to provide business and personal references. If the board asks for only a list of names, addresses, and phone numbers, chances are it will never look at, much less contact, your references (except for curiosity value).

Many boards make you go a step further and get these references to attest to your sterling character and professionalism in letters of recommendation. Having both written these for friends applying to other buildings and received them in my capacity as board president, I have yet to understand their purpose other than to: (1) test the literacy of your friends and colleagues (which, if experience is any guide, may prove seriously wanting), or (2) see what company you keep—all the better if it turns out you're a fellow traveler with board members in their social circles.

What should these missives say? That the applicant is creditworthy to a fault (holds only solid gold plastic); pays all his bills on time (but gives priority to monthly maintenance); is a quiet and courteous neighbor (translation: does not have wild parties or blare his stereo); is well adjusted and considerate (won't be a thorn in the building's or the board's side); and recognizes his responsibility to the larger (co-op or condo) community (will attend annual meetings and do some work).

By now I have perfected my own all-purpose form letter that suits any need. I proffer it to you in the hope that it may be of some immediate assistance and eventually lead to the standardization (and hence demise) of the recommendation requirement. This is what it says:

Dear Board Members:

I write in enthusiastic support of [*insert buyer's name*]'s application to purchase Apartment—at [*fill in apartment number and address*]. I have known [*buyer's name*] on a personal and professional basis since [*insert year*], when we met at the XYZ firm. On both a professional and a personal level, [*buyer's name*] conducted herself [or himself] according to the highest ethical and intellectual standards, with impeccable integrity, absolute reliability, and a generosity of spirit toward her [or his] colleagues.

Since then, [*buyer's name*] and I have remained in close contact. I am confident that [*buyer's name*] will be a wonderful neighbor. She [or he] is sensitive to the needs of others and thoughtful of the larger community of which she [or he] is a member. [*Buyer's name*] is

> responsible in financial affairs and punctilious in honoring her [or his] commitments.
>
> As a long-time co-op owner myself, I know how important it is to have shareholders who are engaged and interested in the well-being of the building and the corporation. I am certain that [*buyer's name*] not only will fulfill her [or his] role as a shareholder, but also will be a welcome addition to the residents of [*address of building*].

Now that you know what to say, and assuming you are grammatically fit, you're probably better off drafting the letter yourself and just giving it to your friend or colleague to sign. But if one of them insists on being the actual scrivener, make sure you see what he or she has written before the letter is submitted to the board, lest your friendship—and your apartment—be in jeopardy.

Loose Ends

There are a host of other documents you'll be asked to sign, seal, and deliver: an acknowledgment that you've read and will abide by the House Rules (so you can't say you didn't know), a slew of legal forms relating to everything from foreign tax credits to window guards. You may even be asked to sign a so-called "Inducement Letter," acknowledging that you know pets are not allowed or guests can't visit without permission (or some other restriction high on the board's agenda), although, as we'll see (chapter 14), these required missives aren't always enforceable.

Special Requirements

Think you're finished? Not yet. Apart from the standard fare just highlighted, a number of buildings make their own unique demands.

Are You Investigation Proof?

In some buildings, it is not enough that you have laid bare your financial soul. They also want to pierce the veil of your secret life. To that end, they require that you submit to an FBI-like background check by some high-class gumshoe. Chances are you will know that you are the target of such an investigation because you get the privilege of anteing up—to the tune of anywhere from $500 (for a standard Pinkerton report) to several thousand dollars for a deeper intrusion into your privacy. Now that money counts more than manners, use of these supersleuths is on the wane, but just your luck, the building of your eye is an investigational holdout. So, if you have any skeletons in your closet—too many parking tickets, smoking a joint now and then, playing your stereo too loud—you had better clean up your act before the co-op commandos get their P.I. on your tail.

Are You Suit Free?

No building wants to have in its midst professional plaintiffs—individuals for whom a wrong glance or a misspoken word provides cause for suing the board, the building, and everyone in sight. Such perpetual complainants not only wreak havoc on day-to-day building life but also spell financial disaster. Some buildings take preventive steps to ferret out these slaphappy suitors by submitting prospective purchasers to a litigation check. This can be done as part of the background investigation by combing through court records to see how often the buyer's name turns up or by calling past landlords to check out how many times and for how much he or she has sued. Of course, it's always important to go back a few landlords, because if there is a problem, the current one would sooner be suit free than candid. The bottom line: too many lawsuits and you won't make the cut.

Buying in a Nonhuman Name

If you thought you had to jump through hurdles applying for yourself, you'll have to navigate even more if you're buying in the name of a trust, as more purchasers are doing, mainly to avoid probate and pass along the apartment to a family member at a discount. The law says that a trust is a "person," which is important because in order to qualify as a co-op with tax deduction benefits, all shares have to be held by persons.[8] (It matters not that they aren't living and breathing.) Although many boards are allowing such transactions, they are used to dealing with real-life persons, and in order to protect themselves (and their buildings), require at least the following when a trust is to be the shareholder:

- **Trust Agreement:** The agreement sets out the terms of the trust, the names of the grantor and trustees, and the assets held. Some boards require that the document be prepared in a standard format by their attorney; others may allow you to submit your own agreement for review by the co-op's counsel. Either way, you'll pay the legal fees, which can amount to several thousand dollars or more, depending on the complexity.
- **Occupancy Agreement:** A trust is not human, so it may own an apartment, but can't occupy it. To give the building control over who actually lives there—now and in the future—the board will ask for an agreement that usually says that any change in occupancy will conform to the requirements of the proprietary lease on subletting, guests, and the like.

- **Guaranty:** Since the trust may have assets that are limited (and subject to depletion) the board wants to be sure the maintenance gets paid. That's why it will insist on a personal guarantee, usually from the grantor and occupant of the co-op.
- **Jurisdiction:** In case of trouble, the board doesn't want to have to go searching for the right person to slap a summons on the trust, so it will likely make you agree in advance to submit to the court's jurisdiction and designate a person to accept service of legal papers.

GETTING A PASSING GRADE—INSIDE TIPS ON PREPARING YOUR APPLICATION

As a litigator schooled in techniques of anal compulsion, I have come into contact with too many similar types for personal comfort. But when it comes to preparing your purchase application (and for no other reason) you could do worse than follow their example. The key is to be sufficiently compulsive and attentive that you get the application complete, accurate, and legible on the first go-round. This way it is easy for the board to give you the green light and resist the temptation to launch a deeper probe into your affairs that will take time and can only mean trouble.

I offer a case in point. Two applications came before our board. One was a hodgepodge, with conflicting numbers and confusing employment data, which took months' worth of phone calls and additional documents to unravel. The other was a model from cover sheet to commitment letter. Immediately and instinctively (shudder the thought), I sensed the handiwork of a lawyer (as it turns out, a tax type, a breed that makes litigators look mellow). He got his answer in a jiffy because the board did not have to do anything—except say yes.

In my years of reviewing applications, I've seen it all. I share with you my inside advice in the hope that you'll be able to steer clear of the hidden traps and make it through the application phase with distinction.

Give Them What They're Looking For

Specific financial requirements vary widely from building to building (see chapter 2), but at a minimum they will be looking for the following in your application:

- Do you have sufficient income to support payment of maintenance and mortgage charges? This is key. If the combined payments do not exceed 28 percent of your (gross) income you pass with honors, but you are still likely to make the grade provided these charges are under 33 percent of your income.

- Is there cash on hand to pay the nonfinanced portion of the purchase price or, if it is an all-cash deal, is there a sufficient stash visible and available for closing? Most banks will not give you a mortgage without proof of the amount needed to close. So if there is a loan commitment the answer is automatically in the affirmative.
- Does the credit report reveal any problems: defaults or late payments on credit card charges, student loans, or outstanding mortgages? Minor infractions may be tolerated (especially if they have been corrected), but anything else here spells trouble. So a disputed American Express charge of several hundred dollars that has been paid late may be overlooked. But a student loan placed for collection or consistently paid late can be fatal. And even minor derelictions, if there are enough of them, can wreck the deal for you.
- Do you have excessive debt? Annual payments of debt, maintenance, and mortgage should not total more than 40 percent of your income (36 percent is even better). The nature of the debt is almost as important as the amount. Large outstanding student loans are a fact of modern-day life, and boards generally will be tolerant as long as they are being paid down on schedule. But it's a different story if you have amassed a load of credit card debt. The board may conclude that you are a spendthrift and force you to reform by vetoing your application.

Although it's nice to have a bank account stuffed with cash, unless the building imposes specific net worth requirements it should not be fatal that you will shoot the majority of your wad in paying for your apartment.

Make It Easy for the Board to Say Yes

By now you may harbor latent hostility against the board for putting you through the financial wringer, but the bottom line is that you want it to approve your application. So make it as easy as possible for it to just say yes.

Don't submit information in dribs and drabs. Get your act and information together and submit a finished product. This means if a net worth affidavit requires the signature of your accountant get it signed *before* you submit it. If you are asked to supply tax returns, don't edit out the pages you don't like. If the application is contingent on financing, wait until you have your loan commitment. A good broker will take charge of the process and be sure all is in order before passing it along to the board, typically through the managing agent.

Usually the proprietary lease gives the board a definite time from receipt of the completed application in which to say aye or nay. You may think you are speeding things along by supplying information as it is ready, but the board likely will conclude that you are trying to set off its time clock before it should start ticking—a tactic not calculated to endear you.

Don't Give Inconsistent Information

You wouldn't give inconsistent information on a college application, nor should you here. Yet we regularly get applications that give one set of numbers on the loan application, another on the net worth affidavit, and a third on the financial statement. One potential buyer who submitted contradictory financial information to the board, and then refused to provide clarifying documentation, lost the apartment—and her deposit.[9] Avoid this mistake at all costs. The board may conclude that you are playing games and drum you out of the corps. At best, it will unleash an investigation into your financial affairs worthy of an IRS audit—requesting bank accounts, brokerage statements, and assorted other documentation you didn't even know you had—to determine which set of numbers is real. This process is not only guaranteed to produce frayed nerves but also may be your undoing. My advice—get it right the first time.

Don't Inflate Your Assets

Think if $10,000 sounds good on a statement, adding a few zeros sounds better? Don't try it. The board is bound to find out and make you rue this exercise in hubris.

Once we had an applicant with attitude who no sooner submitted his package than he demanded approval. But something in the application tipped us off that the $250,000 bank account indicated on his net worth affidavit was overstated. When we asked to see the underlying bank/brokerage statements corroborating that amount, a chastened buyer returned with documentation showing only $50,000 and an explanation placing blame on the broker. Mr. Attitude eventually got his apartment, but it wasn't quick or easy—and I am confident he learned his lesson.

Don't Submit Pounds of Checks

Experienced boards know that every buyer has different financial circumstances and ways of documenting them. The more unorthodox your own situation, the more scrupulous you should be in providing the best-available information. Not long ago we had a self-employed potential purchaser who hadn't yet filed tax returns for the prior year, giving us little to go by. Show us your estimated tax payments and any recent contracts, we asked. What did we get? Pounds of photocopied checks. I was tempted to use them as a doorstop because they certainly didn't show if our would-be buyer was making—or losing—money, or by how much either way. We worked it out, but his irrational response gave us the leverage to ask for (and get) financial and other guarantees of sanity.

Don't Say You're Employed Where You're Not

Sounds too elementary an issue to raise? This blunder is not as uncommon as you think and can mean your ruin. The truth is that if the facts in the letter from your employer and on your credit report are in sync, the board is likely to take them at face value and inquire no more.

Some time back we had a shareholder in our building who announced that he was selling his apartment and moving to Europe. So when we got an application from him seeking to buy a smaller apartment that represented that there was no change in his personal or financial circumstances and that he was employed by the same company—our antennae went up. Three telephone calls to the company elicited three responses that the person no longer worked there. (Nor did it help the purchaser's cause to have a recalcitrant lawyer who insisted that all was in order.) Weeks later, after an exchange of angry phone calls and letters, the situation was resolved and the deal got done. But the purchaser would have done us all a favor if he had been candid from the start.

Don't Let the Board Know You Cheat the IRS

What you put on your tax return is between you and Uncle Sam. But as a board member, I don't want to know that you are cheating the IRS and your application had better not tip me off to this fact. It makes you look untrustworthy—after all, if you don't pay your taxes maybe you won't pay your maintenance. And it puts the board in the uncomfortable position of seeming to condone a tax cheat (even if you are otherwise qualified) if it approves your application.

Yet prospective purchasers not infrequently submit applications that reveal "discrepancies" between the financial information reported on their tax returns and other documentation. Sometimes one almost has to admire their financial bravado. Take the case of the retired couple who purchased an apartment for their adult son to live in. Although their financial statements indicated substantial assets, their tax returns showed nothing—not even Social Security payments. Faced with this apparent discrepancy, the board asked to see backup documentation—brokerage statements, pension accounts, and the like. The documents revealed that there was plenty of money—and that the IRS didn't seem to be getting its fair share. Let's just say that the board got a lesson in creative accounting—and the buyers ultimately got the apartment.

Don't Submit Drafts

Applying to a co-op or condo is the real thing, not a dress rehearsal, which is why I'm always confounded when potential buyers submit "drafts"—of tax returns, financial statements, you name it. Maybe literary types like to put their imprint on works in progress, but boards want the final version—don't give them anything else.

If There's a Problem, Deal With It Up Front

If there is a potential problem with something in your application, my advice is to suppress your instinct to cover it up or bury it in the mounds of paper you are submitting. Odds are, if the board is awake at the switch, you will be found out. The more time and energy the board has to spend to figure it all out, the less charitable it will be toward your situation. So, for example, if your current income is dangerously close to acceptable ratios but a year-end bonus or salary increase is in the offing, get a letter to this effect from your employer. If you have an unusual employment arrangement such that ordinary documentation will not accurately reveal your compensation, get an explanatory letter. If your finances appear stretched to the limit because you are carrying a mortgage on another property that you are in the process of selling, let the board know that relief is on the way.

Sometimes honesty really is the best policy—and in the case of preparing your co-op application, I would add, sooner rather than later.

UNCONDITIONAL SURRENDER

Having gone through the application wars and submitted a portfolio deserving top security clearance, you should accept nothing less than unconditional surrender. The standard co-op contract provides that sale of the apartment "is subject to the approval" of the co-op corporation. That means the board can accept or reject your application; it can't impose its own conditions not agreed to between buyer and seller. And if it does, you can walk from the deal with impunity, as did a rich businessman who, through his corporation, purchased a $5 million pad at the posh Pierre Hotel for use by him and his family when they visited. After he had signed the contract, the board demanded that he enter into a use and occupancy agreement (more restrictive than the proprietary lease) that required him to get prior written consent for guests staying at the apartment. Unwilling to submit to a board-imposed bed check, he demanded his $500,000 deposit back—and got it—because the court said the board had no right to condition its approval.[10] A buyer at another co-op submitted a contract in her individual name only to have the board condition its approval on her purchasing in the name of her personal trust, insisting on a personal guaranty, deposit of maintenance charges, and payment of its legal fees. She, too, got to cancel the deal because it wasn't the one she had made with the seller.[11]

Suppose the board wants to see some more financial heft and asks (or rather tells) you to: prepay a year's worth of maintenance (at $2,000 a month, or an even $24,000 a year); or to get a financial guarantor to sign on the lease (what are parents for?); or tries to impose some other condition not in the contract.

Maybe the board is just exercising a little discretionary muscle. Boards try this all the time. I know; we've done it. What are your rights? If you're hot for the apartment and agreeable to the board's terms, then go ahead. The board is satisfied and the seller is happy (since the deal goes through). But if you think what they're asking for is too big a financial nut to crack and don't want to wind up feuding with your guaranteeing family forevermore, you should be able to just say no.

One way to help avoid potential problems with the seller is to have your lawyer amend the contract from the start to say that board approval must be *unconditional.*

GETTING COLD FEET—WHAT TO DO WHEN YOU WANT OUT

Ordinarily you want to make the board your ally in the admissions process to speed the route to approval. But suppose you have a change of heart. What if after signing on the dotted line and agonizing over your application, you wake up in a cold sweat only to realize that the penthouse overlooking the park is not apartment nirvana after all; you're really a downtown kind of guy. Or the loft you thought was perfect doesn't have the right feng shui so the force will not be with you. Or you learn that a move to Milan is imminent. Is there any way out—without losing that hefty deposit you plunked down when you signed your John Hancock to the contract?

Think and Act Fast

The sooner this revelation hits, the easier your task will be. As long as you have not received back the signed contract, you may be in luck. The standard co-op (and condo) contract provides that it is not binding unless it is fully executed and *delivered* to each party. The practical effect of this provision is equal opportunity reneging. In other words, if the seller can get out of the deal because he's still sitting with (and in control of) the contract, the buyer should have the same right.

In theory, if the contract is not yet binding all you have to do is call, or have your attorney call, the other side, tell them the deal is off, and request your check back. In practice, I'd play it safe and put a stop payment on the check (if you can).

That's just what the purchasers did who signed a co-op sales contract containing a similar provision and then sent it off with their deposit check to the seller's attorney. The seller signed several days later and left the contract with her attorney. While the contract was still with the seller's attorney, the purchasers' attorney phoned to call off the agreement and the purchasers stopped payment on the check. Although the seller cried foul, the court found the purchasers were right as a matter of law. Since the contract had not been delivered to them before the purchasers rescinded their offer, it was unenforceable and they got to keep their money.[12]

It's not always clear when delivery takes place. Back on August 29, 2001, a buyer signed a contract for an apartment, which was then executed by the seller, and on September 10, overnighted back by his attorney. Then came September 11, and the buyer said the deal was off. The seller claimed he'd already delivered the contract, but the buyer, whose downtown office was closed, didn't get it till September 27. Now the two are fighting it out in court.[13] Better to spell out in advance what delivery means in the context of your transaction.

So before you have a panic attack go have another look at the contract (which, of course, you should have read prior to signing). If you haven't received back a fully signed copy from the seller, you may have an easy out.

Let the Board Do Your Work for You

But all is not lost even if the contract has become a binding obligation, because it is still subject to board approval along with the rest of the application. The standard co-op (and condo) sales contract provides that if the purchaser does not go through with the deal the seller gets to pocket the deposit as "liquidated damages." (Though as we'll see in chapter 18, the law looks at these provisions differently.) The theory is that in the event of the purchaser's default it would be impossible to figure out the amount of the seller's loss, so the deposit (usually 10 percent of the purchase price) seems like a nice round number to keep the peace. But the sale—and hence the contract—is subject to approval by the apartment corporation. So as long as you have not acted in bad faith (purposely sabotaged your bank application, been less than candid with the board), if the board rejects you, you're off the hook. It may cut against your emotional grain to be found "unacceptable," especially after you've psyched yourself to prove your bona fides to the board, but with the tens of thousands you'll save, you can afford more than a few shrink sessions.

Far be it from me to counsel you on how to get out of a contract with impunity, but I offer the following tale as a guide. Some years back a friend of mine, after an exhaustive search, found what he thought was apartment heaven and signed a contract, only to learn shortly afterward that he had to head off to Italy for business. Not wanting to lose his deposit, he resorted to creative self-help. Instead of following the broker's advice and coming to the board interview decked out in conservative business attire, projecting an image of rock-solid fiscal and social responsibility, he turned up outfitted head to toe in black leather and sported a decidedly flaky attitude to match. When a board member called some days later and tried to let him down gently, my friend had the last laugh. Since the board had killed the deal, he was home free—off to Rome with refund in hand.

The key to this strategy is that the board remains an unwitting accomplice in the mission to render yourself unacceptable. Should buyer and board be found to be co-conspirators in the quest to avoid the contract, both could be in trouble with the seller.

The Bank Lets You Out

Then there are the outs when you don't want out—the bank won't give you the money. Unless you are sufficiently loaded to pay all cash for your apartment, you should insist upon a mortgage contingency clause, which, in fact, is standard in most co-op (and condo) sales contracts. This protects you as a purchaser by allowing you to cancel the contract and recover your down payment if despite your good faith efforts the bank turns you down.

The deadlines for action vary depending upon your agreement with the seller, but generally you have about seven business days after your receipt of the signed contract to submit your application to the bank and additional time to get the bank to say yes (usually between forty-five and sixty days, but whatever you and the seller have agreed on governs).

If you do your duty, comply with the deadlines, supply all the information requested, and answer the questions truthfully, and still the bank decides based on everything you have submitted that it doesn't want to lend you the money, then you can cancel and get your money back. This is true even if the rejection is due to some special conditions the bank imposes that you can't meet (for example, getting private mortgage insurance). Let's say the bank and the co-op can't agree on the terms of a so-called recognition agreement (this is the document that spells out the respective rights of the bank and the building to the collateral underlying the loan in the event of a default). You still have nothing to worry about. One buyer applied for, and obtained, a low-interest mortgage insured by SONY-MA through Citibank, which required a form of recognition agreement to which the co-op board wouldn't agree. When the seller wouldn't return the down payment, the buyer sued and won because it wasn't her fault that bank and board couldn't come to terms.[14] As long as *you're* not the one at fault for the bank's refusal to approve the mortgage, you're in the clear—and in the black (at least to the extent of your deposit).[15]

But don't let the bank's rejection so rattle you that you forget to tell the seller the news. Most co-op (and condo) contracts give you a set time limit to do this, typically five to seven days, after which you may lose your right to cancel. The result could mean double trouble, with the bank refusing to lend you the cash and the seller demanding that you close or forfeit your deposit. Under their contract, buyers of a co-op had until December 11 to get a mortgage commitment, but they waited till March 12 to tell the sellers that the bank had turned them down, a delay that cost them their deposit.[16]

Although ordinarily I would counsel action, if the bank turns you down you may as well take it philosophically (unless you have reason to suspect improper motives), because the board will surely nix you, too. So stuff that deposit back in the bank (not the one that vetoed you), the better to be used next time around for an even bigger apartment.

To see if you've got what it takes to earn your stripes and join the owning ranks, take the following entrance exams before proceeding onward.

WILL YOU BE ACCEPTED INTO THE RANKS?

What Standard Will You Be Judged By?

Is it a building where the Old Guard has absolute authority over admissions?	Gird yourself for battle and prepare for possible rejection without explanation.
Is the board composed of Moderates required not to reject unreasonably?	They can't nix you without good (and objective) reason.
Are they Libertarians with only a right of first refusal?	They can't say "No." Be complete (and patient) and you should win.
Is it a condo where the Freedom Fighters are in control?	You're in unless they decide to buy (which they won't).

Does Your Application Get a Passing Grade?	**YES**	**NO**
• Have you paid the contract deposit (usually 10% of the purchase price)?	____	____
• Do you have sufficient cash (as documented by bank or brokerage statements) for the rest of the down payment and closing costs?	____	____
• Do you meet the cash requirements of the building?	____	____
• Have you obtained a mortgage commitment (assuming financing is allowed)?	____	____
• Are annual maintenance and mortgage costs no more than 33% of your gross income?	____	____

• Are annual maintenance and *total* debt payments no more than 40% of your gross income?	____	____
• Does your income level meet any stricter standards set by the building?	____	____
• Do you have enough money left over to meet the building's net worth requirement?	____	____
• Is your income regular and on the rise?	____	____
• Have you been on the (same) job for at least a year (longer is better)?	____	____
• Are your assets (and you) within reach of the jurisdiction?	____	____
• Does your application show you've been straight with Uncle Sam?	____	____
• Do all the numbers (on net worth statement, mortgage application, and bank or brokerage statements) jibe?	____	____
• Have you included letters of recommendation from someone who counts?	____	____
• Is it neat and complete the first time around?	____	____

How to Cure a Failing Score

If you've scored 100% you're problem free and ready to be interrogated. If not, you may be able to bump up your grade by doing one (or more) of the following:

- Prepay six to twelve months maintenance.
- Agree to deposit funds in escrow until your finances improve.
- Get a credit-worthier guarantor to sign with you on the contract.
- Present evidence of a cash infusion. (You won the lottery; you got a raise.)
- Show cost-cutting measures. (You're paying down debt; you're selling the property that's been bleeding you.)
- Agree to pay down more than the minimum cash required.
- Flagellate yourself for any errors (past or present), beg the board for mercy, and promise to hew to the righteous path forevermore.

5

Preparing for the Final Assault: Capturing Board Approval

ADVANCE MANEUVERS YOU CAN TAKE

Assuming you remain unwavering in your commitment to storming the barricades, it's time to prepare for the final assault—your meeting with the board. Don't think that just because you've submitted your personal portfolio you can rest on your laurels. (There'll be time enough for that when you're safely ensconced in your new apartment.) Take the initiative. Use the interval between the submission of the application and the interview to scout out the opposition camp and engage in intelligence gathering—especially if you think there may be any doubts about the application.

Let your broker act as advance man. (No reason for you to be implicated in the mission.) If he's on good terms with any of the board members, get him to put in a friendly call to one of them to ask how things are going. If there's a problem, it's best to know about it up front while there's still a chance to act—before the board's position is set in stone. Once board members have locked themselves into a rejection, they're less prone to change the verdict because to do so would acknowledge that they are not infallible.

It's even better if the broker knows some of the shareholders living in the building. See if he'll put in a good word and get them to pass along their endorsement to the powers that be. Since boards usually make admissions decisions with total autonomy, the very fact that constituents will be watching the outcome may increase their incentive to do the right thing.

You also have homework cut out for you. Use the hiatus to inform yourself about the building and the neighborhood (if you're new to it). You never know what may come up at the interview and it's always safest to be prepared. Although (as you will see from reading on) my general rule is to not volunteer anything at the interview, you may score some points by using the information you have gathered to ask a few innocuous questions about the building. This shows that you are interested and intelligent. (Gardens are safe topics, pets are not.)

Who's Calling the Shots

Now that you have gathered every last shred of information the board requested and packaged it in a neat little bundle, who do you think is going to read it all? It may surprise you to know that the board may never even see it.

In some buildings, especially if they have only a right of first refusal, the managing agent often does the dirty work. Since these agents don't live in the buildings, they don't really care who does—so long as the applicant can foot the bill. Dollars and cents are all that count, and many condos don't even scrutinize your finances. If you meet the standardized set of criteria used for buildings under their wing, you're in. And you get your answer with dispatch because there is no need to wait for a board conclave.

But usually the managing agent is only the first line of defense, deputized to marshal the evidence and pass it on to the board for inspection. Contrary to popular perception, this is a much more rough-and-tumble bunch than you may think. If my experience is any guide (and conversations with other board presidents and agents suggest that it is), although there may be a score or more board members, in most co-ops only a handful review and make decisions on applications (let us hope no one with whom you have crossed professional or social swords).

Some boards formally delegate authority to screen and interview to an officially constituted admissions committee. It may be made up of a subset of board members or just a bunch of shareholders who get a power rush from deciding who gets in and who stays out. The truth is that most committees only get to recommend and it's left to the board to make the final cut.

Nor should you be anxious for a full-blown hearing in front of the entire body, because boards get involved only in the most troublesome cases or those where the purchaser refuses to give up without a fight and the specter of litigation looms. The more people who have to pass judgment on you, the greater the chances that someone will have something negative to say.

ACING THE INTERVIEW—DOS AND DON'TS FOR CAPTURING BOARD APPROVAL

With your life's history in the board's hands, all that remains is your meeting with destiny. In co-ops this is a make-or-break session. In condos, although some boards require interviews, they can't reject you, so just play it cool—and relax.

Now that you stand at the brink of victory, resist the urge to call (or to have your broker call) the day after your completed application has been submitted to ask why no interview date has been set. For you the interview may assume life-or-death proportions, but for your examiners it is a necessary evil to be squeezed in between earning a living, chauffeuring the kids, and going about their daily business—for which they get no pay, only the privilege of saying no.

If the board is really on the case, it will have set dates for committee and board meetings well in advance so you know where you stand and can save the Excedrin for another day. But if real life is any guide, this does not usually happen. More often, the interview is an ad hoc affair, scheduled and rescheduled to suit the needs of a changing cast of characters. Within reason, go with the flow. But if the time limit for their decision approaches (this is usually spelled out in the co-op's lease or bylaws) some gentle prodding may be in order.

Once the time is fixed, the battle is half over. The very fact that the board has deigned to meet with you means things are looking pretty good. Chances are that if your application had real financial problems it would have rejected you outright. This spares you the pain of the interview and the board the exposure to a lawsuit. A rejection on paper is likely to be viewed as strictly financial, but an interview opens the board to discrimination and other possible claims.

Boards are coached by their lawyers on what they can and can't ask you. It seems only fair you should know how to answer. I offer my suggestions for making it through the interview unscathed.

Dress the Part

On the fashion front, remember that the object is not to make Mr. Blackwell's best (or worst) dressed list but to fit in. In the interests of full disclosure, I admit I find the notion of conformity anathema and in my capacity as a lawyer have long eschewed the power look in favor of my own aesthetic. But for this one evening, forsake the high road and put practicality over principle. Show up in something your interrogators will appreciate and understand—with the emphasis on dressing "up" rather than "down," an instant sign of board respect. Once you're in, you're safe. As far as I know, dress codes have not yet made it to co-ops and the fashion police do not patrol the halls. So after you're comfortably ensconced let your true colors shine forth.

Play the Role

What counts in court—and in co-op interviews, too—is not so much the truth as the appearance of truth. When you walk in the door, you're on—play your part as if your apartment depended on it. If you've just had the fight of a lifetime, leave the bickering at the doorstep and put a smile on your face. The board will not look kindly upon any couple likely to engage in domestic warfare on the premises (think of the insurance premiums).

Like it or not, these interviews are often family affairs. If children are going to be living in the apartment, the board may require you to bring them along, ostensibly to meet and greet, but in reality to get a preview of their behavior. So do whatever you have to—whether it's bribing your youngsters with the latest Game Boy or taking them to Disneyland—to be sure they're in their best form.

Cut the attitude—even if you resent being interrogated by a jury of your unequals—and turn on the charm. But take care not to give responses that are too pat, lest you reveal that you are a product of your broker's coaching and not your true self.

Prepare Your Pets

You may regard that prized Pekingese as a family member, but the board probably sees it as a potential deal breaker. When it comes to pets, the first rule is that if the building is really one that prohibits them (not one where the lease says no pets but everyone has one), don't think you can sneak in that shih tzu inside your handbag. You will be found out and rue the battle that ensues—even if you win. But assuming that pets are legal, remember that one man's pet is another man's poison. When it comes to your standard four-legged types, quantity and size are what matters, although truth be told some of the smallest dogs make the loudest noises. (The full scoop on pet policies and politics is set out in chapter 14.) If we're talking anything more exotic, of the reptilian or other variety, all bets are off, since you don't know the board members' phobias. My advice: the less said on the subject the better.

But you may not have any choice in the matter, because some buildings demand interviews not only of the masters but also of their pets—at least when it comes to the canine variety. And just as you should dress the part, be sure your four-legged friend is properly washed and coiffed. (Indeed, groomers report a brisk business in interview styling.) It wouldn't hurt to come armed with letters of recommendation from former landlords testifying that your dog is clean and friendly. And a breeder's statement of pedigree is a nice touch of elitism sure to appeal to latent board snobbery.

But even if your pooch does you proud and sits there silently throughout your ordeal, that may not be the end of it. Boards have been known, especially when there is a cranky neighbor across the hall, to impose a probationary period of several months—even on pets that pass inspection.

Don't Light Up

Think you'll calm your nerves by taking a drag during the interview? Don't try it. Your approval may go up in smoke. Faced with increasing complaints by nonsmoking shareholders of health hazards caused by secondhand smoke seeping through apartment vents and into corridors, a number of buildings are trying to make their buildings smoke free. Even if there's no outright ban, it's just not P.C. to light up. So if you think you'll have a nicotine attack during the interview, by all means slap on a patch (and wear long sleeves), but leave the cigarettes at home.

Be Prepared to Talk Money

Usually, if you have gotten to the interview stage your finances are in fairly solid shape. But this does not mean the board will forgo one last opportunity to turn the screws. You may feel flush to be paying all cash for your apartment, but unless the application makes clear where the money came from, the board may wonder if you just got back from a drug-running junket. So be prepared to allay its fears and to show (via explanation and documents) that you came by the loot legally and have not left yourself cash strapped.

The buyer whose finances are borderline can also use the interview for rehabilitation. If you know there is a problem, don't wait till the board starts grilling you and you are forced to take the defensive. Come prepared to explain your current cash flow situation and any improvements that are in the offing (you won the lottery; you got a raise). If you can, make the grand gesture of offering to pay six months' maintenance up front. This shows that you are solvent, serious—and just may put you over the top.

Beware of Loaded Questions

Until these people are your friends (or at least your neighbors) they are your potential enemies, and you should view their questions accordingly. Chances are when that board member asks about your CD collection, it is not because he is a musicologist but because he wants to know how loud and how often your favorite songs will be blaring—especially if he lives downstairs. If someone queries you about who you know in the building, it may be a way to find out if you will be a member of the ally or enemy camp.

If they ask about your last visit to your lawyer, it's okay to say you went to have a will drawn up. But assuming they don't already know from their own check that you're involved in litigation, better play it close to the vest or risk being labeled a troublemaker. If they want to know what you do in your spare time, don't get caught in the culture trap. The last thing you want to let on is that you're an aspiring pianist (they'll find out soon enough when that baby grand gets hoisted up) or an amateur opera singer (*you* may want to know the house practice rules lest there be too much golden silence for you). And if music is your business (a fact presumably disclosed in your application) you just may wind up playing elsewhere. The key is that nothing is as innocent as it seems.

Don't Volunteer Too Much

This is standard advice I give to clients in preparation for a litigation deposition. It also applies here. You may be worried about getting in, but the board is worried about getting sued if you don't get in. Often it is prevented by law (and its lawyers) from asking the questions it really wants answers to and has to resort to inoffensive substitutes. So, for example, asking you how many children you have may be a problem because under antidiscrimination laws family status is a protected category. Inquiring if you'll be living alone is no good either because marital status is also protected.

Instead, the board may ask you whose name the unit will be in or who will be occupying it, hoping you will fill in the blanks it wants answered. When it comes to these kinds of inquiries, let your conscience and common sense be your guide—but remember, the more you volunteer the more likely you are to get into trouble.

Don't Ask/Don't Tell

In the context of co-op politics, this means if the board doesn't ask about sublets, don't tell it. Sublet policies vary widely from building to building, from total prohibition to absolute freedom, with most allowing you to lease out your apartment for a finite number of years. Although many boards were forced to relax sublet rules during the market downturn to stave off shareholder revolt, they still turn up their noses at the thought of renters who put a damper on the building's image—and finances.

Even if the building allows sublets, there is no surer way to make yourself persona non grata than to let on from the start that your intent is to rent out your pad. So if you are a retired couple with another residence in Florida you had better have an explanation for what you plan to do with your apartment while you are sunning yourself down south. (Keeping it vacant is probably okay; letting your grandson crash there is not.)

Show That You Are Civic Minded But Not Power Hungry

Board members love to hear that somebody besides themselves is willing to do some work. So it's a pretty safe bet that expressing a willingness to volunteer for a committee or two will earn you a few brownie points. After all, it's hard to argue with someone who's willing to get down and dirty in the garden or take on the task of decorating the Christmas tree. (Offering to do more serious decorating, as in the lobby, can mean trouble and should be avoided at all costs.) The truth is that most committees do the work but have no power, since the board, not the committee, ultimately decides. Volunteering to run for the board, on the other hand, can be tricky. Unless you have inside information it's hard to know as an outsider whether your interest in co-op governance will win you kudos as a good citizen or brand you as a brazen upstart seeking to overturn the status quo.

HAVING THE LAST LAUGH—GETTING IN WITHOUT BOARD APPROVAL

At this point you may reasonably conclude that this game is not for you. No apartment is worth exposing yourself to the trauma of a full-scale inquisition. At least your rent-stabilized place allows you to retain your persona (and your past) intact and inviolable. But if you still harbor secret longings to own your own castle in the sky, don't give up so easily. With a little initiative you may not only avoid the board interview but circumvent the need for its seal of approval altogether.

Several paths to boardless entry are available, depending on how daring you are at heart.

Buy Directly from the Sponsor

As the entity that creates the co-op plan (whether by new construction or by conversion from rental status), the sponsor makes the rules in the bylaws and proprietary lease—including those defining the board's power to approve sales and transfers in the building. But the first thing the sponsor does is exempt itself from the very rules it has created. (This may seem unfair, but it's perfectly legal.) And the sponsor retains this above-the-law status in perpetuity. No matter that a majority of the building's owners later amend the governing documents to set different or additional requirements for apartment sales—the sponsor does not have to comply.

So when you or I go to sell our apartments to someone, our buyers are subject to the snub of rejection if they fail to pass muster under the board's scrutiny. If the sponsor decides to sell its apartments (called *unsold shares*), it does not have to get the board's approval. To the contrary, the sponsor can sell to whomever it wants, at whatever price it wants, on whatever terms and conditions it chooses. (Of course, if the sponsor tries to dump apartments to financially unfit buyers unable to pay maintenance, as one strapped owner was taken to court for, that may cross the line.)[1] Otherwise this legal loophole also gives you a break. As the person at the other end of the transaction you get the benefit of the sponsor's exemption.

Buying from the sponsor does not, however, exempt you from having to show that you are financially capable. But if your credit is good enough to get a mortgage commitment from a lender for the apartment, odds are the sponsor also will bless the deal—without your ever having had to come in contact with the board. For some people, it's confidences before cash. As one broker told me, buyers will talk sex but not money. To avoid having their (financial) affairs broadcast to the board (and the building) they'll even pay *more* to the sponsor to keep their secrets safe.

Try Going the Foreclosure Route

Chapter 2 gave you the straight talk on what you need to know before going this route and the pros and cons of buying at a foreclosure sale. Let's say you have done your homework and decided you're ready to go for it. If you're successful you may be able to get an apartment at a bargain price and close the deal without having to get board approval.

Co-ops want to encourage banks to continue to lend toward the purchase of apartments in their buildings, and to do that they often make it easier for banks to get rid of apartments they have acquired in foreclosure. Many buildings have lease provisions exempting banks from the board approval requirement when the banks sell apartments they acquired from defaulting shareholders. Instead, sales by a lender in these situations may be subject only to the approval of the managing agent—or some other stepped-down requirement. Even condos often free lenders from their right-of-first-refusal requirement in these cases. It's okay to make individual sellers cool their heels while the board grinds its way to a decision. But if the guys with the deep pockets get hot under the collar about waiting too long, they may get so steamed that they'll take their money and run—and not lend on apartments in the building anymore.

How does all this affect you? If you are lucky enough to get a gem at a foreclosure sale you also may get the benefit of the special treatment given to the lender. At least one court said yes to a real estate investor who bought through foreclosure from a bank an apartment that he intended to sublet. After interviewing the purchaser, the board directed the managing agent to tell the buyer he had been rejected, without giving any reason. But the buyer argued that under the co-op's lease the managing agent alone—not the board—had the right to make the decision, since he bought in a foreclosure sale, and, moreover, that decision had to be *reasonable*. Since the agent merely rubber-stamped the board's rejection and did not exercise its own independent judgment, the buyer claimed, and the court agreed, that both agent and board had acted unreasonably. So the buyer got his apartment despite the board's objection.[2]

And a buyer who purchased a condo at auction from the lender who had foreclosed on the unit had similar good luck. Since the condo bylaws said the board couldn't preempt sales by the bank in such situations, the buyer at the other end of the deal got to walk right through the door.[3]

Armed with this intelligence, should you snatch up an apartment at a foreclosure sale in a building that grants this kind of preference to lenders, you should wind up the beneficiary, along with the bank, of this relaxed admissions standard. Indeed, if you are really gutsy you may even want to challenge the co-op's board's right to interview you. After all, why should its input matter when the exclusive power to decide has been handed over to the agent?

Leverage the Right of First Refusal

As you know by now, in condos and co-ops with a right of first refusal there is no traditional board approval. The board does not have the authority to accept or reject you, only to buy the apartment if it doesn't like you. There is usually no interview, either, because all the board is interested in is your cash, not your character. Best of all, since it can't say no, your success is predetermined—it's only a matter of time.

TRANSFER OF POWER—FROM OLD GUARD TO YOU

The ultimate step in the process is the official transfer of power (a.k.a. the closing), which follows hard upon the heels of board approval. For those of you who have not experienced the legal set up close, here's your chance to see them in action—as a participant, not a Court TV observer. Be forewarned, they come in multiples.

There'll be you and your lawyer. Come with your signing arm in shape (for those piles of documents your lawyer will review and place in front of you) and checks a-ready so you can claim (and move into) your trophy. The seller and his lawyer will attend to collect the cash. If the seller has a mortgage on the apartment, his lender's lawyer will show up to get paid back whatever amounts are outstanding on the loan before he'll turn over the original stock certificate and proprietary lease (co-ops) or deed (condos). The building will have a representative to act as transfer agent. And if it's a condo (where you have to get title insurance, as you would for a house), the insurance company's man likely will be on the spot.

Today's the day you pay the apartment piper. Better to know now while you're calm and collected (and think you're playing with Monopoly money) what the tab will be. You can get an idea of how much you'll have to shell out in closing costs from the charts at the end of the chapter. It costs more to close on a condo than a co-op mainly because when buying the former (but not the latter) you have to obtain title insurance and pay a mortgage recording tax (assuming you're financing the purchase). If you've ever been a stand-alone home owner you know the purpose of such insurance is to protect against any defects in the title to your unit or any problems or liens against the condo building. Unlike health insurance that protects against *future* trouble, title insurance guards against defects that exist up to the time you purchased the policy. There are two kinds, and you'll need both: An owner's policy requires the insurance company to defend your rights in the property and to pay for any title-related losses. The lender's policy (essential to get a mortgage), covers only the bank's interest in the condo for the length of its loan. Then there's a mortgage tax that applies to loans on real estate (condos), but not to share loans used to buy co-ops. It's the City Fathers' way of increasing your financial pain to the tune of thousands.

You'll have to bring real checks for the balance of the nonfinanced part of the price, bank costs, lawyers' fees, transfer agent fees, and assorted building add-ons. You'll also have to even up the score with the seller, paying your proportionate share of maintenance (and maybe assessments, too) for the balance of the month. And if you've gone for broke and bought a really palatial pad you'll be out even more. New York has a so-called Mansion Tax, which imposes a 1 percent tax on the sale of co-ops and condos priced at least $1 million.

This is your victory day, so don't let anything spoil the celebration. I almost scuttled my own sweetheart of a deal by standing on principle. My lender's lawyer demanded a travel fee (of several hundred dollars) for the time it took him to get across the river. What's the big deal? you lawyers out there are asking. Except my legal shark was charging for the same hour ten times over since ours was a bulk closing at the building's conversion. I tried apportionment appeasement, but when that didn't work, I paid the entire amount of extortion.

Be prepared for a few last-minute skirmishes, the better to ready you for your role as a member of the co-op (or condo) rank and file. The seller has a pile of parking tickets totaling hundreds that show up at the last minute as a judgment lien on the condo. (This can happen if they initially escaped detection or were docketed for judgment between the initial and final searches.) Or he decided to play hardball and not pay the last month's maintenance, figuring you'd pick up the tab rather than lose the apartment. In either case, someone's got to pay or the deal won't get done. I'm not saying you should pay, just that you should keep things in perspective (and not lose sight of your ultimate goal).

As soon as the last paper has been signed, you're one of them. After you have crossed that line from prospective purchaser to resident owner, watch out that your political philosophy doesn't undergo a radical transformation. It's one thing to challenge the power establishment when you're an insurgent storming the barricades. But it takes true moral courage once you're a member of the privileged class not to forsake your partisan past and join in the construction of still higher admissions barriers to protect your newly won way of life.

WILL YOU SURVIVE THE INTERVIEW?

Dos	Don'ts
1. Show up on time and ready to charm.	1. Bring your bodyguards with you.
2. Dress for acceptance.	2. Interrupt your interrogators—they know best.
3. Bribe the kids to act their Brady Bunch best (if the board requires their presence).	3. Light up (whether cigar, pipe, or cigarette).
4. Finish domestic feuds before you walk in the door.	4. Break out the Bazooka.
5. Ask innocuous questions about the neighborhood.	5. Bring up your sublet plans.
6. Volunteer for committee (but not board) service.	6. Ask about lobby renovations.
7. Compliment the physical aspect of the building.	7. Say anything about your pets (unless directly asked).
8. Be on guard for loaded questions.	8. Discuss your musical preferences.
9. Use the opportunity to rehabilitate questionable finances.	9. Let on that you're a party animal.
10. Make note of any inappropriate or potentially discriminatory questions (the better to challenge a rejection).	10. Volunteer any information that could be used against you.

HOW MUCH WILL IT COST TO CLOSE?

(Assuming you're buying a $600,000 co-op and paying 20% down)

	Estimated Range	Assumed Cost
• Managing agent processing fee:	$250–$500	$400
• Credit report:	$50–$100	$75

	Estimated Range	Assumed Cost
• Recognition agreement:	$150–$300	$250
• Move-in fee: (may be a *refundable deposit* of up to $1,000)	$250–$500	$300
• Your attorney:	$1,500 and up	$1,750
• Loan origination fee:	(0–3% of loan value)	$7,200 (1.5% of $480,000)
• Appraisal:	$400–$600	$500
• Judgment and lien search:	$250–$350	$300
• UCC-1 filing fee:	$50	$50
• Misc. bank fees:	$500–$600	$600
• Bank attorney:	$500 and up	$625
• Prepaid mortgage interest:	(for balance of month in which you close)	________
• Maintenance adjustment:	(pro-rated for month of closing)	________
		________
TOTAL		$12,050 (plus unquantifiable charges listed above)

Caveat:

For million-dollar-plus pads, there is a Mansion Tax of 1 percent of the purchase price, which adds on an initial $10,000 once the threshold is met, and goes up from there depending on the cost of the apartment.

HOW MUCH WILL IT COST TO CLOSE?

(Assuming you're buying a $600,000 condo and paying 20% down)

	Estimated Range	Assumed Cost
• Managing agent processing fee:	$250–$500	$400
• Credit report:	$50–$100	$75
• Move-in fee: (may be a *refundable deposit* of up to $1,000)	$250–$500	$300
• Contribution to capital fund:	(where applicable, 1–2 months' common charges)	
• Your attorney:	$1,500 and up	$1,750
• Loan origination fee:	(0–3% of loan value)	$7,200 (1.5% of $480,000)
• Mortgage recording tax:	(1.75% of mortgages less than $500,000; 1.85% of mortgages over $500,000)	$8,400
• Title insurance:	(approximately $500–$600 per $100,000 of purchase price)	$3,300 ($550 per $100,000)
• Recording fees:	$250–$350	$300
• Misc. bank fees:	$500–$600	$600
• Bank attorney:	$500 and up	$625
• Prepaid mortgage interest:	(for balance of month in which you close)	________
• Common charge adjustment:	(pro-rated for month of closing)	________

• Bank tax escrow:	(usually 2–6 months of real estate taxes)	________
TOTAL		________
		$22,950 (plus unquantifiable charges listed above)

Caveat 1:

For million-dollar-plus pads there is a Mansion Tax of 1% of the purchase price, which adds on an additional $10,000 once the threshold is met and goes up from there, depending on the cost of the apartment.

Caveat 2:

For purchases of newly constructed condos, the sponsor usually passes on to you the following costs ordinarily paid by the seller.

• Sponsor's attorney:	$1,000 and up	$1,250
• N.Y.C. transfer tax:	(1% of sales price of $500,000 or less; 1.425% of sales price if more than $500,000)	$8,550
• N.Y.S. transfer tax:	(.4% of sales price)	$2,400
TOTAL		$12,200 more

6

Dealing with Rejection: Fight or Flight?

DECIDING ON A PLAN OF ACTION

Got a thumbs-down? Resist the urge to vent your spleen against the broker (he's only the messenger) or even the board (you may say things you will regret, especially if you decide to pursue legal action).

But it may soothe your bruised ego to know that you are in good company. Mike Wallace of *60 Minutes* fame was rejected; as was Steve Wynn, the casino entrepreneur. Madonna and Barbra Streisand faced the same fate. Sean Lennon, son of John, was rejected from his own mother's co-op. Mariah Carey was nixed, as was author Daphne Merkin, supposedly for "dirty writing." Since, as you know, condo boards have virtually no control over sales, the sting of rejection is reserved for thwarted co-op buyers.

The more haute the building, the more likely the criteria are to be idiosyncratic and subjective. So think of rejection as a badge of honor. You have just made it to the Mensa Society for co-ops. If that doesn't work, down a therapeutic dose of vodka and tonic or foaming latte—whatever your particular poison—and wait until those nerves of steel return so that you can plot out a proper battle plan.

Do you want to try appeasement, engage the board in full-scale war, or cut your losses and move on to the next building? To make the choice that's right for you, you'll need to know both the realpolitik of rejection and the legal weapons at your disposal.

THE POLITICS OF REJECTION

What You're Up Against

Rejections tend to rise along with the market. There's always someone waiting in the wings to fill the shoes of the turned-down buyer, sometimes for a higher price, so the seller is less likely to complain and the jilted buyer usually would rather switch to another building than fight, allowing directors to flex their muscles with impunity. By some accounts, the rejection rate exceeded 8 percent during the market peak of the past few years, compared with a mere 1 percent at the last trough of the early 1990s, when boards were faced with disgruntled shareholders desperate to sell. Statistics aside, some boards wear their authority more openly than others. An acquaintance at a downtown building had three prospective purchasers rejected, ostensibly for inadequate finances (though all were loaded), only to have them accept the fourth, who promptly went bankrupt after closing.

The real rate of rejection is probably even higher than the reports suggest. It's an open secret that some buildings look askance at those of certain ethnic origins; others at gays. Some do not look kindly upon unmarried couples of any persuasion; others frown upon newlyweds of child-bearing age or those who are "too old." Prospective buyers steer clear of "unsuitable" buildings so they are not rejected, just never considered.

Some purchasers try their own form of appeasement. One live-in couple I know, who had always vowed not to be shackled by official convention, cast aside their principles and made a quick trip to the altar rather than lose an apartment in a building where the board frowned upon cohabitation without benefit of a marriage certificate.

Hey, you may be thinking, it's not such a bad way to get that guy to finally make a commitment. But for those unwilling to be manipulated (even at the expense of remaining ringless), there are other options out there for dealing with rejection. Although your instinct may be to fight, my advice is to try at all costs to avoid legal warfare (usually the most expensive and least effective way to go) and to first attempt some pacific overtures.

Defensive Maneuvers

Let's say you sense in the interview that all is not well but you can't put your finger on the reason for your discomfort. Was it something you said? Did you criticize the lobby decor? Were your kids less than adorable? Make a beeline to your broker and let him debrief you on all that transpired. Based on his knowledge of past sales and rejects, he is likely to have a sense of the building's undisclosed profile and may be able to tell you where you went astray. And a broker who is savvy and well connected may have a pipeline directly to the board president. If so, he or she can find out from the horse's mouth whether there is a problem (an invitation to engage in some capital-style lobbying on your behalf) or you're home free. In either case, knowing where you stand is an essential first step in crafting your next move.

If you know what the problem is, you're already ahead of the game. Make a peace offering to the board, assuming it's something you can live with. If it's your passion for music that got you into trouble, offer to insulate your practice room or strictly limit your hours of practice. If you're a young couple with limited liquid assets, agree to have your parents sign on as guarantors. If it's the dog that did you in, accept a probationary period—or try thinking goldfish. Who knows—if you're creative and the board is rational, you may hit upon a mutually agreeable resolution short of war.

Saber Rattling

Assuming that the board remains unmoved despite your efforts at compromise, maybe the time has come to give it a taste of its own medicine and a chance to see what it's like to be on the hot seat. Let the board know firmly, but politely (preferably through your attorney), that you are aware of your legal rights and will take action to vindicate them. Of course, if you opt to take this approach it helps if you have the facts and/or the law on your side.

Suppose the board in a co-op operating under the right-of-first-refusal system is foolish (or defiant) enough to reject you outright. Let it know you are aware (as it should be, too) that, like it or not, it does not have this option—and you are sure a court of law will see it the same way. If the board is bound not to withhold consent unreasonably but nevertheless nixes you, remind it that its subjective excuses (or stonelike silence) will not pass judicial muster.

If you believe you are a victim of discrimination, make that clear up front. Your case will be all the stronger if you can arm your attorney with questions you were improperly asked at the interview: What country do you come from? Are you single? What synagogue or church do you attend? How many kids do you have? These are all forbidden areas of inquiry that could help you and hurt the board in the event you sue for discrimination.

This legal saber rattling may get the board to the negotiating table—or at least to talking. (The more it talks, the more likely it will be to offer up helpful tidbits.) Although boards may wear their power with pride, don't think they're not afraid of being hit with a lawsuit. It costs them time, money, and aggravation to defend against such an onslaught and may even expose them to personal liability. And on top of that, they may have to answer to angry shareholders, who may ultimately foot the legal bills and will hold board members responsible if the building has to pay up for having unlawfully rejected someone.

If these tactical measures and threats of war yield no results, you may have no choice but to resort to the long arm of the law to knock down those barriers to entry.

THE LEGAL FRONT

Score One for the Board

The only problem is that for the most part the law is on the board's side. It has long been the rule that, absent discrimination prohibited by law or bad faith, the board can reject you for *any* reason or *no* reason. This state's highest court recognized decades ago that co-ops are like private clubs when it ruled:[1]

> Absent the application of these statutory standards [which prohibit discrimination] . . . there is no reason why the owners of the co-operative apartment house could not decide for themselves with whom they wish to share their elevators, their common halls, their stockholders' meetings, their management problems and responsibilities and their homes.

Nothing much has changed since then. Although you may sense from a chill in the air during the interview that things are not going to turn out right, the board does not have to tell you why it is turning you down—and it usually doesn't for fear of saying something it shouldn't. Most boards are instructed by their lawyers to transmit the news orally through the managing agent so their fingerprints won't show. A letter may be necessary to provide a formal record, allowing buyer and seller to terminate the contract without adverse consequences. But it, too, usually will come from the agent and be sanitized to say no more than that the board has not approved the purchaser's application. Not a lot to go on.

Here are some of the reasons boards have relied on for rejection, all of which have been upheld by the courts:

Money

You don't have enough of it: your income's too low, your assets are insufficient to meet the building's criteria or they're too illiquid to count, your credit is lousy, you've been involved in a bankruptcy, you're seeking too much financing. Far and away, money is the number one cause for not getting in, which is not to say that sometimes it may be used as a pretext to obscure the real reason.

Dissembling

You haven't come clean on your application. Refuse to give the board your tax return? It doesn't have to give you its approval.[2] Overstate your net worth? That's enough for it to say no.[3] Give vague and unresponsive answers? The board can give you a definite heave-ho.[4] Provide inconsistent information? You may find yourself in trouble.[5]

Bargain

You got too good a deal—the apartment is too cheap. Maybe the sellers are splitting up and need to make a quick settlement, or the owner has to get up and go (somewhere else) for a new job. Their loss is your gain—unless the board steps in. Boards sometimes refuse consent to sales if they think the price is too low, figuring they have to protect values in the building. As a matter of law, whether or not they can do this depends on who you are. Since as a buyer you're not yet a shareholder to whom the board owes any duties, the courts have said it's okay for them to reject for a lowball price, but the answer may be different if it's the selling shareholder who complains. (See chapter 18.)

Undersized

Your apartment is too small for your status. If you're a hot shot with a big wad, but are buying a small-time apartment, the board may figure it's really for someone else—a child-care nanny, a poorer relation—and deny your application. After having been turned down by the grand Dakota apartment house, singer Carly Simon sued for return of her down payment, claiming the board had rejected her because it couldn't believe she was buying the $1 million one-bedroom for herself, but must have intended it for her children.[6]

Outlaw

You've said or done something to make the board believe you aren't going to abide by the rules of their regime:[7] Somehow you've let on that you plan to engage in unauthorized empire building or sneak in a Great Dane in contravention of the building's no-pet policy or sublet your apartment in violation of the co-op's policy against selling to nonresident owners.

Untouchable

You or your assets are beyond reach. Could be your net worth is tied up in real estate in Hong Kong (which you call home), and you want to buy an apartment for a relative halfway round the world in New York, where you have no assets (a situation our board faced). Or maybe you're a diplomat with immunity so neither your person nor your property is subject to our justice system. Boards can (and do) reject those who refuse to waive immunity, even if they agree to provide bank guarantees.[8]

Overburden

You're too much trouble. Maybe you're a shrink who plans to practice from home, and the board is afraid there'll be too many patients coming and going, causing wear and tear; or you're a white-collar criminal returned from Camp Fed, with lots of cash and even more security risks.

But take heart. Although the board generally has the upper hand, you may have available options that allow you to take it on and win.

Fight Back with Reasonableness

If you have read this far you know (from chapter 4) that there is a movement afoot, at least in some buildings, to check the board's power to reject by imposing a reasonableness requirement. (Assuming you have done the homework assigned to you and have read the proprietary lease and bylaws, you also know by now whether the board that rejected you had its wings clipped in this fashion.)

In these buildings, the board does not have the authority to just go by its gut in saying yes or no to prospective purchasers. Regardless of its personal feelings about you, it cannot "unreasonably" withhold consent to the sale of an apartment to you. Will this restriction make it easier for you to challenge the board's veto and win? The answer depends on why you were rejected.

The lowdown on the law as interpreted by the relatively few courts that have confronted this issue is that the "unreasonable" term invokes "an objective third party standard." As one court put it:[9]

> New York courts have interpreted such clauses to require standards that are:
>
> readily measurable of a proposed . . . assignee's acceptability from the viewpoint of any landlord, including:
>
> (a) financial responsibility
> (b) the identity or business character of the subtenant, including suitability for the particular building
> (c) legality of the proposed use
> (d) nature of the occupancy

In contrast, subjective reasons based on the "landlord's supposed needs, dislikes, personal taste, sensibility or convenience" generally will meet with judicial disapproval.

How does all this legal theory translate into real-world practice?

Take the relatively straightforward case of the purchaser who sought to buy an apartment to be used as a medical office occupied by one doctor and *two* employees. Although the municipal regulations to which the proprietary lease was subject allowed such occupancy, the board nevertheless conditioned its approval on limiting the occupancy to only one doctor and *one* employee. The buyer sued and won. Given that the board had ignored the clearly objective standard in the municipal ordinance, the court found it had unreasonably withheld consent in violation of the lease.[10]

Or consider the challenge by a woman who applied to buy an apartment from a shareholder in a recently converted co-op. Her extended family had significant assets but complex financial arrangements. At the interview, the buyer couldn't say what she intended to do with her existing apartment, did not know the persons who had been listed as references, and was uncertain about questions dealing with finances, bank accounts, and available funds. Despite the fact that the financial questions were later answered by letter and additional references were provided, the board rejected her, citing her vagueness and unresponsiveness to its questions. Although ordinarily the board could take cover under such subjective excuses, here the court ordered it to transfer the apartment because it had violated its contractual obligation not to "unreasonably" withhold consent.[11]

And finally, another board was taken to task, and to court, for having refused consent to a sale. The thwarted shareholder claimed the board was ticked off at him because some third party sued the co-op over an accident that had occurred in his apartment. On top of that, he said some board members tried to make his buyers give up their future right to rent out even though the lease allowed subletting. Once again the court found that the grounds for refusal were unreasonable and hence a violation of the board's obligation under the lease.[12]

Still confused about how all this legal lingo can help you if you've been rejected? What you should take away is this: if, after serious soul-searching, you believe you were objectively qualified to buy the apartment (financials in order, no dark secrets lurking in your past or present) and the board turned you down for its own subjective reasons (you didn't fit its profile; it didn't like your answers), you should win in a showdown.

Of course, even if you're convinced based on what you've just read that you are right, the fact remains that the board is still refusing to transfer the apartment and let you move in. Short of physical confrontation by the moving men (not a strategy I advocate), the only way to force the board into submission, assuming you've had no luck with any of the tactical maneuvers, is to get a lawyer and sue. But before you decide to go that route you should know what you're getting into and what the potential pitfalls may be. Read on.

Catch Them If They Cross the Line

No matter whether the board is bound under the co-op's rules to be reasonable or not, under the law the board cannot deny consent in bad faith. Although (absent a reasonableness requirement) it can turn you down for *any* reason or *no* reason, it cannot reject you if the reason is its own self-interest. Power has its limits—and if the board crosses the line you should be ready to act.

So if it turns out that you got axed not for lack of qualifications but because the board president had a vendetta against you for having successfully acquired an apartment he coveted (as actually happened in one case), you would get the last laugh (and the keys to the apartment).[13] Or suppose one of the directors was interested in acquiring for herself the very apartment you wanted to buy.[14] Or the board nixed an intrafamily transfer because the daughter refused to pay a "flip tax" that hadn't been charged to other shareholders.[15] Here, too, the courts have upheld claims of bad faith against the board in refusing to approve the sale.

Don't Let the Board Get Away with Discrimination

Although under certain circumstances boards can arbitrarily deny consent, they can never legally discriminate against you. If you think this was the real reason for your rejection, you should consider taking action. When it comes to discrimination, the law is squarely in your corner. But proving that the board violated the law is not easy.

In New York, a purchaser who has been rejected because of discrimination has a broad range of legal weapons (at all levels of government from local to federal) with which to lead the charge. The New York City Human Rights Law[16] provides the broadest coverage, prohibiting any refusal to sell, lease, or otherwise deny housing accommodation to a person based on race, creed, color, national origin, sex, age, disability, sexual orientation, marital status, citizenship, occupation, or the existence of children. On the state level, there's what's commonly known as the Human Rights Law[17] and the New York Civil Rights Law[18] which together ban discrimination based on race, creed, color, national origin, sex, age, disability, marital status, or familial status. Similar protections are found in federal statutes, most notably the Civil Rights Act[19] and the Fair Housing Act.[20] The particular statute you use to do battle is to a large extent determined by where you decide to file a complaint: federal or state court, New York State Human Rights Division, or New York City Commission on Human Rights (something you should let your lawyer worry about).

The problem you will face is how to prove discrimination under the law, because the board does not have to give any reason for rejecting you. To try to overcome this obstacle, New York courts require only that you prove discriminatory *effect*, not discriminatory *intent*. This means that to make out a so-called prima facie case of discrimination (one that will withstand challenge) all you have to do is show the following facts:

1. that you are a member of a protected class;
2. that you applied for and were qualified to buy the apartment;
3. that you were rejected; and
4. that the apartment remained available after your rejection.

How does this work? Let's say, for example, that you are a gay man (protected because of your sexual orientation) or an African-American woman (protected on two counts, race and sex). Assuming that you were objectively qualified to buy and that you were rejected for an apartment that remained available, you have, without more, established a claim for discrimination.

The burden then shifts to the board to show that it denied your application not because of discriminatory considerations but due to other, nondiscriminatory factors. The board would likely offer up a litany of supposedly legitimate reasons for your rejection: you failed to submit all the necessary information, you didn't have credible answers to its questions, you're at a new job, you had to take a loan, you won't be a good neighbor—and more. As the wronged buyer, you get the last chance to prove that the reasons the board came up with are only a pretext to mask discrimination.

These rules setting the standard for what you have to prove to win a discrimination suit against a co-op board were established in a case called *Robinson v. 12 Lofts Realty, Inc.*,[21] decided more than twenty years ago. In that case, a black physicist working for IBM contracted to buy two-thirds of a floor in a co-op building having ten shareholders (all were white and each owned his or her own floor). When his proposed purchase came before the shareholders, they voted to change the informal procedure they had used until then and set up a committee to meet with prospective buyers and obtain background information. The newly formed committee interviewed the purchaser and his wife, at which time its members asked a host of loaded questions, including some about criminal and underworld connections. This new procedure was not followed for a white buyer who happened to be applying at the same time. Although the committee found that the purchaser's finances, references, and answers to its questions were all "satisfactory," the shareholders voted to increase the 51 percent majority needed for approval of a sale to 66⅔ percent, and then rejected the application for being one vote short.

When the rejected purchaser sued under federal antidiscrimination laws, the co-op board claimed it had rejected the purchaser because its members had heard rumors that the physicist intended to use the premises as an after-hours club and because he had been abrasive and uncooperative during the admissions process. Incredibly, the trial judge bought the co-op's argument and found that the reasons for rejection were nondiscriminatory. But on appeal the court reversed, finding that the facts were sufficiently egregious to demonstrate not only discriminatory effect (all that's needed to prevail) but also discriminatory motive.

Although the standard today remains the same—and all co-op discrimination cases, whether brought under local, state, or federal law, still take their cue from *Robinson*—the nature of the facts underpinning the discrimination is usually not so overt. Coached by teams of lawyers in what they can and can't ask under the antidiscrimination laws, board members nowadays rarely fall into the trap of posing such obviously improper questions as did the *Robinson* board. Instead, they go about getting the information they want by more subtle and indirect inquiries, hoping to get you to cough up the facts they can't legally ask for. (Assuming, of course, you heeded the advice in chapter 5 to be on guard for such subterfuge, you will have volunteered nothing.) As a result of the shift to subtlety, it's often harder today to make a discrimination claim stick. But it has and can be done.

Take the challenge brought by prospective purchasers—an African-American man and his Hispanic wife—who contracted to buy a co-op for $205,000, putting down a standard 10 percent deposit, and planning to finance $184,500 and pay the rest in cash at closing. The board claimed their application raised financial concerns—too little income and too much debt—and was confusing because it wasn't possible to tell whether some assets and liabilities were reported once or twice. The board told the managing agent not to schedule an interview until it had received the revised statements, but went ahead with an interview anyway—and then rejected the buyers. By granting an interview *after* a financial statement had been provided, the court said the board's intent had been put into question and allowed the buyers' claim for discrimination to proceed.[22]

But the biggest win by far came in the sublet context in a case that has sent shock waves through co-op and condo boardrooms. An interracial couple with cash (lawyers both) applied to sublet the apartment of their dreams in posh Beekman Place, but were turned down after a face-to-face interview. With the husband's law firm agreeing to lead the charge, they took on the board. At trial the board members claimed their rejection was not due to race but because the husband was "arrogant" and "aggressive." But the jury didn't buy it, maybe because it came out that one of the board members had scribbled "black man" on a pad in discussions about the couple's application. They awarded them $640,000 in damages, plus approximately $900,000 in fees and expenses, for a total in excess of $1.5 million, including $125,000 in punitive damages that Mr. Board President had to pay out of his *own* pocket.[23]

New Battlefronts

As times change, so do the nature of claims for discrimination, with age being the latest battleground. Maybe you think you were turned down for the counterintuitive reason that you're too young. That was the basis for a shareholder suing her board in a tony Manhattan co-op. Three times she presented potential buyers to the board—all thirty-something couples with childbearing potential—and three times they were rejected. After almost a year and a half of thwarted attempts, finally it approved the application of a fifty-nine-year-old divorcée without minor (noisemaking) kids. Even though the $455,000 price for which Ms. Shareholder ultimately sold was higher than that in the initially rejected contract, she said she was damaged due to age discrimination committed against her would-be purchasers because she had to continue paying maintenance and lost interest on the proceeds of the earlier sales. The court agreed and let her claim stand, saying, "the power of a cooperative board of directors to reject purchasers is not unlimited."[24]

Her victory updates that achieved two decades ago by two twenty-something single women who had legally sublet an apartment at an Upper West Side co-op, and then applied to buy. Although they were exemplary tenants, the board said no, coming up with excuses rather than reasons, and finally declaring it had sole discretion to decide. But the court saw through the pretext, said the investigation by the State Division of Human Rights had no basis, and sent the case back for the Division to do its homework properly.[25]

Conversely, it could be that you're convinced you were rejected because you're too old. Pointing to statements made by members of the board that turned down his application to buy a co-op, an eighty-one-year-old buyer claimed he was a victim of age discrimination. The court there, too, found he'd presented enough evidence for his case to go forward.[26]

Beyond age (at either end of the spectrum), other bases are being tested. One Manhattan building that recently turned down a prospective buyer after an interview, finding her finances wanting, got hit with a claim for disability discrimination, and more such suits are likely to follow.

Standing

You don't have to be the actual victim of discrimination to get relief. If you're the selling shareholder, not the willing buyer, nixed for being too old or young (or some other form of discrimination), so long as you can show you were adversely affected by the board's decision, you can make a claim.[27] And because you're an owner to whom the board is responsible, you'll also have a claim for breach of fiduciary duty.

Balancing Act

Despite these reported victories, it's not always easy to predict the outcome where discrimination is claimed, because the facts are rarely clear cut, and judges differ on how much deference to give board assessment of buyers' finances, usually the reason advanced for rejection. Based on my experience and on what I've heard from other boards, I suspect buyers are more disposed to threaten discrimination complaints (legitimate or not), and boards may be more willing to settle than fight, given the potential for significant liability (personal and collective) and the high cost of defense.

So where does all this leave you? If you're a financially qualified buyer who is a member of a protected class (due to sex, race, marital status, or sexual orientation, for example) and you believe the board has rejected you for no legitimate reason, you may have a sound basis on which to proceed. How far you'll get you won't know till the end. It's hard to give general parameters because these kinds of cases depend so much on the particular facts. But here are a few practical points worth considering.

Are You Beyond Reproach?

You already have been counseled to tell the truth on your purchase application. If the board finds out that you've been less than candid (which it will) your credibility will be crushed and with it maybe your case. That's what happened to a couple who claimed the board discriminated against them based on family status because it rejected their sublease application after learning that they had four kids, not two. But the board said (and the court agreed) that the turn down was the result of the applicants' dissembling, not its discrimination.[28]

Did the Board Do Itself In?

It's unlikely, but not impossible, that a board member's ill-chosen words will reveal his true colors and the board's real (and illegal) reason for your rejection. That's why you should take careful notes during the application process, especially following the interview. The first thing any witness who's been grilled by the grand jury does is to run into the arms of his waiting lawyer and spill all that his interrogators have asked before he forgets. So, too, if after your meeting in the lion's den you suspect you may be a target of wrongful rejection, write down what was said while it's still fresh in your consciousness, the better to provide your lawyer with ammunition should you decide to proceed.

Did It Refuse to Talk?

The board doesn't have to tell you why it turned you down. But if you ask and its members still remain mute, their stonewalling may make them look bad and earn you a few strategic points.

Did It Change the Rules?

It's okay for a board to pass rules so long as they're uniformly applied. But if it puts into place some rule or change in the application process specifically aimed just to keep you out, that's another red flag. It's hard to believe this practice still occurs after *Robinson*, but it does. One board's rejection of a purchaser was held discriminatory, in part, because it switched from its usual practice of voting by a show of hands to a secret ballot for the buyer in question.[29] The problem is you may not know that the board has singled you out this way till you're deep into the discovery process.

Did It Rely on Objective Criteria?

Lots of boards expose themselves to problems by relying on unwritten financial standards for admission that are honored more in the breach than in the observance. They figure brokers who do business in their buildings know the rules. If you get in, you probably don't care. But if you don't and you think discrimination is the reason, take heed. Unless the board can point to objective financial criteria (equally applied to all) that you flunked, it may find itself in trouble.

Is Your Rejection Part of a Pattern?

One turndown could be a fluke, or really due to finances. But if others of the same status (for example, all gay men or single women) also got shafted, you may be able to show a pattern of discrimination which could bolster your claim.

Winning Results

What do you get if you slog through the legal morass and win? The answer depends on the particular circumstances and the law you rely on, but these are the general parameters:

Apartment

The apartment you most want is the thing you are least likely to get. Shareholders don't usually dash into court to stop the sale of the apartment they were denied, and even if they did, they would be unlikely to get it because most courts would say cash is enough to compensate you. I'm not saying never. After finding that the co-op board had discriminated against the buyer, one court ordered it under the Federal Housing Act to approve the application and transfer the apartment,[30] but the odds are heavily against your getting such relief.

Regular Money

How much you can get depends on how much you actually lost, but such damages could include lost interest, payment of extra maintenance, and the price differential between the apartment for which you were rejected and the one you wound up with.

Penalty Money

As we've seen, punitive damages can be a big number, and they can hit the co-op (and ultimately its shareholders) hard because they are not covered by insurance. (See chapter 17.) But the facts in the case of the Beekman Place subletters were so outrageous that we're unlikely to see an award of that size any time soon.

Fees and Fines

Under certain circumstances you also may be entitled to reimbursement for attorneys' fees and expenses as were those subletters—to the tune of hundreds of thousands of dollars—and award of civil fines under the law.

PUTTING YOUR LEGAL WEAPONS TO WORK

Now that you know the legal weapons in your arsenal, you have to decide if you're prepared to use them to wage a full-scale attack against the board—whether it has unreasonably rejected you, acted in bad faith, or engaged in discrimination. Be forewarned that legal warfare is only for those with sure resolve, steady nerves, and sufficient cash. Where discrimination is at issue, the government has such a compelling public interest at stake that, assuming you have a real claim, the New York City Commission on Human Rights or the New York State Human Rights Division may take on your case without a fee. If you opt for the private route, whatever the basis for your suit, you're on your own when it comes to footing the bill and everything else. Before you decide to go to war, which can add thousands to the cost of the apartment for which you are fighting, be sure it offers sufficient reward—so that you are assured of sweet revenge, not a Pyrrhic victory.

Here, then, is a look at the different strategic options available to you in pursuit of victory.

Getting the City to Fight Your Battle

If you decide to do battle and don't want to spend a bundle on legal fees, try the New York City Commission on Human Rights. If it takes your case, its enforcement division lawyers will act as your attorney, from the complaint through the trial stage, without a fee. When it gets to a hearing, you may want to bring in your own counsel. Or if you're lucky and your case involves some hot legal issue that impacts a wider audience, you may be able to enlist the aid of one of the interest groups sympathetic to your plight (for example, Lambda Legal Defense, the NAACP, the ACLU). If such a group agrees to take on your cause, you will get not only high-powered representation (for free) but also useful publicity.

If you go the commission route, a human rights specialist will listen to your story and, if it makes sense, send off a complaint to the offending co-op or condo. Although most boards simply deny the charges, the reach of the law can have a sufficient in terrorem effect to get some of them talking. Mediation (which the commission can engage in on your behalf after the complaint is filed) is your best hope for a reasonable and timely solution. Since the substance of such negotiations and any settlements that result need not be made public and do not count as legal precedents, the board may be willing to make concessions rather than risk protracted litigation.

If not, the commission investigates your claim to see if there is probable cause (sufficient evidence) for a hearing. It tries to expedite housing cases, but in fact it takes months, more often years, until a claim gets to the hearing stage.

Calling on State Forces

The drill is similar at the New York State Division of Human Rights, where you can opt to go to file your complaint against a co-op that you believe turned you down for unlawful discrimination. Investigators there are ready to speak with you, and enforcement division lawyers will serve as your counsel without charge through the hearing stage. Although the city's commission is empowered by the administrative code, which gives it jurisdiction to hear cases only within its five boroughs, the state's Human Rights Division draws its authority from the state's Human Rights Law, which allows it to act on complaints statewide.

Bringing In Your Own Hired Gun

If money is no object, you may want to bring in your own hired gun to do your bidding. Going the private route gives you greater control over how your case proceeds and, if you choose well, probably will get you a more nimble and creative advocate than you'll wind up with in the government bureaucracy. Depending on a number of factors, including the chosen statutory framework, your legal eagle can press your case in federal or state court. You can't have it both ways. Nor can you bring a complaint in either court if you already have one pending with the state division or the city commission. (The rule is, you can seek judicial *or* administrative relief, not both.)

Although your attorney can try to run into court and enjoin the sale of the apartment you hope to get, as mentioned previously, such relief is rarely meted out. More likely, your case will wend its way slowly through the system. Justice this way may not be any swifter, but it surely will be more expensive, probably hundreds of dollars an hour. Nor is there any way to predict how many hours' worth of fees will be necessary to do the trick, because the dynamics (and hence the price) of the case are largely determined by how hard the board fights back.

The bottom line is that for most of us, going to court with a discrimination claim against a co-op or condo board is not realistic because it costs a bundle and it takes forever—at least long enough so that by the time the case is resolved you could have had a baby, been divorced, or gotten remarried, with the result that you may no longer fit into the apartment for which you fought.

7

Decor and Decorum: Renovating by You and the Board

VICTORY ON THE HOME (REMODELING) FRONT

For most of us, closing on a co-op or condo marks the end of the hunt for that perfect pad. But for some it signifies only the beginning of the search for residential nirvana. For these folks, to look at an apartment is to reconfigure it in their own images. No matter that the rooms are perfectly proportioned Palladian spaces with their original moldings intact. They want them stripped bare and opened out (an effect they probably could have achieved more cheaply and easily, but with less visceral satisfaction, by buying a loft). Others are content to leave the architectural bone structure standing but see the rooms as three-dimensional blank canvases on which to let loose their creative energy—transforming that pint-sized bathroom into an ode to cleanliness or the standard galley kitchen into a chef's delight. Whether you're of the body-sculpting or nip-and-tuck school of renovating (or even if you want only a cosmetic makeover), your big brothers and sisters on the board (and sometimes even outside agents of authority) will be watching. So you'd better get their blessing before you begin or risk incurring their wrath afterward.

This chapter takes you through the renovation process: from understanding the alteration agreement to getting approvals (from the board, buildings, even your fellow owners); from carrying out your plans to the consequences of noncompliance. On the flip side, it tells what you need to know to keep the board in line (and on budget) should it decide to go on a renovation rampage.

THE POWER OF REASON

In most co-ops and condos, the board rules over renovations. It gets its power fix from the proprietary lease (co-ops) or bylaws (condos), which almost universally require consent before alteration—though, generally, its consent can't be unreasonably withheld. In co-ops, the reasonable standard had better be in the lease, otherwise under New York law the landlord (a.k.a. your board) can *unreasonably* deny your request.[1] In condos, regardless of what the bylaws say, the Condo Act says the board must act *reasonably* in reviewing alteration plans.[2] This imposition of the reasonable standard gives you some leverage should you want to challenge the board's rejection of your planned renovation. Still, the board's power is broad enough that in a job of any consequence its word is final—and the courts are likely to leave it untouched. So if what you want to do to your new place is of make-it-or-break-it proportions, you'd be well advised to get a sense of board sentiment (preferably in writing) before you go too far in the purchase process.

If you bought a penthouse with the dream of becoming a gentleman farmer, and a greenhouse atop your terrace is essential to realizing your pastoral plans, you'd better find out first whether the board will allow you to turn your vision into an architectural reality. If your object is to wrest a marble bathroom out of that blocklike broom closet, you'd better be sure there are enough plumbing lines available to breathe life into your creation—and that the board will let them flow to where they have to go. Or maybe, like many New Yorkers, you're a latter-day Bismarck, hell-bent on expanding your residential territory by annexation. If you're buying in multiples with the intent of conquering and combining, you'll want an indication of board approval up front lest you be left with a string of non-strategic apartments.

When it comes to grand-scale renovations, the board can pretty much call the shots. Since its mandate is to look out for the good of the many, not the philistine pleasures of the few, courts would be loath to second-guess decisions on renovations that could threaten the building's structural integrity, implicate its central systems (heating, plumbing, electrical), or expose it to violations. You're on safer ground with smaller-scale dreams that can be realized within the confines of your own four walls: a kitchen or bathroom makeover in which the plumbing stays intact; a remolding of your interior space through a little wall shifting. Here, board rejection is more likely to be seen as unreasonable.

And if what you want to do is really only skin-deep—a new hue for the walls (via paint or paper), a different coating for the floor (with sanding and polish or just a carpet), a repair of trivial proportions—that's called decorating, not renovating. In many buildings you may be able to proceed on your own without board approval—and without fear of reprisal over aesthetic differences.

THE RULE OF LAW

From the board's general right to grant or deny renovation requests flows the power to fix more specific alteration policies and procedures. These can run the gamut from setting out what types of work need consent to how and when it should be accomplished. For everyone's sake, it's best if the board's construction manifesto is spelled out in an alteration agreement that all owners must sign before they start. That way both sides know in black and white what's allowed—and what's not—and the consequences of noncompliance. In New York there are two basic forms of alteration agreement in use: One is a short and too-simple Blumberg form, the other is a sometimes too-complicated, lawyerly document introduced several years back by the Real Estate Board. But lots of buildings use their own idiosyncratic agreements, so you won't know exactly what you're up against till you see it. The fine points of these compacts will vary depending on the nature of the board and the building but should address at least the following issues.

Submitting to the Authorities

It's the board's job to protect and defend the building (and other owners) against what you may want to do in your own apartment—a task that sometimes requires outside assistance. If you're doing any work of consequence, especially if structural walls or building systems are implicated, the board will probably make you submit your plans for independent review by an architect and/or engineer (of its choosing), for which you'll pay an amount ranging from $500 on up, depending on the grandeur of your vision. Sometimes this is a two-step (or more) process, especially if what you want to do is really big time—a planetarium on your roof for spare-time star gazing, a glass-enclosed solarium for temperature-controlled tanning. You may be asked first for design sketches so the board (and its architect) can see what you have in mind and make a preliminary decision on whether to allow your concept to be realized—or to reject it right away.

If the board nixes it in the bud, it'll usually notify you by letter. It may not give you any reason, because explanation invites litigation. That doesn't mean you can't ask—you should. If board silence still reigns, you're in a better position to claim its rejection was unreasonable (since undefined). Assuming the board favors you with a response—or better, a discussion (which allows for possible negotiation)—you may be convinced (even if you're not pacified) that there was reason behind its rejection: your skyward neighbors object that your planetarium will interfere with their heavenly views; your planned solarium will wreck the roof and its guarantee.

If the board grants you conditional approval, its next step will be to demand detailed architectural drawings so the board (and its architect) can see how you plan to turn your paper conceit into 3-D reality—and whether it threatens person or property.

Signing On the Outside Agents

In addition to dealing with the board (and its agents), you may have to brave the governmental bureaucracy. If all you want to do is change the look (not the location) of things, you're probably safe from government interference. You decide to replace those standard-issue stainless steel fixtures in your bathroom with some Sherle Wagner extravaganza—frolicking cupids, cavorting dolphins. Go ahead and indulge (if that's your taste). You can even put in a seashell toilet and sink to match—and pretend you're the Sun King. So long as everything is in the same place as before, your bathroom's your business, not the bureaucrats'.

But if you decide not only to replace that aesthetically impure fridge with a sleek Sub-Zero but to give your new machine a fitting home by expanding and reconfiguring the rest of the kitchen, then you'll probably have to get the Buildings Department to approve your plans and issue you a work permit before the board will let you begin. And where structural alterations are involved you may even have to bring your apartment into compliance with handicapped-accessibility laws.

If the project is of major proportions (combining apartments, adding exterior structures), getting government approval is necessary not just for you but for the whole building. If your grand design involves tinkering with the past, the landmarks people may also have to sign off, lest your building get hit for being historically incorrect.

Flirting with Disaster

Before you proceed you have to protect, which usually means making sure your contractor has enough insurance in amount and kind to pay off in case of some construction catastrophe. You may resent this requirement, especially if you want to use an inspired, but uninsured, artiste (as I did, but I didn't). And you probably figure everyone in the surrounding apartments has a homeowner's policy anyway. But accidents really do happen, as I was reminded by a contractor working in a nearby penthouse on my floor. In one grand charge he managed to invade both horizontally and vertically, breaking through two separate apartments: in the first case slashing through adjacent walls (and affixed paintings); in the other, raining a plaster shower down upon a closet full of clothes. Should your construction team become similarly overzealous in executing its mission, better have the complainants go against it than try to come after you.

Anyway, you don't really have a choice. Boards require you to get comprehensive personal liability and property damage policies from your construction chief. In most buildings (including my own), a cool $1 million in coverage will do the trick. But since a million doesn't buy what it used to (particularly when it comes to renovations), buildings where real Renoirs, not museum reproductions, grace the walls may demand a minimum of $5 million or more (an amount that may scare off less-than-solvent outfits). If your plans are sufficiently aggressive that damage or destruction could befall your next-door neighbors, try convincing them to participate in a little photo documentary. It will gratify their egos and give you evidence. That way, if the worst occurs and they claim destruction of their fine-tuned Bösendorfer or damage to their hand-waxed floors, you can call their bluff—or get your contractor to make good—depending on what the blowups show.

Your contractors also will have to show proof of workers' compensation and employee liability policies. A good thing, too, otherwise when they claim they were emotionally traumatized on the job by your over-the-top design scheme they may come running to you for recovery. And depending on what you're planning to do, the board may insist on proof of other policies, including an umbrella.

Demanding Security

Most boards won't let you begin any work until you park some cash with them (in the form of a security deposit), to be sure there's money around to cover any loss or expense that may befall the building by reason of your renovation. In my building, we ask our shareholders for a $500 demonstration of good faith (distinctly on the low side, in keeping with our fee-free philosophy). Most buildings start at $1,000 and go up—if necessary, to the tens of thousands. Whatever the amount, you should get it back promptly after the work is done, either in full, if you have carried out your renovations trouble (or fee) free, or minus any legitimate deductions if you have not. In addition, there are usually non-refundable fees of several hundred dollars each to the building *and* the managing agent for the privilege of fixing up your apartment, and many upper-crust buildings impose fees of $100 (or more) for each day of work.

Promise to Pay

Not only does the board want security, it will also make you promise to pay for the work you're having done (a seemingly self-evident proposition). It's not that the board cares about keeping you honest. It's just that it doesn't want you to get into a dispute with your contractor that could spill over and affect the whole co-op if he files a lien. To protect the building from this risk, the board usually makes you agree in advance to discharge any lien within ten days, which (you'll see if you read on) means paying off your bills or posting a bond.

Civil Construction

In an effort to keep the peace and allow you to remodel without driving your fellow shareholders over the edge, most buildings impose temporal limits on renovating your space (weekdays nine to five, or something similar; more restricted times for more ear-piercing projects). For some boards, not only time but season is of the essence. Some demand that you get things done in the period between Memorial Day and Labor Day, when there will be minimal disturbance because the maximum number of owners are taking in the Hamptons scene. Then there are boards that set finite bounds on renovations whenever they're done, requiring you to complete the job in a set period—say ninety business days. To make sure you adhere to construction etiquette, the board may make you pay (sometimes several hundred dollars a day) for every day you go beyond the limit, though, as we'll see, several courts have recently put in doubt the enforceability of such provisions. If that's the case you should be sure to pass the penalty on to the true perpetrator, your contractor, via a suitable provision in the contract.

Not only must you be timely, but you should also be clean and quiet. In case these qualities don't come naturally, they are usually enforced through regulation. It's in your own best interest to follow the rule of reason. Otherwise your neighbors (and/or the board) can take legal action. And the court can decree tougher standards that may put a crimp in your construction style (as has happened)[3]—all of which will surely put you under stress and over budget.

Clean Up Your Act

Lots of shareholders fail to pay fees for what they figure are minor infractions (from late charges to pet fines), and it's not worth board time and effort to go after them for a few dollars. But the balance of power shifts when a shareholder needs board consent to renovate. And boards have been known to use their newly found leverage to collect—making owners pay up or postpone their work. So you'd better be prepared to wipe your debit slate clean as a construction precondition.

Passing Inspection

It's not that the board doesn't trust owners. It's just that it wants to head problems off at the pass. That's why lots of boards require you to submit to periodic and postalteration inspections by their architects or engineers. If execution and plans conform, you have nothing to fear from the investigative brigade—except maybe a little copycat renovation (and you know what they say about imitation). But as plenty of you out there know firsthand, not everyone follows the original plan. You got approval for some pro forma plumbing, but you decide while you're at it to add a hot tub—in the process, digging a hole through your downstairs neighbor's ceiling. Or you realize midway through executing those legal renovations in your duplex that proper flow demands relocation of the staircase, a change that nearly breaks the bearing walls. If the inspections reveal a conflict between plan and reality, the board is likely to make you stop and kick out your crew until you get it right. And no matter which way the chips fall, *you're* the one who'll pay for the visits from these uninvited inspectors.

NO RETURN

Assuming you have played by the rules, you will have bought yourself protection. Once the alteration agreement is executed and board approval has been obtained, you're ready to roll. There's no turning back even if the board changes its mind. Not that there haven't been boards that tried.

The Board's Word Is Binding

After shareholders' renovation plans—including their intent to increase the electrical supply—were reviewed by their Sutton Place co-op's architect and approved by the board, it told them to stop work on the very same day they were authorized to start, claiming it needed to preserve the building's electrical reserves. Unable to resolve the impasse, the owners sold the apartment in its demolished state—and sued. The board claimed it was just exercising its business judgment (see chapter 9), but the court said, That's no defense to the agreement you made.[4]

A shareholder downtown found herself in a similar jam. She jumped through all the bureaucratic and building hurdles necessary to connect her apartment by a new staircase with space she held on the roof—and the board approved. When she was knee-deep in rubble with a hole opened to the heavens, the board told her to cease and desist, citing concerns about the roof. I can't stop now, she told the judge, and he agreed. Because the board had given its word, it had to allow her to finish what she had begun.[5]

The same thing, in reverse, happened to a couple at an Upper West Side condo who got board approval to combine two apartments. *After* the job was done, the board decided they should have gotten a Buildings Department permit and told them to undo it. But the court said what's done cannot (or, at least, should not) be undone, because the board had given its consent.[6]

Even if the board has second thoughts, it can't go back on its word. Assuming your plans have been approved and you don't cheat, you should win if it comes to a showdown.

Of course, if you deviate from the plans the board approved, all bets are off. Take the case of a Village shareholder whose court battles we'll hear more of later (see chapter 9). He got approval and signed an alteration agreement but then violated it by proceeding with a change in the building's heating system without giving notice as required. Since he had defied, not relied, the court made him restore his steam riser from whence it came and where the board wanted it.[7]

Apparent Authority Is Enough

In many buildings, the managing agent signs off on standard alteration agreements. Can the board countermand the agent's approval? The answer is no. One Park Avenue board tried to hide behind its managing agent, which had sent a letter to a shareholder saying the board approved plans to do bed, bath, and beyond work, including opening the brick wall and closing it with a new window. When all that remained was that eye to the sky, the board said, "Stop, there's a bulge in the brickwork." Too late and too bad, the court ruled. She had a right to rely on what the board's authorized representative said.[8]

Likewise, the owner at a downtown condo was entitled to rely on the apparent authority of the board president. Both before and after all necessary permits were obtained, Mr. President had agreed in writing to the owner's plans to add a balcony and five terraces to his loft. Only once he had begun demolition did the board wake up, claiming it didn't previously know about, and now was rejecting, the very plans the president had approved. But the court said the owner doesn't need their consent, because the president is presumed to have authority to enter into contracts on behalf of the building.[9]

In one case, even though the president's approval of designs and diagrams was only oral, it was enough to rescue a West Seventy-second Street shareholder. Because the board president approved the shareholder's design diagrams and the board raised no objection to his alterations until they were nearly complete, the court said the board gave up its right to enforce the provision. Not only did the renovations stay put, but the board had to pay the shareholder's attorney's fees.[10] Still, going this route can be dangerous. If you find yourself in an after-the-fact mess, having proceeded based only on an oral okay, by all means give it a shot. But since, as you'll see, there's also authority out there that says you can't rely on an oral approval, get it in writing *before* you begin.

Affected Owners Have a Say

Not only do you have to contend with the board, but worse, you may also have to deal with your neighbors. The Condo Act requires consent of any unit owner affected by your alterations.[11] Even though the president's word was enough to bind the board in that downtown loft, the owner of the apartment downstairs, who complained that his view and light would be lost, was able, at least temporarily, to bring construction to a halt.[12] No such statutory protection or obstruction (depending on your perspective) exists for co-ops, but the proprietary lease is sufficiently broad to enable the board to look after your rights, provided your claim is rational. Relying on the offering plan that gave "typical" apartment layouts, one shareholder complained fifteen years after she had moved in that her neighbor, or his predecessor, had moved the adjacent living room wall, thereby depriving her of nine inches of living space. She got what was coming to her for such a frivolous claim—nothing.[13]

SPECIAL MISSIONS

Sometimes your mission may be sufficiently complex that it can affect the whole building—with one false move resulting in violations or, worse, refusal by the powers that be to let anyone else renovate. In these cases you'll need approval above and beyond the board and its aides-de-camp to push your plans through the government bureaucracy and to assist in their execution.

Inside Edition

Everyone wants more space, and the best place to start is inside your apartment. Many shareholders do, especially if a baby is on the way and Mom and Dad are squeezed into a one-bedroom. It's a no-brainer, one couple who moved into our building figured, without first asking. We'll slap up a wall and turn the dining alcove into a nursery. Only problem is that under law such a space must have a window, the better to inhale the polluted air outside (and this one didn't). Some boards are philosophically opposed to letting owners carve out additional rooms on the theory that they don't want to foster dorm-style living. But if that's no obstacle, and both sides are willing to suspend disbelief, one way around this predicament (apart from punching a window through the building's skin), is to designate the alteration a "closet." Though your clothes may need to breathe the law doesn't require them to have a window—and once your "closet" is constructed, who's to know if you sneak in a crib?

Expanding Residency

Those with grander plans may embark on a march through the building and gobble up territory as neighbors die or move on. Your quest may be horizontal or vertical, depending on whether the person who passes on has an apartment that's architecturally fit for occupation. Fate may conspire to make available two (or more) contiguous unoccupied spaces for immediate conquest—a tempting but dangerous situation unless you have your battle plan in order. This means (as we'll discuss below) an okay from the board, an architectural sign-off, and a Buildings Department clearance. Don't make the mistake of conquering first and planning later—or you may suffer defeat at your own hands (a humiliating and expensive way to go).

Years back when I was in the market, I answered an ad direct from the owners of a prewar two-bedroom in prime Fifth Avenue Village territory where the price was better than right. The couple had overextended itself, having bought back-to-back two-bedrooms intending to break through into one vast and glorious expanse—symbolic of their earthly success. Only they didn't ask till after the fact how (and how much) their empire building would set them back. When they got the news, they decided it would be cheaper and easier to just buy bigger—which they did, this time on the Upper East Side. No sooner had they become minimoguls with their triplet of apartments than the market and their fortunes suffered a reversal—and they had to unload for less than a song. (Truth is, for reasons aesthetic, not financial, I passed on the deal. But I'm sure some other buyer grabbed the opportunity that resulted from their renovation error.)

Here's what you need to do to avoid becoming a victim of multiples excess:

Is the Fit Feasible?

Unless the apartments are a strategic fit your purchase can wind up a raw power play giving you no territorial advantage. To find out if the fit is feasible you need to bring in an architect (and maybe an engineer) to tell you what walls you can break through without also tearing into the building's gas, electric, or plumbing lines. If you plan to move the kitchen to where the living room once stood, you need to find out if there's a way to bring water to the spigot and power to the fridge. My plans to turn my cookery into a sleek European wonder came to an abrupt halt when I found out it would cost tens of thousands just to bring an electric line from the bowels of the building to my rooftop kitchen.

Assuming the systems check out A-OK, you should next consider whether the area you have staked out will yield a unified whole or a gerrymandered district. For some, the need for raw space to accommodate the pitter-patter of little feet takes precedence over internal logic, so it's quantity, not quality, of square feet that counts. After having a child, a couple I know jumped at the chance to buy the apartment next door; so desperate were they for space that they went through with the deal even though they discovered that there was a structural wall between the two that couldn't be breached (without threatening the building's integrity). But if you've outgrown the need for family-sized barracks and are looking for harmonious flow, you'd better be sure the recombinant apartment will meet your aesthetic expectations.

Is the Price Right?

Looked at from the strictly economic point of view, annexation doesn't always make sense. But even if your underlying motive is self-aggrandizement, not savings, take heed from those overbought Villagers.

Find out up front how much it will cost to carry out your reconfiguration and compare that to the cost of a like-sized ready-made. True, we're a little into apples and oranges here (because no two apartments are strictly identical), but the exercise will give you a rough reality check to see if what you're doing makes dollars and sense. Apart from the price comparison, which at least is a one-shot deal, you need to look at how the maintenance for the combined apartments stacks up against what you'd pay every month for one that comes preconfigured. Whether cornflakes or co-ops, the monthly charges often work out cheaper for the jumbo-size box than for two smaller ones.

Is the Board Willing?

It goes without saying that you can't combine without consent. Don't even think of trying it. When you are found out—from the doorman you stiffed, the neighbor who has it in for you, or your own lack of vigilance—the consequences can be severe. Apart from the usual alteration routine, the board's concern is that you do it legally—or else the building could get tagged by the renovation police. That means bringing in the outside agents of authority.

Are the Bureaucrats on Board?

It used to be that combining your many splendid apartments into one salon meant changing the Certificate of Occupancy for the entire building—a process that could have you pulling out your hair and waiting more than a year. Now it's a relative snap.

All you have to do is file an application (Alteration Type II, for the detail-oriented among you) with the Buildings Department and get an architect or an engineer to bless your plans. All existing exits in both apartments have to stay (so expect double the usual take-out menu mess). The second kitchen has to go, though you can make alternate use of its plumbing for a washer/dryer or a wet bar (assuming your board approves). You'll still need an expediter to shepherd your papers through the system, but since the whole process is truncated so is the cost (probably just several thousand dollars). Only problem is that with the hassle removed an annexation boom is sure to follow, making contiguous co-ops and condos all the more dear.

Buying Space

For some owners it's not enough to amass and annex apartments. Like addicts in need of a constant fix, they lust for more space, even if it doesn't belong to them. Say you cobble together your fantasy from two (or more) adjacent units and now you want to lay claim to a portion of the corridor so you can create a new entrance befitting your new station in life.

After buying apartments 2D and 2E at the short end of an L-shaped corridor in a Greenwich Village condo, the two owners wanted to enclose a small part of the hallway to create a common entrance to their combined apartment. The board said okay and granted them a revocable license, whereby they paid a monthly amount equal to the common charges allocated to the fourteen square feet of corridor enclosed. Mr. 2C, who lived on the long end of the L, claimed that the combiners had illegally divided and conquered the condo's common elements, and he demanded that the wall be removed. But the court let the agreement—and the wall—stand, declaring it was legal because it didn't affect Mr. 2C's undivided interest or his use of the hallway.[14]

As a result of the battle fought, and won, by the Perry Street Boys, it's now clear that a condo has the power to license a part of the common elements for use by a single owner. Shareholders can obtain the same result in co-ops by buying shares allocable to the space and paying monthly maintenance. For the space-starved among you, keep in mind that while this device is usually used to acquire hallway access, it may also be applied to acquire space for storage or an air conditioner condenser that has to sit on the rooftop or other items on your wish list.

Turning the Outside In

Most apartment dwellers yearn to breathe free and to own a piece of the great outdoors atop or attached to their high-rise. But based on what I've seen as board president, the grass really is always greener. I can tell you that lots of those who get their wish then want to turn the outside in and convert their balconies or terraces back to interior space. The rich man's version is to build a greenhouse so that he and his flowers can bloom year-long together. The poorer man's way is to enclose his balcony, creating an extra room for himself—and an eyesore for the rest of us. Either way, you'll need board and Buildings Department approval.

Enclosing Your Flowers

Even for the determined penthouse set, getting the go-ahead for a greenhouse is a daunting mission.

First, there's Buildings. You may see that crystal pavilion as expanding your planting space, but the bureaucracy sees it as increasing the floor area of the building—not something you necessarily have a right to do. To overcome, you'll probably have to invoke the "One Percent Solution." Here's how it works. Most buildings (including my own of 1950s vintage) were overbuilt. To provide an expansion outlet for existing owners (who weren't the overreachers), the Buildings bureaucrats may allow the addition of up to 1 percent more of floor area—which is what your greenhouse takes up.

There's no assurance you'll get any or all of that allotment; it's totally up to the department.

And even if Buildings says it's okay, the board may not. The 1 percent rule applies not just to *your* greenhouse plans but to the *whole* building. If other terrace owners have similar expansionist plans, turf wars could erupt, putting the board in a bind because it can't say yes to one shareholder and no to another. Since by definition parceling out finite space may require selective enforcement, what works for Buildings may not work for your board.

That's not the end of potential Buildings battles. You may have to get a change of C of O. Some buildings' certificates show the number of rooms, not just the number of apartments. If you're lucky enough to live in such a detail-oriented building, you may have to get an amended C of O for the entire building because even though you aren't changing the number of apartments (as when combining), you may be changing the number of rooms with your addition.

Even if you don't need special dispensations, you'll still need Buildings' approval to go ahead with your greenhouse effect. It'll want to be sure your creation is structurally sound, leakproof, weight appropriate—and more.

Then there's the board. It has the obligation to protect and defend the building against damage that may be caused by your pitching a permanent glass tent on the building's roof. Since the board has to repair and maintain the roof, this poses an immediate problem (even if you agree to indemnify the building). Your urban arboretum can wreck the entire roof guarantee. And your neighbors may object to being Trumped as your glass walls go up and their view gets wiped out.

I'm not saying it's impossible, but if the board turns you down you don't have a legal leg to stand on.

Or Yourself

Perhaps you want to be hermetically sealed in one of those balconies that run up and down the building—or something grander. That's assuming your board has no policy against those glassed-in boxes that make a crazy-quilt patchwork across the facade. You'll need Buildings' approval to be sure whatever you're using is up to fire and safety snuff and is sufficiently affixed so that those glass walls don't come tumbling down. And since you're adding a room, if your building's C of O counts rooms (not just apartments) you may have to get it changed.

Just don't follow in the footsteps of the Gramercy Park antiauthoritarian. She went full speed ahead enclosing her terrace, without a nod to board or Buildings' approval and without focusing on the fact that her newly built glass house abutted the co-op's twenty-two-story smokestack, which was in need of urgent repair. Take it down now, the court told her. Not only does the board need to get to your terrace to fix the chimney, but even if it didn't, the structure is still illegal. So after having spent tens of thousands to put up her folly, she was ordered to pay even more to remove it.[15]

Preserving History

If history is your passion, you may want to save it for reading rather than residing in. As the proud owner of an apartment in a landmark building or district you have to secure alteration clearance from the Landmarks Preservation Commission if you want to change the face of time—or at least its external appearance. The purpose of the commission is to preserve the character of those significant pieces of our past still standing amidst the more modern and mundane architectural wasteland. In the Big Apple, where the masses are piled high in undistinguished brick boxes, living among the relative ruins has a certain cachet. But having your place labeled historic by the keepers of the cultural flame can be burden enough to make you see the benefits of joining the contemporary vanguard.

If all you want to do is alter the inside of your apartment, you may be able to proceed without the preservationists. They only get involved when the work needs a Buildings Department permit or the changes will affect the exterior or the interior itself has been designated a landmark (not likely unless your apartment is open to the public). But if you're tampering with the building's outside look (a rooftop retreat, a year-round greenhouse) they'll have to approve your makeover. This means submitting an application signed by the board president (not the managing agent) and getting the commission to grant a permit for minor work or a certificate of appropriateness before you can get cracking. Your failure to comply may result in your building being branded a violator—a designation which may halt the renovation progress of fellow owners and cost you a few stripes.

One shareholder couple who lived in Fifth Avenue splendor opposite the Temple of Dendur learned all this the hard way. They embarked on a renovation program when they moved in, including installation of airtight windows to replace the classically girded but drafty originals. The agent acting for the board said it was okay, as he had for two prior shareholders who were tired of looking through a glass darkly. When the co-op got hit with violations for altering without approval in the Metropolitan Museum Historic District, the agent said, "Don't worry." And no one did—until those culture czars rejected an application by another shareholder and told the building to clean up its act. Then things got messy. The preservationists told the couple to restore historical accuracy in windows at a cost of $400,000. The couple said this wasn't a case of history in the re-making but arbitrary tyranny, since other shareholders had been allowed to keep their updated oculi. Thirteen years later, the couple and their windows finally got a reprieve from the state's highest court.[16]

It's not only individual owners, but whole buildings that can find themselves enmeshed in battle with the preservationists, as did one condominium at the gateway to the historic Soho Cast Iron District. Years back the board thought it would be a great idea to make an aesthetic statement and, under the auspices of the City Walls program, agreed to the installation of a massive 3-D sculpture on the facade of the building. Artwork and owners coexisted in harmony until the beams of the work deteriorated and the board wanted to remove the sculpture, repair the wall on which it hung, and replace it with commercial signs. Only the Landmarks people said no, claiming they were duty bound to protect the work's historic value—and won. The court ordered the board to restore the artwork to the side of the building, forcing residents to live with the masterpiece, like it or not.[17]

These tales should serve as reminders: If you want to spend years luxuriating in, rather than litigating over, your renovations, find out if your building is subject to Landmarks' approval before you begin. For interior work, they'll let time march on without interference. For exterior jobs, expect more vigilant scrutiny. The easiest way is if your building has an approved master plan that sets the standard for future repetitive alterations of architectural features (the incremental installation of windows or through-wall air conditioning). That way your building gets a uniform outlook (aesthetically if not philosophically) and you get Amex-style preapproval. Going it alone is more difficult. The preservationists have window guidelines on how much history can be revised. If you follow their standards, a staff member can probably sign off. Otherwise, you or your board will have to go to those higher authorities (and perhaps even request a public hearing) for approval of an alternate proposal.

WHAT PRICE DELAY

Renovations have a way of assuming lives of their own. To prevent them from going beyond their predetermined existence, boards often impose hefty fees for each day beyond the allotted time the project lasts, which can quickly mount to tens, and sometimes hundreds, of thousands of dollars. But relief may finally be here because of shareholders who have challenged these fees as unenforceable penalties—and won.

Under an alteration agreement that imposed an automatic fee of $500 a day for each day of delay, the board of a Fifth Avenue co-op demanded $32,000 from shareholders whose grand-scale renovations extended beyond the scheduled completion date. They said the delay was due to the owner above them, whose faulty alterations flooded their apartment, and prevented work from proceeding. Besides, they objected, the fee doesn't bear any rational relation to reality. Since the board charged $500 a day for delay (and only $100 a day during alterations), the court agreed that it didn't reflect actual losses sustained by the co-op, and declared it null and void.[18]

Based on a similar $500-a-day delay fee, the board of another Upper East Side co-op demanded $175,000 from renovating shareholders who, it said, went way beyond the six months allowed in the alteration agreement. Sorry, you can't collect, the judge said. It's an unenforceable penalty unrelated to the expense inflicted on the co-op by mere delay.[19]

The good news is that if your board tries to hit you up for a $500-a-day delay fee (or any amount significantly more than what it charges per day *during* alterations), it is likely unenforceable, and if you refuse to pay, you should win. The bad news is now that boards can't use the lever of money to get you to complete work on time, they will likely devise other methods, including more frequent inspections during the project to ensure it gets done on schedule (for which *you'll* pay).

DON'T LIEN ON ME

A central tenet of communal living is keep your nose clean and mind your own business. But like it or not, in the alteration arena your fellow shareholder's dispute can become your headache. Let's say midway through building his metaphorical Taj Mahal he runs out of rupees or decides the work is not up to his princely standards so he just won't pay. The jilted contractor who's been chiseling away on perfectly veined marble for months is not about to walk away empty-handed. He slaps a lien not only on the royal pretender's residence but on the whole co-op.

Unfortunately for the innocent and renovation-responsible shareholders, the law says he can do this. A bunch of boards have tried to get rid of blanket liens stuck on their buildings by contractors for work done to glorify a single shareholder's apartment but with no luck.[20] Since in theory the improved apartment is communally owned by all of the building's shareholders through the corporation, you all get the benefit of its increased value. (A nice legal fiction but in real life unlikely to gain you entry to the defalcating shareholder's palatial digs.)

So long as the lien stays put, it can create a cloud on the building's title and trigger a default under the co-op's underlying mortgage. What all this legal mumbo jumbo means is that the building may not be able to refinance and individual shareholders may have trouble selling because lenders won't want to lend until the mess is cleared up. To be sure it is, most co-op leases give deadbeat shareholders a finite time (usually ten days) to get rid of the lien by paying or putting up a bond. If not, the co-op can take action to bond the lien on its own and then collect from the owner as additional maintenance all it paid (plus attorneys' fees and interest).

In condos, you won't get socked the same way for your neighbor's construction cost overruns. A complaining contractor can put a lien only on the specific unit where he toiled without pay. He can't cover the building with a blanket lien. Remember, condo owners hold their units outright, not as part of a corporation. Recognizing their rugged individualism, the law says no lien can be put on the common elements without all owners giving their unanimous consent,[21] a vote against self-interest not likely to happen.

CRIME DOESN'T PAY

Knowing the struggles you must endure (with board and bureaucrats) before you get to break ground (or ceiling), you may be tempted to cut through the red tape and seek an antiestablishment solution. It would be a mistake—as one enterprising if slightly crooked condo owner found out. He tried to bypass the board and make a deal directly with his downstairs neighbor, offering hard cash to buy her silence and compensate for the inconvenience from his installation of a Jacuzzi overhead. He didn't learn until it was too late that his chosen co-conspirator was my friend—a woman and a practitioner of the law—and a more potent force to be reckoned with than any board member. She revealed what he concealed, with the result that he not only had to get board approval but had the board on his back monitoring progress every step of the way—lest he try some other slick maneuver. And when his finished watery vortex overflowed into my friend's kitchen he paid pronto, knowing she had the goods on him and would use them.

If you don't try to enlist a partner in crime you may, in fact, get the work done undetected. But when you are discovered (and it's only a matter of time) you may wish a snitch had outed your secret plans to spare you the consequences that can ensue after the fact from unauthorized alterations.

Demand a Cure

The reality is that plenty of renovations are done without approval. This solution allows both parties to save face and avoid a showdown. You snuck in a vibrating whirlpool (you say for therapy, not pleasure), but the lease says no motors. The bath stays; the motor goes. (And now you really *are* stuck with a cure.) You've cut a swath through your kitchen (and your neighbor's pipes) in the haste to complete an underground overhaul. You restore the plumbing and the illegal renovation becomes legitimized. Things can get more complicated if you've also bypassed approvals from outside agents. As we've seen, your transgression can put a violation on the whole building and bring a halt to the construction plans of your fellow shareholders. Here the board will (and should) not back down, but will make you cure at any cost.

Still, you're getting off easy if all the board does is demand that you (and your alterations) come clean. I'd counsel compliance before the punishment escalates to the next level of enforcement.

Kick You Out

In most co-ops, renovating without consent is a violation of your lease (or, in condos, a violation of the bylaws) for which the board can seek to evict you. Making you move out will not in itself resolve the alteration altercation. As a result, this method, when used by boards, is usually intended more to scare you into compliance than to secure eviction. Given that there are more direct means to these enforcement ends, an action to recover possession is not usually the first line of defense against renovation offenders. But when used effectively this method may, in fact, raise your blood pressure to a sufficiently high level that you decide to reform. One board in pastoral Queens tried this tactic against shareholders who installed window guards without getting prior written approval, as required. Concerned that their offense would spawn copycat imitators and turn the co-op into an armed camp, the board sought to oust them. The court saved the day, granting the relief but staying the eviction warrant long enough to give the violators a chance to see reason, remove the bars, and restore a sense of serenity to their fellow shareholders.[22] A Brooklyn board got a judgment of possession against a shareholder who shoved her air conditioner through the wrong building wall without permission. But she got ten days' grace to reverse course and remain a shareholder in good standing.[23]

If you are faced with an eviction attack for illicit renovations, know that the odds are de minimis that the board will actually get you out. But it can make life so unpleasant that you may decide compliance is the better part of valor.

Restore the Peace

The more drastic the offense, the more dramatic the relief the board is likely to demand—even to the point of making you undo what you have done on the sly. One frustrated co-op owner, angry at the board's intransigence, staged a stealth attack of the vertical variety—opening an eight-foot hole in his ceiling and putting in a stairway to his attic (an action he later justified by the agent's oral okay). He paid the price for carrying out an unapproved annexation, getting 120 days to retreat and remove his steps to the stars. What's more, the court authorized the board to monitor his disengagement, allowing it to conduct on-site inspections till the deed was undone to its satisfaction.[24]

Another owner, this one of two condo units—foiled by the board's rejection of his expansionist plans—took hammer and chisel in hand and punched a hole through the wall, thereby uniting his domestic duchies. Outraged by his contempt of the law, the board counterattacked and got a judicial order for restoration lest it be required to mount its own force majeure invasion to redivide and conquer the outlaw's apartments. To ensure compliance and future obedience, the defeated owner had to post a $50,000 bond and pay attorneys' fees and damages.[25]

Even if your offense is unauthorized renovation within your own territory and not annexation of adjacent apartments, you expose yourself to the not-inconsiderable risk of capitulation and restoration. One condo owner learned that after ignoring building bylaws and proceeding on his own to install glass doors in an exterior wall. The board went on the offensive, with the result that he got hit with an order requiring him to undo the damage in 60 days and to file a $10,000 undertaking to be sure that he did.[26] In another unauthorized attempt at light and air, a shareholder couple broke through their (and the building's) brick wall to install a window in the living room. They met a like fate and were ordered to return the wall, brick by brick, to its preocular state and themselves to residing in relative darkness.[27] Even if you just install an air conditioner, if it's in violation of bylaws (or a lease) that prohibit obstructing or defacing the building's walls, the board can make you remove it.

The only thing that may save you from less-than-legal alterations is the passage of time—so much of it that the equities turn your way. That's what saved one lucky shareholder. He had opened up a five-foot hole in his floor, which happened also to be his neighbor's ceiling, and stuck in a whirlpool. There he sat in blissful bubbles until thirteen years later, when a newly arrived shareholder downstairs discovered the missing concrete slab. Together with the board, he demanded restoration to prevent the floodwaters from rushing into his apartment. Though the tub violated the board's rules and the Building Code, the court let it stay, figuring if it hadn't collapsed in all those years it was built for the ages.[28]

It should be evident from these self-help sagas that the consequences of renovation contempt are too great to be worth the risk. Through the proprietary lease (co-ops) or the bylaws (condos) the board has the power to enforce control over apartment alterations. Defy its power and it may seek retribution through the courts, which have been constant and consistent board allies on this score. Before the fact you may figure the end result is worth the risk. But after you have committed environmental pillage and raped some South American rain forest to sheath your newly reconfigured walls in slabs of mahogany, the prospect of undoing your crowning aesthetic glory (to say nothing of the cost involved) will make you see things differently. My advice is approval first—then action.

Get a Declaration

If you insist on pursuing the offensive, you're better off taking the legal, not the construction, route. When the board says no, instead of lifting a sledgehammer in revolt you can file a complaint seeking a declaration that the board's refusal to allow the alteration is unreasonable. In legal parlance it's called a *declaratory action.* If you're lucky, the board may back down rather than fight in your chosen forum. If not, at least you get a judge—hopefully with a more objective outlook—to decide your renovation fate. And if he (or she) blesses your plans (legally, not aesthetically) the board has to abide. You can proceed secure in the knowledge that whatever fantasy (or folly) you embark upon will stay standing until you decide it's time to tear it asunder and start anew.

GETTING AWAY WITH MURDER

Although I stand by my advice that crime doesn't pay, in the interests of full disclosure I confess that I carried out my own master plan during the throes of conversion unfettered by the rule of law. Having gained control of my penthouse a month before the closing, when the building stood in limbo between rental and co-op, I took advantage of the renters' rights, to which I temporarily succeeded, and got the landlord to restore the walls (which hadn't seen a paintbrush in twelve years) to a livable hue.

Then I turned to the real renovation work at hand. The apartment I acquired was a testament to 1970s Joe D'Urso industrial chic—which, for the uninitiated, means built-in walls, pillars, furniture, and everything else that can make a room feel claustrophobic—all in gray. This harsh reality stood in the way of my vision of a soft and sensuous Empire salon. It had to go. I drafted a makeshift demolition team, appointing a building staffer as general and letting him fill in the ranks, admittedly not giving a thought to securing establishment approval. I paid no more attention to procedural necessities from insurance to garbage removal to work hours and conditions. (Who knew from alteration agreements?)

But the fates were with me. My neighbor, who could have turned me in to the authorities (such as they were), instead feted me with gourmet treats from her terrace barbecue. I caused no damage (psychic or physical) to anyone around that would engender a claim. I managed to get rid of the roomful of rubbish and tangled steel that remained at the end of phase one, though to this day I'm not sure how. (I suspect the staff palms that I greased helped smooth the way for Sanitation cooperation.)

After deconstruction came reconstruction. I started by bringing back moldings, which I bought in sixteen-foot lengths, unmindful of how I'd get them into my apartment. To make the impossible possible, I called in my chits from ten years' residence and commandeered a crack crew for Saturday at dawn, stationing one staffer down below in the courtyard and another up above in a vacant apartment, which we designated Command Control. Thus strategically positioned, they pulled those planks, tethered on cords, one by one up fourteen floors, all the while hoping against hope they'd avoid the prying eyes and complaints of disbelieving residents (who might get their own creative construction ideas).

That was but a training mission to prepare for Operation Staircase. Since I wanted a staircase to match my neoclassic taste, I removed the construction-site wall that had served as my predecessors' idea of a railing and had it replaced with an iron-and-brass beauty. I'll spare you the travails of my adventures into neighborhoods unknown (but dangerous) in search of artistic (but affordable) ironmongers. I'll just tell you it took an army of blowtorchers to weld the molten metal, and a pair of special agents (willing to risk life and limb) to deliver the precious cargo by riding it in atop the elevator. And when it arrived safe, but higher by a foot than the existing supporting end post, there was much ranting and raving between me and its artistic (but mathematically challenged) creator—until we agreed upon a solution (building up the post to meet the balustrade's mistaken height). As for its installation, a tale in itself, all you need to know is that the only damage done was to my own walls, saving me from the horrors of claims against me and my uninsured artiste.

But now that I've turned philosophical traitor and crossed over to the other side, bound by my presidential oath to uphold (and follow) the rules, I know whatever other renovations I undertake will be disappointingly tame after the liberties I took in those heady lawless days.

RENOVATION AFTERSHOCK

Your grand plan complete (I'm assuming by the book and the law), you settle in as the dust settles, surveying your creation. Just don't get too comfortable too soon. Although you are warm and dry and surrounded by design bliss, your neighbor's work may only have just begun. Turns out your renovations unleashed streams of water, plaster, or other destruction upon the girl (or guy) next door. Or the contractor got injured on the job. What recourse do these people have against you?

Don't get uptight. As a general rule, you are not responsible for the negligent conduct of that independent contractor you hired to do the job. (He, or, more likely, his insurer should ultimately pay for his construction sins.)

But thanks to shareholders who got soaked (for upward of $100,000) by their neighbor's renovations, there may be a chink in your legal armor. After getting payment from their insurer, they sued their fellow owner for almost $30,000 in unreimbursed damages, claiming the neighbor shouldn't get off so easily under the general rule because he had a duty as an owner in a co-op to keep his premises safe for the other owners. Although the court agreed that the innocent renovator had no statutory duty to his neighbor (maybe a moral one to feed the cat or water the plants) it let the case proceed under the rules of negligence, leaving the door open for liability against the renovating shareholder.[29] So you'd better check out your contractor's references to be sure he's competent and hasn't left a path of destruction in his wake, lest you expose yourself to a claim for lack of care.

That's not the end of the lawsuit possibilities. Even though you as a shareholder hire a worker to renovate your apartment, the co-op may wind up potentially responsible if he's injured on your job. In order to assure safe conditions for construction (and other) workers, New York has a Labor Law that, under certain circumstances, imposes absolute liability for injury on the "owner."[30] Relax—if you're a shareholder, you're not the owner for these purposes, the co-op is—even if the injury took place on your renovation job. You condo unit owners are also exempt from liability under the law.[31]

Take the case of the East Sider who hired a contractor to renovate his three-bedroom. When the contractor was injured while cutting wood on a saw, he sued the co-op and the renovating shareholder under this law. The shareholder got off the hook, but the co-op's legal battle had just begun. That's because the law exempts residential one- and two-family homeowners (which has been interpreted to include shareholders) since you have no more power than the parties you hired. It's left to the co-op to sue on down the line until the ultimately responsible party (usually a subcontractor) is held to account and the injured worker gets compensation.[32] My only point in all this is if you get hit with such a postrenovation suit for on-your-job injuries, although you may well be named, you are not the target—and should be let off.

Of course, if you're somehow negligent in connection with renovations done in your apartment, it's a different story—but that's for a book on torts (the law has its own name for everything), not co-ops and condos.

DUELING ON THE DECOR FRONT

It's enough of a hassle redoing your private haven, where you have only yourself to please. Just wait till those directors decide to redecorate the public space: whether the object of their desire is the lobby, the corridors, or something else, the process can be an invitation to war between the board and its constituents—and sometimes among the rank and filers themselves. No matter if your building's constituents are aesthetes or aesthetically challenged, they will surely have a diversity of opinion on whether Miami glitz, English estate, or industrial modern is the way to go. If not, the likely result will be standard lobby neo-Baroque complete with crystal chandeliers dripping with plastic.

In my building, the sponsor made a sneak attack prior to conversion, turning the 1950s modern lobby into a paean of downtown chic. Whereas before going downstairs was like slipping into a pair of comfortable Hush Puppies, familiar but worn, suddenly each morning we had to squeeze into our fashionably new Pradas—gray everywhere the eye could see, except for the black granite floor. And as the final coup de grâce, in place of the steel ship sculpture that had always welcomed us to home port, there were splashes of color paintings that punctuated the blandness and bombarded our already shattered senses.

Even though this took place preconversion, when we had no say, that didn't stop us from acting. A group of building stalwarts circulated petitions to preserve the homey wallpaper covered with Village scenes and save the ship sculpture. In the end, though, the march of time was inexorable. The lobby face-lift went forward, and the corridors were converted from their idiosyncratic (if tired) charm to anonymous gray abstraction.

Most sponsors are neither so brave nor so flush as to take on design duty, a task usually assumed by the building. Once your board lets loose the beautification battle cry, things could get bloody, with the traditionalists pitted against the avant-gardists; the postmodernists against those who are simply moderne. Nor are there any real rules of design engagement to help keep the peace. This is an area where the board reigns supreme. With the power to manage comes the right to remodel. The power to fix cash requirements for improvements gives the board the power to spend the dollars it's fixed (though most condo boards have limits on how much they can spend without approval).

But to be forewarned is to be forearmed. Having seen action in the decor wars on both sides of the power divide—first as a renter without rank and later as the commander-in-chief leading the charge—I know what you're up against. The board unquestionably holds the upper hand here, but that doesn't mean you can't make a difference.

Opening Salvo

Substance comes before style even in matters of renovation. The first item on the remodeling agenda is a reasoned decision that it needs to be done. This sounds more cut-and-dried than it is and can itself lead to open season between those for whom cash is king (and the priority is saving pennies or scrimping on maintenance) and those who prefer a touch of class (and the payoff of enhanced aesthetic and apartment values).

The board can by rights make the decision on its own, but there is nothing more certain to set off an angry mob than owners awakening unexpectedly to the sound of jackhammers in the lobby. And since the rank and file can penetrate director territory with the push of an elevator button or a walk down a hallway, I wouldn't recommend this course of action.

If the board is smart it'll wait for groundswell support and the vox populi to speak. The state of lobby affairs, whether out-of-date or down-and-out, usually stirs the masses to demand decor action (except for the perpetually tightfisted contingent who'd rather see the walls come crumbling down than spend a dime). To get things moving, either shareholders or the board can send around a survey to get a sense of community consensus or call for a vote at a shareholders' meeting. The problem is, none of the results are binding on the board. Even if shareholders weigh in with a resounding no, the board can vote yes (and vice versa).

That's what the shareholders in one East End building found out when the board forged ahead with plans for aesthetic aggrandizement in the face of calls by a quarter of the shareholders for a special meeting to reconsider. Although the anti-improvement faction tried to put a judicial halt to the lobby renovation, claiming that both its price tag and its persona were too haute, the court allowed work to proceed. The board may have acted undemocratically but not illegally. A sympathetic judge told shareholders that the only way to put a stop to the project was to oust the design despots—a bit of advice you should bear in mind if your board decides to proceed full tilt without your support.[33]

I've received calls from shareholders wondering what they can do about boards that have decorated, redecorated, and decorated anew, hoping by trial and error to get it right. Sometimes redesign accompanies regime change, a tangible way for new boards to leave their mark or erase that of their predecessors (like those pharaohs of old who replaced the faces of the sphinxes when they assumed control). Fortunately, in my building, there's been cash on hand and shareholder consensus for all design projects (of which there have been several since *The Co-op Bible* first appeared), enabling our board to proceed with (though not necessarily conclude) the work without controversy.

What Price Glory?

Once the board has gotten (or taken) the go-ahead, the assault on your pocketbook begins. Co-op boards can impose assessments, raise maintenance, use money from refinancing, or dip into reserves (provided it's not sponsor-tagged cash) to fund the aesthetic movement. (Condo boards are more limited in their power to borrow and spend without consent.) Since you're the real cash machine, you'll want to know up front whether your directors are direct descendants of a certain Bavarian Ludwig; lived former lives as Cheops, the pyramid-crazy king; or simply fancy themselves modern-day master builders, intent on leaving a living testament to their reign.

How much the board spends is a function of its philosophy, whom it chooses to carry out its grand plan, and how it agrees to compensate them. Once the renovation alarum has been sounded, it's not uncommon for boards to engage in wholesale destruction and reconstruction, whether or not such extreme makeover is aesthetically prudent or cost effective. Even assuming your directors are more measured in approach, they have to come to terms with the designers. There are decorators, who focus on cosmetics and are typically recruited to modernize lobbies and corridors, and architects, who get involved when structural changes are needed, as was the case with the entrance vestibule to my building.

As I learned from undertaking that project, most design professionals base their fee on a percentage of total construction costs, usually 20 percent. If the project comes in at $300,000, the architect would get $60,000 (plus various extras). Only it's impossible to know going in how much the job will actually cost, because it's not bid out until *after* the bulk of the architect's work is done. By agreeing to such an open-ended price term, the building (and thus, you shareholders) have no protection. If costs run amok due to problems with contractors or the board's decision to use more luxe materials, the architect's fee would jump in tandem (even though he didn't do anything more to earn it). Anyway, most of the design work performed by the architect precedes and, therefore, is not directly related to construction costs. And human nature being what it is, the architect has no incentive to keep costs down if his compensation is tied to them.

Some boards go with the flow, figuring that's how it has to be. We wouldn't, and went through several architects before we found one willing to negotiate what we considered an appropriate fixed fee plus a capped provision for cost overruns during the construction phase.

Equally important is whom the board selects to carry out the designer's vision and how the contractors will do it. In one building I know, all renovations were performed by an "in house" contractor who had a monopoly on both private apartments and public spaces until a new director offered to lend his design expertise to the building *only* if competition were introduced and the job properly bid out, a requirement that resulted in savings of tens of thousands. You, too, want to be sure that your design dollars don't go down a black hole.

Armed with the basics of design economics, you should try to gain some control over the purse strings from the start. Shareholders should ask their commanders-in-armchairs for a budget and demand to know where the money is going to come from. This doesn't mean they'll get one; the board may not even have one. But its response will tell shareholders a lot. If the board is forthcoming with figures on the total damage, shareholders can decide before it's too late whether a little cost cutting will do the trick or it's time to mount full-scale financial opposition so the building (and they) won't go broke in the name of good taste. That will avoid the fallout that occurred in my friend's condo, where the board spent *first* on building glorification and taxed *later* in the form of many-zeroed assessments to pay the bills. (A dangerous strategy under any circumstances, but one that can lead to open trench warfare if owners are asked afterward to fund a change they didn't want beforehand.)

If the board asks for time, claiming a case of your putting the cost cart before the design horse, it's okay to cut it some slack. But in the interim at least ask it for the outer limits so you'll know if it's dealing in the realm of the surreal, and it'll know it'd better get real. And extract a commitment that once its homework is done, it'll give you a dollar-and-cents report before it starts spending.

If silence is the answer, whether a case of stupidity or arrogant stonewalling, there's trouble ahead. I'd start mobilizing insurgent forces. First inform your fellow owners. Next, get them to join together to register their opposition to the managing agent and, board (whether by petition, telephone, or letter-writing campaign), and, if mum's still the word, to take action.

In my building, before we performed cosmetic improvements on the lobby, we told shareholders that the cost was minor and there was cash available. Still, nobody even asked how many design dollars we planned to spend. I'd like to attribute that to a vote of confidence, but I suspect it's more a result of shareholder tune-out (the norm until some crisis gets up close and personal). Since usually the price tag is steep and the expenditure discretionary, you have only yourselves to blame if you don't try to keep the board in check.

Visual Warfare

With the coffers filled (cash or credit will do), the directors should be ready to wage the design campaign. They have several strategic options on how to proceed.

Self-Help

If one or more of your directors is either foolish enough to think they have—or enlightened enough so that they really do have—a transforming vision, the board may choose to go it alone in renovating. This requires it to do its own design intelligence, ferret out resources, figure out costs, pull it all together, and then take the fall for shareholder dissatisfaction. Few boards opt to go solo with the stakes stacked so heavily against them, although, as you know, in my building that's what the royal "We" did.

Bringing In the Lobbyists

Most boards enlist the aid of a lobbyist, one of those legions of decorators out there whose sole mission is to bring aesthetic order to your building's public spaces. No Adam Tihanys among the residential set to leave their idiosyncratic mark of inspiration. That would be counterintuitive to the very nature of most residential lobby design, which aims to achieve a middle-of-the-road marble and brass homogeneity, appealing to all and irritating none. But at least these design divas lend the board both cover and credibility. One of their sisterhood, taking her marching orders from the sponsor, brought our building into present-day conventional design codes—a mold that I took pleasure in breaking once we assumed control.

Calling On the Rank and File

Whether to lessen the load, increase the appearance of shareholder say, or defuse criticism of themselves, some boards form in-house design committees to come up with ideas, screen decorators, and research resources. These can be a subset of board members or drawn from the general rank and file. It's not a perfect system. (The board, not the committee, has the final aesthetic and financial say.) There are sure to be battles along the way. In one nearby building that I looked at but ultimately passed by (thank heaven), the Old Guard fought for (and won) preservation of their namesake chandelier against the cries of the Generation Xers who wanted a taste of twenty-first-century design. In another the fight was over marble or mahogany. Assuming everyone is still talking when the dust settles, the result that emerges from the communal consensus is more likely to be a diluted compromise than a strong, individualized vision. And the more people who are involved, the longer it will take.

No matter. If you are someone for whom aesthetics counts, toughen your skin, get ready to take (and give) some heat, and enlist in the cause of good design. If the board doesn't ask for committee members, volunteer to form your own and don't take no for an answer. You *can* make a difference—even if only by making things difficult. I know whereof I speak.

During the conversion of my building, the sponsor made the mistake of using the corridor outside my apartment as the design launch pad. When I arrived home one evening to find the walls faced in Howard Johnson nondescriptness and the floors covered with green plaid carpets that said Midwest, not Memphis (downtown, that is), I knew it was time for action. I collared the only souls in sight to ask if they were serious (a tactical faux pas since one was a sponsor-scion-cum-decorator responsible for the decor). When that got me nowhere, I called the office with my lament. In an act of supreme enlightenment and common sense, one of the building's owners volunteered to take me around for inspection (and inspiration) to others of their buildings in the throes of conversion redesign. I suspect the motive was more to satisfy a potential buyer and silence a could-be troublemaker than to elicit my design sensibilities, but I didn't care. My only worry was that once he saw my own Chinese-red lacquered walls he'd start eviction proceedings or cancel the invitation. But the tour went ahead on schedule.

I can't say I was cheered by the alternatives or that my individual voice prevailed. But at least disaster was averted—the Motel 6 paper and plaid rugs were soon no more. And I was given a personal preview of what was in store for our lobby with the lines of communication left open for change.

Presentation of the Colors

In the context of co-ops and condos, where there are as many ideas of good taste as there are owners, no design solution is free from controversy. Rather than get embroiled in aesthetic disputes, if it's a minor design project, the board may go its own way and present the owners with the finished product. In the elevator modernization project we completed not long ago, we left the mechanics to the engineers but took control of the interiors, eschewing the plastic laminate that covers the walls of most cabs in favor of stainless steel industrial mesh and studded black rubber floors. Only problem was the black absorbed so much light that nobody could *see* our new creations, which shareholders nicknamed Darth Vader, The Tomb, The Dark Star. We took the hint and fixed the lighting. At that year's annual meeting, a few traditionalists proclaimed the elevators "ugly," but they were quickly silenced by the rest, so I figure we got it about right.

Assuming the project is one of consequence, it behooves the board to give you a foretaste of its chosen design scheme, though it's not required to do so. A show-and-tell for owners should be set up with samples of the real thing. If the hallways are being updated, that means examples of the carpet, wallpaper, and lighting. For a lobby makeover, design sketches together with samples of the finishes and furniture should be made available. Sometimes the board deigns to ask your opinion or gives you alternatives from which to choose. Whether it's a true beauty contest where you get to vote or a fait accompli you'll never really know, since it doesn't have to listen to you. Still, if there's sufficient dissension in the ranks, this is an area where owners sometimes can bring the force of moral suasion to bear, so don't assume you have no recourse against the visual affront being inflicted on you. The board at a nearby downtown building substantially changed its plans for an entrance plaza in response to owners who wanted to make it more child friendly.

Design by Fiat

Although I've given you chapter and verse, that doesn't mean we followed them to the letter when it came time for a little cosmetics on our own lobby. Having had the sponsor's version of good taste imposed on us for years, there were many who were not unhappy that the paper was peeling, the couches dirty, and the lighting fixtures near death. At the annual meeting, shareholder sentiment was for something to be done. The only issue was how drastic to go and who would make and carry out the design decisions.

You have to understand, I am someone for whom aesthetics seriously matter. Rather than taint my living room with some nondescript lightbulb holder, I worked by moonlight for five years until I unearthed the perfect pair of Ching dynasty ceramic figurines in the back room of some antiques shop. It was another six months before they made the transition from their origins as temple-top dancers to their more secular incarnations as functioning lamps—what with mounting, electrification, and custom shades.

So while I like to think of myself as a woman of the people in step with my fellow shareholders, I must admit that when it came to decorating the lobby I threw democracy to the wind and let my absolutist aesthetic take command. At stake was not a complete overhaul but a mere touchup for which we weren't asking shareholders to pony up a penny. Besides, no one was breathing down our necks volunteering their aesthetic two cents. So we sent around a notice and set to work.

Since the paintings had to stay, we decided it was better to join them than to fight them. So we banished the battleship gray that muddied the walls and refinished them with a textured surface built up layer by layer in a shade of white that it took me and my designer friend (whom I pressed into service) days to select. Instead of letting my fingers do the walking in those catalogs of cookie-cutter lighting fixtures, I burned some shoe leather, in the process finding a pair of uniquely wonderful French Deco nickel sconces. The gray modern-pretender couches were replaced by classic Corbusier in steel and black leather. The black floors were polished to a skating rink sheen; the stainless steel cornices glistened. With a few strategic maneuvers the lobby had been transformed from standard issue to a starkly simple International Style gallery.

Though I hesitate to speak for the masses, I can report that the result was achieved and received without incident or any physical violence. A few brave souls even openly pronounced the project a success. And when I overheard a broker waxing poetic to a client about the change, I exulted with aesthetic satisfaction and also saw dollar signs dancing before my eyes.

Playing by the Rules

We are now deep into renovating the lobby vestibule, this time going by the book, with the entire board involved and shareholders kept apprised every step of the obstacle-strewn way. We interviewed more architects than I can remember till we found the right one for the right price who, hopefully, will come up with the right design. What seemed like a straightforward project turned out to be anything but, because we inherited a space with a raised platform across half of it that would require the doormen to sit enthroned six inches above us common folk. We figured we'd lop off the step so we could all be on an equal footing, only to be told by our structural engineer that we'd also be chopping off all the electrical cables in the building, a state of affairs that has forced us to reconsider our options. Now we have to decide whether to move the doormen, cut a limited swath through the concrete platform, or leave well enough alone and go with a coat of paint. I'll let you know what happens.

8

The Rules of Repair

THE FIX IS IN

Nothing lasts forever. Whether through the march of time, an act of God (or man), or some other source, things get broken or outlive their useful lives—both inside and outside your private domain: the electricity shorts, the wires rot, the windows need replacing, the pipes burst, the elevator goes kaput, the paint peels, the roof leaks. The real question is who is responsible for putting in the fix—and footing the bill. Usually, though not always, it is one and the same being.

In and Out

The place to start for answers is the proprietary lease (co-ops) or bylaws (condos). The standard lease in New York sets out the obligations of the co-op something like this:

> The Lessor [the co-op] shall keep in good repair all of the building and at its expense keep in good repair all of the apartments . . . and its equipment and apparatus except those portions the maintenance and repair of which are expressly stated to be the responsibility of the Lessee [the shareholder].

Shareholders (the lessees) usually are charged with the following duties:

> to keep the interior of the apartment (*including* interior walls, floors and ceilings, but *excluding* windows, window panes, window frames, sashes, sills, entrance and terrace doors, frames and saddles) in good repair and to do all of the painting and decorating. [Emphasis added.]

In addition, you as the shareholder (the lessee) are "solely responsible for the maintenance, repair and replacement of plumbing, gas and heating fixtures and equipment" and the "appliances" in your apartment. To complicate matters further, most leases describe (in language only an engineer could love) the point at which these fixtures are considered within the scope of your apartment (and thus your problem) and when they are beyond (and thus the building's headache). I'll spare you the details if you promise to take a look at your lease *before* you talk to the board in the event of trouble.

In essence, you're responsible for gas, steam, and water pipes attached to the fixtures or that *you* installed in the walls or ceilings or under the floors. The board is responsible if the pipes are part of the standard apartment equipment. And it's up to you to maintain and repair lighting and electrical fixtures (including fuses, circuit breakers, wiring, and conduits from the junction box at the riser into and through your apartment). The answer to your question is: the junction box is the point at which the electric wires converge and then branch out to the various apartments. It can be located in the basement (as in my building) or in the hallway or other site generally outside your own apartment.

Basically, it all comes down to the difference between inside and out. You're responsible for what's inside the four walls (and floors and ceilings) and the board is responsible for the common areas and the building-wide systems (heat, water, gas, electric). This same division of labor exists in condos: the board is charged with repairing the common elements and individual owners with repairing their own units.[1] (For the ambitious among you who have pulled out your bylaws, don't get nervous if the language looks different. Condo lawyers have their own way of saying what, for your purposes, is essentially the same thing.)

Living Distinction

Where does all this legalese get you in real life? Some examples will help show you the way—and the potential problems.

1. Your fridge is on the fritz. No more calling on the agent (as you did in your renting days) to haul up a new one, or more likely a reconditioned job no better than the old. It's clearly your responsibility to repair and replace your own appliances.[2] And in case you think you can shift repair responsibility for your wall oven on the theory that it's a fixture, not an appliance, another co-op owner actually sued over this—and lost.[3]

2. Your air-conditioning unit (through the wall or window) conks out, and you're in a lather. Assuming it was permitted to begin with (because, as we've seen, if it wasn't the board can make you get rid of it), if you want cold air it's up to you to get it. Whether you achieve that goal with a trip to the Arctic—or one to Sears—is strictly your call.

3. It's not your stand-alone cooler that collapsed but a unit that provides *both* hot and cold air. Under law, co-ops and condos are required to warm you in winter—but they don't have to cool you in summer. So the responsibility for repairs may turn on the season of the breakdown. If Jack Frost has you iced, the board may have to thaw you out. But if it's the summer sun that has you sweltering, get a piña colada. One Upper East Side condo owner tried to get the board to replace her heating and air-conditioning system. The season was right, but her demands went beyond relief—to revenge.

She wanted a fix not only for her apartment but for the whole line, plus alternate housing till the fix was in, fines placed on the board, even a ban on the board's disbursing the proceeds of a $3 million loan till the repairs were completed.[4] But that doesn't mean you won't win if you go with the right season *and* the correct approach.

4. The socket at your bedside doesn't work, leaving you powerless to finish the closing chapters of Tom Clancy's latest. Technically, since that junction box only brings electricity to a point outside your apartment, you're responsible for restoring the juice. On that theory the co-op board told my friend, who experienced just such an outage right after she moved in, that the task was hers. With discovery of the source of the problem (turns out a leak from the roof ate through the wires) came a change in board attitude, and in the end the co-op paid the cost of restoring the light source.

5. The ceiling is cracking and plaster is coming loose—a little at first, but spreading like some mutant virus. As we'll see, this kind of residential disease, where the symptom but not the cause is readily apparent, can give rise to battling diagnoses between board and owner. If it's a case of a hit-and-run paint job, then get some plasterweld, a new painter, and some Benjamin Moore and go to it. But at least one court has said if the mess was caused by use of a defective bonding agent so that the plaster never properly stuck during construction of the building, that's part of the underlying structure, and repair gets shifted to the board.[5]

6. Those bronze doré sconces you rescued from the ages at the Marche aux Puces don't light when you turn the switch. Since you initially had them electrified and installed, it's up to you to get an electrician unless you want them returned to their original candlelit state. (And if you'll be fooling around with the building's electrical system, you'll surely need board consent as well.)

7. A kitchen pipe bursts, turning your apartment into the Grand Canal. Whether the restorer for the ages will be you or the board depends on where that water pipe was. If it was within the wall, it's the board to the rescue; if it was attached to a fixture, the rescuer may be you. Even assuming the board bears the brunt, it's not always clear (as we'll see) just how much restoring it has to undertake.

8. The door to your apartment is warped and corroded. Seems pretty clear from most leases, which exclude "entrance" doors from your duty to repair, that the job falls to the board—something I wish I had known before I bought my apartment. My predecessors had hacked several inches off the bottom of the front door to accommodate their high-pile shag. Uncertain of my rights, and unwilling to risk exposure to either creeping creatures or accumulating menus, I took self-help and got the super to switch my

shortened door with a full-length version from another (vacant) apartment. I hope you will not repeat my mistake (or misdeed), since in this case the authorized solution is cheaper and easier than my undercover caper.

9. The door's okay, but the lock is shot. If it's the bottom one that the building installed, then the board should replace it. But if you've secured the top spot with a designer lock of your choosing, whether Fichet or Medeco, you're probably on your own when it comes to repair.

10. A power surge melts your plug and incapacitates your VCR (and other electronic equipment). I didn't make this one up—we got such a claim from a shareholder. My answer now is the same as it was then: Come on, get real. The building doesn't control the power flow, and besides, you can protect against erratic electricity with a fifteen-dollar power surge plug. (By the way, the few cases I've seen suggest that not even Con Ed would legally be to blame.)

Of course, you may have your own repair tale of woe. Hopefully, the board will respond apace (assuming it's the board's responsibility). But if it decides to play hardball, there are a couple of approaches you can take to enlighten it and get action.

Ambiguous Advantage

Where the division of responsibility (in the lease or bylaws) is clear, the repair should be swift and uncontested. But as you can see, that's not always the case. Where ambiguity attaches, battles may ensue: the nature of the repair is not specified in the lease; the fact of damage is undisputed but not the cause. Who gets the benefit of the doubt? Here you have the law largely on your side, especially if you live in a co-op, where, as you know by now, you have a landlord to look to.

The law says if there's any ambiguity in the lease (or bylaws), it gets construed against the one who prepared it—that's the co-op or condo. The theory is that the stronger party should pay the price of the uncertainty it created.

How does this play out? The court read relief into the lease for a co-op owner whose bedroom floor had buckled due to rotted "sleepers" and underflooring.[6] They weren't interior repairs (which the lease made the shareholder's responsibility) because they were under the floors, invisible to the shareholder's eyes (and thus excluded from his domain). Rather, they were part of the permanent structure and thus the board's duty under the lease. Another shareholder's kitchen ceiling hung in the (im)balance after the board declined to do anything about the bubbling and chunks of falling plaster. Again, judicial lease reading put the burden on the board.[7] The problem was structural, caused by use of a defective bonding agent so the plaster never stuck to the building's beams and supports from the start. (If you're one of those owners with perpetual ceiling problems, I'd keep this reference handy to fight back next time the board turns you down.)

Exclusive Control

We've all heard of (but preferably not experienced) those cases where the patient wakes up after surgery without an appendix—but with a sponge—in his gut. They get settled quickly. Only the doctor was conscious, so he had to be in control. It's the same thing with co-op (and condo) damage distress. Sort of. A steam pipe behind the walls (and out of view) bursts, turning your apartment into a shvitz bath. Or problems with the building's plumbing system transform your living room into a floodplain. If the condition you're complaining of is within board control (and you didn't do anything to contribute to it), odds are the board will have to fix it.

That's what a court told a Bronx condo board that refused to repair a concealed water leak in the ceiling of an owner's apartment. Since the water came from common area pipes, of which the board was in sole control, the board also had to be the sole solution.[8]

Legal Promise

But probably the best thing you have going for you (at least as a co-op owner) is what's called the Warranty of Habitability, a law passed to protect renters.[9] It says that in every lease there is an implied promise that your apartment "will be fit for human habitation and for the uses reasonably intended" and that you shouldn't be subjected to any conditions that would be "dangerous, hazardous or detrimental to [your] life, health or safety." To make sure this promise is kept, the tenant's duty to pay rent is made dependent on the landlord's maintaining the premises in habitable condition. If he's not, then the tenant can take a rent reduction.

Since co-op owners are also tenants, the courts have ruled that this law protects them as well.[10] For condo owners, independence has its downside, one of which is that the judges have said that you don't get the benefit of this guarantee (though that doesn't necessarily mean you are without remedy).[11]

Before either camp gets too excited, let's take a look at what the warranty really means. It promises a *minimum* standard of livable conditions. When a staff strike at an Upper West Side building resulted in accumulated garbage, flourishing vermin, and invading roaches, the warranty was breached and the tenants got a 10 percent rent reduction for the duration.[12] But when a bunch of Upper East Siders tried to use this remedy of the people to maintain their patrician lifestyle, they found out that neither worn hallway carpeting and exposed wiring (during wallpaper repairs) nor discolored tiles and missing doorknobs in their apartments amounted to a breach. The only reason they were entitled to any rent relief at all was that there were also elevator service problems.[13] Nor does the warranty extend to greenhouses and terraces—those playgrounds of the privileged. Even though a shareholder was denied access to his terrace for months while the building claimed it for needed repairs, he got no maintenance discount, only a good citizen's award.[14]

Most of the kinds of repairs for which you'll want to invoke the warranty are somewhere in between. In those cases it can help you get results. It brought flood relief to a penthouse owner who suffered damage to fabrics, furnishings, and assorted wall mirrors caused by an exterior leak that the board refused to fix. She got dry land, restitution, and a maintenance rebate for the board's breach of the warranty *and* the lease plus thousands more in damages.[15] It helped a tenant whose apartment had broken appliances, cracked windows, nonfunctioning sinks, and toilet and water damage, to boot.[16]

But it won't do you any good for the ordinary nuisances of life in the big city. Shareholder above you pad around like a clodhopper? Better learn to live with it.[17] Got a vibrating fuel booster below you?[18] Too much noise and too little water pressure?[19] Minor electrical problems?[20] To each of these complaints, the courts have recently said, the warranty won't protect you.

Still, it can be a powerful weapon for shareholders. It applies regardless of what your proprietary lease says. Neither the building nor the board can waive it. So rather than getting into a fight with the board over what some lawyer meant by the language in the lease, head straight for the warranty—it stands alone. No matter what the lease says, you have the right to a habitable apartment. And since paying your maintenance is dependent on receiving essential (not luxury) treatment, if your place is rendered uninhabitable you should be able to take an offset.

Real World Relief

How much can you deduct? It depends on how intolerable the situation is. The rule is that you are entitled to the difference between the maintenance you paid and the rental value of the apartment with the offending condition.[21] One shareholder got a 50 percent reduction when his board installed new laundry equipment that drove him nuts and exceeded code standards.[22] Another got 20 percent off for his claimed breach.[23] And if the apartment truly becomes uninhabitable, as in cases of mold (see below), you might really have to move out and not be required to pay at all.

A wildlife rehabilitator who shared his two-floor loft with turtles, tortoises, and assorted reptiles demanded $22,500 a month to relocate when the board didn't adequately respond to his problem with heat, hot water, and mold. Instead, the court ordered the board to fix the mess, and when it didn't, he went back to complain some more. The board claimed it wasn't able to comply because Mr. Rehabilitator refused to be separated from his lizards, so the court ordered a hearing to see if the reptile man should get the money.[24]

If you substantially prevail, you may also be able to get attorneys' fees from the co-op.[25] And if the board has made you suffer long enough without taking action, you might even be entitled to punitive damages, as a number of shareholders have been. (See chapter 17.) Just don't get carried away or you could get into trouble (as have some shareholders who withheld for years, only to ultimately have an expensive comeuppance. See page 239).

Residency Requirement

Since the point of the warranty is to provide habitable conditions for the person living in the apartment, generally you have to be the shareholder in occupancy to claim its protection.[26] If you use your co-op only as a pied-à-terre and don't live there, or if you sublease to someone else, odds are you can't invoke the warranty. In the rental context where the rule originated, the idea is that you shouldn't be able to profiteer by charging your subtenant the full amount while not paying yourself. That rationale broke down in a case where the wife stayed in the family co-op after the husband-shareholder had been ordered out as part of a divorce settlement. This time when the co-op brought an action for unpaid maintenance, the court said it was okay for the nonresident husband to take advantage of the warranty because, otherwise, the co-op could ignore its obligation to fix the problems in the apartment while getting paid full price.[27] Whether the commonsense approach of this judge will be followed by those higher up is uncertain.

Condo Caveat

Condo owners have the same repair problems, but they don't have the same protection; that's what the highest court in New York State to have considered the question said more than a decade ago. A downtown condo owner complained of water leaks and claimed the warranty allowed him to withhold common charges, which he did (to the tune of $20,000 over two years). But the court said there is no warranty, and no right to withhold, in condos—only the bylaws to go by.[28] Another soaked unit owner tried again only recently and got the same answer from the same court. When he tried to go up the ladder and appeal to the judicial top dogs, he was told, Don't bother us—we don't want to hear it.[29] The result is unless those lawmakers step in and do something about it, you fat-cat condo owners have fewer rights than lowly renters.

In the interim, enterprising owners have devised their own strategies to circumvent the ban and level the playing field, with only mixed results.

- Forget about the warranty—you breached your contractual duty to make repairs, a West Side condo owner argued when the board tried to foreclose for unpaid maintenance. Despite its obligation under the bylaws to make repairs when another unit owner failed to, for years the board did nothing and refused to let the owner do anything as water from the defective penthouse windows caused his ceiling to collapse. May not be a breach of warranty, but could be a breach of contract, the court agreed, and let the claim stand.[30]
- Another creative thinker resorted to the Housing Maintenance Code to get relief from leaky drain pipes. We know the warranty doesn't apply to condos, the court said, but that doesn't mean you're out of luck. The board "controls" the building and, under the law, the entity that controls the building is considered an "owner," and an owner is required to keep the building in good repair: ergo, you can enforce the Code against your condo to get relief.[31]
- But the court didn't buy a condo owner's claim that the board had committed fraud in failing to repair the common elements, because it had made an effort (albeit not totally successful) to fix the problem. You can't withhold common charges, it said, and now you have to pay them back—plus interest and attorneys' fees.[32]

Unless and until there's a change in the law, you condo owners can't count on the warranty, and you're not safe if you offset.[33] Indeed, you could wind up worse off than before, forced not only to pay your arrears but also the condo's expenses in fighting you.

Transferring Responsibility

You may be able to make the board fix the problem even if it was caused by another owner. Most co-op leases and condo bylaws require the board to keep the premises in good repair. They often require, or permit, the board to step in and fix an unresolved problem in another owner's apartment that's affecting you. And at least in co-ops, shareholders have that warranty to look to for promise of a habitable place. So what happens if the owner above or adjacent to you embarks on the renovation plan of the century, leaving you with a perpetual leak—and he won't do anything to help? Do you have to suffer in silence—and wetness? Or can you get aid elsewhere? The answer: Go to the board.

That's what one shareholder tried after living for more than four years with leaks that started when the owner atop began renovating—and got so bad that he had to contend not only with the flow of water but also with exposed pipes that were uncovered as the ceiling deteriorated. Tired of soaking in silence, he took the board to court, arguing that it had an independent duty under the lease and the warranty to keep him (and his place) high and dry—and won.[34] I hope your board is on notice that it can't sit back and do nothing. It has to take action against the offending owner; if it doesn't, you can seek—and should be able to get—relief directly from the board. (It's the board's headache to then go after the reckless renovator.)

Caught in the Middle

It's easy to blame those board members, but sometimes they're stuck in the middle, especially in condops where the commercial spaces usually aren't owned by the building but by the sponsor (or some other third party). Odds are that the board has no say over who moves in: maybe a restaurant that starts out Italian, morphs to Thai, and then turns Szechuan, each reincarnation more troublesome than its predecessor; or it could be a garage that pulls down its metal shutters in the wee hours and attracts graffiti artists; or a hair salon whose air-conditioning system drips water into the adjacent wall.

The board may not even know there's a problem until shareholders start complaining. Even then it usually can't take direct action because it has no legal relation with commercial tenants, and its only effective legal recourse is to get the sponsor (or whoever owns the space) to act. If the problem is capable of a onetime fix, odds are it will get resolved; where it's more chronic, like a restaurant that doesn't observe the basic rules of residential propriety—but has a lease that goes out twenty years—the solution may be hard to come by. Even if the sponsor takes legal action to get out the offenders, that doesn't mean they'll go, and slogging it through the courts can take years. For once, at least, board and shareholders should be united in a common cause, and together you may be able to hasten the troublemaker's departure by making your voices heard through complaints to the appropriate authorities.

Equal Access

You can't complain if you won't comply—and do your bit for the communal repair effort. That means giving the board access to your apartment to get the job done. Sounds too simple to need saying? Unfortunately, it's not. Most owners maintain a wide-open-door (and -mouth) policy for repairs *they* have requested. But many change their philosophy if it's work for the commonweal that may not benefit them directly—a cracked pipe inside your wall that rains down on the guy below. Replacement windows that they don't want.

I hate to say it, but it's usually those terrace owners who are the most repair resistant. One board had to go to court to get an owner to provide access and keys so it could fix the roof before the guaranty ran out.[35] Another recalcitrant owner forced the board to get an order allowing it entry to waterproof his leaking terrace and install replacement windows.[36] A third made the board go to court and get an injunction before he would let the building raise his terrace doors as part of necessary roof repairs.[37] In my own building, we had to contend with a few members of the resistance when we installed new windows. But their objections melted—and their doors opened—when they found out the new oculi were assessment free.

Whatever your reason—you don't want to be bothered, you prefer those old casements—give it up. If you make the board go to court to get your door opened, you will lose—and render yourself persona non grata in the process.

All or Nothing

Once the problem is solved, the question is how much more does the board have to do? Is a quick fix enough or does the board have to go beyond repair to restoration of the decoration status quo ante?

In order to replace those wires that rotted, the board chopped through your living room wall, leaving a gaping hole and a gash in your Zuber hand-painted paper. At the very least, the board has to seal the hole (the better to keep out any unwanted creatures) and restore your wall to where it was. Beyond that, nothing's for sure. Since most leases (and bylaws) make *you* responsible for *all* painting and decorating, some boards will say the rest is up to you. The truth is, if your walls are sheathed with a standard color slick, it doesn't cost the board any more to let those contractors slap on another coat (you supply the contents). That's what our board does. If you have some sponge-painted masterwork by one of the new breed of decorative artists or wallpaper-clad surfaces, you are probably on your own.

Sometimes the line between repair form and function is blurred. A pipe burst in the bathroom tearing asunder your ceramic-tiled shower floor. Since you can't wash without a waterproof surface, the board has to provide a replacement, but it doesn't have to go back to Italy—or even to the local Home Depot—to get a color-coordinated match.

There's no sure word from the courts on how far the board has to go to fix most things—a gap that suggests that these situations usually get worked out. If it happens to you and the board leaves you unsatisfied, you can take on the cause and go charging to court. One shareholder did, and was told it's the building's responsibility to restore the standard floor but up to him to pay to bleach it driftwood white.[38] It's cheaper (by far) to get homeowner's insurance than to fight. (If you don't have it, get it.) Some buildings mandate that owners have insurance on their apartment's contents to protect them and the building.

And if the repairs are in an area the board is responsible for maintaining (even though it's part of your apartment), it can do what it wants—whether you like it or not. Parting with those quarry tiles on your terrace (when the board decides to replace them with cement pavers) may bring sweet sorrow—but no cause of action. (See page 278.)

Shifting the Blame

Ownership brings responsibility. Although you should take the board to task if it drags its feet (and dollars) in carrying out repairs that fall on *its* side of the divide, don't expect the board (which really means your fellow owners) to assume *your* share of the repair bargain for work that needs to be done in your apartment. Some street-wise owners have tried to shift their burden to the board by reporting as Housing Code violations repairs they want done. Since the code was intended for rental buildings, it covers a multiplicity of repair sins from peeling paint to pouring water and makes the "owner" responsible for clearing up all violations whether inside or outside individual apartments. In a rental building, this makes sense since the landlord (a.k.a. owner) owns it all. But some renters turned owners figured, Why give up a good thing? Instead of assuming responsibility, they hoped under the Housing Code to make the building, as owner, fix everything, inside and out.

One Upper East Side shareholder sued to require her co-op (as owner) to remove violations ranging from leaking faucets to faulty paint to defective outlets in her apartment to penetrating water without. The court agreed the co-op was the owner and thus, at least initially, it had to cure all the problems. But the board could then charge *her* for everything she had to fix under the co-op's lease.[39]

The answer is more direct in condos. Since you own your apartment outright, you (not the condo) are the "owner" for these purposes. The result is that when a couple of unit owners tried the same tactic as the co-op owner described above, the court told them they had to cure the violations in their own apartments as required by the condo bylaws.[40]

I'm all for creative problem solving, but this one smacks of disloyalty to your fellow owners—who ultimately would be the ones paying for your repairs. And if past experience is any guide, it will only get you back to where you started—with each side's respective repair responsibilities determined by what's set out in the lease (or bylaws).

Fungus Attack

Now that you know the basics of who's responsible for what, and how to get action, I should tell you there's a new danger lurking on the horizon: mold. My only exposure to the stuff was when I opened the refrigerator to find a long-since-forgotten wedge of Brie transformed into an unrecognizable growth. The thought of having that mess cover the walls of my apartment is beyond contemplation. Yet for reasons not entirely clear, mold is the latest battleground between shareholders and boards (and developers). Bianca Jagger sued her Park Avenue landlord for $20 million, claiming that mold caused by an unrepaired leak forced her to move out of her plush (but cheap) rental.[41] Across the avenue, condo owners are hot and heavy into litigation with the developer over construction defects they say caused mold infestation in their ritzy apartments. Lots more are coming down the pike.

Why now? Who knows? Maybe because modern construction techniques use materials molds like to eat. Maybe because the board failed to fix a persistent leak. Maybe because it's the next profitable front in building litigation after asbestos and lead poisoning. The real question is what should you—and the board—do about it.

One Upper East Side couple was faced with the problem. It started slowly with a leak; the leak turned into a flood; then the ceiling started coming down, and brown water gushed out. Although the building patched it up, the couple returned from vacation to find their closet invaded by black mold, and their entire apartment smelled as bad as the blob looked. They packed their bags and left, never to return except to go to court to get the owner to remove the mess. When Mr. Foot Dragger sued them for nonpayment, they responded that the apartment was unlivable (what we lawyers call constructive eviction). The court agreed, saying the apartment was not habitable for nearly two years, so they didn't have to pay rent.[42]

Let their travails be a lesson in what to avoid. You know what they say about an ounce of prevention. Unless the problem was created by new construction, the cheapest and easiest solution is to nip it in the bud: to prevent leaks from turning into mold-hungry conditions. But should fungus attack, civil war between you and the board is not the way to go. It will cost you and the building plenty (especially because insurance doesn't necessarily cover mold), and could ultimately affect apartment values, so before you freak out—and move out—talk it out with the board, and together devise a rational plan of attack.

GETTING ACTION

Hopefully, you will remain comfortably ensconced in your co-op or condo—walls intact, water flowing (not overflowing), electricity on, and free of damage from your renovating neighbor. But in case a problem arises and you need repair action, here are the rules to go by:

1. Identify what needs fixing and where the problem is coming from. Think like a lawyer. If the ceiling is coming down and the possibilities are: (*a*) a lousy paint job, or (*b*) a defective bonding agent, as an advocate in

reporting the problem go with choice *b* (which is the building's responsibility) as opposed to choice *a* (which is yours). (Of course, if there's moisture penetrating inside your apartment from without, that's also likely in the board's bailiwick.)

2. In the real (as opposed to the legal) world of co-op and condo living, the lease and the bylaws are only the beginning—and represent a minimum of what the board is bound to do. Some boards are niggardly and go by the letter of the law, requiring owners to do their own repairs no matter how piddling. Others take a more expansive view (and have a more generous spirit) in interpreting their responsibilities. They'll fix a burst pipe though it's attached to the sink, not in the wall. They'll pay for electrical repairs caused by problems behind the wall.

3. Although the board sets repair policy, the managing agent carries it out—and has some discretion on just what gets done and what doesn't. The board will thank you if it doesn't have to get involved. So, at least initially, approach the agent with terms of endearment, not antagonism.

4. If, when you call, the board disclaims responsibility, try a little legal persuasion. You know your rights by now, but pull that lease (or those bylaws) out to be sure. If it's not clear, you should get the benefit of the doubt under the ambiguity rule. If the problem is caused by something exclusively within the board's control, that's another factor in your favor. And remember, no matter what that lease says, co-op owners have the warranty to work for them.

5. Still no action? One option is to fix the problem (using standard, not super-deluxe repairers) and send the board a bill. If it doesn't pay and the amount is not more than $3,000, you can haul the board into Small Claims Court. If you're right (or the judge agrees), you get your money back. If not, you'll still have an opportunity to see our (after-dark) justice system at work—an experience, I promise you, that will be more entertaining than a night on the town. If you're talking more serious money you'll have to bring a complaint in a real court, which can cost real money.

6. Of course, turnabout is fair play. If it's something you're responsible for and don't fix, the board can get the repairs done and charge you. Enforcement is easier for the board since it can add the amount onto your monthly charges and come after you if you don't pay.

7. If you live in a co-op where the warranty applies, you may be able to deduct part of your monthly maintenance until the fix is in. How much? Let your conscience and reality be your guide. You are sure to get the board's notice—and maybe even action. And should it go after you for nonpayment, you have a warranty defense.

8. If the damage was caused by a renovating shareholder from whom you're getting no satisfaction, don't sit back in silence. Remember, under

the lease and the warranty you still may be able to go directly against the board for repair action.

9. But if what *you* did caused the problem, forget it—you're on your own (and you'll get no sympathy from the board or your fellow owners). You fought for that greenhouse—you fix it when it leaks.

10. Assuming you get the board to act, it's not clear how far it has to go. Most boards will opt for the minimum—restoring your wall but not whatever may have covered it—and have the lease (or bylaws) to back them up. If you want more you may have to take legal action, thereby resolving the question—how much is enough?—for us all.

9

The Ruling Class: The Power, the Glory (and the Limits)

PRELUDE TO POWER

As a member of the rank and file you'll want to know whether your rulers are fit to serve and just how much sway they hold over you. Can they ride roughshod over your liberties or are there limits to the board members' authority? Are they benign despots, latent anarchists, or let-them-eat-cake reactionaries—in which case revolution is just as much in order now as it was then (although the steps set out in chapter 12 promise a path to victory without bloodshed).

As this chapter explains, at least within the confines of the building the board has the power to control your residential destiny—but that power is not unchecked. The law imposes limits on how far it can go. The board's members may hold the reins of government, but the more you know about what they can and can't do the better you will be able to keep them in line and accountable. And don't forget that their power is temporal. Since you, the people, elected them, unless they are sponsor-designated directors (of which more later), you can get rid of them if they abuse your trust.

THE SOURCE OF POWER

If you've ever wondered where your co-op board gets its attitude, you may start at the source of power. Co-op directors don't have to go to shareholders for most of their authority; they get an independent fix directly from the state. New York's Corporation Law (which applies to co-ops) says that the business of a corporation shall be managed under the direction of its board of directors.[1] In the corporate context, this grant gives the board virtual carte blanche to run the company's business affairs as it sees fit—from declaring dividends to raising revenue to selling assets to entering into mergers or other major transactions. As you know, if you are a shareholder in any corporation from AT&T to Zoltek, the decisions board members make can have a significant impact on the company's bottom line and hence on the value of your investment. In the case of co-ops, which function not only as corporate entities but also as quasi governments, the scope of the board's power is even more centralized because it controls every aspect of your existence.

Whereas co-ops are akin to constitutional monarchies, with power concentrated in the board, condos are more like independent republics, with decentralized board power. Condo boards don't have any comparable outside grant. The Condo Act gives them a few specific mandates.[2] But, basically, the board members act as your agents—which means the ultimate power source is the unit owners.

So how do you know what your directors—co-op or condo—are authorized to do? In the case of co-ops, take a look at the building's bylaws and its lease. Not that they're likely to help all that much. Board powers in corporations (which include co-ops) are so well established over time (through statute and cases) that they're considered to be implicitly understood, at least by the legal cognoscenti. Because of this breadth, many co-op documents don't bother spelling them out. Such definition might edify you, but arguably it could delimit the board's power—not something the board wants to do.

It's the reverse in condos. Condo boards have no time-tested or independent power grants. Condo bylaws usually include a specific list of what the board can do. If some power is omitted, it may not be implied, which means your board just can't do it. (A useful tidbit you should store away in case of a rainy-day run-in with the board.)

Whether you live in a condo or a co-op, the board still has plenty of say over you. We'll take a detailed look at the respective spheres of influence of condo and co-op boards later on, but for now it's important to get a general sense of what your directors can do to you.

1. They can fix monthly charges, raising or lowering them (don't hold your breath) as they see fit to cover the building's costs, and decide when and how you pay.
2. They can get you to pony up hard cash to pay for their pet projects by assessing you fees on top of your monthly maintenance in proportion to your ownership interest.
3. They can enter into contracts for anything from satellite dishes to professional services and bind the building (and you, its owners) to ante up the agreed-on price.
4. They can lead the building headlong into legal battle by bringing or defending lawsuits on behalf of the building.
5. They can retain hired guns to wage their chosen warfare, as well as other outside professionals (accountants, engineers, and architects) to suit any need they believe exists.
6. They can pass or repeal House Rules that regulate everything from pets to parking spaces, bicycles to baby carriages, guests to grilling—and in the process establish the building as a democracy or a dictatorship.

7. They can hire and fire staff (though they'd better know the ins and outs of the union contract before they exercise their muscle or you could wind up paying for their mistakes).
8. They can retain a managing agent to run the day-to-day affairs of the building.
9. They can invest the building's cash reserve fund (which can amount to millions) even if they don't know the difference between a T-bill and a taco.
10. They can decide whether your renovation plans make it off the drawing board to the drawing room by withholding or granting consent.
11. They can indulge their passion for empire building through capital improvements from modernizing the elevators to installing new windows to restoring the roof. (Though condo boards usually can't alter without owner approval beyond set dollar amounts.)
12. They can borrow on behalf of the building (but in condos, they can hock owners only so much without their consent).
13. They can decide (in most co-ops, but not in condos) if your buyer gets in or stays out and (if authorized) make you pay up for the privilege of selling your apartment by imposing a flip tax.
14. They can (in most co-ops, but not in condos) tell you how and when you can sublet your own apartment and hit you up for fees when you do.

In case you haven't gotten the drift, the board has the power to do most anything necessary to run the building—all the while using your currency as the coin of the realm. As you've probably realized by now, condo boards can't spend your money as freely as co-op directors, or control the sale or the use of your place with the same iron hand. But as we've seen (and we'll see still more), these differences can be a mixed blessing.

THE REQUIREMENTS OF RULERSHIP

Given the reach of your rulers' power, you may think they need haute qualifications to match their vaunted status. Alas, apart from the Corporation Law, which mandates that co-op directors be at least eighteen years old, *no* requirements exist for taking on the mantle of board commander and no compensation is allowed under buildings' governing documents.

Usually (except for sponsor designees), board members have to be owners or spouses of owners—so they have to live by their own rules. The bylaws of some co-ops, including my own, also require that directors be occupants, on the theory that absentee shareholders are on a par with absentee landlords—out of sight, out of mind. If a residency requirement is what you want, it had better be spelled out in the bylaws or else your directors may be able to rule from afar.

One Queens co-op board tried to prevent a shareholder who owned, but didn't live in, his apartment from seeking election. Since the bylaws didn't restrict director eligibility to residents, the court said it couldn't either. Nor did its after-the-fact attempt to amend the bylaws to keep nonresidents off get it any further. The out-of-town shareholder got to run.[3]

Condos are more prone to have absentee rulers. The reason is that corporations, partnerships, and other nonbreathing beings more typically own condo units—and usually their officers or directors can run for election even though they don't reside there.

Just because the law doesn't safeguard against incompetent directors doesn't mean that shareholders and unit owners can't take steps to protect themselves by fixing qualifications for office and standards of conduct for directors once elected. (Some strategies for doing just that are set out in chapter 11.)

No Dirty Tricks

But the board can't set qualifications that single out, and effectively ban, a particular candidate from running. Remember how the Republican Establishment tried to keep Sen. John McCain off the ballot? Well, the board members at one Park Avenue co-op used a similar tactic in order to forestall a former president, whom they'd removed and didn't want back. Two weeks before the election, they amended the bylaws to require that no person could be a director unless (1) he had a college degree, and (2) had not sued the co-op or any of its directors. The only shareholder who fit the specifications was Mr. Ex-president, a Polish self-made immigrant who previously had brought a lawsuit against two board members. He had the last laugh, however, when the court enjoined enforcement of the requirements, finding they had been rammed through solely to keep him from running.[4]

THE SIZE AND STRUCTURE OF POWER

Apart from the substance of board power, you need to know the mechanics. In the case of co-ops, the Corporation Law pretty much dictates the rules on board size and structure, which are then incorporated into the building's bylaws. Although not bound by them, condos follow their co-op leaders on many of these governmental matters.

What's in a Number?

No magic number of directors is necessary to make up the board. The size of the board should bear some rational relation to the size of the building.

Though, in truth, the smallest buildings often have the largest boards. That's because it's not unusual for a building of a dozen (or fewer) units to opt for participatory government by making every shareholder a board member. Once a certain critical mass is reached, direct democracy becomes unwieldy, so a representative government is fashioned by delegating power to a finite number of directors.

Board size varies all over the lot. All the Corporation Law requires is that there be one or more directors.[5] In my building there are 229 apartments and seven board members—presently, two sponsor and five resident owner-directors. Logic (not law) dictates that most boards have an uneven number of members. Since there's no vice president to break any deadlock, the board depends on the odd man out to do the trick.

In both co-ops and condos, the bylaws dictate how many directors sit on the board—usually giving a range instead of a fixed number for flexibility. Our building's bylaws, for example, require that there be not less than three nor more than seven directors.

Changing the Number

But the bylaws (and thus the numbers) are not set in stone, and both can be changed to suit the building's need. Suppose the board wants to increase its number because there's more work than workers and it needs a few warm bodies to do the job or in order to stack the deck in favor of one faction. Or the board may have to decrease its size if some of the sitting directors have had enough and want out from their obligations but there aren't enough willing souls to fill the empty seats.

Whether addition or subtraction is your goal, it can be accomplished by amending the bylaws. (See chapter 12 to learn how.) In co-ops, as you will learn, usually there are two possible routes to amendment: board action or shareholder vote. (In condos, only the owners can amend the bylaws.) Either way may be okay for adding directors. But if board action alone were enough to decrease their numbers, any board could stage a legal coup via amendment and get rid of its political enemies or insurgent minority members (although under the law no decrease can be used to cut short the term of any incumbent director).[6] To prevent such abuse and safeguard democracy for the masses, some buildings, including my own, require that any *reduction* in the number of sitting directors be put to a vote by the shareholders at the annual meeting.

This nod to the democratic process goes only so far when it comes to co-op and condo politics. What if a board seat became empty because a director kicked the bucket or simply bid adieu? New York law and most co-op and condo bylaws allow the remaining directors, by majority vote of the board, to fill the vacancy without notice to the shareholders.[7] (There may be different procedures for filling vacancies resulting from an increase in the board of directors.)

In either case, the right to choose returns to you at the next annual meeting when elections are held. But in the interim it is the voice of the power elite, not the people, that has spoken. Assuming your interests are one and the same, it matters not whether a director got to office by board appointment or popular election. But remember who got off the hook when Gerald Ford was appointed, rather than elected, by the people. I'm not saying capital crimes are a big worry in co-ops or condos, but if you're dealing with a factionalized board you should watch out that it doesn't use the opportunity created by an unforeseen opening to appoint one of its own (and one of your enemies) to push through its agenda.

The Magic Number

No matter how many or how few directors sit on your building's board, power can be concentrated in the hands of even fewer. All the board needs to conduct building business is a minimum number of directors to act, what lawyers call a *quorum*. This is usually a majority of the entire board. The law says that co-op bylaws can require a greater proportion or fix a quorum at less than a majority, but not less than one-third of the entire board.[8] Using simple arithmetic, you can see how this works. If there are nine directors on your board, only five need show up (assuming a majority)—only three, if there's a one-third quorum—for the board to take action.

Most actions require only a majority vote (of those present, not the entire board) to bind the board and the building. The result: a small fraction of directors can decide your residential fate. Using the same nine-member board, a little lower mathematics makes the point. If five directors are present and make up a quorum, only three are needed to bind the board. If three directors are all that's needed (for quorum and attendance), only two must cast their vote for something to be an act of the board. So though you may think you have nine directors representing you, it is possible for only a small fraction of them to be calling the shots. (And take my word, no matter what the law says that's the way it usually is, because only one or two members are usually doing most of the work.)

What all this means is that attendance counts, a thought you should keep in mind when deciding whether to vote for that jet-setting investment banker. He may be a wiz with numbers, but unless he's there to work his magic, he may not do you much good. Unlike annual meetings, where absent shareholders can designate stand-ins to cast their ballots, no-show directors can't send in a substitute. Reflecting the reality of our technological era, the Corporation Law was changed to allow a director to be "present" by telephone or other telecommunications hookup (unless the certificate or bylaws say otherwise),[9] and under some circumstances, the board can make decisions without any meeting if *all* members consent (in writing) to the adoption of the action.[10] But the nuts-and-bolts business of most co-ops and condos is conducted face-to-face at monthly board meetings, which your elected representatives had better attend if they want to be counted (and you to be represented). You can find out if they are ever-present or perpetual delinquents by taking a look at the board minutes, which record (but don't give a grade for) director attendance.

THE PATH TO GLORY

Once the directors are on board, it's one person, one vote. But there are distinctions in their paths to glory (and the length of time they can bask), depending upon whether they come from the sponsor or rose through the resident-owner ranks. Understanding how the road to rulership works will help you manipulate the system and maximize your chances of winding up with competent leaders.

Divine Right—Sponsor Anointment

As founder of the republic, the sponsor gets to select the initial members of the government. The law allows, and most offering plans and proprietary leases (co-ops) or bylaws (condos) provide, that so long as the sponsor owns unsold shares, it has the right to appoint a set number of directors from its ranks.

Since the sponsor usually starts out with control, it can designate a majority of the board—a selection process over which you have absolutely no say. The plan may provide that if the sponsor owns 50 percent of the shares it can designate three directors; if between 25 percent and 50 percent, two directors; and if less than 25 percent, one director to the five-member board.

You may or may not like the sponsor or its policies, but the reality is its people probably know more than you (or any of the newly elected resident directors) about managing a real estate enterprise because that's what they do for a living. So declare a temporary truce. Allow fraternization with the enemy (if that's how you perceive the sponsor's representatives) so that your directors can gather intelligence from its generals and begin to understand how the system works—a necessary prerequisite to the smooth transfer of power. All the better if sponsor and shareholder representatives believe they're serving a common cause.

Endless Limits or Finite Control

But the sponsor's power over the people is of finite duration. Under law, the sponsor must give up voting control (in noneviction plans) five years after the conversion or as soon as more than 50 percent of the shares (or, in condos, common interests) are sold—whichever comes first.[11] (In newly constructed buildings, the rule is the sooner of two years or less than 50 percent of the shares or common interests.)[12] If your founding fathers are democratically inclined, they'll pass the baton peaceably to the new generation of owners. That's what happened in my building when the sponsor voluntarily ceded control to us before five years were up, even though it still held a majority of shares.

Assuming your sponsor is unwilling on its own to relinquish its franchise, the question becomes, What are its voting rights? Is the sponsor limited to designating its nominees or can it *also* cast its shares for the remaining candidates, thereby effectively extending its reign even *after* five years or sale of more than 50 percent of its shares, especially if there's a mole in your midst or, at least, a sympathetic shareholder willing to do the overlord's bidding. The answer depends on what your bylaws and offering plan say. If you are governed by a standard "voting control" provision that merely forbids the sponsor from exercising voting control over the board after it owns less than 50 percent or five years, then the courts have ruled that sponsors can double-dip. They can handpick their own nominees prior to elections (based on the number of shares they hold). They can *also* vote their shares at board elections so long as the candidate they support isn't on their slate or payroll.[13] One sponsor of an embattled downtown building managed to keep control of the seven-member board after five years had passed by selecting three designees and then voting all its shares for a friendly resident owner. Even though the sponsor had given him a mortgage in which he had no personal exposure on default, that wasn't enough to disqualify him.[14] The sponsor can even solicit proxies from shareholders for candidates of its choice.

If you're lucky and your building has a "will not elect" clause in which the sponsor agrees not to elect a majority of the board, you owners will have more say sooner over building affairs. In one co-op that had such a proviso, the sponsor nevertheless tried to double-dip: to designate its three directors and then vote its shares for the remaining four members of the seven-person board. Sorry, the court announced, the offering plan says that after the initial control period, the sponsor can vote its unsold shares for *not more than one less than a majority of the directors to be elected.* So you get to pick only your three, and no more.[15] Just recently, the sponsor in a Lower East Side condo was limited to voting for no more than two directors out of a five-member board on the strength of a similar provision.[16]

Hopefully, your founders were men of the people and left you with governing documents that expressly restrict the sponsor's ability to elect board members, in which case it can probably vote for only one less than a majority, and you owners should be able to run your own show.

Democratic Election—Voice of the People

Unlike sponsor nominees, directors from the resident owner ranks have to be elected. But often that's a mere formality. Unless there's some catastrophe afoot in the building, the election is often uncontested, so the power of a board seat is there for the grabbing (which is not to say that some don't actually use it for good). And the truth is, you're probably relieved that somebody else stepped forward so you can sit back and have the privilege of complaining without having to deliver.

Even if there are more candidates than seats, the contest is still no guarantee of quality assurance. Before they stand for election, directors of public companies have to show they know how to run their businesses. And despite the bad rap politicians get (not without cause), at least the election process exposes them to the glare of public scrutiny—with the result that by the end of the campaign we know the good, the bad, and the ugly about them.

Co-op and condo commanders are not subject to any such competency checks. Usually candidates give their pitches at the annual meeting and then it's time to vote.

Power of Incumbency

Once your directors are in, they can be hard to get out. Maybe they can't suit up in a bomber jacket and fly onto an air force carrier as one incumbent we all know did; still, they have the power of office on their side.

First, they have name recognition; they don't have to advertise to get it. Lots of shareholders, assuming they're satisfied (or at least not dissatisfied) will automatically hand over their proxies. The board can also solicit proxies on its behalf and refuse to do so for other candidates. A couple of shareholders at an Upper East Side co-op challenged the board for voting, and then soliciting proxies, for an incumbent slate, but the court said, It's their right.[17] In some buildings, boards (or a subset of directors) act as nominating committees that recommend, and may even control the flow of, candidates, a process that can, like New York–style primaries, determine the result before the real election is held. Just like professional politicos, if the election is contested, the board may seek to give its slate the most advantageous ballot position, by putting the names of the chosen directors first or marking them with asterisks, not something I'd suggest, because it only gives the opposition ammunition in the event of a challenge.

Finally, there's what I'll call the *in terrorem effect*: shareholders who are afraid to go on record as voting against the incumbent for fear they'll exact retribution when it comes time to pass on sales or alterations. This is

New York, not Iraq, and if your board's claim to power is vindictiveness, it's time to get them out. As discussed in chapter 11 there are ways to do this while keeping your vote secret.

What Are the Limits?

How long can your elected representatives stay in office? Under law and most co-op bylaws, each director's term of office lasts until the next annual meeting and until his successor has been elected and qualified.[18] The Condo Act says that the terms of at least one-third of board members shall expire annually[19] so that their terms can last longer. Although the law limits the length of time sponsor-designated directors can stick around, it doesn't impose term limits on board members chosen from among the residential ranks. Term limits on resident directors have to be set by the buildings themselves—which deal with the issue in three basic ways:

1. No Limits

Assuming your bylaws are silent on the subject (as ours are), directors can exercise power in perpetuity—or so long as the voters don't kick them out of office. If you're lucky enough to have competent generals at the helm, then silence is golden—offering the prospect of carefree continuity in leadership. But if the forces of darkness have taken over and won't let go, then you'd probably wish the founding fathers had spoken on the subject.

2. Absolute Limits

Taking their cue from the Power Corrupts School, some buildings impose fixed term limits on their directors. If that's the case, their bylaws may say that no person may serve on the board for more than three or four (or some other number) of terms. Once they've done their duty, they're sent out to pasture—although (unlike other ex-officeholders) they get to keep their residences and follow their successor's progress firsthand.

3. Qualified Limits

Then there are buildings that require directors to take a break every so often from the intoxication of power and return to sobriety and the people—after which they can resume their reigns. Such bylaws may say that no director may serve for more than three or four consecutive terms, but may again be eligible for election after one (or more) years of absence from service. Requiring this round-trip helps keep them humble and makes it harder for any board member to get too comfortable in office.

Should There Be Limits?

What's the best way to go? Truth is, I'm of two minds on the matter. In the real world, outside my residential domain, I'm an advocate of term limits. I don't sufficiently trust any of those politicos to want them turning their offices into lifetime sinecures. Besides, there's always some up-and-comer anxiously waiting in the wings to dethrone the incumbent.

But in the co-op and condo context there is not an endless number of able or willing bodies. Experience has taught that a few take-charge types get things up and running when the building converts to protect their own investment and continue to run the show unless and until suitable replacements emerge. I have no doubt that there are some corrupt commanders who have become entrenched, but there are ways to get rid of them short of imposing arbitrary term limits, which would also unseat competents. You may say that as a board member since my co-op's conversion, I'm self-interested (or, more accurate, self-destructive). Still, on balance, I'd vote no to term limits for board members.

THE RULE OF THE REGIME

Now that you know how those directors (or managers, as they are called in condos) got to be members of the ruling class, it's time to address the question you really care about: How much control do they have over your life? Most of us live in such fear of our boards that we assume a reign of terror comes with co-op or condo territory. In fact, it's only relatively recently that courts determined the standard by which board action should be judged and in the process made directors near dictators.

How It Came to Be

So just what fueled this power trip? It all was sparked by a steam riser. A frustrated co-op board president, upset that his fellow directors challenged his right to move a steam riser as part of a kitchen renovation, figured he'd show them who was boss and took them to court in a case called *Levandusky v. One Fifth Avenue Apartment Corp.*,[20] thereby assuring, if nothing else, a place for himself in posterity. The board initially approved his renovation plans and only later learned that as part of the redesign he intended to move the riser in his apartment, a change that required consent. When the building's engineer advised against it, the board said no to the plans—unless they were modified so that the riser stayed put. Not one to listen to authority, Mr. President went ahead with the work anyway and hired a contractor, who severed the riser. The board issued a stop work order. He went to court to have it set aside.

Three courts, four years, and several hundred thousand dollars later, New York State's highest court came out on the board's side and held that the "business judgment" rule prevented it from reviewing the board's decision. (Litigation being the rational process that it is, ultimately Levandusky agreed to reimburse the co-op for much of the legal fees it had incurred fighting to make him keep the riser where the board said it should be in exchange for his being allowed to move it where he wanted.)

In anointing the board with the power of the "Rule" (as I'll call it for ease), while also making Mr. Levandusky move his steam riser, the state's highest court rejected what's called the "reasonableness" standard, which had been used till then to judge board conduct. Under that test, if you challenged board action it was up to the directors to show that their decision was reasonable. So if you attacked their plans to shoot the building's wad in a beautification binge or to embark on a maintenance program to render it fit for the ages, *they* had to justify what they had done. But in adopting the Rule the court turned the tables, shifting the burden of proof from the board to complaining shareholders.

Lest you condo owners think your boards must be more democratically inclined, forget it. The courts have made it clear that the Rule also protects your board of managers.

What It Means to You

You're probably thinking: So what's this Rule and why should I care? Reduced to its essence, the Rule says that courts should keep their hands off decisions made by your board members unless they do something really outrageous—like act beyond the scope of their authority, or engage in bad faith or self-dealing, or treat shareholders (or unit owners) unequally. Though the results may show that what they did was demonstrably dumb, shortsighted, or inexpedient, as long as they didn't breach any of their so-called fiduciary duties (of which, more later), the court won't question (or let you question) their use of power. In other words, in most cases what the board says goes, as if at this point you needed some court to tell you so.

The Rule was plucked from the corporate boardroom, where it had its start. Courts figure that when it comes to the complexities of running a corporation, the big boys and girls know best how to run the show and that black-robed judges who deliberate in chambers, not commerce, shouldn't second-guess the decisions that result from managerial savvy. In order to protect these directors, the Rule assumes that they act in good faith and use honest judgment in carrying out corporate business.

In the corporate context, directors owe their shareholders duties of loyalty (they can't act for their own self-interest) and due care (they'd better not be guilty of gross negligence), among others. Even if the outcome shows their decision was wrong, unless shareholders can prove that they breached these duties, the board's decision is final and unreviewable.

Directors at IBM or Intel take actions that affect shareholders' pocketbooks (making you richer or poorer as goes the company's stock price). But co-op and condo boards control not just your fortune but your life. That's pretty heady stuff—enough to give a novice, which many a board member is, a Napoleon complex—unless you pull them down to size. Nevertheless, courts figure that what's good for corporations is good (at least by analogy) for co-ops, which, after all, are a species of corporation even though they're also home sweet home. And what goes for co-ops goes for condos, so the courts have said. Even if decisions by their boards don't involve corporate rocket science, the theory is that directors (not judges) know best what a building and its residents need.

In case you haven't figured it out, the real reason the Rule is such a tough nut to crack is because *you* are the nutcracker. That is, it's up to you, the rank and file, to prove that the directors in your building did something wrong. Because of the ruling in Mr. Levandusky's case, it's now your job (or more probably your lawyer's) to show that the board breached its duties to you. It is not enough for your lawyer to show that the board's action was unreasonable or even stupid. You have to show that it acted in bad faith or self-interest or that for some other reason (for example, discrimination) it should not be able to hide behind the Rule. To you nonlawyers out there, trust me, this shift makes all the difference.

I can tell you from personal hard-fought experience that in the corporate world the Rule gives directors so much protection that they're virtually immune from shareholder attack. In the co-op and condo context, the Rule is potentially more potent. Though owners may believe that the board has done them (and the building) wrong, few of them have the financial fortitude to do legal battle. And even if they do, most of the time the courts won't do anything anyway. All in all, it's not a system that encourages director humility.

How Far It Goes

How does all this legal theory shake out in the real world of your building? The board has control over every aspect of your existence—from the cradle to the grave, and sometimes beyond. Thanks to the *Levandusky* court that power is on the upswing. Since there's no outside authority to look over a board's shoulder and second-guess the decisions that it makes, the board can pretty much do what it wants. We'll take a detailed look at a board's various spheres of influence down the road. But for now, here's a sample of how it can invoke the Rule to protect its actions from your challenges.

1. Mundane Matters

Take those House Rules that dictate everyday conduct in your building. To the untutored they may seem trivial, but to anyone in the know they're what controls your quality of life. Owners have tried, without success, to overturn board-imposed rules that prohibit installation of washer/dryers,[21] parcel out parking spaces,[22] ban motorcycles[23] (Harley hogs, beware), order removal of whirlpools,[24] limit the hours during which brokers can show your apartment,[25] and set renovation guidelines à la Levandusky. Since the board is the ultimate arbiter, the courts generally have refused to review the rules it passes.

2. Territorial Control

Penthouse owners are big on suing because they have more to protect. But their challenges have only confirmed the board's ability to intrude into their private paradises. Courts have let stand—without question—board decisions to ban planters, replace quarry tiles, remove secret gardens, expand general rooftop hours over penthouse owners' objections, even appropriate individual terraces for the greater repair good.[26]

3. Apartment Sales

Whether it's power to say yes or no to sales or to impose transfer restrictions, the Rule protects (co-op) director action from challenge. Using its shield, boards have set financial (and other criteria) for admission, imposed payment (and other objections) to departure, and prevented estates from selling (and winding up their affairs).[27]

4. Sublets

Under the Rule, co-op boards have broad discretion to regulate how and when shareholders can sublet and how much it will cost, and as we'll see, now condo boards are trying to get in on the act.[28]

5. Share Allocation

Under the Rule, it's up to the board to assess the factors that warrant an increase or decrease in the number of shares assigned to an apartment and to decide whether a reallocation is in order.[29]

6. Management

The Rule gives the board power to establish budgets, fix assessments and maintenance charges, decide whether or not to make repairs, what repairs to make, and how much to spend—even to gain access to owners' apartments to carry out repairs.[30]

7. Abort Justice

The board can even stop shareholders from suing if it goes about it the right way. The same building that battled over Mr. Levandusky's steam riser and first brought us the Rule finally saw the light and decided it had had enough litigation. Five years later, when a bunch of shareholders tried to sue the board on behalf of the co-op (what the law calls a "derivative" action) because it allowed several shareholders to combine apartments without changing the building's certificate of occupancy, the board wanted to put a quick end to it. It appointed a committee of directors that on its own investigated the facts and then voted to terminate the action. Two years, ten thousand–plus pages, and who knows how many thousands of dollars later, the court said that under the Rule it could not question the board's decision to end the suit. What's more, the Rule applied not only to the board but also to the specially appointed committee.[31] Score another one for the ruling class.

Reducing all this to a nutshell: most board decisions are final and untouchable. Even if you go to the expense and trouble of suing, the court won't even *review* director action, let alone *reverse* it. So don't waste time and money (yours and the building's) in futile pursuit. As we'll see, there are less expensive and more effective ways to make sure your directors are working for you.

THE LIMITS OF POWER

Even in co-ops and condos the totalitarian state has not yet arrived. Board power has its limits, which you need to understand in order to keep your directors from crossing the line. This section teaches you the essentials of power politics.

The Board Must Do Its Duty

As we've seen, the Rule grants board members immunity from most challenges to how they run the building. In return they owe you so-called fiduciary duties. If they violate them they lose the Rule's protection and are ripe for attack. A short primer on the subject should set you straight.

A fiduciary duty is one that arises out of a special relationship of trust and confidence. As defined by one court long ago, it is "a punctilio of an honor the most sensitive." It can exist in a variety of everyday situations. Your broker may or may not be making you a bundle, but odds are he's bound by a fiduciary duty to you. A Realtor acting as an agent in selling your co-op probably stands in a fiduciary relationship to you. Your lawyer may or may not be your friend, but he is likely your fiduciary. The idea is that when someone is in a position of trust and power over you, often because of superior information or knowledge, he or she has a duty to do right by you—to act for your interest and not to put his or her own personal agenda first.

In the world of Wall Street corporations this notion has been around so long it's ingrained in the legal consciousness. Corporate directors owe the company and its stockholders an obligation of trust and confidence and must act for their common interest—though judging by Enron and WorldCom and all the other scandals, that doesn't mean directors always abide by it. The rationale is that shareholders, as the real corporate owners, expect to get their fair share of the profits, so when a director benefits at the expense of the corporation he violates a duty to shareholders by preventing them from getting their due.

When our friends at the *Levandusky* court transferred the Rule from the corporate boardroom to co-op directors, with the power came the duty of directors to use it for the general welfare of the co-op and its shareholders—a duty that expressly has been held to apply to condo boards as well. The contours of this directorial duty in the residential (as opposed to strictly corporate) context are still evolving. But certain things are pretty clear. Board members can't use their positions to engage in self-interest or bad faith. They can't act beyond their scope of authority or treat their constituents unequally.

Self-Interest Is Out

Director self-interest can assume different shapes. The most obvious is the raw power play, in which a board member uses his or her position to extract some special privilege. Sometimes the grab is a littler subtler but no less invidious, as when a director turns a building transaction to personal or professional advantage. Whatever the form, self-interest is forbidden.

No Perks for the Powerful

The Rule says that board members can't put their personal interests ahead of the building or its collective owners. Although they may get a healthy dose of ego gratification from wielding the scepter, apart from this emotional high, directors are not entitled to get anything you don't. The nature of possible power perks is limited only by how inventive your commanders are and how invincible they think they are. Some may seem relatively innocent. The board decides that since you don't express any appreciation, it'll give its members a gustatory pat on the back. It holds an annual meeting of the mutual admiration society at Alain Ducasse and sends you the tab for its high-priced repast. Illegal? No. Unethical? Debatable. Unwise? For sure—unless the board wants to encourage class warfare. Better to hold a year-end fete for all (staffers on up) and show it's a board of the people. Or take the case of the condo board members who were held to account for getting $50,000 for themselves and only $10,000 for the other owners in negotiating for the sale of common interests.[32]

Whatever the perk, even if it's more symbolic than substantive, the principle is the same: Directors can't get them and owners should see that they don't. So if the super is hanging the gardens of Babylon from a board member's terrace; or suppliers are supplying the board, not the building; or a delinquent director has worked out a sweetheart deal for deferring maintenance fees; or the co-op's contractor is painting not only the town but the board president's apartment red (at no charge)—it's a pretty safe bet that board members are putting their self-interest first.

Avoid Temptation

To you directors out there, my advice is to resist the urge to take advantage of your position. Experience has shown that shareholders assume the worst. So when it comes to special privileges you'd better have nothing to hide—unless you're prepared to have the masses come knocking at (or down) your door.

I'm no Girl Scout. (Indeed, I never made it to the merit badge stage.) I admit to having borrowed a few pens and pencils from the office supply room and even a legal pad now and then. And sometimes I have gone so far as to swipe an extra packet of Equal from Starbucks when I realize I have none left for my morning coffee. So it's self-preservation, not sanctimoniousness, that keeps me off the take.

Thankfully, the kinds of things I covet are not those that suppliers or contractors usually hand out. Only once did I see my director status as a means to an end. We hired a staff member who proudly announced that he was a member of the Masai tribe from Kenya—and pulled out photos of himself and his brother clad only in Kente cloth and silver adornments to prove his heritage. An avid collector of ethnic jewelry, I lusted after those hammered silver beauties, and knowing that he made runs to Nairobi already envisioned how those circlets would look gracing my bare arm. But I caught myself before things got out of hand and made a trip to Craft Caravan instead.

I suspect the staff does come to my apartment faster to fix a leaky faucet. But, hey, some people get the best tables at Nobu and they are envied, not indicted. And shareholders show no shame in calling upon me to use my influence to expedite work in their apartments. So I figure what's good for Peter is good for Paul. No more—no less. That's my credo.

Conflicts Must Be Controlled

What Are They?

Sometimes it's not special perks but divided loyalty that you have to watch out for. A board member has a personal interest in some co-op or condo transaction that he also is considering in his role as a board member. What's best for him as an individual may not be what's best for the building (or its owners). Unless the so-called conflict of interest is controlled, there can be trouble.

Dual Role in the Opposition Camp

So long as the sponsor is in control, the potential for conflict is obvious, which is why courts have said that sponsor-dominated condo and co-op boards owe you an extra-high standard of duty.[33]

If they breach it the consequences can be severe. One court declared that sponsor-appointed condo board members could be held *personally* liable for a variety of breaches of duty, including failure to correct deficient construction of the units, to determine realistic cash requirements, or to establish adequate reserves.[34] Another court, finding that sponsor-affiliated directors had breached their duties to the co-op by bringing it to the brink of financial ruin, ordered that they shift control to shareholder representatives.[35] It's clear that sponsor-appointed directors owe a duty to the corporation, rather than to the sponsor.

Usually, though, with sponsor-dominated boards it's more a case of legal influence peddling than illegal breach of duty. You proud new apartment owners want to increase monthly fees to pay for building enhancements appropriate to your new station in life. But the sponsor would prefer to fatten its profits by keeping charges (which it has to pay) at rock bottom to help it sell apartments. The reality is that so long as the sponsor retains control, it holds the purse strings. To some extent sponsor tightfistedness is legally sanctioned. So running to court to get the board to open its wallet is not necessarily the best solution. There are other defensive tactics you can try to keep the sponsor in check (see chapter 11).

Division Among the Loyalists

Even after the sponsor is long gone, there's plenty of room for conflicts among the remaining resident loyalist board members. Let's say your building is installing new windows or modernizing its elevator. That architect par excellence by day who dabbles at night as a board member offers to do good for the building (and himself) by taking on the job—at a discount. Or the suspendered wunderkind who just made partner at some fancy law firm (and also sits on the board) knows the building is looking for a legal general and is ready to serve his co-op (and himself)—for a fee. Or that high-flying real estate broker who lives in the building offers to sit on a board committee that passes on sales and subleases in which he (and his competitors) have an interest.

Assuming you're an all-in-the-family type, you may be asking "Where's the problem?" The architect gets the business and the co-op gets a bargain. The lawyer gets a client and the co-op gets professional courtesy. The broker gets a commission and the building gets a new shareholder.

The point is that each of these transactions (and any others where directors stand to gain at the co-op's expense) have within them the seeds for communal destruction. Although there are those who are so selfless that temptation doesn't cross their consciousness, odds are they're missionaries, not board members. For the more human directors, the wiser course is to steer clear of potential trouble and (as those lawyers would say) avoid even the appearance of impropriety.

How to Know If They Exist

Half the problem with these conflicts is knowing them when you see them, which, as I've learned firsthand, is not something that comes naturally to either board members or shareholders—most of whom are untutored in the basics of legal logic. As a start, it's not a bad idea to require new board members to undergo a little sensitivity training (from the co-op's lawyer) so at least they understand what they're not supposed to do.

How do you know if any board member is engaged in double dealing? The easiest way is to keep your eyes and ears open (a sea change in attitude from the renter's nose-to-the-ground mentality). If your next-door neighbor, the interior decorator, has been retained to redo the lobby, you should start asking questions. (In my friend's building, failure to take action before decoration in such a case resulted in a serious suit after it was done.) If the co-op's treasurer, the CPA, is now also the building's paid accountant, that's another red flag.

Observation alone may not suffice. So take an activist stance and ask the directors at the annual meeting (or before, if the issue is pressing). Let's say the board is engaged in some major improvement project. You have every right to know what companies it has considered and selected for a deal on which it will be spending millions of dollars of your money and whether any directors are in bed with them (so to speak). In fact, you will probably earn the board's grudging respect (if not admiration) by showing yourself to be an informed citizen. If its answers don't cut it, and you have reason to suspect a sweetheart deal, it may be time for shareholders to seek out a lawyer.

Another source to go to are the minutes of board meetings, which are usually made available to shareholders (see chapter 11). If they are properly kept, they should record when a director has a conflict and whether he voted on the transaction (as well as how the others voted)—information you need to know as a first step in deciding if any wrongdoing is afoot.

How the Board Should Handle Them

My best advice for you and your directors is that the board stay sufficiently wide of the mark so there's no room for debate over divided loyalties. But if conflict rears its head, here's what the board has to do (at least under New York law) to protect you—and itself.[36]

The director with the interest in the deal must come clean to the other board members. One Sutton Place co-op had to sue its resident lawyer/director to get back his ill-gotten gains. He recommended a law firm to contest the co-op's tax assessment—apparently without telling his fellow directors that he had cut himself (and his firm) a deal to share half the fees.[37]

So long as the director's up front with all the details he or she can take part in the discussion and even vote. But the transaction has to be approved by a majority of the board (not counting the vote of the director with the possible conflict). If the interested director controls more than a majority of board votes, as may be the case with the sponsor, then the unanimous vote of the remaining minority is required. Or the director can disclose such an interest to the shareholders (don't count on it) and if everyone still votes yes—it's a done deal.

How You Should Handle the Board

In the wake of corporate scandals, with executives being hauled off in handcuffs, new legislation has been passed demanding that public companies adopt codes of ethics and conflict-of-interest standards for their top dogs. Although the law doesn't apply to co-ops and condos, odds are that, eventually, some of its requirements will filter down, so better to take preventive action now (rather than wait for some judge or lawmaker to impose mandatory restrictions) and adopt a written conflicts policy that directors must agree in writing to abide by. Depending on how tough you want to be, here's what it should say:

1. Spell out in plain English what a conflict is (as much for director edification as for enforcement). For maximum protection, the definition should be broad enough to include any situation in which a director's interest may diverge from the co-op's or condo's—for example, when a director decides to sell or refinance his apartment.
2. Ban receipt by directors or agents of any financial benefit or arrangement from vendors or contractors in exchange for business decisions, whether in the form of cold cash, free or discounted services, or worldly goods.
3. Set out procedures to be followed if there is a conflict. They should include full disclosure by the interested director and, even better, an agreement not to be present during discussions or to vote on the deal.
4. If you really want to get tough, prohibit board member professionals—whether attorneys, accountants, or architects—from acting for, and getting paid by, the building in their official capacities. And if you want to get even tougher, impose a ban on the board's retaining any consulting or contracting firm in which any of its members has an interest.

No code of conduct is foolproof. But by putting your directors on notice of their duties (in black and white for all constituents to see) they can't say they didn't know—thereby solving a big part of the problem.

Bad Faith Is Out

Even when the board is not looking out for its own self-interest, it may still be breaching its duty to you by acting in bad faith. What does that mean? Although courts haven't precisely defined "bad faith," they've made clear that this standard is intended to provide a check on boards' potential power to regulate your conduct, lifestyle, and property rights. Basically, if you think you're getting shafted and (honestly) can't think of any legitimate reason for board action, it's probably acting in bad faith—in which case it loses the Rule's protection.

It may help to take a look at how the courts have come out on the issue. Arbitrary and capricious action by a board is likely to get its members branded as bad faithers. That's what happened to one board that terminated the garage lease of a unit owner without giving any reason. The court told the board that had brought the action to recover possession of the garage space "No reason, no relief"—and threw out its claim.[38] Another board approved owners' alteration plans to construct walls, then refused to sign the necessary building permits and made them tear down what they had spent thousands to put up. That's bad faith, and the unit owners won.[39]

If the board rejects a sublet or sale in bad faith, its decision will be reviewed and overturned.[40] As we already have seen, if the board nixes a sale for personal profit or vendetta, its bad faith means your sale proceeds.[41] When a co-op board tried to hold up sale of an apartment by making shareholders settle lawsuits against the co-op first, the Rule was of no help.[42] A director in another building not only demanded that the shareholder discontinue the litigation against him but also insisted on a commission. He fared no better.[43]

The point is that bad faith on the part of directors can take many forms and affect any aspect of co-op (or condo) life. If their action doesn't pass the sniff test, remember that relief may be at the ready.

Equal Justice for All

The Rule demands that directors treat the troops uniformly. They can't use their power differently to play one shareholder against the next. In co-ops and condos, it's equal justice for all. If you've been singled out for disparate treatment the courts will strip board members of the Rule's protection and review their transgressions.

We've just seen how the court took a Park Avenue board to task for passing director qualifications intended solely to keep the past president off the ballot.[44] The same thing happened to the board of a Greenwich Village co-op that passed a flip tax that ostensibly applied to sales by all deceased owners, only it was suspiciously implemented right after one shareholder had gone to meet her maker (and presumably couldn't complain from the beyond).[45] And when another board imposed a sublet fee that, by its terms, applied only to the single owner of commercial units, and not to any of the residential units, it, too, was struck down.[46] The court stood by one shareholder who attacked when the board decided, supposedly for security reasons, to install bars on only her windows.[47] Another court went after a board that wanted to build a roof garden and a rooftop chimney just to harass a penthouse owner.[48] Having treated their constituents unequally, these boards could not seek refuge behind the Rule.

From where I sit, it's not always the board that's at fault. Although the sublet rules in my building have been clear and immutable from Day One, that hasn't stopped many owners from declaring themselves a little more equal—and thus exempt. We've had owners sneak in tenants under cover of night (only to find out that my building's board never sleeps), claim they didn't know the rules (ignorance of the law is no defense), and cite financial hardship (even though they bought as insiders and stood to make a killing). One couple even went so far as to transfer ownership from one to the other in order to start the allowable sublet period running anew—thus skirting the spirit, if not the letter, of the law. Despite the pressure to resort to a more rough-and-ready form of law enforcement, my building's board has not cracked and continues to dispense evenhanded (though sometimes unpopular) justice.

Assuming that you are not guilty of fostering inequality (in which case, no matter what the law says, you don't have a moral leg to stand on), you have a right to expect your board to treat you likewise.

Staying Within Bounds

Powerful as it is, the board is not above the law. The legal system adopted by the sponsor in the form of bylaws and proprietary lease is both the source and the limit of the board's authority. The Rule won't protect the board if it steps beyond the bounds, as a bunch of directors at a Soho co-op found out when they tried to take the law into their own hands. Although the co-op had no sublet fee or flip tax, the directors demanded that a shareholder who wanted to sublease a commercial unit in the residential loft building pay tens of thousands in such fees—and thousands more for fixing the co-op's staircase, as a condition for allowing him to rent out his space. Not only did the court order the board to approve the original (demand-free) sublease, it also required the directors who acted without authority to hand over $100,000 in punitive damages.[49]

Shareholders have taken on a number of these overreaching boards. One board decided on its own to do away with sublets and passed a rule prohibiting them, even though the building's proprietary lease gave shareholders the right to sublet.[50] Then there was the board that took matters into its own hands by just saying no to a proposed sublet though the co-op's bylaws prohibited the board from unreasonably withholding consent to any sublease of less than twelve months.[51]

In each case the voice of the people prevailed as these fiats issued from on high were struck down by the courts. Directors were told that they'd better stay within the limits of the law. It's up to the masses, not the power elite, to change the fundamental documents governing the co-op and condo regime. And procedural due process requires that owners be given notice of any significant change and a right to vote.

10

Widening the Gap

THEY'VE GOT YOU GOING . . .

Power begets power. In the interim since this book first came out, boards have amassed even more, thanks to the courts that have interpreted the Rule to allow directors to act unchallenged on virtually every matter that affects your lives and pocketbooks. Indeed, recently they were granted the *ultimate* power to evict a shareholder and terminate his apartment ownership for engaging in objectionable conduct.[1]

You might say this particular shareholder asked for it. No sooner did he move into his Upper West Side digs than he decided to stir things up. He demanded video surveillance, twenty-four-hour door service, new mailboxes. He complained that his upstairs neighbors, an elderly, retired professor and his wife, who'd been living there peacefully for more than twenty years, were blasting their music and running an illegal bookbinding business that used toxic chemicals. He got into a fistfight with the professor and then pressed criminal charges (which later were dismissed). He distributed flyers to his fellow shareholders warning of the "psychopath" in their midst and accusing the professor's wife of having an affair with the board president's wife. He made alterations to his apartment without board approval. He commenced four lawsuits—against the couple, the co-op management, and its president—and tried to bring three more.

Enough! the board finally said. The proprietary lease provided that the co-op could terminate a shareholder's tenancy if two-thirds of the shareholders decided his conduct was "objectionable." Notice of a special meeting went out to everyone, including Mr. Objectionable, who didn't show up. No matter—by a unanimous vote of nearly seventy-five percent of *all* outstanding shares, the owners decided his conduct was, indeed, objectionable and voted to terminate his lease. When he wouldn't leave, the board brought suit to eject him, and the court—this state's highest—said, You gotta go. Even though the law says that a co-op has to prove its claim of "objectionable" conduct by competent evidence to the satisfaction of the *court*, the judges said, we'll defer to *your* decision under the Rule. A deal was struck, and Mr. Objectionable was forced to sell his apartment, but how much he got after having to pay for his former co-op's attorneys' fees and other expenses is anybody's guess.

The decision caused a schism in Co-opland. Reactionaries figured the more power for directors, the better. Liberals saw the potential for abuse given the often internecine nature of co-op politics. How far off normal (or, at least, acceptable) does a shareholder's conduct have to be before he's declared an objectionable persona non grata? Is it like pornography—you know it when you see it? Should your neighbors, who may not be your friends but could be your enemies, and most certainly are not objective, be allowed to play judge and jury in deciding your residential fate? Can a finding of objectionable conduct provide cover for boards to stifle dissent or prevent owners from enforcing their rights or thin the ranks of nuisances or cut loose elderly residents in need of special assistance?

It's too soon to tell, but attempts already have been made to expand the definition of objectionable. One board in a downtown co-op used it to oust a shareholder who threatened the safety of everyone in the building. She had a history of gas odors, smoke, and fires in her apartment, including one for which she didn't call the fire department, but just walked out. Although the board (and more than two-thirds of shareholders) voted to evict, it got tripped up on a notice technicality, requiring the court to give the firebug another chance—but not before acknowledging that the co-op's claim had merit and suggesting that it get it right and then come back.[2] In a reverse twist, a co-op claimed, and the court seemed to agree, that its sponsor's conduct was objectionable because it was rerenting instead of selling apartments that became vacant.[3]

While boards are trying to broaden the definition of objectionable, they are attempting to reduce the number of participants necessary to make the decision so that *on their own* they can identify and oust an undesirable shareholder. The seven-member board in one building acted solo in bidding adieu to a shareholder without even giving him a chance to tell his side of the story, saying the co-op's lease gave them the right to terminate the lease of a shareholder whose conduct was "objectionable or improper." I don't care what the lease says, you can't do that by yourselves without having shareholders vote; it's for the court to decide, the independent-minded judge of a lower court chastised the power grabbers.[4]

The board at a downtown building did them one better. Relying on a lease provision that said a vote of two-thirds of board members can establish a shareholder's objectionable conduct, they tried to get rid of an owner who was vicariously objectionable. Mr. X had sublet his apartment to someone named Trouble. Mr. Trouble renovated without board consent and without bothering about permits, in the process causing a fire in the apartment wall and severing a cable that cut off the building's heat. The police searched Mr. Trouble's place not once, but twice, and each time arrested him for drug possession. During the arrest, the police damaged the locks on the building's front door. When the lock was changed, Mr. X didn't give

Mr. Trouble a new key, so he sued the co-op for illegal lockout. The board wrote letter after letter to Mr. X telling him to evict his bad-seed subtenant, but he didn't answer and renewed the sublease until finally, sanity or self-interest kicked in, and he got the renter out and regained possession.

Too late and too much, the board figured, and before he returned, it called a meeting to decide what to do. Mr. X and his attorney came but weren't given a chance to present their case, and, ultimately, the board—but not shareholders—voted to terminate his lease. When he wouldn't go, the directors went to court for help. Instead they got an earful. You guys acted in bad faith because you didn't let Mr. X have his say. And you went beyond the scope of your authority because you weren't even properly elected. Because you screwed up, you don't get the benefit of the Rule, and now a judge, not you, will get to decide if Mr. X's conduct was objectionable.[5] Although it gave the directors a tongue lashing, the court didn't answer the key question: Can a board *on its own* evict shareholders for objectionable conduct?

Now that fellow shareholders can watch to see if you've been good or bad, you'd better mind your manners all year round. It's not just for behaving badly, but also for doing wrong that the board can get rid of you. Ask the shareholders in Forest Hills who said, but didn't show, that the board had illegally terminated their lease for discrimination. Because the true reason was not racial animus, but operation of a business, the court said the board has the power without more to send you packing.[6]

It's probably no surprise that you can be drummed out of the corps if you don't pay your maintenance, but in some buildings you may not be able to sell your shares for fair market value. Adding insult to injury, the board of a Bronx co-op evicted a shareholder for not paying her maintenance, and then said, We're exercising our option under the bylaws to repurchase your shares at *book*, rather than *market*, value. The despairing owner, who had paid $45,000 for her apartment and was being offered only $5,000, complained that the board's decision was "unjust and unconscionable." "No," the court said; it may be a rotten deal, but without a showing of misconduct by the directors, we can't do anything about it.[7]

. . . AND COMING . . .

Not only do boards have more power than before to kick you out, but they also have greater authority over who can enter their domain, as disappointed shareholders found out when they sued the board for rejecting their prospective buyer based on the possibility she might have a babysitting business in the apartment. There's nothing we can do, the judges said; so long as the board acts within the scope of its authority, it doesn't matter what we think.[8] (Sometimes, though, the law overrides the board, as one condo owner who wanted to use her apartment for a day care center found out—see page 319.)

Another turned-down buyer, who had bought at a foreclosure sale, had no better luck when he went after the board that said the price was too low and would depress the value of other apartments. They've got the power, was all the court said.[9] And a shareholder who claimed the board had impeded his efforts for several years to sell his apartment so that one of its members could buy it on the cheap got nowhere, even when a director finally bought the place at a foreclosure sale. Since there's nothing to show the board acted improperly, the court ruled, they've got the power.[10]

Even condo boards have had their hand strengthened in guarding the gates. When an owner tried to lease his apartment in his high-rise for an obscene amount a month to the ambassador of Yugoslavia, the board said no. Although Mr. Ambassador agreed to offer a bank guaranty for a year of common charges, he wouldn't waive diplomatic immunity. That's discrimination, the owner complained, sensing the dollars slipping from his fingers. But the court said, No, it's not. They've got the power.[11]

. . . AND IN BETWEEN

It's not just the big stuff where boards can intercede. As the following real cases (all decided since *The Co-op Bible* first appeared) show, their presence can be increasingly felt in your every move:

- Like Dorothy, you want your own yellow brick road to lead you home, only you prefer yours painted pink and don't bother to ask permission. The board has the power to make you return your sidewalk to its original hue.[12]
- You don't want to go to the lobby to pick up your food, so you tell the delivery man to put the steaming hot package in the elevator and let it ride up alone. The board has the power to say no.[13] And you've got to wonder about a shareholder who, rather than riding down to the lobby to get her sesame noodles, goes to court and—for good measure—adds a claim for emotional distress because the staff neglected to screw in a lightbulb for four days. (Thank God she's not one of my flock.)
- You want to sip champagne and luxuriate in your own private whirlpool, which you install without seeking approval, as required by the lease, for all appliances. The board has the power to make you take it out.[14]
- The board says okay to your request to build a ten-by-twelve-foot wooden deck, but you decide that bigger is better and construct a

concrete patio nearly twice the size, meant to last for the ages. The board has the power to make you remove it.[15]

- Shareholders can't agree, so the board decides for you and adopts a rule governing the use of apartment vestibules. In the name of the Rule and the greater good, it has the power.[16]
- After fifty years of shading you from the sun, the board says that awning on your terrace is in violation of the house rules, and besides, the guy downstairs needs the space to install a through-wall air conditioner. It's got to go and, what's more, you're lucky the board didn't try to terminate your lease and get *you* out.[17]
- You've been minding your own business and enjoying the privacy of your condo when the board decides to build a shed for the benefit of *all* on the common area adjacent to your plot of heaven. They can do it, and there's nothing you can do about it.[18]
- You go ahead and build a greenhouse that's grander than the plans you submitted to the board. It can cut you, and your glass structure, down to size.[19]
- You think you know better and don't like the contractor your board has hired to renovate the lobby. Too bad. The board has the power to decide.[20]

Power itself is not a dirty word. Someone has to be in charge or chaos will prevail. The real question is whether power is used or abused. If the latter, as we've seen, the board loses the protection of the Rule, and the law will be on *your* side. As in the real world, most of the time the problem is not that co-op and condo rulers use their authority improperly but that we may not agree with what they're doing. Remember, you elected them. You have the ultimate power of the ballot and, working within the system, you may be able to get them to see things more your way.

11

Restoring the Balance

GET READY FOR ACTION

Now that you know the power you're up against you can prepare to swing the pendulum back the other way. This chapter teaches you how to work within the system to redress the imbalance and make sure your directors are working for you. It tells you what powers you possess as a member of the owning ranks, how to pass the good citizen's test (a prerequisite to taking action), how to gather and process the information you need to know what's really going on, what to look for in your elected representatives, how to get maximum mileage out of your vote and the voting process, and how to keep your representatives responsible to you once they're in office.

PEOPLE POWER

By now you know that the board pretty much runs the show when it comes to managing the day-to-day affairs of the building. That doesn't mean that you constituents have been stripped bare. In fact, under New York law, shareholders have the exclusive power to make decisions on many fundamental and extraordinary matters of co-op governance. The Condo Act is less specific in setting out what decisions condo owners have to make, but the bylaws can (and do) spell these out. So let's begin tipping the scale back your way by taking a look at some of the affirmative authority that's in your hands.

Electing Your Rulers

The cornerstone of any democracy, co-ops and condos included, is the power of the people to select their representatives. You, as a shareholder (by law) or a unit owner (by standard practice), have the exclusive right to elect your directors. The power to choose works only when there is choice. In the context of co-op and condo elections, where there are often more seats than sitters, this power may seem elusive. But the ballot lets the board know it can be held to account. And if it screws up, would-be directors are sure to emerge from your ranks to challenge the incumbents, thereby creating choice—and returning power to the people when it's most needed.

Removing Directors

Even if there's no real choice in electing directors, you always have the power to get rid of them. Most co-op and condo bylaws say that, as owners, you can vote to remove your directors with or without cause. Under the law governing co-ops, it usually takes a majority of owners to get rid of them[1] (this is often the rule in condos, too). The board also may be given the right to self-police and to remove directors who have done wrong—but only shareholders can vote to remove without cause. We'll hold off on the mechanics of removal (until the next chapter) in the hope that your differences with the board can be resolved without resort to such extremism.

Ousting Officers

Under law, shareholders have the power to get rid of any officers whom they elected.[2] Since in most co-ops (and condos) the board, not you, gets to elect the officers from amongst its ranks, it also gets to remove them. So don't count on this one to get you very far.

Legislating Change

Unlike the outside world, where you have to wait for your pork-barreling representatives to hammer out a deal to get legislative action, as an owner you have it within your capacity to effectuate such change on your own. In condos, it takes two-thirds of unit owners to change the bylaws;[3] in co-ops, by law at least a majority of shareholders must vote to amend (although most co-ops require a two-thirds vote). The problem is that in co-ops the law also allows the board to change the bylaws on its own (where provided in the building's certificate or in the shareholder-adopted bylaws).[4] Even if it has the power to act solo, it should have the wisdom in most cases to refrain, especially if the change involves something of questionable benefit to shareholders (like increasing the number of directors). Lest the board get carried away in making changes unpalatable to the populace, the shareholders have the right to repeal or change any bylaw it adopted. And the compact between you and the co-op (the proprietary lease) also requires shareholder consent for change (usually two-thirds).

Disenfranchising Deadbeats

It's up to shareholders collectively to impose limits on the voting rights of your fellow owners. Let's say the board wants to disenfranchise those of you who don't pay your maintenance on time. Unless the building's original certificate of incorporation says no money, no vote (not likely), the board can't ban deadbeats from the ballot box. Shareholders have the sole power to take away the vote by amending the certificate. (In condos, it's the bylaws that regulate the vote.)

Selling Out

Apart from having a voice in the procedures of government, you have the ultimate say. As shareholders you have the exclusive right under the law to consent to sale of the co-op's assets or to authorize its dissolution.[5] These extraordinary events would affect the very existence of the co-op and your investment in it. So, the decision should be (and is) up to you. What all this means is that if the board gets the bright idea of converting your co-op to a condominium it can't do so without your approval.

Controlling the Flow

Condo owners, on the other hand, don't have to wait for D-day to have a say in matters of real substance. Most condo bylaws require owners to give cash consent to the board beyond certain fixed limits—whether spending what's on hand or going to the well for more. (Not a prerogative usually available to co-op shareholders, whose boards can spend to their—though not necessarily your—hearts' desire.) Control of the flow means accountability of your condo commanders.

Deciding Your Fate

As we've seen, condo owners are also on top of their boards (and ahead of co-op shareholders) on the transfer front. Under the right-of-first-refusal provision, standard in most condos, the board can't say no to any proposed sale of your apartment. What's more, a majority of your fellow owners must say yes before the board can even exercise its right-of-first-refusal (though, as we've seen, this may be done by power of attorney).

While offering some redress, these powers (at least in co-ops) don't tip the scale too much in your favor when it comes to the everyday affairs of the building. If real equality and accountability are what you're after, you'll have to go the next step and take on the powers that be.

RULES OF GOOD CITIZENSHIP

But before you go challenging the establishment full tilt and expose yourself to scrutiny from your fellow owners, you had better be sure your own conduct is squeaky clean. After all, you don't want some minor transgression to stain your reputation as a good citizen and thereby squelch an incipient countermovement. To be sure you do not fall victim to such fate, I offer up my Ten Commandments for model citizenry.

The Ten Co-op Commandments (Good for Condos, Too)

1. Get In an Ownership State of Mind

Rule One is to remember that you now own a piece of the rock—you are no longer leasing out pebble beach. So change your mind-set to fit your new station in life. With ownership comes responsibility (and, hopefully, rising property values). No more blaming that absentee landlord if the building isn't a model of efficiency, the staff are surly, or the balance sheet is off balance—you *are* the landlord. So start thinking like one and stop blaming everyone else for what's going on.

2. Give the Directors Their Due

Since the board is the power establishment, you may as well show a little respect. I admit, humble is not my style. But a little sucking up—nothing obvious, mind you (that would be bad form and counterproductive)—may provide some insurance protection for the day when you need the board's help (which, I promise you, will come).

Let the board know you've arrived and are appreciative. A phone call to introduce yourself, say hello, or volunteer your service is not a bad idea. One recent recruit even made a courtesy call, much to my surprise and delight. Instead of accosting board members when you corner them in the elevator with every complaint you have stored up, try some friendly chitchat; a thank-you note now and then wouldn't hurt, and acknowledgment of a job well done will positively send your stock soaring. And if your problem is authority figures, go see a shrink—don't show outright contempt (especially if the board is competent).

3. Knowledge Is Power

The key to protecting what is probably your most important investment is being an informed citizen. This means keeping your eyes and ears open and using your smarts to get the scoop on what's going on so that you can fend off disaster before it occurs. It also means knowing your rights as an owner and using them to keep the board (and the balance of power) in check.

4. Silence Is Not Golden

Board members are not psychics, so if you have something on your mind, let them know—whether it's staff sleeping on the job, corridors that are unkempt, or kids that need quieting. Don't sit back in silence and wait until you're so tightly wound about it that you uncoil your pent-up anger on some unsuspecting director. As your frustration mounts, their patience will ebb—not a formula for getting what you want. So take the time to say what's on your mind.

5. Do Unto Others (You Know the Rest)

I advocate this credo not to preach but to be practical. After all, even if your neighbors are not your friends, they are your business partners. So you'd better learn to get along with, if not love, one another. Try being civil; cordial is better still. And think twice before you remove their clammy underwear from that still-spinning dryer or decline Trick or Treat duty. They may repay you in kind when you need their political support.

6. Exercise Your Franchise

I don't care if you've soured on the system and haven't voted in a national election in the past decade, you had better get yourself to these polls. The outcome will affect your pocketbook more immediately and directly. Since you can cast your ballot in person or by proxy, you have no excuse for not doing your citizen's duty.

7. Use the Power of Assembly

The board has to report to the owners at the annual meeting. Go and hear what it has to say. If things are going gangbusters, you can rejoin the silent majority for the time being. If not, you'll have a chance to speak your peace and your mind. And if it turns out that matters are really out of hand—you'll have an opportunity to do some consciousness-raising and start organizing those insurgent forces.

8. Avoid Getting Caught Up with Counterinsurgents

Every building has a cadre of troublemakers whose mission it is to do in the directors—and who won't let the truth get in their way. In my building these agitators tried to enlist the support of the masses by floating rumors of unjust board firings and other supposed sinister director doings. Do not be seduced by their facile propaganda. Ultimately the truth will out and their mission will come undone—taking your credibility along with it.

9. Don't Complain If You Won't Act

The directors may be in charge, but you are not exempt from your duties as a member of the body politic. By all means, voice your objections; criticize board action if you think it's doing wrong—the First Amendment is alive and well in co-ops and condos. But barking commands without being willing to help doesn't go over big and is more likely to engender board anger than action.

10. Currency Is Next to Godliness

In co-op (or condo) parlance this translates to pay your maintenance on time. There's no longer a deep-pocketed landlord to make up the shortfall if you don't send in those monthly checks. It's your resident comrades who'll have to pick up the slack and who won't thank you for the privilege. The best way to ensure peaceful coexistence is to pay up.

THE ART OF INTELLIGENCE GATHERING

Once you've mastered the rules of good citizenship you are ready to take action. The first thing you have to do is educate yourself so that you know your rights as a co-op or condo citizen and how to use them to best advantage. Even if you've tuned out the latest international incident, are tired of scandal, or have taken a break from sexual politics, you'd better make it your business to know all that's doing within the confines of your building.

Several avenues of intelligence gathering are available. First, as part of good government, the board voluntarily should keep you abreast of what's going on. Then there's legally mandated disclosure. Under the law, the board must hold annual meetings,[6] prepare financial statements[7] and make available minutes of shareholder meetings.[8] In addition, the Condo Act specifically gives unit owners the right to inspect books of receipt and expenditures,[9] access not statutorily granted to shareholders. And if you're smart, you won't stop at those official information services but will seek out unofficial sources as well.

Mass Communication

I should (and I will) tell you that the board is supposed to keep you informed on a regular basis of everything that's happening—it's also politically expedient. One of the first things every lawyer advises client boards is to feed the populace enough information, via newsletter or other house organ, to keep them satisfied and at bay.

This sounds good in theory, and in practice it works fine if there are a few warm and semiliterate bodies on the board. But in many buildings, including my own, no budding journalists have emerged to take on the task. From my perspective, it doesn't seem fair (to me or to the shareholders) to be my own propaganda mill. And frankly, after having spent hours getting things done, I'm not inclined to start turning my deeds back into words.

Apart from such concerns, board experiments in the free press can be dangerous. One shareholder sued his board for defamation, claiming it had printed critical comments about him in its newsletter. He didn't get very far on the legal front because the court said the comments were protected by privilege, requiring him to prove that the words were false and malicious. But the whole affair had a chilling effect on co-op communication—at least in his building.[10]

Financial History

Both co-op shareholders and condo owners have the right to receive annual reports setting out the financial condition of the building; these reports usually include a balance sheet and a statement of income and expenses certified by a licensed public accountant. You should get this document as soon as possible after the fiscal year ends. There's no surer sign of spring in New York than the blooming of daffodils and the stuffing of shareholder mailboxes with financial facts—hopefully, sufficiently in advance of the annual meeting so they can sink in. In my friend's building, these figures didn't arrive one year until the roses were in full flower in late summer, causing a postponement of the shareholders' meeting till fall. Not a critical mishap, but an indication that the board's financial state of mind is too casual for my comfort. Whenever you get this report, read it—it will diagnose the financial health of your building and help give you a sense of the board's competence (or lack of it).

From the annual report, you can see how much your board spent over the year in running the co-op (or condo) and for what, how much the building took in from monthly charges and other revenue-raising activities, and whether it (and you all) ended the year in the black or the red. It lets you compare expenses and income for the year just past with the figures for the previous year so you can see what progress (if any) is being made in cost control. It sets out the building's assets and liabilities on a comparative year basis and shows if the cash flow is positive or negative and by how much.

Apart from giving the big picture, it lets you focus in on specific details. You should look for how much cash is in your building's cash reserve coffers and how your directors invested it, what the co-op's underlying mortgage is and how much the collective you paid in interest, what the co-op's current real estate taxes are and whether they're going up or down, how much the building paid in income or other taxes—the answers should all be there.

And even if you're the kind of person whose mind goes blank at the sight of numbers lined up like sentries, there's no excuse for not reading the attached notes, which are penned in plain (albeit accountant-style) English. From the narrative you should be able to tell: (1) what capital projects are upcoming and how much they'll cost; (2) whether the board has developed a plan to assess the needs and cost of future major repairs and replacement; (3) whether the building is getting the benefit of any real estate tax rebates; (4) whether there have been any special assessments; (5) how large a percentage of unsold apartments the sponsor owns; (6) whether there are any material lawsuits against the building—and more.

Future Prediction

Although the law requires the board to recount the financial past for you, it doesn't make it give you a future prediction by way of a budget outlining how much it plans to spend (and on what) and how much it'll get from you in maintenance charges in the coming year. Most co-op boards don't; many condo boards do. As far as I'm concerned, since you're paying the freight, you have a right to know. (We send our shareholders a budget before each year-end setting out the projected numbers for the next year.) This way you can raise questions about how funds have been earmarked while the money's still around (and something can be done) instead of being left to complain after it's all gone.

There's no logical reason for directors not to provide this information. Assuming the board has done its duty and prepared a budget for the upcoming year, it's no big deal for it to send copies to you. If it hasn't figured out the forthcoming expenses and revenues (or worse, doesn't want you to know), that ought to tell you that maybe the problem isn't the budget but the board. Don't be bashful. Ask your directors at the next annual meeting, if not sooner, to start distributing copies of the budget to you all *before* it spends your cash. If it declines your request without rational response, I'd start thinking about getting new directors.

Annual Assembly

Not only do you get to read how your money was spent, you get to question the big spenders in the flesh at the annual meeting. New York law and most co-op bylaws require that the board hold an annual shareholders' meeting to elect directors (of which more later) and transact other business.[11] (Condos follow suit, though the Condo Act is silent on the subject.) Let the board talk first; power has its privileges. The president should report to you on the highlights and lowlights of the year past and what's going to be in the limelight for the coming year—everything from personnel problems to the physical plant, capital improvements to everyday affairs, as well as all that's hot on the financial front—the cash reserve fund, maintenance increases, special assessments, and refinancings on the horizon.

Then it's your turn to show your stuff and rally the troops, if necessary. Everyone who counts will be there: the directors (from the opposition and loyalist camps), the building's accountant (primed to respond to owners who did their financial duty), the general counsel (to keep peace in the event of incipient or actual dissension), and the members of the rank and file.

Take the opportunity to get the facts and gain some tactical advantage. Put the board's members on the hot seat. Ask how they're investing the building's stash of cash and what rate of return they're making for you. If there's some major project looming, get them to tell you which and how many contractors have bid on the job and how much it will set you all back. If maintenance has been headed skyward, find out why and what plans, if any, they have to contain costs and bring them back down to earth. The point is, now is the time to put up or shut up. If everything is rosy, give them a round of applause and a landslide re-election victory. If anything needs fixing, use the forum to find out what you can and then light a fire under your fellow owners.

A final word of advice: You want to get at the truth, not deliver an empty tirade—which will only brand you a troublemaker. We have one shareholder who delivers an annual litany of complaints—from the water temperature in the washing machines to the extravagant use of postage. His pet peeve, though, is dogs, which he wants banned from here to eternity despite (or because of) the fact that we have more pets than people in our building. I'm no animal lover; the only four- (or more) legged creatures I have are the ants on my terrace. But I'm politician enough to know that outlawing pets will lead to revolution in the ranks—not something for which I care to take the fall. So every year I invite him to exercise his citizen's power and organize fellow shareholders to demand change, secure in the knowledge that our canine population (and its masters) will live happily ever after. Or at least until the next year, when he will treat us to another harangue—and skewer himself in the process.

Shareholders know whose lead to follow and whose not. So if you want to use the annual meeting to establish your credentials as the voice of the people, get the facts and stay focused on the real issue.

Attendance Substitute

In case you can't make it to the annual meeting, you can get a copy of the minutes, which, under law, co-op boards are required to prepare and make available to you as a shareholder.[12] Don't go running to pick up your copy hot off the press, because these minutes are written in a way that only a lawyer could love—reciting the order of business without much more. Better call that civic-minded neighbor who attended to get a more complete, though unofficial, version of what happened.

Source List

The law requires that co-ops and condos keep a record containing the names and addresses of all owners together with their ownership interests. For co-ops this is spelled out in the Corporation Law, which entitles shareholders (on five days' written demand) to inspect and copy the information as long as they are using it for any purpose reasonably related to their interest as shareholders.[13] In condos it's not so clear: The Condo Act doesn't specifically give you owners this right, and the cases addressing the question have come out with opposite answers. One says that a list of unit owners is a public record, so there's no reason why the board *shouldn't* give it to you;[14] the other says there's no reason why the board *should* give it to you because you can get it on your own.[15]

If the time comes when you want to mount a proxy battle to elect an insurgent slate of directors or counter the sponsor's campaign to stack the board with resident sympathizers, having access to name, address, and ownership records will enable you to communicate with all your comrades (resident and nonresident alike) when you seek their support for the cause and ask them to designate you or someone in your camp to vote their shares via proxy. The board may still have an advantage because lots of times it has shareholder phone numbers, maybe even e-mail addresses, which the law doesn't specify you have a right to.

Recorded Action

In a few locales, owners are legally empowered to see their government at work. They get to act as flies on the wall—where they generally can be seen, but not heard—at monthly board meetings. New York does not provide for such legalized owner eavesdropping, though some buildings' bylaws give owners a ticket to admission.

While (usually) you can't see your directors live in action, you may be able to read what they did (or didn't do) in the board minutes. New York law requires corporations, including co-ops, to keep accurate minutes of what went on at their meetings.[16] Unlike minutes of the annual meeting, you don't have a legal right to see these, but most boards make them available voluntarily, and if they don't, I'd be suspicious. That doesn't mean the board has to photocopy up a storm and send copies of the minutes to every shareholder, nor make special deliveries to those who want them—both requests which our board has received. Usually you can go to the offices, where the co-op's books and records are kept, during normal business hours. (There are no provisions in the Condo Act regarding board meetings, but most condos follow the same practices.)

Now, I caution you up front—board minutes don't ever tell the whole truth; at most they offer a piece of the truth. There is an art to their writing that only a lawyer can comprehend. The key is to not say too much (which could get the board in trouble) or too little (which could lead to accusations of nondisclosure). As the only lawyer on the board in my building, I have been ridiculed relentlessly for my parsing techniques. But having been involved in lawsuits in which the minutes held the key to victory or defeat, I'd prefer to be safe rather than sorry.

With that caveat in mind, there's still plenty of information you can glean from their pages. Want to know if there's an assessment coming down the pike? The minutes should give you a pretty good idea by telling you what capital improvements and repairs are on the agenda and how the board plans to pay for them. Want to know if any of the directors has a financial interest in these (or other) building transactions? The minutes should disclose the nature of the conflict and whether the board followed the proper voting procedures. Want to know if there are staff problems that could expose the building to lawsuits or if the building already is enmeshed in legal proceedings? The minutes should provide an early indication. Want to get a sense of the board's track record in approving and rejecting potential purchasers? Once again, the minutes should supply the answer.

So, although minutes aren't a perfect substitute for the real thing, this monthly recordation should keep you up-to-date on the doings of your board. Ask to see them. If nothing else, your requests (assuming there are enough of them) will force the board to start keeping a full and accurate account of what it's been up to.

Unofficial Sources

If you've been reading closely, you know that sometimes the best information comes from outside official channels. Suspect some physical building problem? Go directly to the staff. (They'll know before the board will.) Need the latest market price update (apartments, not stocks)? Try the broker down the hall. Want to know who's been violating the House Rules? Ask the doorman. Even board members can provide helpful tidbits if you catch them in their good-neighbor (unofficial) state.

HOW TO EXERCISE YOUR FRANCHISE

Having staked out the available information, you are ready to go to the polls as an informed citizen and vote your conscience—and your comrades into office. By cloaking them with board authority you are empowering them to act on your behalf and spend your money. So you want to make sure you're electing the right candidates, or at least the best your building has to offer.

Procedures for Victory

Before you go to the polls, you should know how the system works: what qualifications you'll need to vote; how to cast your ballot when you can't be there; how many votes you have; how to maximize their power; and how to avoid being disenfranchised. Here is the lowdown.

No Quorum/No Election

The first thing you need to know is that your presence matters. In most co-ops, if owners of less than 50 percent of shares are represented, the meeting can't go forward and those directors get to stick around until another election is called. So if change is what you're after, you'd better show up.

You have only yourself to blame if you don't. For years the shareholders at a fancy East Side high-rise were too busy to bother going to the annual meetings so no elections were held, and the directors perpetuated themselves in office by appointment. They got a rude awakening—and a quorum—when the board told them that nearly $5 million worth of work had to be done for which they'd pay in assessments and maintenance hikes. Those newly energized owners got together an opposition slate, only to be challenged by the entrenched lifers, who claimed their proxies were invalid because they had faulty acknowledgments. But the court said the proxies were okay, giving the new guard three seats, and further ordered an election for the remaining six members of the nine-member staggered board, finally giving the shareholders a say.[17] Let this be a lesson: Don't wait till catastrophe strikes before going to the polls to vote, because by then the damage has been done.

One Man/One Vote

You may logically think that in co-ops and condos the one man/one vote rule means one apartment/one vote. You'd be wrong. Taking its cue from the laws governing corporations, which provide for one vote per share, voting in co-ops is determined by the number of shares, not the number of units, you own. In condos, voting usually goes by the percent interest you hold. (So you might get one vote for each .01 percent interest in the common elements attributable to your apartment.) This means all apartment owners are not equal in the eyes of the law. The bigger the apartment, the more shares or the greater percent interest, and hence, the more votes you have. In life, as in co-ops, it's the lords of the manor (a.k.a. those penthouse owners) who have more clout than the average studio-owning Joe.

Apartment size is not a political divide on most issues. So rest assured that no matter how big (or small) your pad, your fellow owners generally have a common interest in voting with you according to the competency of the directors, not the count of their shares. But there are issues involving real money (for example, transforming that rooftop into an urban playground or the basement into a temple of fitness), where the big spenders may speak with a louder voice by virtue of their vote. If that happens, remember that in numbers there is strength. All you have to do is rally support (and votes) among the commoner folk in the building to silence the hotshots' thunder.

Absentee Ballot

In case some higher calling keeps you from fulfilling your duty to attend the annual meeting, you can make your presence felt by proxy. This is an absentee ballot that lets you name somebody else to vote in your stead. Assuming your board is on the case, it should automatically send you a proxy, together with the notice of the meeting, well in advance of the actual meeting date. The law governing co-ops requires that you be given notice at least ten (and not more than sixty) days before the date set for the annual meeting.[18] The Condo Act doesn't require setting a record date, so if you bought your apartment after notice was sent you should still be able to vote.[19] Under either system you have plenty of time to sign, seal, and deliver it—including, of course, filling in the name of your stand-in. All this has been made easier for shareholders because the law says you can transmit your proxy by fax, telegram, or other electronic wonder.[20] No more having to submit a signed original before the meeting date. If at the last minute that trip to L.A. is canceled and you can make it after all, just revoke the authority and exercise your franchise in person.

Since the right to be represented at the meeting and to vote by proxy in corporations—co-ops included—is granted by law, even if your co-op's bylaws are silent on the score they can't deprive you of your due. It's the opposite in condos. Since the Condo Act doesn't give owners the right to vote by proxy, it has to be granted in your bylaws. You can designate anyone you want in the proxy; it need not be another shareholder. If you have faith in your directors, the easiest thing to do is to make the proxy run in favor of the entire board or one of its members whom you know to be functional.

And if two or more people own an apartment together, fear not if they're not all around to sign the proxy. So long as one of the owners authorizes it, it's valid and the votes will be counted.

Poll Tax

To be worthy of the privilege of voting you should be a citizen in good standing. In some buildings this means you'd better pay up maintenance and any other outstanding sums before election day or risk losing your franchise. In case anyone tries to bar you from the polls, what you now know is that in co-ops your delinquency can disqualify you only if the building's certificate says so. (And most don't.) In condos, the bylaws may say that you can be disenfranchised for not paying. (For the reason behind this distinction, see chapter 16.)

Power Voting

Most of the time a vote is just a vote. But sometimes a vote is more than a vote. This is the case if your co-op has what's called cumulative voting, which the Corporation Law expressly allows, though it must be in the co-op's certificate to be valid.[21] This technique allows you to get maximum voting power out of a minimum number of votes and enables minority shareholders to get their feet in the door and their man on the board. With regular voting, you just divide your votes equally among the candidates. But with cumulative voting you can multiply the total number of votes you have times the number of directors up for election and then cast that total amount of votes for a single candidate or among as many directors as you want. The Condo Act is silent on the subject of cumulative voting, though presumably the bylaws could opt for it.

Here's how it works. Suppose you hold 300 shares and have 300 votes for each of the three directors up for election. Instead of casting 300 votes for each director, under cumulative voting you can vote all 900 shares (3 × 300) for one nominee. By concentrating your voting muscle on one candidate, you geometrically improve the odds of that candidate's election.

How can this system help you? Suppose the sponsor is still in control. If shareholders pool all their votes and cast them for a finite number of directors, they can get their partisans on the board—to act as a governmental gadfly and keep the directors honest. Or what if there are different factions among the resident board? With cumulative voting you can push more of those in your camp into power. Or let's say you think that the incumbents have become too entrenched. Try using super-voting to break their stranglehold and get an insurgent in among the establishment group. Unhappy with how the board was spending owners' dollars, one shareholder at a Park Avenue co-op used the power of cumulative voting to get elected, only to be outmaneuvered by the board, which then increased the number of directors to dilute his limited voice. My building is among the minority of co-ops that still provides shareholders with this potential weapon. But I'm happy to report that, thus far, it has not been used to dislodge sitting directors or plant an agitator in our midst.

Classified Counterattack

In order to take the muscle out of cumulative voting, some boards try to amend the co-op's documents to provide for classified or staggered boards. Under this system, instead of electing all the directors at once, you elect only a certain number each year. So, for example, if there were three "classes," one third of the board would be elected each year and each director would serve for three years. Reducing the number of directors to be voted on at one time mathematically reduces the chances that a minority faction can elect a director with power voting. If you don't want to give up the power that comes with minority participation, vote no to this one.

Secret Ballot

Suppose you want to vote for somebody in the opposition camp, but fear retribution from the incumbents in deciding your renovation and sales fate. There are several ways around this dilemma. If the managing agent is independent, it can be in charge of counting the ballots. If you think it's too close for comfort to the board, ask that an outside independent service be brought in. Another way is to devise a system akin to that used at the real polls, allowing you to sign in with name and apartment number (so that no impostor can vote your shares) but to submit an anonymous ballot so no one knows *whom* you voted for. (By definition this procedure can't be used for proxies, because you're not there to sign.)

Democratic Nominations

Most bylaws don't spell out procedures for conducting nominations, even though the process used can affect the election outcome. Assuming that's the case, it's probably okay to accept nominations from the floor, and at least one court has said just that in response to a bunch of condo owners who tried to force amendment of the bylaws to provide for a more controlled process.[22] Even better is for the board to request anyone who wishes to run to make known that intention in advance so that it can send out the names and biographies of all candidates to owners *before* the meeting. In contrast to nominating committees, which tend to perpetuate the incumbents, free-for-all nominations allow the will of the people to prevail.

Tallying the Results

In real-life elections, you may be able to get minute-by-minute tallies, not that the candidate with the most votes necessarily is victorious. In co-ops and condos, the directors with the most votes win, but most boards don't announce how many votes each candidate pulled in; that doesn't mean they shouldn't provide the information if it's standard building practice or there's good reason. Only one demand was ever made in my building, by an unsuccessful candidate who couldn't believe he didn't win. Rather than start a war over nothing, we silenced him by telling him how many votes had been cast in his favor.

Voting Tips

Now that you've got the proceedings down pat, you'll want to be sure you select candidates of substance. But how do you know if those would-be directors are fit to serve? In the case of a novice (especially if the person is also a building newcomer and you have no scuttlebutt to go by) it's no easy task. Here are a few suggestions to help make the election process a model of informed democracy.

Make Them Talk

Even if the seat is uncontested, building policy should mandate that a candidate address the masses. This way you can tell straight out whether the office seeker has the gift of the orator's tongue—not a prerequisite for every board member, but surely a quality to be sought after in the president, who has to communicate his or her vision to the troops and lead them through battles with accountants, architects, and agents—to say nothing of potential civil war at home. After the candidates have finished speaking, you'll also know what their agendas are (assuming they've thought that far). At the very least, you'll get an instant intelligence and character reading. If they ooze unctuousness, display attitude, or appear brain-dead, it's a pretty sure bet their election will mean trouble for the building and unpleasantness for you. My advice is to look for someone who's action-oriented, with common-sense smarts and enough pit bull instincts to take on the status quo if need be.

Get the Lowdown on Their Backgrounds

The urge to serve is noble, but it's nice to know that the members of the board also have the right stuff. Taken together, the body politic should have a head for business (from staff management to contract negotiation to capital projects), eyes that don't glaze over at the sight of numbers (of which there are plenty—for example, budgets, financial statements, and balance sheets), a brain that works on several wavelengths (from economic to aesthetic), and an ear attuned to shifts in shareholder and staff sentiment that left unchecked could lead to unrest.

It doesn't much matter whether these collective attributes are attained by vocation or by natural instinct, so no one profession is a proxy for success. Although it's trendy to trash lawyers, it's good to have at least one on the board (for free, not as a paid general counsel—that could give rise to conflicts) to keep the legally uninitiated out of trouble. A number cruncher, to look over the shoulder of the outside auditor and double-check the co-op's tax returns, is also an asset to the board. Beyond that, business execs, engineers, architects, and even creative types (as long as they're moored to reality) can bring something to the table.

Psych Out Their Political Philosophies

Even though candidates need not announce their party affiliations, their building raps should tell you what you need to know about their political philosophies (and how they will affect your life). Chances are that the neighbor who wants board-sponsored dog inoculations, fines for offending Rollerbladers, and leashes on children will bring with his election a storm-trooper regime. The candidate who lets her kids use the lobby as a playground, allows her dog to roam free, and blasts her CD player till midnight presages an era of uncontrolled anarchy. For the sake of everyone's sanity, let us hope some middle-grounders also join the race. You can scope out their political leanings from their building behavior.

Ask What They Plan to Do

Don't be bashful. If they don't offer up any vision of a brighter tomorrow, ask them what they see in store for the building's future and how they plan to get there. Appropriately asked questions should help you get a fix on where they're coming from, what they see as the issues, whether they have given them deep (or any) thought, and how they sort out priorities—which may or may not be the same as yours. Of course, if you don't like the answers, your only alternative may be to throw your own hat into the ring and subject yourself to examination by the electorate.

Home In on Hot Topics

If there is some burning issue brewing in the building (which probably ignited their candidacies), get them to focus on their proposed solutions. Suppose there's a heavy dispute with the sponsor. Do they plan to wage legal warfare or try friendly persuasion? The difference can mean thousands to you. If it's decorating that's on the horizon, you'll want to know if their taste tends to gaudy grandeur or downtown minimalism—and, more important, whether they plan to bankrupt the building in the name of good taste. If it's a case of financial distress that's sparked the controversy, find out if they plan to spike the maintenance, hit you up for an assessment, refinance the mortgage, get a credit line, or raise revenue in some more unorthodox manner.

Require Remedial Education

Why not try something radical—demand that your directors know what they're doing. Or at least see to it that novices get enough information so that they don't get themselves and the building into a mess. There are a couple of ways you can do this. Require them to take a crash course from the building's counsel in the basics of director duties. (Prevention is a lot cheaper than litigation.) If you have a competent managing agent, include in your contract a provision that the agent will give remedial instruction to new directors. Or ship them off to school. There are courses (good, bad, and indifferent). Some are sponsored by co-op councils, whose "professors" have an interest in becoming your building's professionals. Others are offered by universities (continuing education departments) whose motive is disinterested and more purely educational.

Returning Incumbents

If it's an incumbent seeking re-election, let past history be your guide. Has your maintenance remained fairly constant over time or risen in line with inflation? Is there cash on hand for the major projects that need doing and are they getting done? Is the physical plant (inside and out) being kept in good working order? Are the staff on the case and responsive to your requests? If the answer to these queries is in the affirmative, then you know someone must be doing something right.

Just because the building appears to be running smoothly doesn't mean all of your directors are doing their duty. It only proves that at least one person is on the job. So long as things in your building seem to be going swimmingly, you probably don't know (or care) who's carrying the laboring oar. But what if the only take-charger got hit by a car or decided to move or finally said to hell with it? Although I'm not saying the walls would come tumbling down if no number two person was waiting in the wings to pick up the slack, all you need do is remember Dan Quayle and his *potatoe* to appreciate the potential problem.

Set Up Standards

Apart from these self-help measures, the Corporation Law allows shareholders to establish written requirements and procedures for nomination of directors.[23] How tough you make the standards is up to you. At the very least, you should require that nominations be submitted sufficiently far in advance so that you know who's running and can avoid the shoot-from-the-hip, decide-from-the-floor syndrome. You may also want to fix minimum qualifications—all maintenance paid up, no rules violated. Whatever the standard, it has to be set out in the bylaws to be valid.

Dealing with Sponsor Directors

When it comes to sponsor directors, doing your homework won't do much good because you have no say in their election. The sponsor gets to pick its representatives and bypass the election process altogether. But as we've seen, the sponsor has to give up voting control the earlier of five years after the conversion or sale of more than 50 percent of the shares (or, in condos, common interests).

Strategies for Defeating Sponsor Sympathizers

Even after the sponsor no longer has automatic voting control (because five years have passed or it owns less than 50 percent of the shares), it can continue to keep control by voting its shares at the election for sympathetic shareholders. It can even take the offensive and solicit and vote proxies from among the shareholders.

But a united shareholder front can wage a number of defensive maneuvers to fend off the assault. If you're lucky, your work will have been done for you by the offering plan or the bylaws—a few of which expressly limit the sponsor to voting for less than a majority. (See chapter 9.) More likely, you'll have to try another tack.

If the sponsor has decided to wage a proxy battle, counter its strategy with a voting blitzkrieg of your own. For added assurance get a campaign going to solicit proxies—the more the better—among shareholders (resident and nonresident alike) naming a friendly board member as designee. Communication with the masses is made easy because, as you now know, at least in co-ops you have the right under law to get the names and addresses of all shareholders.

For maximum advantage, agree in advance on a single slate of pro-shareholder candidates to keep sponsor sympathizers from being nominated for a seat and to be sure voting power is not diluted among excess candidates. Hold an unofficial primary among shareholders before the real thing so you know the election eve outcome in advance and can avoid unwanted surprises.

Tactics for Taking Control If You Don't

But if somehow you are outmaneuvered and the sponsor secures control, there are still strategies you can use to check its raw exercise of power. One tactic your board representatives should try is establishing an executive committee at any meeting where the resident directors constitute a majority. New York's Business Corporation Law[24] and most co-op bylaws provide that a majority of the board may vote to set up an executive committee (consisting of one or more directors) to run the day-to-day affairs of the building between board meetings. Such a committee can't control budgets or maintenance charges or fill board vacancies, but it can have plenty of clout over the business dealings of the corporation. Just don't get carried away and try to use the executive committee to suspend regular board meetings. One faction of a warring board gave it a shot, only to be chastised by the court that condos aren't banana republics.[25]

Sometimes the best bet is just lying in wait until sponsor absenteeism gives your shareholder-representatives temporary control. Unlike annual meetings, at which you can have someone vote in your place, at board meetings the sponsor can't act as proxy holder for absent directors. So unless it produces actual bodies or has them present by phone (which the law allows), it can't exert control. Your team should be alert to this possibility and ready to act if such a power vacuum occurs.

Another approach is for one of your own directors to get named president. (Officers usually are elected by directors from among themselves after the board elections.) A victorious sponsor may offer up the post as a gesture of appeasement to the vanquished, thinking it's all show and no substance. Take it—or, if noblesse oblige is not the order of the day, ask for it. Although a populist president can't change the power structure, she can influence the agenda and steal the psychological edge by taking charge at board and annual meetings.

KEEPING THE BOARD ACCOUNTABLE

Once your directors are in, you want to be sure they remember who elected them and don't let the power go to their heads. The best way to do this is to assume your proper role as a responsible citizen and engage in participatory democracy. Instead of letting them set the agenda (and then complaining), tell them what you want done. A word of caution: Be politic in how you proceed. Some methods are calculated to get action and others to stop it dead in its tracks. Based on my interaction with shareholders (sane and insane), I offer my advice on the Dos and Don'ts of action for accountability.

Dos

Be a Big Brother

Let them know you're watching them—and what they're doing. No need to be obnoxious or obvious about it, especially if they're doing a good job. But be evident enough so they know someone's looking over their shoulders. It's just human nature that with so many eyes upon them, board members will be more accountable than if you cede them total autonomy through apathy.

Try Friendly Persuasion

If there's some item on your wish list, whether a playroom for those pent-up toddlers, a sundeck for their shut-in parents, or something more mundane, bring it to the attention of the board by leaving a neighborly note for one of its members stating your case. And if it's something involving lots of money, include any ideas about how to pay for it. A phone call's okay, but not tactically the best way to go. You may get the director on the line while she's otherwise engaged and therefore is indisposed to your (or any) idea.

Set Your Own Agenda

If friendly persuasion doesn't work, go the next step and ask that the item be put on the agenda for the next board meeting. Assuming that the directors take up your cause, which logic, but not law, dictates they should, you will have scored a double victory. First, your proposal will get a full (and hopefully, fair) hearing in front of the entire board. (Maybe it will even invite you to attend and present your case in person.) Second, even if you don't get immediate action, there will be a record of your request in the board minutes, which may later prove handy to document the board's do-nothingness.

Get Up Close and Personal

If you can't beat them, join them. Infiltrate the inner sanctum by joining a committee that reports to the board. Maybe there's a need for a new member to help vet admissions or explore a capital idea or make the garden grow. If there are no such bodies, volunteer to head up the creation of one. By getting close to the co-op's (or condo's) commanders you will have access to the board's inner workings (and its ear)—and can more easily influence decisions.

Don'ts

Demand Action Anonymously

Anonymous shareholders don't go over big with directors. There's something spooky about getting demands from unnamed sources. If anything is worth doing, it's worthy of your name. Having had unidentified requests for action on various building matters breathed into my answering machine and stuffed under my door, I can tell you that my reaction always is determined inaction. So, if you hope to get the board to act, you'd better begin by giving your name, rank, and apartment number.

Communicate with Graffiti

The "art" of subway graffiti may be dead. But it's alive and well (albeit in more refined form) in many a ritzy co-op, where it has become a form of urban protest used by otherwise law-abiding citizens to voice their discontent with board action. In my building, shareholders have used signs posted in the lobby and the laundry room as makeshift canvases for scribbling their own action agendas. No self-respecting director would respond to such subway sloganeering. And even shareholders who agree with the messages usually take offense at the method—which sends the wrong signal about the building. (It's property values over principle.) So, unless you're the next Keith Haring, use a notepad instead of a wall when action is what you're after.

Complain with Unclean Hands

A cardinal rule, especially for those shareholders who take a holier-than-thou attitude, is to hew to the mark (and the House Rules) yourself. Don't set yourself up as the resident saint: the shareholder who professes perfection and demands it of all her fellow residents but doesn't practice what she preaches. My building's would-be Mother Teresa lectures the populace on manners at each year's annual meeting, then clogs the halls with baby carriages, lets her dog pee in the tree pit, and puts the luggage cart in the elevator, expecting it miraculously to walk to the lobby. I promise that someone will catch you in the act, not only jeopardizing your shot at canonization, but also making you persona non grata.

Lose the Forest for the Trees

Don't get me wrong—details count. But they have their place. As a shareholder, don't make the mistake of badgering the board on nit-picking trivia to the exclusion of things that really count. You'll look stupid and the board won't take you seriously when it matters. The board in my building was deep into negotiations for multimillion-dollar building makeovers and mortgage refinancing. But at the annual meeting the item atop our constituents' agenda was why our building's low-tech but effective communications hub (a.k.a. the bulletin board) had been moved. If you want to retain credibility, get a grip before you complain.

12

Taking the Offensive

HOW TO GET ACTION WHEN THE BOARD WON'T ACT

I hope that the strategies outlined in the previous chapter will help you keep your directors men (and women) of the people. But suppose the balance is becoming too one-sided for comfort. The board is losing contact with its constituents and assuming a bunker mentality. Instead of listening to what you want—whether the issue is changing the admissions policy, doing away with flip taxes, or relaxing the sublet policy—it has embarked on its own private agenda. Don't wait till mutiny is on the horizon and things could get ugly. There are a number of avenues open to you to get action when the board won't act—from taking your case to the people to calling a special meeting—and if all else fails, you can even revolt without bloodshed and stage a (legal) boardroom coup. (The law makes these remedies more explicit for shareholders than condo owners.) Although it's often expeditious if you have a counselor to lead the charge and take you through the legal technicalities, if you follow the steps set out in this chapter you should be able to get pretty far on your own.

Having Your Say—and Satisfaction

Let's say the board won't listen to reason—or to you. You have a plan to fix the building's ancient plumbing system without breaking its bank. Or you want to turn tar beach into a rooftop arcadia and think the building should hire a landscaper to explore the feasibility. The elevators have outlived your cat's nine lives—and then some. So you want the co-op to bring in an engineer to give them a new lease on life. But the board insists on following its own counsel, giving short (or no) shrift to your proposal. Don't get mad; get even.

Take It to the People

If the board is foolish enough to ignore your requests, go directly to your fellow shareholders. Try making your case in a shareholder proposal at the annual meeting. The first step is to get your proposal to the people. You can prepare a draft and ask the board to mail it together with notice of the meeting, but it's not clear that the board has a legal duty to comply. As any of you stockholding activists know, getting Microsoft or IBM (or any public company) to transmit shareholder proposals (whether for environmentally

friendly manufacturing or slimmed-down CEO paychecks) is not easy. Although the requirements for public companies don't apply to co-ops, the theory is the same. The board is there to serve the general corporate good, not individual shareholder interests. So don't be surprised if the directors turn down your request to act as messenger. Of course, there's nothing to stop you from delivering your message yourself. If you're really serious about your plan, get that shareholder list and start licking stamps.

Or you can make your pitch directly to the populace at the meeting. Unless your proposal is out of order (because it's obstructive or purely personal), the board should let you speak. The problem is that shareholders may not get to vote—at least not at this meeting. Assuming official notice of the proposal was never sent around, absentee shareholders would be in the dark and denied a vote. Do not regard such a result as a defeat, just as a delay—the better to enable you to marshal support for the next step—calling a special meeting.

Call a Special Assembly

If action is what you're after, you don't have to wait till the next annual gathering of the clan. Most co-op bylaws (based on the Corporation Law)[1] say that if a certain number of shareholders agree on the need for a special meeting to consider some shareholder initiative, it has to be held. (Condo owners don't have a comparable legal right, but their bylaws often take their cue from co-ops.) There's no set percent needed to trigger action. A typical co-op provision may require the secretary to call a special meeting to put your proposal to a vote when requested in writing by shareholders owning at least 25 percent of the shares. One (not very democratic) condo I know of makes victory a prerequisite for a special meeting, demanding that a majority of owners issue the call. (For what to say, see the form on pages 216–217.)

So if you are initially thwarted, remain true to your cause. All you need do is get the required percent of your comrades to affix their signatures to a petition demanding assembly and your proposal will be presented and voted on. And if enough of them vote for passage, it becomes the law of the co-op. You should take some satisfaction in the knowledge that *all* shareholders, those reactionary directors included, must abide.

Just don't get macho and try to go it alone. One shareholder thought he had a brilliant idea to conduct a study for a new sewage system, but the board didn't see it that way. When he couldn't present his brainstorm at the annual meeting because the mike was on the fritz, he went to court and demanded (but didn't get) a special meeting.[2] Since the board acts for the co-op it doesn't have to cave in to every individual request. But as long as you get the necessary show of (written) support from among the ranks, you will get its attention—and your assembly. And, hopefully, the requested change in the regime.

Write the Ending

It's a long shot, but you may be able to skip the meeting and go directly to the desired result. The law allows shareholders to consent in writing without a meeting.[3] (No such comparable provision exists for condo owners.) This remedy rarely gave relief because it required unanimity. Everyone had to say (and write) yes—one lone dissenter and the proposal was dead. But things have gotten a little easier for would-be activists. The law was changed so that the co-op's certificate can say that you need only get written agreement from the holders of the same number of shares it would take to pass your plan if it had been brought to a vote at a shareholders' meeting. Assuming amendment of the proprietary lease or bylaws requires a two-thirds vote of shareholders at a meeting, you can skip the meeting if you can get owners holding that many shares to sign. If a resolution requires a majority vote of shareholders, that's how many have to consent in writing. Then you have to deliver the signed consent to the co-op—and notify nonsigners of your victory. Although still not a sure thing (unless your co-op has only a few noncontentious shareholders), if you can get enough of your fellow owners to agree in writing to your proposed resolution, you can write a happy ending and avoid the hassle of a meeting. Here's a sample of what it should say:

Written Consent of Shareholders

The undersigned, being the holders of outstanding shares of (*name of co-op corporation*) having no less than the minimum number of votes that would be necessary to authorize such action at a meeting at which all shares entitled to vote thereon were present and voted, do hereby consent to adoption of the following resolution without a meeting on written consent:

Resolved:

1. State the resolution or action to be implemented.
2. That the board is authorized and directed to give prompt notice of this action to all shareholders.
3. That the board is also directed to file this consent with the corporation and to take all necessary and appropriate action to implement this resolution.

Dated: ________, (Year)

Signatures/Addresses/Apt. nos./
Number of shares of consenting shareholders

____

____

____

Demanding Elections

Maybe the problem is not that the board won't listen to your proposals but that it ignores your existence altogether. In a supreme act of arrogance (or apathy) the board decides to govern solo and doesn't bother calling annual meetings for election of directors as required. Do you have any recourse (other than voting the despots out of office)? Shareholders are protected by established legal remedies, but condo owners are more on their own (or dependent on what their bylaws say) in getting redress.

Try Self-Help

Under the Corporation Law governing co-ops, if no annual meeting has been called as required by the co-op's bylaws, then holders of 10 percent of the shares may, in writing, demand that a meeting be called for the election of directors.[4] Three conditions must exist for shareholders to have this right: (1) passage of thirteen months from the last annual meeting (or one month after the date fixed in the bylaws for the annual meeting); (2) failure to elect a sufficient number of directors to conduct the business of the co-op; and (3) failure of the board to call a meeting within two weeks after the expiration of the thirteen-month period. Assuming all three apply, then shareholders owning at least 10 percent of the shares should demand (in writing) that the co-op's secretary call a meeting to hold elections, specifying the date (which should be not less than sixty or more than ninety days from the date of the demand). For what the demand should look like, see the form on page 218.

On receiving this demand, the co-op's secretary has five business days to act. If he or she doesn't, you shareholders can take matters into your own hands. Any one of you who signed the demand can send out a notice to your fellow shareholders calling for a meeting to elect directors.

A big turnout on election day is nice, but once you've issued the call, you don't have to worry about how many shareholders show up at a special meeting to elect directors. However many attend, in person or by proxy, is considered enough (or, in legalese, a quorum) to hold the election and vote in new directors.

Shareholders' Demand to Call Special Meeting for Election of Directors

To: (*Name of Secretary*)

Secretary of (*Co-op's Name*)

The undersigned being the holders of at least 10 percent of the votes of the shares entitled to vote in an election of directors, demand the call of a special meeting for the election of directors for (*name of co-op corporation*) to be held on ______, (Year).

This demand is being made because more than a month after the date fixed in the bylaws for the annual meeting (or more than thirteen months after the last annual meeting) there has been a failure to elect a sufficient number of directors to conduct the business of the ______ co-op corporation, and further, more than two weeks after this specified period there has been a failure by the board to call a special meeting for the election of directors.

Signatures/Addresses/Apt. Nos./
Number of shares/Shareholders

____

____

____

Use the Courts

If self-help is not your style, you can always resort to that time-tested method of using judicial intervention to compel or enjoin the holding of an annual meeting for elections.[5] Of course, that requires bringing in an attorney to do the legwork and get a court order.

Legislating for Change

Shareholders are the co-op's legislators. It's up to you to make fundamental changes by amending the co-op's bylaws (lease and certificate of incorporation).[6] You don't have to wait for the board to institute change. (Although many co-op bylaws allow the board to amend the bylaws, any bylaw adopted by the board can be changed or repealed by the shareholders.) This gives shareholders real power and ultimately allows you to override unpopular board decisions if you can muster the necessary (usually) two-thirds vote from fellow shareholders.

Unit owners have the Condo Act to help you.[7] It says that at least two-thirds of you (in number and common interest ownership) must vote to amend the bylaws. Although there's no separate statutory framework outlining the procedures as there is for co-op owners, the same basic procedures usually apply.

Taking the Initiative

Let's say the market is not sizzling and you can't sell your apartment, so you (and many of your fellow shareholders) want to be able to sublet. But the board won't budge because it's afraid the co-op will be turned into a hotel. Or maybe you think the board is becoming entrenched and you want to impose term limits, but the board's members think they should have lifetime tenure. You can accomplish these changes, and more, on your own by amending the co-op's governing documents.

Before you begin, you'd better be sure you're going by the book or your effort and energy may be for naught. Using that time-honored tradition of passing around a petition or resorting to some other ad hoc technique may get your voice heard. But the board doesn't have to listen to what you're saying because a petition is not a legally binding document for these purposes.

Here are the procedures to follow:

1. Call for a special meeting. By now you know the drill.
2. Have the secretary send out a notice of the meeting that states that its purpose is to vote on a provision to amend the bylaws. A proxy should be attached that includes the specific resolution to be voted upon. (For an idea of what a resolution should look like, see the form on page 225.)
3. At the meeting, be sure to keep an accurate record of the vote.
4. Assuming the proposal passes by the required number of votes, the co-op's (or condo's) bylaws should be officially changed and all owners promptly notified. Regardless of how they voted, all are bound by the new law of the land.

Leveraging Your Legislative Power

Given the political dynamics of co-ops and condos, usually it's the board (not you) that gets the legislative ball rolling. Maybe it wants to change the number of directors that sit on the board or increase its power over the admissions process. Whatever the board's goal (and sometimes it *is* for the good of the building), it probably can't achieve it without the shareholders—and their votes. So take a cue from professional politicos and use the chance to demand something in return.

In my building the board wanted to get rid of the right-of-first-refusal provision, which tied our hands when it came to sales and subleases, and amend the proprietary lease to give us the right to just say no to financially unfit purchasers. Some able shareholder constituents lobbied for relaxed sublet rules as the price for their vote (though we ultimately decided to let well enough alone).

Truth is, if you can manage to convert your comrades to your cause you're ready to graduate from guerrilla in training to generalissimo. At the very least, you belong on the board, where you can use your moral suasion for the power of good. Don't say never—until you read the next chapter and see what's involved.

THE ULTIMATE WEAPON: BOARD REMOVAL

Hopefully, the measures just outlined will help you gain the upper hand and put the board in its place. But if, despite all your efforts to work within the power structure to effectuate change, certain board members show no sign of reform, it may be time to get rid of the wrongdoers themselves. There are several approaches—ranging from street smart to courtroom—depending on the severity of the situation and your own personal style.

First, consider a few ways to convince those directors to do the right thing.

Saving Face

The simplest solution is to try to get the misbehaving board members to go on their own. Maybe they're so out of touch they don't realize how low they've sunk in the shareholder polls. If you let them know that you mean removal business they may depart voluntarily—thereby sparing themselves embarrassment and you a potentially messy fight with individuals you won't have to vote for but will have to live with. CEOs of Fortune 500 companies resign under pressure all the time rather than face the stigma of separation (usually pocketing a bundle for their cooperation). Even our thirty-seventh president, faced with the writing on the Watergate wall, figured it was better to stand tall and bid adieu than be given the boot. Your board members' offenses may not be of such compelling magnitude, but they still may prefer resignation to confrontation. So give it a shot.

Popular Persuasion

No one's budged from the boardroom? A little public pressure brought to bear by the populace may get those unruly board members to recognize it's time for a change. In one co-op I know, the shareholders took to the streets and picketed for days in front of their building (not good for sales or morale) until the Old Guard voluntarily moved over and made room for the new. So take a lesson from our forefathers and protest peaceably in support of your cause: hand out leaflets, distribute a newsletter, slap on a placard. Going directly to the people is easier and quicker than any legal route.

Natural Order

If regular elections are imminent and the wrongdoer's term is up, you can avoid the hassle of the removal process—just don't re-elect him (or her). Of course, this means you may have to do some serious campaigning for the insurgent candidate (including proxy solicitation) or maybe even volunteer to serve yourself. The key is to be certain there's a suitable replacement willing to run *and* able to get elected. To be sure the election is conducted according to Hoyle (with neither side stuffing or shorting the ballot box) you dissidents may want to bring in an outside company to run the show. If those in power don't agree, you may have to go to court to get the outsiders in, but such relief should be readily granted.

The Last Straw

But assuming those directors are truly incorrigible (or convinced without reason that they are right) and won't go voluntarily, you'll have to get rid of them. Most co-op (and condo) bylaws provide that any director may be removed for cause by a majority vote of the owners at a special meeting called for that purpose. In addition, shareholders have the benefit of the Corporation Law, which provides an independent statute-based right to oust directors.[8] The Condo Act doesn't provide for unit owner removal of a board of managers. But it's a distinction without a practical difference. Whether co-op or condo, you have the inherent right under the law to remove board members for cause.

"Cause" means director misconduct in carrying out the affairs of the co-op or condo. A director breached his fiduciary duty to you. He violated the bylaws. He put his personal interest ahead of the corporation's. You'll know it when you see it—or worse, experience it. Just remember, no matter what your bylaws say (or don't say), the law says that before you can remove any director you have to give specific charges, adequate notice, and a full opportunity for the board member to be heard and defend himself.

Here, then, is a step-by-step guide to ridding yourselves of the wrongdoers.

1. Get the Lowdown

Before you can act, you have to know the rules you're playing by. That means reading your building's bylaws to see what they say on "Director Removal" and "Special Meetings." Typically, they provide for calling a special meeting if requested (in writing) by shareholders (or unit owners) representing a 25 percent ownership interest, and for removal of a director by a majority vote. But your building's documents may require different percentages for either or both. You've got to know the numbers before you can proceed. Too few signatures (or votes) and your efforts will be for naught.

2. Avoid a Pyrrhic Victory

You want to be sure that your victory achieves real results. It's one thing to have removed the rotten apple from the board; it's another to see that he's replaced with a satisfactory successor. That's not always as easy as it sounds. In lots of buildings the bylaws let the remaining board members fill vacancies (until the next regular election). That means (at least technically) they could re-elect the very scoundrel you shareholders just showed the door. Although they're unlikely to act so imprudently (for fear that they'll be the next ones out the exit), the replacement they choose may not represent the will of the people. One way to avoid this problem is to amend the bylaws at the special meeting to provide that directors removed by the electorate may only be replaced by them. (Of course, proper notice must be given in advance that the amendment will be taken up at the assembly.)

3. Call to Arms

Once you know how many dissidents you'll need to rally, you're ready to snap into action. Circulate a petition among your fellow owners requesting that a special meeting be called to remove those board members who have abused your trust. If enough owners sign on to the cause, you've passed the first hurdle. The owners' written request should be forwarded to the secretary, who in most co-ops and condos is the official charged with putting out the call. Here's what the request should say:

DEMAND FOR CALL OF SPECIAL MEETING

To: (*Name of Secretary*)

Secretary of: (*Co-op's Name*)

The undersigned being the holders of at least (*number must meet bylaws requirement*) percent of the shares of the above-named corporation demand that pursuant to Article ______ of the bylaws a special meeting be called for the purpose of: (1) voting upon a proposal that shareholders hear certain charges preferred against (*names of directors*), determine whether the conduct of such directors or any of them was inimical to the co-op corporation and, if so, to vote upon their removal and vote for election of their successor(s); and (if needed) (2) voting upon a proposal to amend the bylaws to provide that vacancies on the board of directors arising from the removal of a director by shareholders (or by resignation of a director against whom charges have been preferred) may be filled, for the unexpired term, only by the shareholders.

Signatures/Addresses/Apt. nos./
Number of shares of shareholders

____

____

____

4. Set the Date

Assuming your request has valid signatures representing the requisite number of shares (or ownership interest), the secretary—whether an Old Guard loyalist or a member of your opposition camp—*must* call a special meeting. This means sending out a notice to *all* owners (including those offending directors) telling them the time, place, and purpose of the gathering. The notice should look something like this:

NOTICE OF SPECIAL MEETING FOR REMOVAL OF DIRECTORS
(AND AMENDMENT OF BYLAWS)

PLEASE TAKE NOTICE that a special meeting of shareholders of (*name of co-op corporation*) will be held at ______ Street, City of ______, State of New York, on ______, (Year), at ______ o'clock A.M. (or P.M.) for the following purposes:

1. To consider and vote upon a proposal that shareholders hear certain charges preferred against (*names of the directors*), determine whether the conduct of such directors was inimical to the corporation and, if so, to vote upon their removal and vote for election of their successors.

2. To consider and vote upon a proposal to amend the bylaws to provide that vacancies on the board of directors arising from the removal of a director by shareholders (or by resignation of a director

against whom charges have been preferred) may be filled, for the unexpired term, only by the shareholders.

This notice is being issued at the direction of (specify shareholders calling meeting), the persons calling the meeting.

Dated: ______, (Year).

____

Secretary

5. Battle with Proxies

Now it's time for real action. Together with the notice of the meeting, the secretary will send out proxies enabling those owners not able to attend to vote their consciences. As dissidents, you will want to include as part of the proxy a resolution for removal of those overreaching directors. (And, if necessary, one for amending the bylaws to enable you to elect their successors.) The usurpers no doubt will seek to solicit proxies in opposition to the resolution. So get ready for door-to-door combat. In the tradition of your best Girl Scout cookie–selling days, start knocking on doors and get your comrades to give you (or a fellow dissident) their proxies so you can vote out those power abusers at the meeting. The more proxies you get, the better. But even if you get the required majority, it's still not a sure thing—because owners can revoke their proxies (and be seduced by the incumbents) up until the actual time of the meeting.

The resolution you'll want your fellow shareholders to vote on will vary depending on the nature and degree of director wrongdoing. A sample follows to help you get started:

RESOLUTION OF SHAREHOLDERS REMOVING DIRECTOR(S)

Whereas (*insert name*), one of the directors of this co-op corporation, has on various occasions been derelict in his duties as a director and (select from, and elaborate on, one or more of the following, as appropriate)

has engaged in waste of corporate assets;

has usurped an opportunity that belonged to the co-op;

has used his position to advance his personal gain;

has breached his fiduciary duties to the co-op corporation.

It is hereby resolved by vote of shareholders representing at least (*number must meet bylaws' requirement*) percent of shares outstanding that (*name of director*) be, and hereby is, removed from the office of director.

And if you need to amend the bylaws, you can use the example below as a guide:

Resolution of Shareholders to Amend Bylaws

It is hereby resolved by vote of shareholders representing at least (*number must meet bylaws' requirement*) that the bylaws of the (*name of co-op corporation*) be, and hereby are, amended as follows:

1. There are to be deleted from the present bylaws the matter as follows:

   (Specify that portion of the bylaws that currently allows directors to fill board vacancies created by shareholder removal.)

2. There is to be added to Article ______ of the bylaws the following new matter:

   Any director may be removed from office for cause by the shareholders owning ______ percent of outstanding shares of the corporation at a meeting duly called for that purpose. The vacancy created by the removal of a director pursuant to the foregoing provision, or by resignation of a director against whom charges have been preferred, shall be filled only by vote of the shareholders. Said vote may be taken at the same meeting at which removal of the director was accomplished or at such later regular or special meeting as the shareholders may decide.

6. Showdown

Assuming you have done your job well, the sweet smell of success will fill the air by the appointed day. Don't do anything to screw it up. Although your inclination may be to ram through a vote and get rid of the miscreants, as a champion of the people you must let the democratic process proceed.

Failure to do so can cost you dearly—as a bunch of overanxious insurgents at one condo found out. Since they didn't give the accused board members an opportunity to meet the charges before the owners voted, the court said their removal was improper.[9]

So let the directors have their say. Odds are if they're really such bad dudes, the more they talk the deeper into a hole they'll dig themselves. Once they've uttered their last, it's time for a vote. If the requisite number of ballots (in person or by proxy) are cast for expulsion—the power grabbers are out and a new democratic day is about to dawn.

Even if the existing bylaws give the owners the exclusive right to vote to fill the vacancy, you'd better have an insurgent ready to fill the shoes of the ousted incumbent. Otherwise, you'll be left with an empty seat (that could have been warmed by a partisan)—and a Pyrrhic victory.

Tell It to the Judge

Finally, there's the judicial route to ouster. The Corporation Law (which, as you know, applies to co-ops) provides that holders of 10 percent of outstanding shares can bring an action to remove a director for cause.[10] If you can't get the necessary vote required by your bylaws for calling a special meeting and/or removal and you still believe that right is on your side, you can try this approach. Be realistic. Odds are if you can't persuade your fellow shareholders that the directors should go, you won't convince the judge. And you dissidents likely will be the ones funding the lawsuit while you wait to find out. But if you're determined, the law gives you the option.

13

Government in Action

COMMAND CONTROL

Once the board has been elected it's time to divide up the spoils—the seats of power. This usually is a back-room affair presided over by the directors with no shareholder (or unit owner) say. Your building's bylaws dictate the procedure. There's got to be a president, treasurer, and secretary to carry out necessary corporate functions. Vice presidential assignments often are handed out to all the rest so at least they have a title for their trouble. Although anyone who's gone through high school elections has a pretty fair notion of what these positions entail, a little refresher course (co-op style) will help you see how your real-life officers stack up against the ideal.

Commander in Chief

The president is like the CEO of a multimillion-dollar corporation—without a paycheck. Not a prescription for success, or one necessarily calculated to attract the brightest and the best, except to the extent that they want to defend against incompetent shareholder pretenders or protect their own investments. Before complaining about ego-inflated presidents, owners should keep in mind that putting up with a little attitude in exchange for service gratis is not such a bad deal.

The president bears ultimate responsibility for the physical, financial, and psychic well-being of the building. If your co-op or condo has a good commander in chief, she or he will have a vision for the future and a plan for how to get there. Long term, this means carrying out capital projects, seeing to preventive maintenance, spearheading legislative change, acting to ensure adequate cash flow (by refinancing, raising revenues, or other means), and identifying and taking advantage of corporate opportunities as they arise.

Short term, it involves supervising efficient building operations and keeping the peace among staff and shareholders. At any time it means being able to take the heat from whatever source (while staying cool) and to dish it out when necessary to light a fire under agents, lawyers, consultants, and the like to get things done. Since the commander is also the chief communicator at board and annual meetings and the most visible sign of authority, he or she is sure to be the target for anything that goes awry. Frankly, that's a lot to ask for no fee.

The point is somebody really needs to be minding the store, especially in co-ops and condos, where (as we'll see) most functions are outsourced to third parties. Although shareholders are quick to complain about the power of the office, they want it at their disposal twenty-four hours a day—on matters that are usually more plebeian than presidential. I've been asked to stoke the boiler, settle disputes over barking dogs, make flowers bloom (would that my powers were so supreme), command the holiday decoration patrol, stifle fledgling musicians, even advise on how to get Social Security payments.

Financial Officer

The treasurer is in charge of the building's dollars and cents. Above all, he has to know how to read, understand, and reconcile numbers. He should be reviewing the monthly financial statements to see that all is in order and to look over the bills, preferably *before* they're paid (though in most larger buildings the agent has authority to pay without prior approval up to several thousand dollars). If the building is lucky enough to have a reserve fund or other stash of cash, the treasurer should be checking out investment possibilities and getting maximum mileage with minimum risk. It's up to the treasurer to keep an eye on the co-op's outside auditor and to be sure the state and local authorities get their due (via the co-op's or condo's tax returns) on time and error free. He should also see to it that shareholders get the financial facts via an annual report (prepared by the building's outside accountant) and his own reprise, delivered at the annual meeting.

In the wake of financial scandals that have rocked corporate America, some have suggested requiring the creation of audit committees in co-ops and condos to interface between management and outside accountants, like those that exist in public companies. It's a good idea in theory, but in reality often it's hard enough finding *one* in-house financial expert, let alone a committeeful.

Keeper of the Flame

The secretary is the keeper of the corporate seal and the overseer (and executor) of most ministerial functions. He is responsible for taking and maintaining minutes of board and annual meetings, signing transfer documents, affixing the seal to official papers, witnessing signatures on legal documents, and filing forms with state and local agencies. It's up to the secretary to accept and file proxies for annual and/or special owner meetings.

In real-world corporations, these functions are often the province of the general counsel, who tends to be the most compulsive, detail-oriented individual in the organization. In co-ops and condos, it's usually the managing agent who is delegated to take care of these brain-numbing, but necessary, tasks (since no shareholder in his or her right mind would volunteer for such duty).

Would-Be Commanders

Then there are the vice presidents—whether one or many depends on how the board's philosophy plays out against individual director demands. If you're lucky, and their turf is well defined, they may actually lighten the presidential load. Assuming the sponsor is still around, it's a good idea to make one of its directors a vice president so he or she can sign official documents for the corporation without bestirring your directors in residence.

Now that you know the official version of the co-op/condo hierarchy, you might as well toss most of what you've just learned out the window. In real life it's often one or two directors who assume almost the total load.

CARRYING OUT THEIR MANDATE

So what should those directors (however many are on active duty) be doing? You probably know them best in their bad-cop incarnation: intruding into your individual affairs, telling you whether or not you can proceed with your alteration plans, when and what you have to do to sublease or sell, and how much you'll have to pay for these privileges of ownership. (All of which are dealt with in other chapters.) But if they're doing their jobs, they should also play a good-cop role—acting as financial watchdogs for the institution and you to protect and defend all the money they've used their police powers to collect from you (and other sources). This means maximizing cash (and other assets) within their control, spending wisely, and coming up with creative strategies to raise more.

Just because the financial management function seems so basic doesn't mean it's being carried out. The reason: it's up to the board to do it. Most other functions are delegated: the agent is charged with supervising daily operations; the staff with carrying them out; the auditor with uncovering accounting irregularities; the general counsel with keeping the building out of legal trouble. But it's up to your co-op or condo commanders themselves to see to it that the building is run like a model of financial efficiency—not a role that necessarily comes naturally.

Ordinary Spending

Top on the list is how the board is spending your money. You can get the plain facts (and an indication of board philosophy) by looking at the budget and financial statements. By now you know the essentials: Is the budget at break-even, does it reflect reality, how much are the co-op Big Three (real estate taxes, mortgage interest, and labor), and what's the board doing to keep expenses in check? (For a refresher, go back to chapter 3.)

The surest sign of potential trouble ahead is a spike in any of the trio or a sudden rise in legal costs, any of which can presage maintenance increases. Don't wait till the situation has gotten out of hand and your maintenance has gone berserk. At the first hint of surging costs, find out the reason. Maybe it's beyond the board's control, like the hike in real estate taxes over the past few years. Maybe it's a temporary phenomenon (the building got hit with a backlog of water bills). Or it could be a harbinger of increases to come—in which case, better find out cause and effect and what the board is doing about it.

Reality Check

In addition to budgeting the building's financial future, the board should conduct a six-month review to see how its predictions stack up against reality. That way it can make adjustments (by cutting spending or increasing maintenance) before things veer too far off course. Ask your board members if they are using such a backstop, especially if the gap between anticipated and actual expenses is growing.

Extraordinary Spending

Apart from everyday spending, there can be extraordinary expenditures for capital (or other) improvements. How your board handles these projects can secure (or sink) the building's financial future to say nothing of the impact on the fabric of shareholder society. Many of the specifics are discussed in other chapters, but here's a recap of what you should focus on.

First up: Does the job need doing or is it a testament to director self-glorification? Whether it's state-of-the-art elevators, a pristine roof, or a remodeled lobby, the issue is likely to spark shareholder debate. Though ultimately it's up to the board, no matter what you think. Assuming it decides to proceed, you (and it) should ask: Does the building have the money to do it? If not, where is the cash coming from—a maintenance increase, an assessment or a loan from some willing banker? While condo owners have more control over spending than their co-op cousins, however you slice it, the result is you'll be paying more. (How much more depends on how creative your board is in raising revenue.)

Manner of Spending

Wherever the money is coming from, the board's goal should be to get the best job for the least money. Sounds logical but it's not necessarily what happens. Several reasons may account for this lapse between the ideal and the real. Is the board doing some serious comparison shopping? Just as you wouldn't buy that new PC without checking out the competition, the board shouldn't proceed with anything big without banging a few heads together (financially not physically). It goes without saying that every project of consequence should be bid out to at least three to five contractors (not handed out Halliburton-style). And to help ensure that the bids are kosher, they should be opened by the managing agent *only* in the presence of a board member. Alternately, sealed bids can simultaneously be submitted to the agent and at least one director. Equally important to *how much* is being spent for the job is *who* is doing it. Is the board seeking out its own master builders or accepting without question those handed over by the managing agent? Such recommendations can be a double-edged sword: On the one hand the agent may know better than the board who's good and who's bad. On the other, the relationship with their chosen may be too close for comfort. Worse, is the job going to some board-friendly firm, creating a potential conflict of interest? (See chapter 9.)

While you probably don't know zip about building or bids (I didn't) that doesn't mean you should turn over total autonomy to board members. Ask them to take you through the selection process (from my experience something that rarely happens). Their answers will give a sense if the price (and process) is right.

Maximizing Reserves

In addition to spending, there's savings. Let's say your building, like you, is lucky enough to have socked away a tidy nest egg (a.k.a. a cash reserve fund) to secure its financial future and allow it to realize its capitalist dreams. What is your board doing to make the money grow? Is it languishing in the managing agent's chosen bank, rocketing to new highs (or plunging to new lows) in the stock market, being stashed in bank certificates of deposit or Treasuries, or getting stuffed under some board member's mattress? Bet you don't know.

Well, you ought to start paying attention as if that money were your own—because it is. Although it may be in the building's bank account, not yours, as a part owner in the enterprise you have a proportionate interest in the money. And you can be sure that if the board runs low on cash it'll come to you for more (via assessments or flip taxes or some other device). Don't wait till it gets to that point to focus on the building's finances. I'm not saying you have to become an investment guru, but you should be aware enough to know if what your board is doing makes good dollars and sense.

In most buildings the objective is maximum return with no risk. Add to this the need to have access to at least part of the money for upcoming projects, so that most investments must be relatively short-term. These safety and liquidity requirements limit the kinds of investments the board can make to a pretty small universe. Moreover, the rock-bottom interest rates of the past few years have put a crimp on returns no matter the strategy, though now that they're moving back up it's a good time to refocus.

Who's Calling the Shots?

The first thing you should ask is who's doing the investing and what qualifies that person. Don't assume it's the treasurer. Just because that's logical doesn't mean that's what's happening. There may be an investment committee appointed by the board or one of the directors may take the assignment on an ad hoc basis. It doesn't so much matter what the investor's title is so long as he or she has common sense and some basic investment savvy.

Beware of Wall Street types in your midst who volunteer their expertise—and their interest rate prognostication, letting the building's cash languish in a money market account until their crystal balls say the time is right to lock in a rate. If they could really time the market they wouldn't live in the building, they'd own it. Equally dangerous are those who follow the path of temptation and stampede with the bulls, convinced they can defy the avenging demons and get the building's money out before things turn sour. Most often, though, the problem with these self-appointed money managers is not hubris but sloth (or worse, ignorance).

What Are the Rules?

There are no rules dictating how the board should invest your money. Most co-op and condo bylaws give the directors power to establish reserves for capital purposes but don't say anything about what to do with the money once they have it. That doesn't mean you can't request that the board or a shareholder (or a condo unit owner) committee establish building investment policy and parameters. Especially if there's sentiment to get involved in anything other than risk-free investments, everyone should know and understand up front what they're in for.

In the absence of any written manifesto, the only thing reining in directors' "irrational exuberance" or other potentially costly tendencies is that good old fiduciary duty, which (as you know by now) requires the board to act in your best interests. When it comes to money, that means preserving the building's principal and achieving maximum return with minimum risk.

How to Make Your Building's Money Grow

You have probably figured out by now that investing the co-op's or condo's cash reserve fund involves a strategy more basic than one of those *Idiot's Guides*. In most buildings it's a steady stream of Treasuries and bank certificates of deposit (and maybe some high-grade commercial paper). But basic doesn't mean brain-dead. How your board buys these instruments, from whom, and what it pays, all affect the building's ultimate return.

Going with the Government

Take Treasuries. For those of you who belong to the motorcycle school of investing and wouldn't know a safe vehicle if you saw one, Treasuries are rock solid. They represent obligations from Uncle Sam to you, ranging in maturity from three months to thirty years, that pay interest that is state and local tax free while you wait. (For those who care, they're called bills up to one year, notes if they have maturities of two to five years, and bonds if they go out for a longer term.) Your board can buy them through banks, brokerage firms, or directly from the Federal Reserve Bank. If it buys through a middleman, the more it buys (usually in lots of at least $200,000) the less it pays and the higher rate of interest the building gets.

We started out as relative novices, instructing sponsor staff to purchase them through its bank, but they couldn't tell us the rate in advance so we skipped a step and bought directly from our bank—which is what many boards do. But no matter when or how much we bought, we always got less than the rates quoted in the *Wall Street Journal* for comparable maturities. It didn't take long to figure out (as our banker confirmed) that we'd do better going to the source and buying at government auction, which is what we do now. (Treasury auctions are held weekly for three- and six-month bills, monthly for one-year notes, and less frequently for longer maturities.)

By buying directly from the Fed, your board cuts out the intermediaries who shave off a sometimes not insignificant piece of the interest rate spread, allowing your building to keep more for itself. Your condo or co-op also will get the same interest rate as the big-time investors who bid competitively at auction for tens of millions of dollars' worth of these instruments, even though by comparison it's a relatively small-time operation. And your board will pay no fee for the privilege of buying direct, which it will if it goes through a middleman. There may be times when buying on the secondary market makes sense—if you want maturities not then being offered by the government or if there has been a favorable change in the interest rate environment that you want to lock in. But by and large, your board will do better for the building by buying at auction.

Banking on Dollars

When it comes to certificates of deposit (CDs) the differences can be even more dramatic depending on what your board does—or doesn't do. For the uninitiated, a CD is a bank deposit with a fixed interest rate for a finite period of time—from three months to five years, and sometimes beyond. Usually, the longer they go out, the higher the yield they offer. Whatever the current interest rate environment, banks, like supermarkets, offer promotions—CDs with above-market interest rates to acquire cash in maturities they need. The simplest thing is for the board to stuff any excess cash into the same bank where the building does its business. And that's what many boards do (often not even bothering to move it from a checking to a money market or a time-deposit account). But that route is guaranteed to produce subpar results because commercial banks almost always pay a lot less than savings banks. (And even among savings banks the differences are huge, depending on their interest rate profile and the CD special of the week.)

It was my then eighty-year-old mother who clued me in to the existence of "The List" every Thursday in *Newsday*, which gives rates for all the banks in the New York region (and is the favorite investment tool of the geriatric set). Using the List and letting my fingers (and the managing agent's feet) do the walking, our board began transferring the building's funds in troughs of $90,000 (to be sure all accounts, including accrued interest, stayed under the $100,000 FDIC insurance limit) to the banks with the best interest rates. On average, we consistently got at least a full percentage point higher than we would have if we had let the money sit in our regular bank.

To any board members out there thinking of giving this a try, let me caution you, banks don't make it easy for you to give them your building's money. Many demand that someone show up in the flesh, corporate documents in hand (a fax is not good enough), to open the account. Since the Patriot Act, it's gotten more complicated because now many banks demand that directors supply personal information to prove that the corporation's account is not a front for terrorist cash.

The end result was worth the effort (and it will be to you, too, assuming your building has cash on hand of any consequence). Using a strategy so simply any idiot savant could follow it, we wound up with a laddered portfolio of the highest-yielding CDs and Treasuries—earning us tens of thousands in extra interest.

To the Pros—And Back

Things have a way of coming full circle. In the first edition of *The Co-op Bible*, I recounted our adventures with the tassel-loafered investment pros, who drowned us with glossy brochures but hadn't heard of the List—and couldn't offer rates to beat those we were getting on our own. Finally, we found a broker who we thought would deliver, and, hoping to make life easier, put our building's money under one brokerage firm's roof. It worked for a while, but now that our wonder boy is long since gone, we're back to investing on our own—and getting better results. The only satisfaction from the financial round-trip is that our current Mr. Broker finally confessed that they couldn't match the rates on Main Street because brokerage firms rake in their money on fat commissions from stocks and mutual funds and aren't competitive on the slim margin, plain vanilla investments that co-ops and condos make.

But necessity is the mother of invention. With rates low, new investment vehicles have come to market: CDs of fixed maturity (usually at least five years) tied to the S&P Index or the Dow, that guarantee principal (and sometimes a small set amount of interest), and allow boards, risk free, to take advantage of potentially higher stock market returns. Your board has to shop around because the terms vary significantly: not all provide a full guarantee, and some accept only individual, not corporate, cash, but the potential return is worth the effort.

Investment Recap

The truth is, if your board is willing to commit the time, has common sense, and exhibits even a modicum of investment know-how, it probably can do better on its own (assuming it makes these kinds of elementary investments). It's easy to put together a laddered portfolio of Treasuries and CDs in a proportion dependent on their relative rates and your building's needs. For most co-ops, the state and local tax-free status of Treasuries is not of consequence as it is now pretty clear that they don't have to pay federal or state income tax on their interest income.[1] If your building is really loaded and your board wants to do a little legwork, it can go beyond the List and take a look online for the highest CD rates nationwide.

In the event that your board is more passive than aggressive, dealing with a money manager may be the best (indeed, only) alternative. The results will be reasonable (if unremarkable), but at least the money will be put to work. And it wouldn't hurt for the board to pull out the List every so often just to check how the investment "pros" are doing against your brownie-baking grandmother.

Making the Most of Your Money

In addition to getting the most out of your cash reserve dollars, your board should aim to get maximum results from the other cash within its control. I'm not suggesting any esoteric investment strategies—no derivatives, no hedges or straddles, no high-flying hog futures (even though once they made a mint for a certain First Lady who read the *Wall Street Journal*). Just the kind of basic things you would automatically do to manage your own money but that your board may not be doing with the building's cash because no one is thinking about it. Here are a few simple suggestions, culled from my building's own experience, that bolstered our co-op's bottom line and can do the same for yours.

A Clean Sweep

I'm sure most of you pride yourselves on putting your money to work. Whether you have one of those fancy-sounding cash management accounts or do it yourself, the idea is to sweep excess cash off the noninterest-bearing sidelines and put it to action in accounts with yield. It's no different for co-ops and condos. Although the board has to have enough money in the building's checking accounts to pay bills, there's no point in keeping extra dollars there earning nothing. In my building, first we consulted with our accountant to determine a safe level to keep on hand to cover monthly expenses. Then we established a threshold beyond which everything automatically is transferred to interest-bearing accounts. As elementary as this move was, it earned us extra thousands in interest each year.

No Mixed Money

You wouldn't think of pooling your hard-earned dollars in a bank account with strangers—and your building shouldn't, either. Yet it's not uncommon for sponsors and managers to combine money held in escrow for several of their buildings into one undifferentiated account with themselves as agents. This is bad business for several reasons. First, your building loses FDIC protection for the first $100,000 since its money is not broken out from the rest. Second, if the agent gets into financial trouble your co-op may have a harder time getting its money back if there are competing claims to the same account. On our accountant's advice, my building's board long ago decoupled the co-op's money and had it put in a stand-alone account.

Keep the Benefit of Your Bucks

Sometimes someone else is getting the benefit of your building's money and you or your board may not even know it. This can happen in different ways. Maybe as part of its management agreement your building is obligated to put its dollars in the bank with which the agent does business. Or it could be that the building's mortgage lender requires your co-op to deposit its real estate tax payments (which can amount to hundreds of thousands, if not millions, a year) into an escrow account in a bank it calls its own. These arrangements can pack a double whammy. Your building usually doesn't get any interest on these accounts, and the lender (or agent) gets the benefit (for its own business purposes) of having large compensating balances on deposit with its bank.

This is a mistake our board made. Our building converted with an underlying mortgage on which we had to make monthly payments into an escrow account in the bank of the sponsor (which held our mortgage). It was only when we got up to financial snuff and sought to transfer the money to interest-bearing accounts that we realized we'd been bested. The deal (right there in black and white for us to have seen had we known to look) was that we got *no interest* and the sponsor got the benefit of our balances sitting in its bank. We have since learned from the error of our ways. When we refinanced we took control of our escrow accounts, which we now invest exclusively for the building's benefit, adding thousands more a year to our coffers.

Unless your building is already locked in as we were, your board should see to it that the building reaps the benefit of its own dollars and doesn't let somebody else get the bang for its buck.

What's in a Name, or Whom Do You Trust?

Sounds like a simple enough question, but in the co-op or condo context, the issue is in whose name are your building's bank accounts? It's best to have operating accounts in the name of the co-op or condo itself, with signatory authority given to appropriate officers of the managing agent (so they can pay the bills) as well as to building officers (so they can move the money in case of a dispute with the agent). You should think twice about putting money in the name of the managing company "as agent for" the building because if the agent goes bust, your building may have problems getting its hands on its own cash. Or if the manager is fired, it may hang on to the account—for a while—to try to hang on to the building's business.

Reserve account funds, to which the managing agent doesn't need access for operational purposes, should be in the co-op's or condo's name with at least two of your building's officers serving as joint signatories, provided they are the kinds of neighbors you not only trust with your key but also with your cold cash, which is not always the case. Although problems are rare, the concern is real, which is why we tried to institute our own internal system of checks and balances by having the names of one sponsor director and one resident director on our accounts. But the sponsor's policy of self-protection is complete control or no control—not shared responsibility. Now that we've come of age and have the votes, our accounts each have a pair of resident directors as signatories (one looking over the other's shoulder).

THE SUBORDINATE RANKS

Even if your board is doing the building proud, it can't do it alone. It'll need an array of support personnel to follow through on the board's orders—from legal generals on down to foot soldiers. Who your directors engage and how they use their services can spell the difference between the success or demise of the board's regime.

Generals (Counsel, That Is)

At the top of the heap and reporting directly to the directors is the general counsel—usually brought in to keep the building and the board out of trouble. Odds are you don't know the jumble of names that your co-op's or condo's firm goes by, and even if you did it wouldn't mean much (unless you happen to be one of the brethren). I'm not saying you have to get up close and personal with your building's legal watchdogs. But for your own benefit as an owner (paying your proportionate share of attorneys' fees), you need to know a few legal ABCs: Who are these pin-striped warriors? How did they get appointed? Are they allied or independent? What are the terms of their engagement? And, perhaps most important, what are they doing?

Mea Culpa

Okay, I admit it, I was wrong the first time around, or, at least, unfair to the lawyers, an opinion that, I suspect, was colored by my experience with counsel during our building's conversion. So I hereby recant. The truth is, as in any profession, there are competent (and not so competent) practitioners, co-op and condo lawyers included. The real problem is not the lawyers, but the system (a subject deserving its own discussion, in chapter 19), which neither fosters efficient use of counsel nor generally allows them to perform to best advantage. Unlike corporate counsel, who are typically viewed as an integral part of the management team, attorneys for co-ops and condos are often brought in on an ad hoc basis, a kind of piecemeal service that may prevent them from getting an overall picture of building operations that is necessary to represent the best interests of *all* owners, rather than the sometimes individual agendas of boards.

The reasons are both economic and philosophical. Directors want to hold down costs. Moreover, unschooled in legal logic, they don't always know when to call in the hired guns, with the result that they may under- (or over-) utilize them, either of which can cause trouble.

Give Them Assignments That Make Sense

How the board uses its legal firepower is as much a reflection of its managerial ability as of the competence of the counsel it retains. Since you're not privy to all the business transactions the board engages in and it doesn't have to consult you before it brings in the legal brigade, how do you know if its response to a particular situation is rational or based on raw emotion? A quick way to get a pretty good idea is to check out those annual financial reports. If the line for legal expenditures has gone from just plain zero to a many-zeroed number, your antennae should go up. Ask the directors at the next annual meeting (or before) to tell you why—there may be a legitimate reason. But if you keep your eyes and ears open there are plenty of telltale signs all around every day to indicate whether the board is using its legal army strategically.

1. Who's In Charge

The first thing your board has to get straight is who's who in the attorney/client relationship. It seems self-evident, but it's not. The lawyer for a co-op or condo may find herself answerable to a single director (who has assumed de facto control), a multitude of disparate voices, or a surrogate director in the person of a managing agent, often making it difficult for her to figure out who the true client is. On the other side of the divide, there may be a power or comprehension gap among board members, raising the danger that directors (without realizing it) abdicate their roles to outside counsel, turning them into decision makers rather than advisors.

2. No Celebrity Appearances

Assuming your directors are clear on how the relation should work, when do they use it? Some boards bring out the big guns at annual meetings to wave the flag and rally the troops. Accountants usually show up as part of their regular engagement. But most by-the-clock lawyers require an appearance fee. If there's dissension in the ranks, a contested election ahead, or some specific issue that requires their expertise, by all means have them come. Otherwise, it may not be necessary. Thanks to the relative quiescence among our constituents we have managed to conduct our meetings lawyer free.

3. No High-Priced Prose

Every building has its share of social misfits who refuse to comply with the norms of communal living—and who need to be not so subtly reminded that sometimes conformity is a virtue. Maybe they don't understand the function of that chute in the compactor room or they forget that the lobby is not a roller rink and that the corridors are not dog runs. If your offending neighbors are receiving missives complaining of conduct on stationery bearing some hydra-headed firm name, you know the lawyers have been called in to reform them—not necessarily the best way to go. A lawyer's presence increases the stakes and the price—for letter-writing campaigns that your board and agent should be able to handle on their own.

When the offenses get to the point that they potentially endanger the welfare of the building and its residents (and the need exists to make a record prior to terminating the perpetrator), it's time for your board to bring in the legal scriveners. We called them in once to send a warning to a shareholder after billiard balls had been spotted flying out of his apartment window into the night (thankfully, missing a passing patrol car). Although it cut against my principles to pay for a letter I (or the building's agent) could write, the in terrorem effect of that legal letterhead worked like a charm, and no projectiles have been spotted since.

4. No Grudge Matches

Then there's the problem that occurs when reason is dwarfed by a personal vendetta or by the unrelenting (though irrational) need to be right. As a litigator, I'm embarrassed to admit I've been the hired gun for corporate CEOs who would rather fight to the death (leaving destruction and piles of legal bills in their wake) than settle with their rivals for a pittance. The same mind-set has been known to take hold of boards, especially if a shareholder does something to push the wrong buttons or challenges its authority—whether violating a House Rule, ignoring sublet restrictions, or refusing to pay a penalty. One co-op board achieved the status of New York lore by spending $70,000 in legal fees over a dispute with a shareholder who refused to install window guards that cost $900.[2] I'm not saying the board should have sat back and done nothing, but as with any crime, the response should be proportionate to the offense.

My advice to members of the rank and file is to take action at the first sign of your board's battle cry, or before you know it the directors may have you fighting (and funding) the next Thirty Years' War. As soon as you sense a whiff of litigation in the air, find out what it's for and whether it makes any sense. (Trust me, your layman's instincts are probably just as good as the lawyer's.) If you conclude that the board's response is rational, get it to give you a legal budget so you know how much you'll be contributing to the war chest. If not, it may be time to vote in new building leadership before the situation gets out of control. At a minimum, you should require that the board provide regular reports from the field and impose reasonable limits on its military budget.

Sometimes it's not the board but a shareholder who's the warlord. (Inevitably, a resident attorney who can pursue a cause without cost.) It's harder to limit the board's use of counsel when it's responding to the attack of an aggressor. Take the case of the Park Avenue lawyer who decided to target his co-op. For years, he refused to pay maintenance and assessments, claiming his posh digs were rendered uninhabitable by a variety of urban plagues (seeping odors, creeping roaches, leaking water, invading rodents, excessive heat). He waged a war of attrition, with board efforts at negotiation going nowhere. But after four years of fighting, the court ordered him to pay all that he owed and to reimburse the co-op for the nearly $400,000 in legal bills it had chalked up in the process.[3]

It's hard to say whether logic prevailed on either side. And this case should serve as a reminder to you all that whether the board is using counsel for offensive or defensive purposes, it's doing so with your cash (though insurance ultimately may kick in for some or all of it). So you'd better see to it that it abides by the rule of reason (whether it takes a shareholder resolution or revolution) to achieve that end.

5. Legal Necessity

All this is not to say that there aren't times when the board really needs to bring in a lawyer, more now than ever as managing buildings becomes increasingly complex and subject to legal regulation. Counsel should be involved in any major corporate transaction. When we refinanced our underlying mortgage, and whenever we engage in capital projects, we use counsel to be sure the building is protected from the fine contractual print—and so should your board. Any change to governing documents (bylaws or proprietary leases) is easier and more likely to get done right if there's an attorney around to follow the legal rules. And if there's even a hint of a dispute that could ripen to full-scale litigation—a rejected purchaser, a renovation contretemps, a turned-down sublet—the best way to dissipate it is to bring in the big guns to serve as a buffer between board and shareholder.

6. Going Direct

The co-op or condo's counsel deals with the board as your elected representative—not you individual shareholders, who in many buildings amount to hundreds of voices. But there are exceptions to every rule and circumstances where it may be okay for you, as an owner, to call direct. Let's say you and your fellow shareholders want to mount a dissident slate. As we've seen (chapter 9), the board legally has the power of incumbency on its side, and there's nothing you can do about it. But no matter who's running, it's in the best interests of *all* owners that elections be conducted in a procedurally fair way. If you don't believe that's happening, before engaging in legal battle with the board, you might contact the building's counsel to see if she can help implement appropriate procedures. Or if you believe any of your directors is engaged in wrongdoing (not just something you disagree with), reporting the transgression to the building's counsel may be the quickest way to get attention and action.

Get the Right Generals

Now that you know what they should do, the question is where to find them. A few big-name firms have practitioners in their real estate departments who represent co-op and condo boards. Then there are smaller boutique firms that do nothing but. Price is often a function of firm size; the larger the firm, the higher the hourly fees tend to be. In general, rates at small co-op boutiques can range from around $175 an hour for associates to $400 plus for partners, while at larger firms they can run $500 (or more) an hour for the top brass.

In addition to how much it pays, your board should know how (and when) to pay it. Many lawyers request retainer agreements that require payment of a specified amount up front, monthly advances and/or payment of lawyers' legal fees if they have to sue to get paid, though my building's board has been more comfortable paying as we go.

There's no magic formula for ferreting out competent counsel. As with the search for any professional it's seek (through persistence, references, and trial and error) and ye shall, hopefully, find. (If I name names, I'll only get myself in trouble.) My building has used several outfits, depending on the nature of the problem, and always remains on the lookout.

Special Forces

In addition to general counsel, your board may need special counsel for specific missions. You don't have to (and certainly wouldn't want to) get caught up in all the details. But you should know enough so you can tell if your board is recruiting and using its services to maximum advantage.

Certiorari Corps

Every year (in January), as co-op owners in New York know, the city in its wisdom decides how much your building is worth and affixes an "assessed value" to it. This number (together with the tax rate) determines how much real estate tax your co-op must pay. We're talking real money here—hundreds of thousands, if not millions, of dollars a year (often the biggest single item in the budget). It's a case of taxation by stealth. Unlike homeowners—or even your condo-owning cousins, who get individual bills—you may not even realize you're paying real estate tax (or if you do, how much) because it's billed as an undifferentiated part of your maintenance. If no one complains, the authorities are only too happy to increase the value of your building (and hence the tax you pay) every year. To stop this upward spiral, there are legal minions whose sole professional function in life is to battle the bureaucracy to get the amount of assessments reduced. Since they get paid only if they succeed (usually up to 25 percent of the savings), there's no downside to bringing in these so-called certiorari attorneys.

Your board should use them to file an annual challenge—and if it's smart, it should also demand a volume discount, as we did, because often they have to file several times over just to get the tax down to where it was before they started. Both the board (and you) should be aware that the whole process is an annual ritual, with the lawyers the surest winners. Each year the city raises your co-op's assessment (or rate); the lawyers get it lowered (if you're lucky); and get a fee for their efforts, so even if the co-op wins, it loses, because it realizes only a part of the savings. Then the entire cycle is repeated (how many times, not even your lawyer knows for sure).

Rebate Brigade

Then there's another branch of the legal service whose mission is to get a good chunk of your money back if you make capital improvements to the building. New York City gives a gift to encourage upgrading the premises, but only a tiny band of the bar (called J-51 lawyers, after the name of the filing) know the rules on how to collect it. Let's say your building just put in new windows or is modernizing the elevators, projects that can amount to millions. If your board knows what it's doing, it should bring in one of the J-51 crew when it starts to see if the project can reap these bonus rebate dollars, which are deductible as an offset against the co-op's real estate tax bill over approximately eleven years.

Improvements made within three years of the building's going co-op automatically get this windfall. After that there are a number of hurdles to jump before your building can lay claim to the cash and, as discussed above, with apartment prices sky-high, many buildings have priced themselves out of the benefit. (No need to bore you with the details; that's what the lawyers are for.) They collect a fee only if your co-op gets the cash, so there's no reason for your board not to use them.

Operating Lieutenants

Although the lawyers should keep the board (and building) out of serious trouble, day-to-day duty is handed over to the operational forces, better known as managing agents (unless your building is self-managed, a rarity in all but the smallest buildings). In case you're wondering whose yours is, just check out that brass placard that's been plastered to the building's facade or affixed (less obtrusively) to a wall in one of the elevators announcing to the world at large that so-and-so has taken control of your territory.

Getting Their Marching Orders

The first thing you have to understand is that managing agents don't really "manage"—at least not in the white-collar McKinsey & Company corporate sense of the word, a mistake I made coming from a law firm environment. It took a while for expectation and reality to come to a modus vivendi, but I think I've finally figured out what the agents are supposed to do. Here's the deal: They screen, but don't necessarily find, staff recruits (though the board should make the actual decisions on hiring and firing), and ensure that those enlisted perform up to snuff. This means the buck stops with them when it comes to building cleanliness, though you have to understand that their hands are tied by union rules. You pay the bills, but they write the checks for items both big—such as payroll, taxes, and mortgage—and small—such as cleaning agents, rock salt, and hand tools. But don't count on them to shop around for the best deal or the cheapest price. They collect the maintenance and usually are empowered to unleash the wrath of the law on nonpayers. They prepare annual budgets (for board approval) and keep directors up-to-financial-date with monthly statements. They see to the health and welfare of the physical plant and all the systems we take for granted (the water flows, the AC purrs, the electricity lights). They field complaints from shareholders and owners and, theoretically, solve them. They handle a myriad of ministerial corporate functions from processing governmental filings to keeping co-op records to administering board and shareholder meetings to implementing sales and sublets. All this is spelled out in a management agreement between the agent and your board, so if you're really a glutton for punishment, ask to see it.

If the managing agent is doing his job, you probably won't notice his existence; you'll merely experience a subliminal recognition that everything seems as it should be. In my building, it's only when things go awry (in someone's own apartment or the building at large) that shareholders call me in search of the agent's phone number so they can register their complaints. Assuming they've got a legitimate beef, I encourage them to voice their protest.

As an owner, be thankful you don't have to get involved in the daily dealings with the agent that the board does. But that doesn't mean you're absolved from your duty to know the management basics so you can tell if your agent was properly selected and is carrying out his mission.

Nature of the Relationship

There's a delicate balance between boards and managing agents because, by definition, boards are monogamous, devoted only to their own building, while agents are polygamous, responsible for serving multiple residential mistresses. The way the system works, agents simply don't have the time to fully commit to any one building. If the board of any building asks too many questions or makes too many demands (even if they're in the best interests of the co-op or condo), the agent has less time for the others—a scenario that can lead to tension in the relationship. Cracks are even more likely to develop if the agent has an autonomous rental mind-set and isn't used to answering to directors (or anyone else), but to getting the job done the quickest (though not necessarily the most efficient) way.

Whatever firm your board selects, it shouldn't tie the knot for more than a few years at a time and should leave itself an out, given the changing realities in the industry and the marketplace. Either party should be able to say good-bye to the other on thirty or sixty days' notice. Change for improvement is fine. But beware boards that succumb to the presidential syndrome and make a clean sweep of managing agents (and everyone else) to signal their new administration's arrival.

Beating the Bushes

Assuming your board is legitimately in search of new agents, what should it (and you) be looking for? For shareholders with short memories, about a decade ago the Manhattan District Attorney conducted an investigation into corruption among property managers that led to more than eighty indictments for bribery and extortion, and lots of guilty pleas. As a result, a few firms collapsed, some were gobbled up by other outfits, and many cleaned up their act on their own. More recently, similar investigations have hit many roofing companies for engaging in kickbacks. In the wake of all this, there's been lots of reform talk, from mandatory licensing for agents to requiring that companies pass outside financial inspection, but little in the way of concrete action. Given past history, the first (and foremost) qualification your board should be sure of is the irreproachable integrity of the managing agent—not only for your on-site operative but also for the institutional culture of which he is a part. If there's a hint of scandal, stay away.

How do you or, more precisely, your board know? It's not easy. The industry has lots of small players that lack many of the controls that are standard in corporate America. Talk to fellow directors at other buildings to see if their experience has been good, bad, or, more likely, in between. Assuming your board is satisfied with its accountant, he can point it in the right direction. Our accountant has declined to work for co-ops or condos whose agents lack satisfactory financial controls and could compromise the building's audit. If the accountant stays away, so should the board. Since most management firms are not public companies, it's hard to get reliable financial (and other) information. Your board can hire a corporate type P.I., but such intelligence collectors don't come cheap, as we learned when we tried to hire one.

There are plenty of active duty agents to choose from—ranging from pint-sized platoons that control a handful of buildings (with a few hundred apartments) to a few battalionlike outfits in charge of tens of thousands of apartments. Conquest and consolidation are coming to the fragmented co-op management ranks, with a few relatively mega-sized companies attempting to assume command of the largest buildings and bring corporate economies of scale to the residential set.

Size alone is not what counts, though the outfit has to have enough critical mass to provide backup support to your operating lieutenant. What's important is not just the absolute number of buildings the firm has conquered but how many posts each agent is assigned. If your co-op or condo is one of those towering cities within four walls, you may have an operative on location full-time. But usually the agent has to do duty for six or seven (or, increasingly, more) buildings. My advice is to stay away from any firms that spread their agents too thin.

How much should your building pay to keep its operations under control? Expect to pay anywhere from \$325 to \$1,000 per unit. The reason for the discrepancy is that the more units in the building, the less per unit the firm can afford to charge. So the fee for a Park Avenue prewar with fifty palatial apartments could be \$50,000 (50 × \$1,000) while that for a two-hundred-unit high-rise probably would be closer to \$80,000 (or only \$400 per unit). If your directors are smart, they will set a cap on annual increases, so if they choose to renew they won't have to negotiate all over again. My advice to you (and your board): Don't settle for grade-B operatives—skimp on something less strategic.

Approving the Operatives

Once you've got your agent trained to meet your requirements (not an easy task), you don't want him deserting the fold and taking his (and your building's) intelligence to another co-op camp. Yet sometimes it's in his firm's interest to transfer your operative to another assignment or promote him within to a corporate post. Although such shifts serve the management company's purposes, they may run counter to those of your co-op or condo. To prevent this from happening or to protect your building's interests if it does, your board should insist on the right to approve any new operative—and, if it doesn't, the right to terminate the relationship, a lesson we learned from hard experience.

Reporting to His Superiors

Should you find yourself in need of your agent's services (whether to fix that leak in your bathroom or to facilitate a sublease application), be sure to get the chain of command straight before you communicate. As part owner (and payer of his salary) you're the boss, and he reports to you. No more assuming the supplicant's stance, passively waiting to attract his attention. There's no need to overtly pull rank, just let your demeanor bespeak your superior station. And if he doesn't respond to (not necessarily resolve) your problem within twenty-four (or, max, forty-eight) hours, go straight to the top and tell the board president—who's in a position to decommission him if he chalks up too many demerits.

Paymaster General

With the agent paying out the money that you're pouring in, somebody has to be watching where it goes, and the one who comes closest is the accountant brought in by the board from the outside to keep an eye on the building's finances. (If perchance your building doesn't have one, you know right off the bat something's wrong.)

The accountant's task is to check out those financial statements you receive each year to be sure they accurately reflect the building's cash flow, its revenues and expenses, and its cash in the bank—and that they are not some figment of a director's imagination (or, worse, defalcation), though ultimate responsibility lies with the board. To do this, he'll look on a sample basis at some of the backup documents to see if the transactions reported are real. He'll talk to management. He may communicate with selected building vendors to see if their services and fees are as stated or are otherwise. Or with banks to be sure the building's got its balances right. He'll ask for representations from the co-op's (or condo's) lawyers that there are no lawsuits being fought that could "materially" affect the building's condition. (Having responded to these letters in my professional capacity, I can tell you they're an exercise in who can outdisclaim whom.) And after all's said and done, if everything meets with his approval, he'll bless the statement (in accountant-speak, give an unqualified opinion).

In response to the changed regulatory environment, accountants recently have come out with a new standard applicable in connection with auditing co-ops and condos that requires more detailed financial reporting up the chain of command in an effort to ferret out irregularities before they become major problems. It's too soon to tell what, if any, effect it will have on the transparency and accuracy of building finances, but it's a step in the right direction.[4]

Probably the only contact you'll have with your numbers man will be to receive his financial benediction in front of those annual reports. And he'll receive you live and in person at the shareholders' meeting, where you can ask about anything in the statements (assuming you've read them).

Foot Soldiers

Last, but certainly not least, are the foot soldiers, those uniformed sentries who stand guard at the door (protecting us from the evils that lurk outside—and the occasional errant deliveryman), the porters assigned to render the premises spit-and-polish clean, and the maintenance crew (a.k.a. handymen, in civilian parlance) responsible for keeping the building (and your apartment) systems in shipshape order. Although on the organizational chart these recruits may be at the bottom of the chain of command, as anyone familiar with co-op or condo living knows, they are the real power brokers.

Want to know when the apartment next door is going on the market and for how much? They have the answer. Want to keep your affairs (so to speak) under wraps—whether that means sneaking up an illegal washer/dryer or an illicit lady of the night? They know who's been naughty or nice. Want to get something done in your apartment, legit or not? They control the how, when, and who (and have good memories, to boot). So it's not surprising when it comes to enforcing the rules against them that building commanders and their constituents display a schizophrenic attitude—wanting to maintain good order in the ranks without upsetting the status quo.

There's no surer way to ferret out your board's political disposition than by observing how it deals with staff problems—from hiring and firing to everyday discipline. I know some buildings where the board governs with heart more than head, and wouldn't let anyone go even if he were an ax murderer, and others where the directors cut the staff no slack, banning them from watching TV during lunch.

I'd say we're more like the New Democrats—fiscally conservative but with a social conscience, one that I can assure you has been tested. We've had calls appear on our phone bills to the far corners of the earth, from Malta to South America, for what building purpose one can only imagine. We've had staff try to dictate to the board how to manage the building, who to hire for what, and those who ooze obedience to our face but plot to stab us in the back.

Let me state for the record: most of our crew (and I assume yours) are longtime and top-notch and have gone beyond the call of duty. I've had staffers bring wound dressing to save my dying trees, risk bodily injury to hang precariously positioned paintings, and haul bookcases (that missed fitting into the elevator by an inch) up ten flights of stairs. But when problems arise (such as those discussed below), the system (that is, the union contract) dictates the solution—it's not necessarily the way our board would choose to go, but we have no choice.

Whether your board opts to go by the letter of the law or grants staffers more latitude is a function of its (and your) philosophy. Before you can decide if it's doing the right thing, you need a short lesson is union basics.

Reverse Command

Although the union contract won't make its members rich, it gives them lots of latitude. They have vacation days, birthdays, doctor days, sick days, and self-selected days that inevitably fall on either side of a weekend. I can handle that—everyone's entitled to a break from the routine. But on top of that they have a sabbatical policy (more generous than any academic one I know) that allows them to take up to six months every five years—no matter if their departure throws the co-op or condo into chaos.

We had one staffer who insisted on taking the waters at a spa in midwinter (because it was off-season and off-price), leaving us with no one to stoke the boiler in case of emergency. Three times he demanded, three times he was asked to delay till spring thaw. No matter. He flew off to sunny Florida without so much as bidding adieu to the board or sending us a postcard with regards (or regrets). Instead, the board got a letter from his doctor, after the fact, advising us that the sojourn was a little medically necessary R & R. Another staffer took a leave to visit folks back home, committing in writing to return on a specific date some months in the future. He didn't show up on the appointed date—or for weeks thereafter, leaving us to wonder if he was MIA. When he finally reappeared and the board talked termination, we got another medical note, this one advising us that the delay was due to a broken body part.

Our board has come to expect that staff leaves are likely to be extended by some medical malady. Since illness (be it psychic, pseudo, or sometimes real) is an independent category for up to a year's leave according to the union contract, you can see the problem. And it's compounded by an underground brotherhood of doctors that exists to serve building staff. We've received medical excuses ranging from emotional distress to inability to perform spousal services to diseases of unknown origin. They come from a creative (though I wonder if licensed) crop of physicians. And when that well dries up, then we get letters from sympathetic in-house shareholder shrinks anxious to help and unaware of the consequences of their kindness. So long as there's a "doctor's" note (no matter he's not a Harvard or even a Guadalajara grad), there's little the board can do by way of discipline. (Believe me, I've checked this out.) So you may as well grin and bear it—and wait for some misdeed catastrophic enough for termination, which, as you'll see, is not an easy proposition.

Lifetime Tenure

Ever wonder why that doorman who could pass for Rip Van Winkle is still on the job? Or the porter who never met Mr. Clean? Or the handyman who isn't handy? The answer is simple: it's next to impossible to get rid of them (something I learned the hard way and want to help you and your board avoid).

It takes professors five years to get tenure, lawyers closer to eight. But under union rules building staff attain that protected status in sixty days. (Supers get it in six months.) This means that for the first two months they're on probation and the board can remove them for *no* reason or *any* reason. By the time they've registered in your consciousness (and the sixty days has passed), they're in—for life. The only way to separate them is if they're not doing their duty *and* the board can document their dereliction (as lawyers would say, prove cause exists).

Take it from me, this is no easy task. Just think of the pile of evidence against O. J.—and he walked—and you'll get a sense of the burden the board faces in trying to prove a staffer is fit to be fired. We had one character who didn't clean much *on* the job but arm-twisted shareholders to let him clean *off* the job in their apartments (for a fee, of course). Neither delivering packages nor getting cleaning to its rightful owners was high on his agenda. But the coup de grâce came early one morning when a board member found him fast asleep at the door—so deeply had he dozed off that not even the director's return roused him. Still, we were advised we might not have enough to terminate him. So we deputized our super (back from the spa) to act as P.I. and some months later at 5 A.M. he caught the perpetrator in action (more accurately, inaction) and snapped a Polaroid of the sweet dreamer. With this photographic smoking gun in hand (to say nothing of his prior MO), we terminated him.

Although our staffer couldn't wield a mop, he sure could work the legal system. He sued for unemployment compensation. He filed a union grievance demanding reinstatement. He commenced a civil rights action claiming discriminatory discharge. And if he could he would have embarked upon multidistrict litigation.

Our board fought back. We succeeded in getting those unemployment checks cut off and in the process got the judge to rule that our man was discharged for cause—a finding that undercut his other claims. The board turned out for his arbitration in full force, accompanied by counsel, agent, and assorted attachés. (Such a show of strength, we had been advised, was necessary to prove we meant business and to secure a modicum of justice in this less-than-objective tribunal.) Instead we were left to cool our heels as our worthy opponent maneuvered for delay. The third time we finally had a showdown and ultimately worked out a deal that resulted in the staffer's departure—and his return nevermore.

From Induction to Separation

The lesson to be taken from this saga is that your board should recruit with care lest you all be stuck with unwanted staffers. If despite the board's best efforts separation becomes necessary, a quick surgical strike is better than protracted warfare. But if your board has to do battle, it had better be prepared to fight fire with fire if it hopes to prevail. These are the rules your board (and you as owners) should follow for keeping good order and discipline among the foot soldiers.

1. Leader of the Pack

Above all else, the board has to bring in a staff sergeant (a.k.a. superintendent or resident manager) who is up to the task of turning a many-tongued crew into a cohesive multinational force fit for building service. Having lived through three different leadership styles, I can tell you this assignment matters. For years we had an ex-KGB sergeant who ruled with fear and intimidation, which he applied to staff and residents alike. When our commandant finally headed out (for the retirement hills) shortly after the building went co-op, everyone on the board agreed we needed a reprieve. So we engaged a mild-mannered super with a poet's soul who promised to use psychology instead of scare tactics. Whenever a problem arose (whether it was a broken elevator or burst pipes), he penned (and posted) advisory verses, but rarely got around to fixing the situation about which he had waxed poetic. He didn't last long.

I think we finally got it right—a super who relates to the residents (goes for acupuncture and reads *The New York Times*) now keeps the peace among a staff that hails from many continents and maintains the premises in top working order. Unless your board gets the top staffer right, the rest won't really matter.

2. An Ounce of Prevention

Hiring competent staff to complement the super's command is not easy. Since union members get the same pay whatever building they're at and no matter how long they've been there, whether four or forty years (except for summer replacements and new recruits), there's no incentive for them to move. To the contrary, the longer they've been stationed at the same post, the larger their tips are likely to be. So unless they're green recruits, your board should be suspicious about why they're switching.

It's okay for agents to identify and screen candidates (usually they have piles of well-thumbed résumés). The super, if he's plugged into the underground network, may come up with more promising plebes. But board members familiar with the building's dynamics had better interview the candidates and make the final cut. Only they can tell if the latest arrival will promote peace or spark an international incident.

3. No Second Chances

As far as I'm concerned, the union contract forces boards to be more coldhearted than compassionate. There's no room for second chances if the new recruits haven't proved their mettle within the first sixty days. After that they're untouchable unless you can prove sufficient cause for removal. This usually means spending the next year documenting (and living with) their deficiencies and creating a paper trail befitting some high-stakes litigation. So when in doubt, get them out—the faster the better. And even if the sixty-day period has elapsed, sooner is still better than later. The longer they stick around, the greater sympathy their departures will generate among the arbitrators and the more it will cost to remove them.

4. Keep a Dossier

Having come of age during the Vietnam era, when the CIA was busy compiling dossiers on many a conscientious objector, I have a natural distrust of the process. But if you want your board to stand a chance in ridding your building of incompetent recruits you have no choice but to keep files on them. I'm not saying this should be a covert operation. To the contrary, the supposed infraction should be spelled out (by the super or the agent) and staffers should be given an opportunity to read and respond to any charges. Nor am I suggesting that every misdemeanor is grounds for removal. But the day may come when some misdeed is the straw that breaks the camel's back—galvanizing the board into action. Unless those other shorter straws previously have been drawn and documented, you may be stuck with the offender for a long time to come.

5. *Go on Record*

When it comes to staff removal, what shareholders (and unit owners) have to say counts the most with arbitrators. They figure you're paying those salary checks, so you're entitled to service. In order for your complaints to be heard they have to be in writing and they must be added to those overflowing dossiers. As a board member, I have to spend hours, sometimes days, whiling away my time at disciplinary hearings. And I take the heat for any staff problem. So, as far as I'm concerned, the least shareholders can do is give board members the ammunition necessary to win.

But my experience is that it's not easy to get. Sometimes shareholder silence is a matter of principle. Standing up for the (perceived) underdog is what comes naturally. It's okay to grumble to me that the sergeant at arms is asleep at the door, but it's bad form to offend the offender. Some shareholders carry this philosophy to the extreme, taking on the perpetrator's cause, pleading for clemency while complaining to me of incompetence. My rule to shareholders: Don't complain to the board about staff if you won't go on record.

6. *Petition If You Must*

Some shareholders take things a step further and rally behind the endangered staffer, circulating petitions to save his sinecure (which, in any event, have no legal effect). In case you're thinking of going this route, a few words of advice. First, get the facts before you forge ahead. Just because that doorman gives you a cheery hello doesn't mean he's doing his job. We've had those in our ranks who excelled at neighborly chitchat but not at security clearance, allowing unannounced visitors, unauthorized move-ins—and more—to pass through our portals. I'm not saying you owe the board blind allegiance, but assuming they've been doing a competent job, give them the benefit of the doubt and ask why they want him out. Since they'll have to sit at the hearing (maybe for days on end), chances are there's a reason. But based on more than one petition that's circulated in my building, it's generally fight first, facts later—not a winning strategy. When the facts finally out, the movement falters and those who gave uninformed assent are forced to recant.

7. *Or Go Full Throttle*

Of course if you really think the board has done wrong in firing that staffer and are willing to go to the mat, you can challenge its decision in court. One group of dissident shareholders did just that, getting an injunction against board action. No matter, the board tried to evict the super from his apartment. But he fought back—and won—(at least temporarily) until the shareholders could be heard on the subject.[5]

8. Be Prepared to Do Battle

Unless the staffer is prepared to go quietly into the night (which is rarely the case), your board had better be ready to go the distance if it decides separation is necessary. Papering the evidence trail is only the first step. Next it has to get a lawyer to take on the case. In most instances of union arbitration this doesn't mean seeking out a member of the co-op bar, it means going to the Realty Advisory Board (RAB). Assuming your building has paid its annual dues (which amount to several hundred dollars), the RAB is obliged to provide your co-op or condo with counsel. (The staffer's union dues buys him counsel, though most recruits know their rights better than their appointed attorneys.) As I learned, not all RAB lawyers are equal, which means your board had better know whom to ask for.

Even if your board has snagged the right legal eagle, if it wants to win it had better arrive en masse. As I hope my true-life story of the staffer who worked the system (and us) shows, it's not enough that your co-op's agent shows up on behalf of the building and you. Sitting there all day is part of his job (for which he's getting paid). Arbitrators won't take his story as seriously as what your directors have to say, since they've been dragged away from other gainful employ to say it. They figure if board members are mad enough to take off—and show up—the dismissal must have merit. Better still if a few shareholders make an appearance (in person or by affidavit) to testify, although from my experience getting them to come is not easy.

And even if the board does everything right, your building probably will still wind up paying a price to forgo the risk of an irrational decision and be able peaceably to get rid of someone who deserved to go—long ago.

Now that you know the facts, there's no reason to guess how your board is doing. The following quiz will give the answer. Take it to determine if owners can sit back or the time for action is at hand.

HOW DOES YOUR BOARD RATE?

Planning the Future	**Yes**	**No**
• Does it prepare an annual budget?	____	____
• Does it provide you with a copy?	____	____
• Do its estimates comport with reality?	____	____
• Does it check to make sure with a six-month review?	____	____
• Does it distribute annual audited financials on time that accurately reflect the building's condition?	____	____
• Does it keep maintenance constant or increase it modestly in line with inflation?	____	____

	Yes	No
• Does it take advantage of refinancing opportunities to bring mortgage costs down?	____	____
• Does it look for ways to raise revenue or cut costs (without cutting service)?	____	____
• Does it engage a CPA to audit the co-op's (or condo's) finances?	____	____

Managing the Money

• Is it investing your reserve dollars for maximum yield with minimum risk?	____	____
• Is it putting any other excess cash (beyond reserves) to work?	____	____
• Is it keeping your building's accounts segregated from those of other buildings?	____	____
• Is it setting aside large amounts due periodically into escrow accounts?	____	____

Manning the Fort

• Has it retained able general counsel on an as-needed basis?	____	____
• Is it using counsel judiciously?	____	____
• Does it have special counsel file annual tax protests?	____	____
• Does it use special counsel to get tax refunds for capital improvements?	____	____
• Has it engaged competent agents to manage the building?	____	____
• Are they doing their duty?	____	____
• Does it respond when you call on its members?	____	____
• Has it brought in a good resident manager?	____	____
• Does it hire competent staff?	____	____
• Does it follow the "up to par or out in sixty days" rule?	____	____
• Does it see to it that dereliction is documented?	____	____
• Does it follow through with staff separation as appropriate?	____	____

Communicating with Constituents

• Does it hold annual meetings every year on schedule?	____	____
• Does it provide a full report on the state of the building?	____	____
• Does it give you a chance to ask what you want?	____	____

Yes No

- Does it keep you advised of major developments throughout the year? ___ ___
- Is it responsive to criticism or action requests? ___ ___

Improving the Common Ground

- Does it see to it that the physical plant is in good shape, including all building systems? ___ ___
- Does it carry out major capital improvements at the right time and for the right price? ___ ___
- Does it bid out the projects to at least three to five independent contractors? ___ ___
- Does it carry out redecoration without riots? ___ ___
- Is it able to improve the building without assessing you? ___ ___

Serving the Electorate

- Does it respond to renovation plans quickly and civilly? ___ ___
- Does it treat sublease requests reasonably? ___ ___
- Does it handle sales applications promptly and fairly? ___ ___
- Does it repair what it's supposed to in and out of your apartment? ___ ___
- Does it go to bat for shareholders or owners with building problems? ___ ___

Acting Beyond Necessity (Bonus Points)

- Has it done something special for you—a fete for all, a garden paradise, a gym for the ages? ___ ___
- Has it (safely and legally) made a pile of money for the building? ___ ___
- Has it locked in a long-term mortgage at rock-bottom rates? ___ ___
- Has it *decreased* monthly charges? ___ ___
- Has it replenished the reserve fund without coming to you for contributions? ___ ___

Putting Itself First (Demerits)

- Do board members get anything (besides a headache) that you don't? ___ ___
- Does any board member serve as a paid professional for the building? ___ ___

	Yes	No
• Do you get attitude instead of an answer when you request action?	___	___
• Does it consistently (and inexplicably) turn down sales and sublease applications?	___	___
• Does it show favoritism to friends and allies in making decisions?	___	___

SCORING THE RESULTS

Scoring Key: Give your board members 1 point for each yes, 2 points for each bonus yes, and deduct 5 points for each demerit yes.

40–50 Points: You have a model board. Say thank-you and re-elect its members with a landslide.

30–40 Points: Your board members are doing a credible job. Give them encouragement and volunteer to help the cause.

25–30 Points: Your board is slipping below what you should tolerate. Give its members one last chance to shape up, but get those insurgents ready.

20–25 Points: Enough is enough. It's time for action!

14

Everyday Skirmishes

DEFINING THE CONTROVERSY

Life in the trenches of the rank and file can be a daily class struggle. Whatever you want to do—whether it's something as seemingly innocent as ordering in, acquiring a canine companion, installing a washer/dryer, lighting up a drag, getting a communications hookup, even celebrating your religion—there's the board to contend with. And in the exclusive realm of your own private terrace (for those fortunate enough to have one) the board also makes its presence felt, telling you everything from how and what to plant to when you have to turn over your territory for the common good.

To an outsider these might seem like minor annoyances. But as the president of my building's board, I can tell you it's the small stuff that resonates with shareholders and threatens to lead to revolution if left unresolved. I've received hate mail from shareholders about the lack of lights on the Christmas tree, the loss of our bulletin board, and the lateness of tulip bulb planting—but nary a peep about issues of financial moment or capital improvement. The key (for everyone's sake) is to prevent these everyday skirmishes from escalating into more serious blood feuds.

Here, then, is a user-friendly guide to getting your way while keeping the peace.

THE MENU WARS

As any diehard New Yorker knows, few topics are more calculated to spark dissension than the menu controversy. For those of you who have had your heads in the sand or who are committed cooks unmindful of the piles of menus left at your doorsteps, I refer to the practice of those well-trained delivery brigades who use the building access they have gained to make a single dim sum drop-off to cover the corridors with restaurant propaganda. Worse still are those who lurk outside, forcing their way in behind some unsuspecting soul to carry out their mission. At one point things got so out of hand that one West Side building got a court order requiring the restaurant to pay for cleaning up its menu mess. Since then the delivery brigades have, to some extent, forsaken their guerrilla tactics and gone mainstream with direct mail.

At the height of the menu wars, the board in my building made a hit list of the top twenty raider restaurants in our territory and then got a translator to draft a communiqué in Cantonese warning each to cease and desist its practices if it hoped to retain delivery rights. It took only a week before signs of defeat appeared in the form of leaflets haphazardly strewn throughout the hallways. We had to get tough if enforcement was what we were after. The problem was, our board members couldn't even agree among themselves. The litter-free crowd wanted to take decisive action, while members of the coupon contingent favored the status quo so they could keep getting free soup.

In truth, your board can promulgate a House Rule and impose its will on the people, but on an issue that incites such passion I wouldn't advise doing anything without first getting a sense of shareholder sentiment on the subject.

We finally instituted a log-in-log-out system, figuring it would allow us to identify (and deal with) delivery offenders who lingered too long. I offer up some other options that we have considered in the hope that they will suggest ways your building can avert civil strife while keeping the populace sated.

Search and Seizure

As a champion of the Fourth Amendment (the one against unlawful search and seizure), I have a problem with this option. But some of our doormen have deputized themselves and require deliverymen to submit to paper bag inspections—and now, emboldened by the Patriot Act, even conduct pat-down searches of those with unnaturally bulging jackets—to see if they're trying to sneak in any offending literature.

Civilian Escort

In buildings where there is a surplus of staff there is also a ready solution. Have the concierge accompany the would-be raider to the appointed apartment or floor and stand guard while the drop-off is made, thereby ensuring that the food arrives promptly and piping hot without forbidden detours for illegal purposes.

Checkpoint Charlie

Another possible solution is to require the recipient of the delivery to go down to the lobby and pick it up. Since the whole point of ordering in (aside from not cooking) is to remain comfortably sedentary in your apartment—and not necessarily at your fashionable best—requiring residents to bestir themselves and dress for dinner inevitably invites protest. A shareholder at one co-op was so upset that she had to go downstairs rather than have food ride up alone in the elevator, that she took the board to court—and lost.[1]

Limited Authorization

Then there is the option of limiting delivery privileges to those who abide by the no-menu rules. This can be done by having the board prepare (and leave with the doormen) an approved list of restaurants to be allowed entry to the building. The problem here is that one man's offender is another's favorite purveyor. Once you have gotten addicted to a certain restaurant's moo shu you don't care if the establishment's law-abiding or not, you just want that quick fix. (Believe me, I know. Until I broke free of the habit, one year I ordered so much from my preferred provider that it sent me hand-calligraphed calendars for Christmas.)

Start Cooking

If all else fails, your board may have no choice but to impose a total ban and make shareholders go cold wonton. I live in a building where people renovate, but rarely use, their kitchens, so I'm not sure this option would go over big. Still, we keep it in reserve just in case the infiltrating armies get out of control.

BARKING UP THE RIGHT TREE

Battles with the board over members of the animal kingdom are writ even larger. The legion of cases out there attest that the loyalty of some people to their charges is matched only by the hostility of others. Whatever side of the philosophical divide you're on, you need to know your rights so that you can be sure your brand of justice prevails.

Basically, there are four ways that co-ops and condos deal with pets:

1. Carte Blanche

A few buildings are open zones that unconditionally welcome all God's creatures in the pet family. If the proprietary lease and/or the House Rules are silent on the subject—or better yet, expressly allow your friends of the four-legged (or feathered or finned) variety—your troubles are over, initially. Pack up your pooch and start pampering her in the style to which you've gotten her accustomed. Just don't count on the ability to exercise free pet will. Since lawyers usually draft the documents that create co-ops and condos, and they want to be sure to give their client boards an out (even if it's not used), absolute animal autonomy is rare, at least on paper.

2. Advise and Consent (or Revoke)

A step down from unfettered freedom are the provisions many buildings have that require you to get board consent (usually in writing) before you bring in your pet. What the board giveth, the board can taketh. These same provisions often say that it can revoke the very consent it has given—presumably after you and your schnauzer have become best buddies. But the power to revoke often has more bark than bite. As you will see (if you read on), the law protects your pets (and you) against eviction once the board knows about them and does nothing.

In my building, officially (according to the lease) we live under such an advise-and-consent regime, though in reality it has been enforced more in the breach than in the observance. As long as pets mind their manners, they are unchallenged by the authorities. This laissez-faire attitude is changing as more and more owners are acquiring pets in multiples, forcing us to come up with some way to control the population explosion and attendant problems.

3. Status Quo

Then there are the so-called grandfather clauses that allow owners' existing dogs (and other charges) to live out their natural lives in peace and harmony free from fear of eviction. But once their numbers are up so are your pet privileges. You can erect a shrine in Fido's memory or keep his ashes in an urn near your bedside. But you can't get another living, breathing canine cast in the same image to take his place in the here and now.

4. Blanket Prohibition

Finally, some buildings take a hard line and just say no to the harboring of any and all creatures. As you'll see, whether no really means no depends more on board action (or inaction) than on what's written.

The Pet Law

Whatever the rules of your building, you're probably safe if you opt for one of the minimembers of the animal kingdom that can be confined in a gilded cage—whether a pampered hamster, a frog prince, or a goldfish. Unless there is a specific prohibition against such creatures or they are a nuisance or a health hazard, they don't even come within the radar screen of most no-pet clauses. Assuming your preference is for something more warm and cuddly, and even if your building operates under one of the restrictive systems, that's not necessarily the end of the story. In New York City, where civil liberties are a cherished tradition, even dogs have their due in the form of the Pet Law.[2] Other municipalities throughout the state have similar provisions. For those of you thinking about taking on the powers that be on behalf of your pooch, here's what the law says:

> Where a tenant in a multiple dwelling *openly and notoriously* [emphasis added] for a period of three months or more following taking possession of a unit, harbors or has harbored a household pet or pets, the harboring

of which is not prohibited by the multiple dwelling law, the housing maintenance or the health codes of the City of New York or any other applicable law, and the owner or his or her agent has knowledge of this fact, and such owner fails within the three month period to commence a summary proceeding or action to enforce a lease provision prohibiting the keeping of such household pets, such lease provision shall be deemed waived.

Now for what it all means. The law was originally passed to protect renters from retaliatory eviction by landlords who used pets as a pretext to get their masters out. It has since been held to apply to co-ops on the basis of the landlord-tenant relationship that exists between shareholders and the board. But condo owners had better beware. Not even the judges can agree whether you and your animal family get the benefit of the Pet Law. In one court the strict constructionists won out. Because the law refers to leases, they said it protects only pet owners who are tenants. Since condo owners are not tenants and the board is not a landlord, the Pet Law doesn't apply. On the strength of that, they put out the owner's dog and other animal friends.[3] In another court (of equal stature but kinder heart), the pragmatists prevailed and came to the rescue of Petie. The law includes multiple dwellings and doesn't specifically exclude condos, so it's only right that unit owners get its protection. And it's only fair, they figured, that pet owners in co-ops and condos be treated the same. So Petie got to stay because the board failed to bring a no-pet enforcement action within three months.[4]

This split in the courts (and the jurisdictions they rule) means that right now if you and your pet live in a condo in Brooklyn, Queens, or Staten Island, you can use the law to save your pets from eviction. If you call Manhattan or the Bronx home, it won't do you (or them) any good. No doubt before long the dogs will have their day in court (this state's highest) and the issue will be resolved so that all or none (not just some) get the Pet Law's protection.

The anomaly for condo owners is that although you may not be able to invoke the law (depending on where you live), if you rent out your place your lessee probably can. That's because now there's a landlord (you) and a tenant (your renter) whose pet gets protection. For the same reason, if you're a rent-controlled or rent-stabilized tenant remaining in a building that has been converted to a condo, you and your dog get the benefit of the Pet Law.[5]

Civil Disobedience (the Bolder the Better)

The way the law (assuming it applies) works is that if you have kept your pet "openly and notoriously" for three months and the board has knowledge of this fact but does not act to enforce the restrictive pet provision in the lease, it is waived. You get to keep your pet as if the prohibition never existed. The first thing you need to focus on is what's enough to pass the "open and notorious" test. This is not as simple as it sounds, and seasoned jurists—let alone untutored boards—have disagreed.

Take the case of the seventy-five-pound rottweiler acquired by its owners in spite of a no-pet provision. Mother and son took the dog for excursions three times a day, using the main elevator and making introductions of their newfound friend to the neighbors and staff as they passed through the lobby. When almost six months later the building tried to oust the happy family the court said it was too late, the lease provision had been waived.[6]

Poor Coco didn't fare as well. She, too, was acquired in contravention of a no-pet clause. The court held that the co-op board had a right to enforce the policy even though it waited seven months from the time Coco moved in because her owners had not harbored her "openly and notoriously" for more than three months. But the dissent cried foul, finding that Coco's parents took her for constitutionals three or four times a day: from the eighteenth floor to the elevator, from the elevator to the lobby, from the lobby through the hallway, from the hallway to a promenade—a schedule that could not have been missed.[7]

The Hoodys' prized springer spaniel also had to go even though the board waited more than half a year to act. He had the misfortune of having been adopted by the wrong family—which owned an Upper East Side condo not entitled to Pet Law protection. The judge said he wanted to help but his hands were tied by his brethren's hard-hearted ruling.[8]

It may not be necessary to publicly parade your pooch to pass the "open and notorious" test. We have Miss Muffy to thank for that. The owner of this tiny Maltese kept her five-pound charge in her apartment. Her paws did not touch the pavement. When she was taken out, she was carried—I can only assume a Vuitton bag serving as sedan chair. No matter, the court ruled. The law doesn't say that an animal is harbored "openly and notoriously" only when it is taken outside or allowed to roam through the halls. Miss Muffy had been seen and petted by building staffers who had come calling at her apartment to tend to problems. She didn't have to go out and play to be protected.[9] You don't have to be a dog owner to get help from the law. It saved Clyde, the cat, from eviction when, years after he'd been spotted in the apartment by the super, the workmen, and others, the board tried (unsuccessfully) to oust him.[10]

Boards Fight Back

Boards are ever inventive in devising new strategies to circumvent the law. One tack is to plead ignorance. They tried it with Rocky, the chow puppy, who moved in with Max after his wife died. Even though more than three months had passed, the board said he had to go because the lease said no pets. Max fought back, arguing that everyone—the janitor, the porters, the security guards, had seen him from the start walking Rocky to the courtyard three times a day. The board counterattacked, claiming that what they knew couldn't be imputed to it, since they had no duty to tell. But the judges saw things Max's way. Under the Law, the knowledge of the staff is equivalent to that of the board or the managing agent (even if he only came once in two years).[11] Strike one for boards.

Another approach is to say you agreed not to have a pet. Before allowing the new owners to close on their posh Fifth Avenue co-op, the board made them sign an inducement letter, representing that they knew the co-op wouldn't let them have a pet. Sign they did—and then moved into their apartment with a puppy, anyway. When the board finally got around to taking action, it was too late under the Pet Law, so instead they accused the dog owners of fraud in signing the letter. That didn't work either. The letter recites that they were told about the co-op's no-pet policy, not that they would abide by it, the court said. Anyway, the law is superior to the letter.[12] Strike two for boards.

Then there's the condo board that tried an end run. Rather than wait for a judgment ejecting a renter and his three dogs that it claimed were running unleashed in the hallways, the board demanded an injunction up front requiring the dogs to go now. Sorry, it doesn't work that way, the judges ruled. It's decision first, action later.[13] Strike three for boards.

Nor can directors stop the clock from ticking as those at a Riverdale co-op claimed they were entitled to in order to investigate a shareholder's claim that she was exempt from the Pet Law because of a disability. Having concluded their investigation and brought their dog holdover action six days *after* the three months allowed by the Law, they waived their right.[14]

Sometimes owners are more action oriented than board members. One condo owner, unhappy with his do-nothing board, brought a lawsuit to compel the board to enforce the no-pet provision it had waived against a fellow owner, not a winning strategy—and for his frivolous pursuit he was ordered to pay their attorneys' fees.[15]

Canine Countdown

Don't be intimidated just because you receive something in writing telling you your pet has to go. Before you pack up your pooch and head for the hills or decide to have it out with the board, take a look at that piece of paper in front of you. Whether it's a polite communiqué from the board, a stern warning from its lawyer, or even an official-looking notice to cure, the law is now clear: it doesn't count—at least not for purposes of tolling the ninety-day period within which the board must act to avoid waiving the no-pet policy. Unless the board has actually started an action against you (and given you notice) within three months, all the rest is ill-advised sound and fury signifying nothing.[16]

If you plan to engage in your own act of civil disobedience, take advantage of the knowledge gained by the struggles of pets that have preceded. You might be able to sneak in a parakeet or a few tropical fish or even a (very quiet) cat and remain undetected. But there's no way of hiding dogs in perpetuity. Since the tiniest types are the most vocal, even a teacup dog will eventually be found out. But by then you run the risk of a heart-wrenching divorce. You're probably better off putting your pet principles to the test up front. Despite what happened to Coco, if you parade your pup through the corridors unchallenged for three months you should win if the board belatedly tries to take you on. And even if it sends you nasty notes, or does anything short of starting a lawsuit within the allotted time, remember that it has no legal impact.

Succession Rights

Alas, even a dog's days are numbered. Having fought the good fight and won the right to make your home his, what happens after he goes to his just reward? Does the waiver of the no-pet policy you won for your first dog carry over to his replacement? Or must you return to do battle with the board and establish anew your dog's unchallenged presence for three months? In other words, does the Pet Law apply to your dog's tenancy or to yours? Believe it or not, this has been the topic of some heated judicial debate.

The highest court to have spoken has said that the waiver applies to the dog's life, not yours. What happened was that a couple acquired a Great Dane named Xam (not an easy dog to overlook) in violation of their lease, which prohibited pets. The landlord didn't do anything for eight years and admittedly gave up his right to do so. Then Xam went the way of all Great Danes. No sooner had Xam II arrived on the scene than the landlord this time around acted to enforce the no-pet rule. Already attached, Xam II's parents claimed that the landlord's waiver should apply to their new pup. But a trio of judges said the board could only give up its right to get rid of real-life, flesh-and-blood creatures living with you, not those who weren't even yet a twinkle in your eye.[17]

Let's say you got to keep Fido because the board didn't object for more than three months after it knew of his existence. When Fido takes his earthly leave, you can't automatically bring in Fifi or son of Fido, but must win a new waiver the same way as the old. Unless your board is brain-dead or takes a laissez-faire attitude toward pet enforcement, it will be harder the second time around since it is sure to be wiser both to the law and to you.

But there may be help on the way—proposed changes in the Pet Law would allow the waiver initially obtained to apply to your dog's successor.[18]

The Unprotected

Don't count on any help from the Pet Law if your pooch has not mastered (or at least learned the basics of) Emily Post's etiquette. It will not protect a pet that creates a nuisance, causes damage, or interferes substantially with the health, safety, or welfare of the residents. So if he's chewing up the rugs, wailing into the night, terrorizing the kids, or otherwise spreading destruction in his wake, all the parading around in the world will not earn him protected status.

Nor will the law apply if an unauthorized occupant tries to make a dog a partner in crime. Take the case of the mother who moved into her son's co-op four years after he moved out—bringing her dog with her. Under the co-op's lease, Mom had no right to occupy the apartment without board consent (which she didn't bother to get). Since she was an unauthorized occupant, the dog also was unprotected. The result: Mom was ordered out unless she found a new home for her pup in thirty days.[19]

Even in pet-friendly buildings, if you overstep the bounds of reason you are looking for trouble. One such co-op allowed shareholders to have one pet without question but required written consent for two or more. The problem was, our pet lover had eight: three dogs, three cats, and two birds. What to him was the sweet sound of his children at play was chaos to his neighbors (up and down, right and left), all of whom complained of squawking parrots, scratching cats, and barking canines. He had a menagerie, not a companion, and since the animals were causing a nuisance there was no help to be had from the Pet Law. He got to keep only two—and his neighbors got to sleep.[20]

Quality of Life

Even if your dog is allowed to stay because the board has waived the no-pet policy or the building approves of pets, that doesn't mean the welcome mat will be rolled out. Boards can (and do) pass House Rules dictating their conduct. The board can require that your dog be carried or on a leash as he passes through public places (in case he gets too frisky with his fellow canines or friendly residents). It can relegate your best friend to second-class status by insisting that he ride the service and not the passenger elevator (a case of discrimination ripe for some enterprising ACLUer). It can impose limits on pet height and weight (a practice that may better be applied to the building's shareholder-masters). And to top it all off, the board can (if properly authorized) impose fines for breach of any one or all of these offenses.

So if your pet's quality of life is as important as your own, you should check out the building's rules before you buy in. Though it's true that regulations can subsequently be changed, the existing state of affairs should give you a pretty good idea whether the board and the building are pet-friendly or pet-phobic.

HARBORING ILLEGALS

When it comes to the washer/dryer controversy, I admit I am not an unbiased observer. While I plead personally innocent (you can come and inspect my closets), I have friends in my own and other buildings who are harboring fugitive machines, so you might say my silence makes me a co-conspirator. Some rationalize their infraction by saying their private launderettes are taking the place of dishwashers (and thus not using any extra water), and others offer no excuses except their own convenience.

For those of you in the dark, I refer to attempts by owners to skirt the nearly universal ban (except in prewar buildings) against having your very own washing machine. As most of us know, descending to the bowels of the earth to wash your clothes is a New York tradition so ingrained it almost seems normal. But for some it can be a scary place and an even scarier process. You have to understand, most of my friends can write great briefs, but they can't wash them. So although wielding a pen comes naturally to these people, mastering the use of fabric softener, or even finding their way to the site of the machines, does not. I had a colleague who got locked in the basement on his first domestic outing and learned the hard way that there's no washing and no exit after ten P.M. He had to call on his cell phone for a rescue team (embarrassing but effective). Another friend, unfamiliar with standard detergent measures and a proponent of the theory that more is better, left a trail of suds in his wake and had to make a hasty retreat lest he be found out.

Having suffered my own inconvenience and indignities in the laundry room, I can understand the desire of some to avoid such trauma by having a machine of one's own in the privacy of one's apartment. But as a board member bound to uphold the no-washer rules, I feel obligated to put enforcement over emotion.

Fugitives Forever

That doesn't mean all shareholders feel likewise. Let's say you've greased the doorman's palm to cast a blind eye as your new personal launderette is hauled through the lobby and up to your apartment. Are you home free or are there still potential perils? What you should know is that there are no mandatory waivers when it comes to washing machines. You may be as attached to your washer/dryer as you are to your Weimaraner, but the law doesn't see it that way. After three months your pet may be safe from expulsion, but not your home laundry. Even if you are allowed to keep your appliances with the knowledge of building staff, that doesn't preclude the board from enforcing a no-washer rule provided it acts with reasonable dispatch.

That's what happened when the board went after a bunch of shareholders who were in violation of the co-op's rules prohibiting installation of laundry machines and dryers. They claimed the directors had waived their right because staff knew of the machines' existence. No matter, the court said. Under our old friend the business judgment rule, the board had the right to enforce the rules meant to protect the building's plumbing and electrical systems. All the more so because the building's lease (there and in most co-ops) said that failure by the board to act doesn't mean it waives its rights. There's no statute of limitations for washing machines,[21] but if the board sits on its rights long enough, you may win. One washaholic, who claimed she had her machine since the building went co-op, complained when the board waited nearly fourteen years to enforce its antimachine rule. Although the judge agreed that her lease had a no-waiver clause, still, he said, there's a question of whether the directors waited too long.[22]

Sometimes you get lucky. One co-op owner admitted to washing in private without written permission. But she got away with it (at least temporarily) thanks to an agent who mistakenly had given her old (prohibition-free) House Rules with the lease.[23] Don't count on such screw-ups to rescue you.

And to any would-be lawyers among you, don't think you can twist the language of the antiwasher rules so that no means yes. It won't work and could cost you legal fees (yours and the board's). One tenant of a Clintonesque turn of phrase said her "use" of a portable washer did not violate the building's lease provision against "installation" of such a machine. She lost and the machine had to go—or she would.[24]

Caveat Emptor

For those of you who are guilty but undetected (and want to stay that way), a few words of caution. Don't go advertising your sleek, new Euro-cleaning wonder to your neighbors. (They'll only want to follow your lead, causing a system overload and your collective downfall.) And don't flaunt it when repairmen come a-calling. And as for building staff, generous tipping is still the best defense against loose lips. But if despite all your precautions you are finally found out by the board (and it's not singling you out), you may have to give up your private laundry and join the denizens of the deep to get clean clothes.

AVOIDING COMMUNICATIONS SNAFUS

Now that we're in the new millennium, the battleground has shifted from keeping clean to staying connected—an area of friction sure to expand as new telecommunications toys come to market. Cable, direct TV, and cellular antennae are the main playthings (and potential troublemakers).

If you're a technological junkie or just want to stay au courant, can you get wired at will or does the board have a say? It's only fair to tell you at the outset that I'm unplugged myself. I pulled out the cable connections when I moved into my current quarters (rather than have to live with those overgrown wires); I swear by my decades-old dial phone (though in deference to my more modern friends I bought a touch-tone—that's more on the fritz than off). Having given you full disclosure that I'm technologically impaired, I leave it to you to take my advice for what it's worth.

On the cable front, there's relative calm: There used to be battles over buying in bulk back when cable companies demanded that boards deliver whole buildings to get cheaper rates. Now cable combatants generally require boards to deliver 70 percent of all residents to get bulk rates, which can be 30 percent or more off what you'd pay individually. This system provides a lower-priced linkup to the many who want it and freedom from cable coercion for the few who cling to their rabbit ears. One hitch you (and the board) should watch out for: if the subscription level goes below the set guarantee, the building usually has to agree to make up the shortfall, which means those of you who are cable free may wind up subsidizing the viewing habits of the addicted.

But why settle for a mere fifty channels when you can have a thousand (and surf till you drop)? Such desire to escape the bounds of underground cable wires and scour the heavens in search of endless signals already has spawned numerous disputes over satellite TV, and more are on the way. In order to protect viewers from landlord interference, the Federal Communications Commission passed a rule back in 1996 prohibiting any (governmental or nongovernmental) restriction that would interfere with the installation, maintenance, or use of satellite antennae (less than one meter in diameter) to receive video programming that are within the *exclusive use or control* of a property owner.[25] Two years later, it amended the rule to expressly apply to apartment dwellers (renters and owners) who have exclusive use areas.[26] The result is no matter what the board says, the Fed says you, too, can install a dish on a balcony, balcony railing, patio, yard, deck, or other similar area that only you can use.

Indeed, before the rules were fully promulgated, owners of a penthouse in our building, without seeking board consent, installed a satellite dish on the exterior wall of their terrace in order to beam back Polish TV. Rather than go to war, especially since the reach of the rules was not yet clear, we agreed to let them keep it, and they agreed to indemnify the co-op. Reasonableness begets reasonableness and when, several years later, Polish cable had arrived, they voluntarily removed the dish.

As board president I don't much fancy the federal government preempting our members' power. Nor am I thrilled at the prospect of satellite dishes sprouting like Topsy on our rooftop terraces. (Though the real problem will be in those buildings with scores of attached, but unused, balconies.) You should know that the way the law stands, unless there are safety concerns, your board probably can't impose any rules on satellite dishes requiring prior approval or application fees or fines. So long as you set up a free-standing dish on your balcony or patio or mount a dish on a table or other stable object, it's your business. If the board tries to interfere with your viewing pleasure tell its members the FCC is on your side.

Given that few apartment owners can lay claim to exclusive space, having your own satellite dish remains a prerogative of the privileged. The rule's protection doesn't extend to common areas such as the roof, hallways, walkways, or exterior walls of the building. Nevertheless, junkies desperate for their latest dose of reality TV have been testing the legal limits. One condo owner installed a dish on the exterior wall of his unit, but the board made him take it down—and the court agreed that it wasn't an area of exclusive use.[27] Another apartment dweller affixed a dish to his window guard. That's no good either, the judicial response came back.[28] Doing him one better, a tenant in a multidwelling building mounted two dishes upon boards jutting two feet into the air space outside his window. Same answer: Your flying antenna is not protected by the rule.[29] Yet another viewer, desperate for a media fix, strung a wire from her fifth-floor apartment and laid claim to the roof with her dish. Take it down or you'll have to go, the judge said.[30]

Only one satellite insurgent thus far has prevailed, not because she was right but because the landlord was wrong. She attached the dish to a piece of wood that was first affixed to a window guard and then to the windowsill, supposedly with the building's permission. But the landlord waited so many years to demand removal that the court figured by that time she'd suffer withdrawal, and let her keep it.[31]

Of course, the board can consider installing a master rooftop dish, in which case all you'd have to do is buy a decoder box. Although operators have thus far made few such inroads, based on questions posed by shareholders about the possibility during the last few annual meetings, boards may soon be beaming up signals—and maybe a few shareholders.

With cellular phone traffic already overloaded, telecommunications giants are bombarding boards with offers to mount antennae and turn their rooftops into gold. Chances are you don't even know—you should. Here's why. The promise of riches (annual rental fees can be in excess of $25,000) comes with strings—and wires and refrigerator-sized transmissions—attached to your building's roof and exterior. Apart from aesthetics, there have been rumblings that the electromagnetic fields generated by these antennae cause cancerous tumors. (Though thus far plaintiffs have gotten nowhere in the courts for lack of scientific evidence.) Absent health hazards, your board probably has authority to sign one of these deals on its own. But given that you'll all be entering the great technological unknown together, I think board members should tell you first and hear what you have to say.

PRACTICING WHAT YOU PREACH

You can watch what you like, but can you practice what you preach? As everyone knows, in this country separation of church and state is the law of the land. But what about church and co-op (or condo)? I know there's a difference—one has the imprimatur of government; the other is strictly private. Still, I'm sure you figured that in or about your apartment you can practice your religion as you please. You'd be wrong, or, at least, not entirely right. Boards have interfered even with faith-based matters. In co-ops and condos it's not Constitutional privileges like the Establishment Clause or the right of free exercise that reign supreme; it's what your governing documents say—or don't—about religion that counts.

Owners at one condo wanted to celebrate Sukkoth by erecting a sukkah, a temporary structure symbolic of the impermanent dwelling that the Jews lived in while wandering through the desert after their flight from Egypt. The first time, they made the mistake of constructing it on a common walkway that interfered with others' use. Take it down, the board demanded, and the court agreed. The next time they got smarter and constructed the sukkah on their balcony. Again the board told them to remove it, fined them $1,000, accelerated all common charges, and denied access to the swimming pool and the exercise room. This time the owners had the higher authority on their side: They had sole access to their balcony, and nothing in the condo's bylaws said they couldn't put a sukkah on it. Instead the board claimed it was a prohibited alteration, but the judges didn't buy it—and the sukkah stayed.[32]

Owners of a different persuasion at another condo waged a similar crusade with their board over statues of Saint Jude and the Blessed Mother, which they had placed against the outside wall of their unit, where they stood for six years until a new regime came into power and demanded that they take them away. The owners complained the board was interfering with their religious freedom, and the board complained that the owners' statues were giving the impression that it was endorsing their religion. Besides, it said, the bylaws prohibit obstructing the common area. The court chastised the board: It's the condo's documents, not the Constitution, that counts, and the statues haven't violated them because they aren't bothering anyone or blocking the way.[33]

In my own building, it wasn't the free exercise of religion but the right to celebrate the pagan ritual of Halloween that created the controversy. An overzealous couple, who never made it out of the 1960s and aren't big on observing boundaries, let their festivities tumble into the hallway so that everyone had to navigate an obstacle course of carved pumpkins, paper goblins, flying witches, and cotton spiderwebs just to get to their apartments. "Get that stuff out of the corridors" the complaints came pouring in, and because our House Rules prohibit blocking the common areas, we could—and did. Same principle, different result: The bottom line is that simple restrictions on obstructions may, if violated, effectively impinge on your right to practice what you preach.

What if the board decides to get more aggressive: Can it ban religious displays outright? Here at home the question apparently hasn't yet been put to the judicial test, but if those Florida judges are correct, the answer is yes. The problem, at least in the first instance, is that board members get to play Constitutional scholars and decide what's "religious" and what's not. Even though the Supreme Court has said that a menorah is "secular," the condo board decreed it was "religious" and couldn't be displayed, but a Christmas tree was commercial and could be.[34] Another Florida board passed a rule prohibiting religious services in the auditorium or on any common elements, and the court said it was okay as a reasonable restriction to prevent division in the ranks.[35]

Even if your building's governing documents allow (or don't prohibit) religious displays, does the board have to give equal opportunity to every faith that wants to participate? At least one court said yes. If the board is going to allow red and green Christmas bows and wreaths, then it has to let Jewish condo owners put up blue and white Hanukkah bows.[36] In my co-op, we have always taken an inclusive approach, celebrating the holidays with a decked-out Christmas tree and a modernist menorah, eggnog and bagels and lox, thus avoiding religious warfare.

LIGHTING UP

With laws prohibiting you from smoking at work, and play, and practically everywhere else, the last refuge is the privacy of your own apartment, though even this sacred territory is coming under increasing siege by shareholders demanding that boards protect their space from smoke infiltration. At least one couple took the board to the mat, and to court, claiming that secondhand smoke endangered their health and forced them to sell their apartment at below market price. Despite the fact that the board had investigated the complaints and taken remedial action, it couldn't identify the source of the smoke or resolve the problem. It wasn't obligated to seal off the apartment, the court ruled. Under the lease, the shareholders had the responsibility to maintain the inside of their unit.[37] No doubt, however, this is not the last judicial word on the subject.

Rather than wait to be sued, the board of an Upper West Side co-op took self-help, passing a rule requiring all new owners to register—and then kick—the habit, by banning smoking in their apartments, though preexisting shareholders could continue to puff away with impunity.[38] From my experience, dividing the populace into haves and have-nots is not a winning—or enforceable—strategy. Sure enough, a year later the rule was repealed and smokers no longer had to sneak into the apartments of their grandfathered neighbors to inhale.

Thankfully, secondhand smoke hasn't been a big issue where I live, because those affected usually deal with the issue firsthand, forcing their smoking partners to go out in the street (or find a friendly terrace) to satisfy their addiction so they won't contaminate their own apartments. We had one couple who complained that the smoke from the Havanas that the guy next door savored was penetrating through the walls and into their place, but, fortunately, they moved before it became a heated topic.

Whatever side of the divide you're on, the smoking debate is only beginning. Antitobacco shareholders, helped by their hired guns, are sure to test the legal limits of nuisance or warranty of habitability or other legal theories in order to snub out the cigarettes of the propuffing contingent. How it all works out remains to be seen.

PROTECTING YOUR TURF

Whether you're lighting up or not, real (and legal) luxury is having your own supply of fresh air. As any of you lucky enough to have a piece of the country in the city know, owning a terrace is a rare delight to be savored daily and never taken for granted. I count myself among the fortunate, having managed to parlay my one-bedroom apartment into a duplex penthouse during the conversion of my building. The event was an epiphany. Whereas before I was indifferent to the beauty of nature around me, I have since become acquainted with species of flora and fauna I never knew existed but that now share my personal refuge. I wake to the warbling of sparrows and the caw of crows. I have butterflies and dragonflies. I still count it one of the minor wonders that in New York City the bees can find out how to get to my potted petunias with pinpoint accuracy even though taxi drivers regularly get lost amidst the winding downtown streets.

And although I once viewed gardening scornfully as an anti-intellectual suburban pastime, I have become a convert pursuing my passion with a compulsion that comes naturally to Type A litigators. I traveled by train to the Brooklyn Navy Yard through neighborhoods threatening and unknown in search of the most aesthetically (and functionally) perfect planters, waited for months for them to be constructed, and then had to lug them up two flights of stairs when the talented, but eccentric, craftsman who made them broke his arm in a motorcycle accident. I get to the Green Market at 7:30 A.M. in planting season so as to have my pick of the roses, only to be met every week by the same band of neurotic gardeners, each of whom has the identical mission in mind. I mulch and feed. I water and weed. I call the nursery at the first sign of infection or infestation. And on a cool summer's eve, I just sit back and survey the results that nature and (wo)man hath wrought.

So I can relate to those owners who are prepared to fight to the death to defend their turf against any restrictive rules promulgated by the board that might diminish the use or enjoyment of their pastoral retreats. The first thing I did was check out the penthouse-relevant provisions in my proprietary lease. If I had taken their restrictions on everything from grilling to gardening at face value, I would have had second thoughts about my purchase. Lest you be experiencing similar trepidation, let me tell you that the level of board enforcement often is inversely proportionate to the strength of the roof. Be forewarned: the newer the building, the fewer the thousands of pounds of soil the roof likely can tolerate. The degree of shareholder compliance is dependent on who lives downstairs. (Count on duplex owners to be the most law-abiding.) And remember, terrace dwellers are a minority (especially if we're talking a handful of penthouses, not rows of balconies) whose interests may be at odds with those of the rest of the resident owners. So it may be in your own best interest to become civic minded and get on the board (at least when roof or related work is on the horizon) so that your voice gets heard. Don't count on those terraceless directors (who may harbor latent hostility) to look out for you.

Now for the specifics: what you can expect in the way of real-life intrusion into your individual realm and how you can keep the board at bay.

Fending Off Invasion

Your terrace is (or should be) your own private fiefdom for your use and your use alone. Most leases (in condos, bylaws) make this plain by stating that the owner should have and enjoy "exclusive" use of the terrace, balcony, or portion of the roof adjoining a penthouse. Nevertheless, given the scarcity of outdoor space in the city, it's not surprising that turf wars have been fought between the haves and the have-nots. Take the case of the penthouse owner who had plenty of shares allocated to his apartment for his terrace. But when the board fixed the roof, it seized the lion's share of his territory in the name of the people—claiming it as common property for the common man. Mr. Penthouse fought back the invading armies and won—restoring his terrace to its original boundaries and making the aggressor pay for his legal trouble.[39] Let this be a lesson to shareholders; just because you have to pay to fix the roof doesn't mean you get to use it.

Nor can *you*, as a penthouse dweller, seek to expand your private territory by attaching a piece of the common ground and redefining your borders with potted plants. One determined couple tried to extend their terrace by fencing in a larger adjacent garden for their private use. They remained thus, safe and secluded from the outside world, until the board decided to remove the fence, allow in the masses—and worse still, use the area as a playground. The shareholders claimed they had made it their own for so long it should stay that way. Since their lease didn't include the garden, the walls came tumbling down—and the masses came pouring in.[40]

Even though your fellow owners can't gain a foothold in your inner sanctum, that doesn't mean they won't be allowed to sit at the border and breathe down your neck. One couple, blessed with a duplex co-op that had French doors opening out onto two vast terraces, decided to claim a third—even though it was separated from their apartment by a brick wall—when they found out that the board was going to redevelop the space as a sitting area for their fellow shareholders. The only thing they got from their attempted annexation was an order requiring them to pay $287,000 in attorneys' fees.[41] If there is a legitimately carved-out common roof garden adjacent to your terrace, you can't keep the neighbors out of the public space. And if the board in its wisdom decides to increase their hours of enjoyment (even though it may decrease yours), you're out of luck. Our old friend the business judgment rule lets the board pretty much set the timetable.[42]

The War of the Roses

Assuming your boundaries are undisputed doesn't mean your disputes with the board over terrace rights are over. For most of us the lure of outdoor space is giving free rein to our green thumbs. The problem is that unlike our country cousins, who can just dig a hole and be done with it, we city dwellers have to haul the soil skyward and dump it in aboveground planters before we can even begin. Boards can (and do) dictate the how, why, and wherefore of the whole process. Through the lease and/or the House Rules, they can specify the size, weight, and construction of planters. (The New York City Building Code independently mandates maximum roof load, though it's not like its inspectors come calling without cause.) The board may require that no planters be installed without prior written approval. And in extreme cases (as where the roof is in danger of collapse), the board may ban planters altogether—something I'd want to know before plunking down a pile of cash for a blooming paradise only to find that I was stuck with a concrete wasteland.

Just because your planting regime may be regulated on paper doesn't mean it will be enforced in real life. In my building (and most others) the rules require that no plantings or structures be installed without prior written board approval, but we cast a relative blind eye to the English gardens and tropical rain forests that were taking root until we recently redid our roof. Before we began, we undertook an investigational tour and banished offending plants and planters, which didn't cause any wars because we had given everyone affected ample notice of this deforestation (and safely stored their complying shrubs for the duration). Not everyone takes it in stride. One Upper West Sider took the board to court rather than remove his multi-ton planted forest. After having repaired the roof twice at a cost of several hundred thousand dollars, the board decided to enforce the building's ban against planters. But the antiauthoritarian penthouse owner restored his forest nevertheless and let it grow for almost ten years before the board finally got serious about the ban. No matter that it waited long enough for his forest to reach the enchanted stage. Since the board had the absolute right (under the lease) to restrict planters on the roof, they had to go when the directors gave the order.[43] Another gentlewoman farmer lived in lush green splendor while the couple below existed in waterlogged misery. So grand had her garden grown that it threatened to go through the roof, further jeopardizing her already beleaguered neighbors. Unwilling to endure any more (and all efforts at repair having been for naught), they sued the farmer and the co-op, with the result that the garden was removed—never more to bloom without court approval.[44]

The bottom line is that if the board decides to enforce the building's planting rules (even if later rather than sooner) it will win, absent extraordinary circumstances. After our restoration was complete, at the advice of our engineer, we implemented new requirements for plants and planters, which are necessary to obtain a warranty on the roof. So you might as well do it right from the start. For your own benefit (not the board's). Otherwise you run the risk of tending that flowering cherry from sapling to full-grown tree only to suffer the trauma of having to chop it (and the planter) down when it's in its full glory.

The same holds true for anything else you plan to add to your secret garden, from decking to fences to greenhouses. You had better follow the letter of the law or else proceed at your own risk, which is not inconsiderable. Unauthorized roof installations may run afoul not only of co-op policy but also of governmental codes, which could put a violation on the whole building. To say nothing of the leaks or other damage that could ensue, causing potential trouble on all sides of you (since water travels in mysterious ways). The result is, the board has no choice but to act as enforcer. And if you make the board go to court to get compliance you may be sorry. One unlucky shareholder was ordered not only to remove the deck he had paid to put up but also to reimburse the board for legal fees it had spent to get the order.[45] Another shareholder didn't build, but laid claim to a preexisting greenhouse on the terrace adjacent to her penthouse, which she used to shelter people, not plants. No matter that she wasn't the construction culprit, it still had to go because it violated the building's C of O, subjecting the co-op to civil and criminal penalties.[46]

Whether or not you do everything by the book, you may not be totally out of the woods. If the board decides it's time to fix the roof it can (pursuant to lease provisions of most co-ops and bylaws of condos) remove whatever you've got on your terrace so that work can proceed. One downtown forest ranger preferred to risk roof collapse rather than allow the board to dismantle his private Sherwood. He refused access to complete roof repairs and went to court to keep his trees safe from invading forces, but he lost because his forest jeopardized the guarantee for the entire roof.[47]

Who pays for the removal and subsequent reforesting of Nottingham depends on what the lease says. But it's not uncommon for leases to give boards the right to remove and restore—all at your expense. What is unusual is for the total cost of repairing the roof to be passed on to the terrace owners, rather than be paid for by the co-op or condo through *all* its owners. The sponsor at one co-op, afraid of scaring off terraceless owners by making them pay for a benefit they wouldn't enjoy, shifted the burden in the proprietary lease exclusively to those entitled to fresh air access. When they protested megasized assessments of $5,000 to more than $100,000, the court told them the cost was there in black-and-white for them to see, and they had to pay.[48]

Cease-Fire

The first thing I did when I closed on my apartment was to pick up my Weber kettle drum. Only when I got home did I realize: (1) I had to assemble it before I could use it, and (2) the proprietary lease said "No cooking."

I managed to overcome both problems—the first by reading the instruction book and using my best Tim the Tool Man skills to put together the barbecue; the second by taking stock of the smoke signals and the sweet smell of mesquite pouring forth from my new neighbor's terrace. Putting two and two together, I figured there's safety in numbers among the grilling set and went to work igniting my Match Light coals. I have never looked back. A nonexistent cook indoors, I have become something of a gourmet chef outdoors. And to match my prohibited pursuit I cook only forbidden foods—hamburgers loaded with carcinogens, franks with sulfites that will kill, and baked potatoes piled with artery-clogging sour cream.

As you've probably figured out, I'm as addicted to my grill as to my garden. For those of you similarly afflicted, it may be possible to pursue your passion while keeping peace with the board if you keep in mind a few pointers. Just about every co-op lease says "No cooking" (at least outdoors). The trick is to figure out when it really means what it says. If your building is one with balconies stacked up and down the facade, then no probably means no. There are too many of these appendages and they're too public. Since the board can't let one shareholder grill and another go hamburgerless, it runs the risk that everyone will light up in unison and incinerate not only their burgers but the building.

So how do you know? A friend of mine who lives in a balconied apartment at the top of the line figured she was safe since the smoke could only go skyward. But after searching in vain for a single minihibachi to serve as legal precedent, she gave up on the idea. If grilling is a necessity to you (as it is with my next-door neighbor, who continues undaunted through the dead of winter), then you'd better ask someone on the board before you buy. Since this is not something you can get away with, it's better to know up front where you stand. On the other hand, if there are only a few terraces tucked away and scattered about the building, no may mean yes—or at least don't ask, don't tell.

Those of you who are unnaturally upstanding citizens know that not only does your building have barbecue rules, so does the city's fire code. It requires that all grilling be done outdoors, ten feet or more from any combustible surface. Penthouses may be legal but terraces beneath overhanging structures are not. Fire escapes are an automatic no, no matter their size. Though that didn't seem to register with the intrepid griller I once passed toasting marshmallows in a bonfire outside his window, making a mockery of his fire escape.

And forget about those trendy gas grills (not for purists anyway). It's illegal to bring a propane tank into a New York City building or to refill one anywhere in the city. More important, it can blow you and the building up, since it's equal to four sticks of dynamite. Which is why my building's board sent in our enforcer when we spotted one on an isolated terrace. It's not like the barbecue patrol goes sniffing in search of high-rise violators, so you're probably pretty safe from the law (though not necessarily from yourself). But if you have a nasty neighbor with whom you've been dying to get even, there may be a little poetic justice in turning him in to the authorities, who will come to investigate specific complaints if you call.

Unforeseen Conflicts

Some shareholders are so imaginative in their intent to make the fullest use of their terraces that they create conditions the board (and thus building rules) never contemplated. For example, a few of our penthouse dwellers have decided that their woodland retreats would not be complete without water, which they (not nature) have supplied in the form of wading pools weighing many a pound. (I'm not talking about those little plastic kiddie blow-up jobs but full-fledged suburban aboveground types.)

Frankly, I should have figured this out. When I first moved up to the penthouse floor, I was greeted by cabana-outfitted residents strolling the corridors. It seemed a little odd, but I figured this is downtown, where individuals still feel free to express their own personal style. I didn't think anything further of my encounters, and everything went swimmingly until our manager discovered the man-made ponds on an inspection tour of the water tower. Not having any antipool provisions, the board had to resort to its general police powers to get the job done.

The same thing happened with hammocks. Some terrace residents got carried away with the fiction of the great outdoors and decided to use the roof railing as trees, to which they affixed their hammocks. Their not-so-gentle rocking threatened to unseat the rails and throw themselves overboard. So we were forced to intercede to protect those who would not protect themselves.

I thought I'd seen it all, until recently a shareholder (thankfully at another building) tried to push the envelope still further, converting the outdoor space of his duplex penthouse into a basketball court, without board approval. The board told him to cease and desist: Your court doesn't comply with the Building Code, which requires that roofs used for recreational purposes have fencing ten feet high. Besides, the noise is driving the neighbors nuts. It's not a roof, it's a terrace, Mr. Delusional replied, and it's not the bouncing ball, but the roof surface the board installed that's creating the racket. This time reason prevailed, and the home team was enjoined from ball playing.[49] Who knows what's next?

I hope you and your board learn from these experiences and enact some creative new terrace laws.

Feet of Clay

Given their defend-to-the-death mentality, it's not surprising that terrace owners are equally protective of their terrace surface (a topic that I admit is near and dear to me and my aesthetic sensibility). Odds are your terrace (if you have one) was originally covered with terra-cotta quarry tiles in the classic English garden manner. These building blocks acquire a patina with age that lends credence to the notion you're not getting older, you're getting better (which doesn't apply nearly as well to most people). But as may be expected in an age where commercialism wins out over charm, when it's time for roof repair many boards vote to replace those characteristic quarry tiles with characterless cement pavers.

More than a few terrace owners have gone to war with their boards over this aesthetic controversy. Given my personal preference I hate to admit that it's a losing battle, but the answer from the courts is always the same: since the board has the obligation to repair roof terraces it gets to pick what surface to use under (you guessed it) the business judgment rule.[50] It matters not that the offering plan describes the terraces as having been surfaced with quarry tile. Or that they have been thus since the beginning of time (or at least the building). Or that the board is aesthetically impaired or unmoved. The board has the law on its side. Since you don't have a legal leg to stand on, you'd better be creative. Appeal to the board's sense of reason and fairness, argue the facts (the roof will last longer; values will increase), or do whatever's necessary to make it see things your way. If plan A doesn't work, try plan B. Consider getting those affected to pay for the difference between quarry tiles and pavers. The truth is the cost differential isn't necessarily that great, which is one reason (in addition to aesthetics) that we opted for quarry tiles when we resurfaced our roof.

Occupied Territory

As if all this isn't enough, terrace owners have to worry about the possibility of being displaced from their territory and forced to hand it over to occupational forces for the good of the building. This happens when repair work has to be done on the building's roof or brickwork. Most co-op leases have language broad enough to allow the board to take over use of the terrace to hang scaffolding, store materials, or do whatever's necessary. I watched as a terrace across the street from me was turned into a construction site for nearly two years, wondering (with more than a little self-interest) what recourse its owners had. The answer is probably none (unless negligence plays a part).

Whether or not you are so disposed, courts require you to be selfless, giving up the use and enjoyment of your terrace so that building work can be done. The theory is that as a shareholder you, too, are a beneficiary of necessary repairs (though you may be the only one ousted in the process). And don't expect anything for your trouble. One penthouse owner tried to recover after his board laid claim for months to his terrace to hang and store scaffolding necessary for carrying out building-wide construction. All he got from the judge was a slap on the wrist, a ruling, and a lecture on his duties as a good citizen.[51]

15

Boarder Wars

DRAWING THE BATTLE LINES

No doubt you like to think your apartment is your castle with you as ruler of its residents. Especially after you've plunked down thousands and thousands for it. In condos—where freedom reigns—you may, in fact, be king of your realm's residents. Most condos don't give the board any real power over your right to sublet (and only limited say over who stays with you). But as any shareholder who's lived in a high-rise palazzo for any length of time knows, in co-ops it's the board that acts as gatekeeper of the fortress and of your individual threshold. Whether it's total strangers (a.k.a. subtenants), family intimates, invited guests, or live-in roommates, the board, not you, has the final word on who stays (and for how long) and who goes. That doesn't mean you can't win in the boarder wars. But you have to master the rules of your regime before you can proceed to share your space, or rent it out, if you want to outmaneuver them.

LEVELING THE SUBLEASING FIELD

In most co-ops *subleasing* is a dirty word. Having made the transition from occupier to owner, many board members (and plenty of shareholders) forget where they came from. Instead, they shut the door behind them, figuring in the process they'll weed out the hoi polloi and keep the building haute. Personally, I don't subscribe to the social caste school of subletting. Having rented for the better part of my adult life, as have most New Yorkers, I'm not about to turn traitor. And anyway, an outright ban on sublets makes no sense because it only fosters disobedience in the ranks.

Reasoned Regulation

That doesn't mean there aren't legitimate reasons for boards to set some sublease parameters. So before you go on the attack, take a moment to understand what they are, how they impact your building (and you), and whether the restrictions your board has imposed are a rational response.

Cash Flow (for the Building's Sake)

Number one is money—or more precisely, the moneylender. True to their button-down nature, most bankers want to see a steady and sure stream of cash before they'll lend millions to refinance a building's underlying mortgage. As far as they're concerned, that means the apartments had better be occupied by owners who are committed to sending in those monthly maintenance checks (rather than risk losing their equity). If they see too many apartments rented out to tenants who aren't struck with the same fear of God to pay up, the bankers get nervous. As a result, they may deny a loan or extend it on less favorable terms. I can tell you that when we refinanced our multimillion-dollar mortgage, one of the first things our friendly banker wanted to know was how many subletters were in our midst.

So how many is too many? There's no bright line test or set number. Under 25 percent sublets, you're pretty safe. Anything beyond that is sure to invite closer scrutiny of the building's finances and a possible black mark on its credit.

Cash Flow (for Your Sake)

The same problem can put a crimp in your own refinancing plans. When it comes to individual apartments, what's tops on the banker's list is the state of your finances. But if the building's creditworthiness is compromised by too many sublets, the situation can come back to haunt you.

Community Cohesion

Then there's the issue of what I'll call the concrete community. If you believe one of the benefits of buying into a co-op is having your neighbors set in stone, you're for it. The only way to achieve such stasis is by banning sublets (which still isn't foolproof, because purchases and sales and life's normal progress bring change). On the other hand, if you think home is a state of mind and you don't care who you're surrounded by or how long they hang around, then you'd probably favor sublease freedom. But if it's left totally unchecked, freedom can lead to anarchy, or at least to revolving-door residents—especially if your building is near a university where dorm space is in short supply. If you want to vicariously relive those days of carefree existence then maybe you won't mind an invasion of students or other temporary residents and the decibel level that often accompanies them. But you may find that such exuberance wears thin pretty soon when you are a mere observer, not an active participant.

My building takes the middle ground on subleases. We allow them for two years out of every five-year period but with no lease less than a year. This last point is key. Reasonable people may differ on how often you should be allowed to sublease in any given period, but requiring tenants to stick around for at least a year goes far toward eliminating the dorm syndrome.

Rootless Residents

Another regular plaint is that subtenants are stakeless. Unlike their shareholder counterparts, who have socked every last cent into their places and are now financial prisoners for life, these folks are here today and gone tomorrow (or at most a year or two from now)—free to fly the coop when their lease is up. Some boards figure that since renters have no financial stake, they are guilty of a kind of moral turpitude because they lack any interest in the long-term integrity and well-being of the building. My experience as a board president is perversely the reverse. I find that renters as a group demand the best the building has without a thought as to who's footing the bill.

Cover-Up

There are also those pseudoreasons lawyers arm their client boards with in encouraging them to maximize their power (and sublease restrictions): too much wear and tear, too little control over building residents, and more. Since these problems can be addressed by issue-specific rules and not outright bans, I'd view them as more a cover for snobbism than sincere concern.

Double Trouble

Finally, I'll admit that as a board president I'm not a great fan of subleasing—but my reasons are practical, not philosophical. For every sublease there is an owner and an occupier. The result is that there are double the number of people who feel free to vent their spleen.

THE SUBLET SYSTEMS

Ultimately, it's not what the board thinks about subleasing but what the building's documents say on the subject that controls. The problem is, these documents usually give the board such broad discretion that, practically speaking, it is both creator and enforcer of the sublease rules under which you live. But as you learned in the discussion of the purchase process (see chapter 4), there are differences depending upon the political bent of your board. Let's revisit the philosophical spectrum and see what effect it has on your ability to sublet—without a fight.

Certain Victory Under Libertarian Rule

You will recall that for a prospective buyer seeking to break down the entry barriers buildings with Libertarian leanings offered the prospect of easiest access. Since the board cannot reject you, its only way of keeping you out is to exercise its right of first refusal and buy the apartment. Given the overwhelming odds against this, you are virtually assured of success from the get-go. In most buildings, if the free market rules for sales, it also rules for sublets. These co-ops (a small but growing number) take their cue from condos (see below) and, as with sales, give the board only a right of first refusal on proposed subleases.

Suppose you have tired of your privileged existence as the owner of that prewar palace and you long to return for a while to something more proletarian—a log cabin in the woods, a one-room retreat up north. If you have bought into a Libertarian building, then you (and your proposed subtenant), not the board, hold the balance of power. To be sure of who's in control all you need do is check out the lease and bylaws. A typical right-of-first-refusal provision would say something like this:

> Within thirty days of receipt of the notice and such other information as the Board may reasonably require from the Contract Lessee [that's you], the Board shall exercise its exclusive right to sublease the apartment (or designate another to sublease the apartment) on the same terms and conditions.
>
> The right of first refusal may be released or waived by the Board of Directors, in which event the Board shall send written notice thereof within the time [above] set forth to the Lessee. If the Lessor does not notify the Lessee by notice to such shareholder of its (or its designees) election to sublease the apartment, then the apartment may be subleased free and clear of the provisions of this paragraph.

What all this means is that the board can't just say no to your proposed subtenant. It has a set period (usually thirty days after it's been notified by the owner of the planned rental) to match the lease terms. So if you have an offer to rent your one-bedroom for one year at $3,000 a month with a security deposit up front, the board has to come up with a candidate willing to meet those terms or make up the shortfall itself. Unless it has a prospect waiting in the wings, it has to hire a broker or advertise to find someone to rent your apartment under these predetermined conditions. The only reason it would go to all this trouble is if the person you've proposed is such a miscreant the board figures he'll bring dishonor to the ranks (and to it).

More likely it'll try to make trouble (or at least difficulty) for you. Although it can't say no, it may try to throw its weight around by asking for additional information. If something is missing—say, a letter from your sublessee's employer or a professional reference—it can make him produce it. Or if there's an inconsistency (the salary on his credit report is different from that on his W-2), it can ask for clarifying information to get at the truth. The real problem (from the board's perspective) occurs when the application is complete but incurable. It shows your proposed tenant has lousy credit or has defaulted on student loans or has judgments from here to eternity against him. No pile of paper will change the facts.

The board can take one of two tacks. It can ask that your proposed tenant get a creditworthier guarantor to sign onto the lease. Or it can play hardball and continue its informational onslaught, knowing the results will be futile but hoping the process will frighten you away. Since most shareholders (and sublessees) don't know their rights, they allow themselves to be intimidated when they really are in control. Don't fall into this trap. If you're in a rush to rent out your apartment and your tenant has no objection to having someone act as guarantor, by all means accede to the board's demand—for although it can't deny, it can delay the inevitable. But if the board is unrelenting in its quest for (useless) information, you can call its bluff and just say no more. Unless the board is willing to cross the line from aggressive upholders to active violators of its co-op's laws, it'll have no choice but to let your chosen tenant have the key.

Battle Royale Under the Ancien Régime

Although the times they are a-changing, the royalists still hold sway in most buildings. If you are a shareholder under the ancien régime, then it is likely that your board has an iron grip over approving (or rejecting) not only sales but also sublets. Just so you know what you're up against, here's what a typical Old Guard sublease provision would say:

> The lessee [that's you again] shall not sublet the whole or any part of the apartment or renew or extend any previously authorized sublease, unless consent thereto shall have been duly authorized by a resolution of the directors, or given in writing by a majority of the directors or, if the directors shall have failed or refused to give such consent, then by lessees owning at least 66⅔ percent of the then issued shares of the lessor. . . . *Any consent to subletting may be subject to such conditions as the directors or lessees, as the case may be, may impose.* There shall be no limitation on the right of directors or lessees to grant or withhold consent for any reason or for no reason, to subletting. [Emphasis added.]

If this is the regime you are living under, then the board can reject a sublease application for any reason or no reason. Indeed, the courts have even authorized boards to be unreasonable in their rejection, thereby sending you back to the drawing board (and the marketplace) in search of a suitable tenant to fill your shoes. No matter that you lost time and money in the process.

Absolutism Isn't Absolute

Although the Old Guard's power to pass on subleases is formidable, it is not impenetrable. There are a few cracks in those palace walls that may allow your subtenant to pass through despite board opposition. I doubt that any of them are of sufficiently widespread applicability to get you very far, but it never hurts to be prepared.

1. A Higher Legal Authority

The board can reject your applicant for any reason or no reason, but it can't reject him or her for an illegal reason. Just as the board couldn't turn down your purchase application for reasons of bad faith or self-dealing,[1] it can't reject your tenant's application on any of these grounds. So it can't say no to your sublease because one of the board members has his eyes on your apartment for his secret amour, whom he'd like to have on hand but not at home. Nor can it refuse to interview your prospective tenants as a means to coerce you into signing a release (or taking other action), as one Fifth Avenue shareholder claimed happened to him.[2]

And above all, it can't say no if discrimination is the real reason. As we've seen in the purchase context, whether the discrimination is based on race, creed, color, sex, national origin, family status, or sexual orientation—it's illegal. That doesn't mean it's not happening; it's just hard to prove. But after a Beekman Place co-op (and its board members) several years ago got socked with a $1.5 million judgment for rejecting a couple's sublease application on grounds of racial discrimination (refer back to chapter 6), you can be sure boards will begin seeing the legal light (unless they want to risk bankrupting their buildings). If you suspect that's the real reason for the board's turning down your sublease, I'd remind its members real fast of the possible fallout (financial and otherwise) of their decision and urge them to reconsider.

2. No Doesn't Mean Never

Under the ancien régime, the board can say no to any sublease you present it with, but it can't just say no. One board operating under this regime figured since it had the absolute right to approve or reject sublease applications, it could cut to the quick and deny them *before* they were made. So it unilaterally passed a rule saying no more sublets. Unhappy at this dictatorial turn of events, the shareholders fought back and nipped the board's power grab in the bud. An outright ban on subleasing is not for the board to decide but for the shareholders to approve via a lease amendment. (Here a 75 percent vote was necessary to make it happen.)[3]

You may be asking, Can't the board achieve the same nefarious end by just turning down all applications *after* they've been submitted? The answer is yes—if you let them. I'd argue that if the board is doing this on a consistent basis it's effectively enacting an illegal amendment without your consent. If that's what's happening in your building, it may be time for the shareholders to get a lawyer to stop the board in its tracks.

Bringing Up the Rear Guard

Although the movement hasn't yet reached groundswell proportions, shareholders are getting smart, stripping boards of absolute authority and demanding that they be held to a reasonableness standard in passing on subleases. We've seen how the New Moderates have had their wings clipped in deciding the fate of purchase applications. The same holds true when it comes to subleases. Check out your lease to see if there's language to the effect that "the board shall not *unreasonably* withhold its consent" with respect to subletting. If that's the case, your board can't just thumb its nose and turn down your tenant without serious consideration and explanation.

One Brooklyn board found this out the hard way. Although the co-op's lease expressly prohibited the board from *unreasonably* withholding consent to any sublease of less than twelve months, it summarily denied not one but two applications by shareholders for permission to sublease. Not only was the board found to have overstepped its bounds but it had to pay damages for its hubris.[4]

Another board that failed to abide by its duty to not *unreasonably* withhold consent to subletting was brought up short by a shareholder after it refused even to give her an application. Although she had sublet before without trouble, the board decided that too much renting out was going on. In order to cut back, it passed a resolution providing that shareholders could sublease for a total of twenty-four months; after that their sublet status would be decided by lottery. Not being a gambling woman, the shareholder refused to enter the sublet sweepstakes and instead opted for the legal arena. She wound up the big winner. The court chewed out the board for disregarding her sublet rights, where it had a duty to be reasonable, and awarded her a $3,500 jackpot in punitive damages.[5]

If your board must be reasonable but comes back with a no response to your sublet request, hold the board's feet to the fire and make it tell you why. Has your applicant failed to come up with all the requested financial data? Does the information he has produced show he's a financial deadbeat? Is he planning to use the apartment as more than a place to call home, whether for commerce or, worse, some criminal activity? Are big-time renovations on the horizon for a short-term stay? If the board gives you (and your sublessee) a cold shoulder and a summary turn-down, you can get it in hot water for violating its obligation to be reasonable.

One last point to remember: No matter what the co-op's regime, if you have financing the bank also has a say. Under the standard recognition agreement, you can't sublet without your lender's approval, though as with co-op New Moderates, banks can't *unreasonably* withhold their consent. So getting their okay for your sublease is usually a formality.

Condo Freedom Fighters

Under most condo regimes for now sublet freedom (or anarchy, depending on your political persuasion) is the order of the day. Condo bylaws usually give the board only a right of first refusal regarding proposed subleases (or sales), a practice some freedom-loving co-ops have adopted. As you know by now, this means the board can't turn down your sublease; all it can do is exercise its right to lease your apartment on the same terms and conditions that your prospective tenant agreed to—not something it is wont to do unless your tenant is a diplomat with immunity or a Material Girl with an entourage. Even that diluted power is watered down still more in most condos. Whereas in Libertarian-leaning co-ops the board can on its own vote to exercise its right of first refusal on a sublease (or sale), in most condos the board can't act by itself but must get a majority of the owners to consent. Given the short time frame it has in which to act and the difficulty of getting a majority of owners to agree to anything, the chances of the board's intercepting your sublease are near nonexistent.

But where there's a will there's a way, as creative condo boards seeking to exert authority traditionally exclusive to co-op directors have found out. Their empowerment started slowly. One owner thumbed his nose at the condo board, renting out his apartment without executing a lease or offering the board a right of first refusal as required by the bylaws. After he did this a few times, the board decided to restore law and order. It got the court to prohibit Mr. Violator from leasing without complying with the rules.[6]

That minor interference with condo leasing may be developing into a trend thanks to courts that are beginning to uphold blanket leasing prohibitions by condo boards using power given in their bylaws. When one board discovered that owners had leased out their unit in violation of bylaws that said no leasing, and took action, the court said it's a reasonable restraint on alienation, and they have to abide.[7] (For a property refresher, see chapter 4.) And when the board at another condo sued owners for payment of fines for breaking the regulations relating to leasing of their units, the judge there said the rules were within the managers' authority.[8]

It's enough for boards if the leasing restrictions are in the bylaws, but as far as courts are concerned, it's even better if they've been approved by the owners themselves and then included as an amendment. Thus far, leasing bans in condos have not yet blossomed into a full-fledged movement because even though such restrictions may be okay as a matter of law, they are viewed negatively in the marketplace, where buyers and sellers like the freedom of renting to whom they please. Still, if I were buying into a new condo, I'd double-check to see what their bylaws said on the subject, and even if your preexisting condo is presently restriction free, it is no longer safe to assume it will remain thus forever.

Running the Gauntlet

Assuming you faithfully followed the rules of engagement to purchase your own apartment, you know the drill for filling out board applications: Don't lie, don't cheat, don't be inconsistent, be neat and complete the first time around. (For a refresher course, go back to chapter 4.) It's usually the broker who shepherds your subtenant through the application phase. And for the 15 percent fee (of the first year's rent) he pockets from your lessee he should get it right. But now that you're a seasoned pro in your own right, why not pass on the benefit of your battle scars for your tenant's sake as well as your own? Ask to see the application after it's completed but before it's submitted to the board. This way you can see firsthand if you're satisfied with your tenant's finances. Unless you're convinced that he's ready, able, and willing to pay you on time, it doesn't matter what the board thinks. If you spot any problems of the curable variety—a missing document, some inadvertent inconsistency—you can see that they're corrected before the board is asked to give its stamp of approval. Even better, now that you're on the inside you can (and should) try to cut the board off at the pass with a friendly call to one of its members.

Usually the application that your tenant has to turn in is a subset of what's required in a purchase application. The board wants to see that your boarder is financially fit and not a social misfit. This means handing over at least a credit report, income verification, professional and personal references, and proof of employment. The board will be looking for this paper trail to show that the tenant can handle the rent (it's not more than 28 to 33 percent, max, of his annual income intake) and has credit that passes muster. Since your tenant is only on the line for the monthly rent and not the underlying value of the apartment, the board doesn't really need to know his net worth down to the last cent or the secrets he shares with the IRS. (Though with some rents reaching the six-figure realm, boards are sure to dig deeper.) On this theory our sublet application is akin to that for purchase minus tax returns and net worth statement. But some boards demand blood, requiring the full-scale dossier of a purchaser for the scaled-down responsibilities of a renter.

Avoid a Pyrrhic Victory

Although you may condemn the board for turning down your prospective tenant, the truth is it may have done you a favor. That's because your financial obligations linger on after you have moved out and your tenant has moved in. Whether or not your tenant forks over the monthly maintenance on time (or at all), *you* remain primarily on the hook for payment. If your sublessee stops sending those checks, it's up to you to hire a lawyer and bring a nonpayment action to get paid or to get back possession of your apartment.

If he refuses to leave when the sublease is over, it's up to you to bring a holdover action to get him out. This can take months and cost you plenty—a fact not likely to escape the attention of any street-smart subtenant, especially if he senses you're selling the place and need to get him out in order to clinch the deal. It may be cheaper (and faster) to pay some legal extortion than to drag him through the legal wringer.

Worse still, what if it turns out he's a really bad dude and is doing something illegal in your apartment? If you don't bring an action to get rid of him, the board can do the dirty work for you, naming you as a defendant together with your less-than-savory subtenant. Remember what happened to Mr. X who sublet to a crazy drug dealer? (See page 187.) You can be hit for your refusal to act with stiff monetary penalties, attorneys' fees, and (in rare cases) even suffer the ultimate sacrifice—forfeiture of your apartment.

Given these realities, it's in your own best interest to find someone who's financially and legally able, even if it means turning down a few frogs to get to the sublet prince. I always get nervous when shareholders submit sublease applications showing their prospective tenants to be financial toads, because it indicates that they don't understand the consequences—or that they're too busy keeping their financial heads above water in their current whereabouts to care.

RULES OF THE REGIME

Not only can the Palace Guard turn thumbs-up or -down on your prospective tenant, under the standard co-op lease allowing it to set *conditions* for subletting it can decide when and under what circumstances the fortress gates will be rolled up to allow in sublet subjects. In most condos, it's the freedom fighters who control the how, where, and when if you want to sublet. Under the standard condo bylaws giving boards only a right of first refusal, they have no power source from which to draw to set any other conditions. The Condo Act says condo bylaws can have provisions governing leases and sales, and as we've just seen, at least one court has upheld a condo bylaw that allowed the board to ban subleasing. But for the most part, condo boards do not impose sublet controls akin to those of their co-op cousins. So if you live in a condo you should be wary of any sublet rules that come down from on high because they are still the exception, not the norm.

In co-ops, sublet rules are standard fare, to be understood if not tolerated.

The specifics of these rules vary all over the lot, but in type they usually fall into one of the following categories.

How Often?

When you get to rent out your place is usually not a function of free will but of board prescription. The way this works is to limit your sublet privileges to a set number of years within a given period. For example, you can sublease one out of three or two out of every five years (as is the case in my building). Less frequently, the board may set a residential lifetime cap—allowing, let's say, two sublets for the duration of your tenancy (however long that may be), to be taken when you choose. Although you may resent board intrusion, at least limiting sublets by setting time boundaries applies equally to all.

How Long?

Just as important as how often you can rent out is the length of time each sublease can be. In some buildings, the board lets you decide. In others it decides for you, typically requiring that no sublease be less than six months or one year (as in my building). The rationale of the rule is obvious from the results. Say you can sublet for two out of five years. Without any limit on lease length, you could have a succession of students or other temporary types coming and going at your (and their) will. With a one-year threshold, the possible traffic jam is reduced to a trickle of one or two people in the same time frame. So if you value stability over transience, this one's for you.

How Many?

Some sublet rules target the body politic rather than the individual shareholder. This is the case where boards limit the total number of apartments in the building that can be sublet at any one point in time. The cap can be either a percentage (say, 20 percent) of all units or a finite figure (say, 40 out of 250 apartments). This kind of rule usually turns up in buildings that are sublet prone, a condition that can create credit problems for the building when renters go over the 25 percent mark. If such a regulation exists in your co-op, you have to be careful that it's coupled with a rule limiting the time each shareholder can rent out. Otherwise the same lucky shareholders can hold on to the sublet slots.

Hard Luck

Then there are the so-called hardship clauses that give the board power to decide, usually on a case-by-case basis, whether special circumstances exist that warrant any exemption from the otherwise antisublet policy. These circumstances can run the gamut: a shareholder got transferred on business to some far-flung locale for a year, another has to go tend to an ailing aunt, someone else tried with persistence (but without success) to sell his apartment and wants to lease till things turn around—and who knows what else. As far as I'm concerned, that's the problem. It's strictly up to the board to decide whether your hard luck is tough enough to grant you an exemption. Even if it exercises its judgment with Solomonic wisdom and shareholder-blind objectivity, it is sure to be exposed to claims of selective enforcement (or exemption) by those whose stories didn't pass the hard luck test. Better to pass a rule that applies to all equally so everyone knows where they stand from the start.

The board can even impose rules on how to carry out its rules. For example, if properly authorized, it can condition your right to sublease on your being current in your own maintenance payments.

Just because the rules exist doesn't mean they're easy to find. If all's gone as it should, sublet rules passed by board resolution should find their way into (or be attached to) the proprietary lease. But sometimes they are sent out by a separate communiqué and don't make it into the official document. That's no problem if you were around when they were passed—as long as you know *what* they are it doesn't matter much *where* they are. But if you bought in years after the fact, you could be in for a rude surprise. That's what happened to one shareholder who decided to sublet his apartment after he'd been living there for a while. A sublet fee (20 percent of maintenance) had been legally passed (in this case, by shareholder-approved amendment) and communicated by letter to all then-existing shareholders, but never made it into the lease. Too bad. He still had to pay the $7,500 sublet fee, the court said, because it's not the board's (or building's) duty to educate potential purchasers on the requirements for subletting or any other transaction under the building's lease. Its only duty was to notify all the shareholders at the time the resolution was adopted, which it did.[9] So if you think subletting may be on your personal agenda, don't take what the lease says at face value because it may not be the whole story. Find out what other rules lurk out there in the co-op netherworld and get copies of whatever exists in writing so in case the board forgets (and it's in your interest) you can remind it.

A potentially worse problem exists if there are no specific sublet rules—just that broad ukase authorizing board czars and czarinas to set whatever conditions their dictatorial hearts desire. That's the situation that a lawyer friend of mine found when she moved into a posh Village co-op. Unable to kick her professional habits, she asked about subletting and the answer came back from above that although there were no written rules the board was "easy" on the issue. Neither she nor I (whose inside advice she sought) took comfort in the results of her investigation. Although such an expression of sublease sentiment is nice, it is not enforceable. Since the board had not carved out any rules from its power grant, the board retains the grant's full force to use when it sees fit—leaving shareholders to wonder what response they'll face when they try to sublet. (And whether that response will be the same for all.)

Making Your Own Rules

Regardless of what rules your regime operates under, there are those unwilling to abide by convention (and determined to rent their places out in a hurry). If you're one of them, you may decide to go undercover and rent your apartment without benefit of board input (or interference). It's been known to happen, and I'm sure some of you out there have tried it (with greater or lesser success), whether or not you're willing to come clean. For the undaunted among you, I offer the following guidelines culled from my experience as board president and counterintelligence agent.

Make the Doorman Your Accomplice

The most common route to boardless entry is slipping the guardians of the gate a couple of hundred bucks to let your subtenant pass through. I believe in using the power of the dollar when it can achieve results, so it's on logic, not principle, that I object to this method. As any high-rise resident knows, there's not one but at least four sentinels standing guard at the door on an around-the-clock basis. In some buildings they work military-style in teams, thereby doubling the number to eight. And there's no way of knowing in advance precisely what time or on whose shift your subtenant will show up with his stuff. Paying off all those would-be talkers is too pricey and too unwieldy—not that many people can remain silent. And paying off just one will not assure success. Besides, if your building is anything like mine, the mere presence of a moving van (whether conspicuously out front or hidden in back) is sure to set tongues wagging and put the gossip mill into high gear—not a formula destined to keep your tenant's secret for long.

Avoid Clutter

You stand a better chance of skirting the system if your tenant moves in light—a toothbrush is okay, furniture is not. This way the aura of legitimacy attaches upon his arrival as your "guest." If he's careful, it may stick even after he's outstayed his legal welcome and become a resident outlaw. Of course, unless your subtenant takes minimalism to the extreme and has renounced all creature comforts, this approach requires leaving your furniture in place. Then he has somewhere to hang his hat and you can charge extra for the privilege.

One of the shareholders in my building gave this a try just after the building converted, in an open challenge to the authority (and intelligence) of the new board. She moved out with only suitcase in hand and not even a nod to board subleasing requirements. Her designated replacement moved in, similarly unencumbered, to her fully furnished studio. It took only one leaky faucet for the super to figure out what was going on and report the undercover activities to the board. The fugitive was removed and the owner learned her lesson. When she next decided to sublease she realized that going to the board was likely to yield more trouble-free results than going behind its back.

Use a Resident As a Ruse

Another novel approach is to lease to somebody already living in the building with another legal resident but who's ready for a room of his own. A grown child who's anxious to fly the coop but doesn't want to go too far from the nest. A roommate who's had a falling out with his owner-companion but not with the co-op. The benefits of such an arrangement for the subversive sublessor are obvious. There's no need to pay anyone to sneak in an illicit tenant because they've moved in as legal residents. (Who's to know their status is about to change?) Nor is bringing in their belongings a problem because they're already there (albeit in a different locale). Even furniture deliveries, if properly handled, shouldn't raise any suspicions as long as they're directed to the old haunt, not the new illegal den.

As a board president I hate to admit it, but this subleasing ruse works pretty well. Indeed, I got the idea from someone in my building who did it and who managed to pull the wool over the board's eyes for over a year. It was only when a dispute over the ownership of the subleased apartment caused the perpetrators to come running to the board for help that they unwittingly professed their offense. Another shareholder whose apartment was furnished but who had not been in residence for a while told us that after his housekeepers had cleaned the place, his son was moving back in. Every weekend he accompanied the "cleaning" couple, who came with shopping bags supposedly full of stuff to render the premises spic and span until the brooms and mops departed—and the couple stayed—a situation our board had to deal with.

Paying the Price

Bottom line, I'd advise against going the illegal sublet route. I'm not saying it can't be done. There are exceptions to every rule. But the odds are against you. Unless your building is so huge that no one knows (or cares) what's going on, chances are your secret will out—whether through some nosy neighbor, a disgruntled doorman, or your occupier's own carelessness. Once you are discovered not only can the board take steps to evict you and your tenant, but if your boarder gets mad enough he can go after you himself.

That's what happened when a Bronxville owner decided to rent her two-bedroom apartment without bothering to ask the board for approval (as required) or to tell her tenant it was an illegal sublet. No sooner did the board find out (within a matter of a week) than it declared war against the offending owner. It did everything it could to legally rub out her illegal tenant—from threatening eviction to removing his name (and hence his existence) from the mailbox and doorbell. Finally he could endure no more. He sought justice (and vengeance) from the shareholder-landlord who got him into this mess in the first place. And he won—getting damages not only for expenses in moving and in finding a new apartment, but also for aggravation. Even punitive damages for the owner's moral culpability.[10]

For those cynics out there who don't believe the long arm of the law is meant for them, let this be a lesson. Proceed at your own (considerable) risk in renting out on your own.

WHAT PRICE VICTORY?

Assuming you have emerged victorious in the boarder wars (whether through outsmarting, circumventing, or complying with the board) and have a tenant safely in position, what are the financial ramifications? This is a two-pronged inquiry. How much can you profit and how much will it cost you?

What You Can Charge

After you've presumably paid through the nose to get your little piece of high-rise heaven, why not recoup some of your outlay when you sublease? I'm not suggesting rent gouging. (After all, I'm a lawyer with a conscience.) But if market conditions permit, you should charge enough so that you can cover your monthly maintenance and mortgage payments and then some. Done correctly, subleasing can be both salutary and profitable.

Legal Lowdown

As you may imagine, where big bucks are involved the board is not far behind. A few co-ops have tried to impose limits on what you can charge your subtenant. (Check out your bylaws and proprietary laws to see if you are at risk.) One shareholder took the board to court when it approved his subtenant only on condition that the rent not exceed the maintenance he paid plus a 20 percent surcharge and a $1,000 deposit.[11] Since these rent limitations were only contained in the corporate guidelines and not in the proprietary lease, our shareholder got to charge what he wanted. (I should also tell you that he was a holder of unsold shares who, like the sponsor, was exempt from most rules anyway.)

Profiteering is prohibited in the rental context. Both the New York City Rent Stabilization Law and Code prohibit tenants from charging their subtenants more than the legal stabilized rent (the rent they pay) plus a 10 percent surcharge if the apartment is decked out with the tenant's furniture. The theory behind this legislation is that tenants lucky enough to have a dirt-cheap lease shouldn't profit at the expense of their law-abiding landlords, who are stuck charging below-market rates. Any attempt to limit what you as a shareholder can charge for a sublet makes no sense because in this situation you *are* the landlord. If perchance your building's documents do impose limits, shareholders should get together and get rid of them.

What the Board Can Charge You

It's a different story when it comes to how much the board can charge *you* for the privilege of subletting your own apartment. Lots of co-ops impose sublet fees for reasons that are philosophical or financial. (Although most condo owners can still rent out their units without board interference, now that the courts have said it's okay for condos to ban subleasing, fees as a condition for allowing the privilege may not be far behind.) Let's say the board wants to keep out the renting riffraff but it can't get an amendment passed banning subletting outright. It may be possible to make the price of subleasing so painful (especially if shareholder sentiment is on its side) that it is effectively, if not actually, outlawed. Alternately, it could be that the building's coffers are not overflowing and a refill is necessary. Rather than pick your pocket when it may be empty (through assessments or the like) it's easier and politically more expedient to make you pay when you have some (hopefully positive) cash flow from leasing out your place.

Power Source or Vacuum

Contrary to what you may think, the power to charge you a sublet fee does not flow ineluctably from the state of directorial grace. The building's lease and bylaws must affirmatively give the board this power before it can exercise it, though the former, which has to be amended by shareholders (usually by a two-thirds vote), is more important than the latter, which often can be changed by the board alone. Suppose you've been subleasing freely for a while when your board announces it's imposing a sublet fee. Don't assume this is the natural order of things. Find out whether there is a power source legitimizing its actions or whether it's engaged in an illegal power grab.

The easiest way to do this is to check out your co-op's governing documents to see if there's a sublease provision saying that the board can charge such a fee. A modern lease would say something like this:

> Any consent to subletting may be subject to such fees and/or conditions as the board of directors may deem appropriate in its sole discretion, including, but not limited to, payment of a sublet fee determined by the board of directors.

Even if the words *fee* or *money* are nowhere in evidence, that doesn't necessarily mean you can lease out for nothing. Lots of leases that came into being when co-ops came into existence—and haven't kept pace with changing legal developments—might contain a general proviso allowing the board to set "conditions" for subletting without express reference to hard cash. Although courts have been requiring more specificity when it comes to making shareholders pay, most judges would probably allow the board to charge a fee.

Whatever the particular variant, such provision is what lawyers like to call an enabling clause because it's the engine that drives board power. We'll discuss in detail what this provision means and how it works. But for now all you need do is note its existence or absence. If it's nowhere to be found, odds are your board is overstepping its bounds in setting a sublet fee, so the shareholders should get their own lawyer to stop the board's illegal march.

That's what the owners did at the Hotel des Artistes, that Art Deco architectural gem off Central Park West, when the board, hoping to reduce the number of sublets and increase revenue in one fell swoop, decided to impose a sublet fee equal to 100 percent of annual maintenance to be phased in over three years, starting in the first year with a hefty 33 percent surcharge. Faced with an angry mob, the board had to scale back and agreed to freeze the fee at $1.33 a share (which was then equal to 33 percent of maintenance). A majority of shareholders ratified the charge at the annual meeting.

But that wasn't enough of a reduction to keep a group of angry shareholders from challenging the board's taxing power in court. Although the lease gave the board power to reject subtenants for any or no reason (except discrimination) it didn't contain the magic words giving the board power to impose *conditions* on sublet approvals. Without the specific power to fix sublet fees or the general power to set conditions on approving subleases, the board was running on empty. If it wanted to sock owners with the fee it had to get the consent of two-thirds of them and amend the lease. The result: the tax was declared null and void and the board was ordered to return all its ill-gotten gains.[12]

In most co-ops these clauses are incorporated at the founding into the governing manifesto before shareholders have a say. Thereafter it's next to impossible to add them, because shareholders won't vote to tax themselves. When my building was converting, our lawyer urged us to adopt one of these clauses so we could later sock it to our constituents in the form of sublet fees. I'm proud to say that our democratic roots won out over our newfound directorial status and we said no. The decision was made easier because our co-op came into existence with sufficient cash that we had (and still have) no need to go to shareholders for more. And frankly, the thought that someday (when my board stint is over) one of my neighbors might be dictating sublease fees to me was scary enough to convince me that power wasn't necessarily a plus.

Tribute Takes Many Forms

Like it or not, what you should understand is that the standard co-op provision subjecting sublet consent to such conditions and/or fees as the board may impose is like a grenade waiting to go off (if it hasn't already). When the board in its sole discretion decides to pull the lever, it can make you pay a fee without asking for your permission. The particular form the board chooses for inflicting its fiat can vary from building to building. These are among the most common kinds of sublet fees you will find in proprietary leases:

1. Fixed Price Pain

A set dollar amount per share annually. At $4 per share, if you owned 400 shares your annual contribution to the kitty would be $1,600.

2. Maintenance Take

A percentage of your monthly or annual maintenance. Let's say your maintenance is $1,000 a month or $12,000 a year and the board had set a 10 percent surcharge. Your tithe would be $100 a month or $1,200 a year.

3. Graduated Fee

In order to discourage subletting, some boards increase the percentage of sublet fees the longer you rent out. So, for example, the first year you might have to pay 10 percent of maintenance; the second, 20 percent; and the third, 30 percent—or more.

4. Rental Cut

A percentage of the monthly rent you charge your subtenant. Assume you're getting $2,000 a month and the board imposes a 5 percent monthly surcharge, you would have to fork over $100 a month to the building.[13]

5. One Month Rule

An annual payment equal to one month's sublet rent for the year. If you let out your place for $1,500 a month, you would have to hand over $1,500 a year (one month's rent) to the co-op.

A word of caution—The fact that your lease includes one of the above—or some other form of tribute—doesn't necessarily mean it's enforceable. The law changes faster than most leases and, as we'll see, it's now pretty clear that types 1 to 3 would pass muster, while 4 and 5 would not.

In addition to the sublet fee itself, the board can add on extras under the same power provision. It can ask you to deposit funds up front or to reimburse it for possible legal expenses, anticipated wear and tear caused by your subtenant, administrative costs for processing the application—and any other items it dreams up that seem to make sense.

Equality for Almost All

The Business Corporation Law that governs all corporations, including co-ops, says that each share must be equal to every other share of the same class.[14] Only there's an exception to every rule. As we'll see, flip taxes don't have to be assessed on an equal amount per share, and for a while boards figured sublet fees didn't have to be either. But a few savvy shareholders who knew their rights got the courts to see things their way. It started with Mr. Wapnick, a shareholder who challenged a provision in his co-op's bylaws that gave preferential treatment for sublet consent and fees to original purchasers. That's not fair. All owners should be treated alike, he argued—and won.[15]

Only his victory caused a crisis among the sponsor elite, who thought the ruling meant that their above-the-law status—and with it their exemption from sublet restrictions and fees—might be over. Their fear was short-lived. A shareholder at another building said he shouldn't have to pay an increasing percentage of the sublet fee when holders of unsold shares (the sponsor) were exempt. Sorry, the answer came back this time from the court. The big boys are entitled to privileged status because they have obligations you don't—including the duty to renew the leases of all those rent-stabilized tenants who stuck around and didn't buy—which they couldn't fulfill if they were subject to the same pesky requirements you are. You've got to pay the sublet fee, the court ordered the shareholder, even though it questioned the board's authority to charge an increasing percent when the bylaws provided for only a *reasonable* fee to cover actual expenses and attorneys' fees.[16]

All doubt was recently laid to rest. The board of a Park Avenue co-op told a shareholder, who had bought her apartment as an insider when the building converted and sublet for more than a decade, that she could do so no more. What do you mean? she demanded. The bylaws say since I'm an original purchaser, I can sublet without board consent, even though everyone else needs approval. The bylaws are in violation of the law, the court said. You can't have superior subletting rights over your fellow shareholders. It doesn't matter that the board let you get away with it for years—you have to stop.[17]

What's the net result of all this legal sparring? Whether it's sublet restrictions or fees, all similarly situated shareholders—that's you, me, and most everyone else (whether original or subsequent purchasers)—must be treated equally. (The only ones who get a pass from the rules are sponsors, because they are *not* similarly situated due to their special obligations.)

What this means for you is that a sublet fee based on a fee-per-share basis or a percentage of maintenance is probably okay—and maybe even a graduated fee, if it's not unreasonable. But any other method would likely run afoul of the present state of the law and be unenforceable.

Reasonableness for Some

Just how much the board can hit you up for the privilege of renting out your own apartment isn't exactly clear, and it depends on whether the building's documents reflect an intent to discourage subletting or contain a reasonableness restriction. In one building where the minutes disclosed the board's policy to curtail sublets, and the bylaws allowed for a maintenance surcharge, the court upheld imposition of increasing fees: 20 percent surcharge for the first year, 30 percent for the second, and 60 percent for the third.[18]

Shareholders fare better where reasonableness rules. One unlucky shareholder couldn't sell his apartment but found someone to sublet it for an amount that covered his monthly mortgage and maintenance payments. Only the board demanded payment of a sublet fee up front equal to 30 percent of his annual maintenance (several thousand dollars in real money). Since he didn't have the cash, the board said no deal—and eventually his apartment was foreclosed. He fought back, claiming the board's fee was unauthorized and unreasonable and had brought him to ruin, for all of which he wanted financial retribution. Since the bylaws didn't give the board a blank check to set *conditions* on subletting but limited its power to imposing *reasonable fees* for specific items (such as the co-op's actual expenses for attorneys' and service fees), the court said the shareholder had a legitimate complaint.[19]

The same reasonableness standard saved the day for another shareholder who claimed that a sublet fee, varying from 20 percent of maintenance for the first year, 30 percent for the second, and 50 percent for the third year of the sublease was too high to be enforceable.[20] Assuming your building's documents contain such a limitation, you should have protection from carte blanche sublet fees.

Achieving Equilibrium

How much say shareholders really have in setting sublet fee policy depends to a large extent on whether the rules are already in place when you buy in or whether the board has to come to you for initial or increased authority. Whatever the situation, knowing your legal rights will help insure that the rules are as shareholder-friendly as possible. Here, then, is a recap of the key points to keep in mind in deciding what action to take.

1. No Power/No Glory

If there's no enabling clause the board doesn't have power to charge you *any* sublet fee. The fact that the board has authority to approve or reject a sublease doesn't by itself give it the right to condition approval on payment of a fee. If the board tries it, counterattack promptly.

2. Conditions Mean Money/Fees Make It Sure

As long as the board is empowered to subject its subletting consent to such *conditions* as it may impose, it can probably make you pay a reasonable fee—though increasingly, to protect themselves, boards also want specific authority to set *fees*. Just how much is reasonable is open to debate. When in doubt get together and demand a reduction. Unless the building is in a real cash crunch, the board would probably rather switch than fight.

3. No Blank Checks

If the board has to come to you for authority, don't ever give it carte blanche to set fees or conditions at its discretion. Demand at a minimum that the board be held to a (written) reasonableness standard. Better still, insist upon a specific cap on what it can charge (say, up to 25 percent of annual maintenance). This way if it needs (or wants) more it has to come to you for approval. Also you'll know the worst-case scenario rather than getting hit with a surprise when the board can hold your sublease hostage.

Giving the board the unilateral right to fix fees smacks too much of taxation without representation for my taste. Even if you trust your current directors implicitly, there's no assurance they'll be around forever (or even next year). When a new crew takes over you could be in for a rude and expensive awakening—after it's too late to do anything. And though you may be an arch opponent of subleasing, wanting to keep the building pure and secure, the day may come when necessity takes precedence over theory and you have to rent out your pad. Remember, you're not subjecting just your neighbors, but also yourself, to the possibility of unrestrained financial pain.

Beware Fellow Shareholders

Even if you reach a modus operandi with your board on sublet fees, that's not necessarily the end of the story. In some buildings, shareholders are more determined to ban subleases than the board. If enough of them (usually two-thirds) band together they can change the lease and bylaws to provide for whatever sublet fees they want—reasonableness and the rest of the shareholders be damned. That's what happened at the posh Sherry Netherland, after war broke out between the majority owners who lived in suites and the minority owner-investors who rented out their studios. Using the power of the ballot, the majority (74 percent) pushed through an amendment increasing the sublease fee (the minority would have to pay) to 20 percent of rent they received.[21] In another large co-op an antisublease shareholder faction approved a lease amendment giving the board power to set a sublet fee of up to 50 percent of annual maintenance.

What the board can't do alone by resolution shareholders can do together (if there are enough of them) by amendment. And although the board may sometimes be your enemy, shareholders aren't always your friends.

ALTERNATE PATHS TO GLORY

Now that you know the financial and administrative costs of passing through the sublet gauntlet, you're probably asking: Is there a way to avoid it all and restore residential self-determination? There's no (legal) way to escape if what you're after is a true sublease. And you've been forewarned of the consequences if you go the illegal route. But if you're looking for something short of a sublease—let's say, a share with a roommate or an extended stay of a family member—there may be help at hand. It all depends on who's staying and for how long.

Is It a Roommate?

Or can you say it is and sneak in a subtenant (which is what you really want to know)? For the answer we need to look at what's called in the legal trade the Roommate Law.[22] This is what it says:

> Any lease or rental agreement for residential premises entered into by one tenant shall be construed to permit occupancy by the tenant, immediate family of the tenant, *one additional occupant*, and dependent children of the occupant provided that the tenant or the tenant's spouse occupies the premises as his primary residence. [Emphasis added.]

Or in plain English, in addition to immediate family, a tenant can share his or her apartment with one other person not named in the lease (and that person's dependent children) without fear of eviction.

Now for what it means in real life. The law wasn't passed to help fat-cat co-op owners. It was intended to give rental tenants the right (for economic or personal reasons) to live with nonfamily members without fear of being kicked out for breach of occupancy lease restrictions. So gay life partners were protected, as were unrelated tenants who lived together out of financial necessity. But courts, in their wisdom, figured that since co-ops and proprietary lessees also have a landlord-tenant relationship, the law should apply. And so, by judicial fiat, it does.[23] The law does not apply to condos because residents are owners, not tenants.[24] It didn't used to matter because condo owners could rent out pretty much as they pleased without board interference. Now that at least one court has said condos may prohibit subleasing (though most still do not), you could ultimately be caught between a rock and a hard place—neither able to sublease your apartment nor be protected by the Roommate Law.

Terror in the Boardroom

For a while this law had boards running scared. To understand why, you need to know a bit of urban legal history involving an eighty-nine-year-old Upper West Sider named Anna. Anna broke a hip and was forced to move to a convalescent home in California. With the approval of her co-op board, she sublet her apartment for a year to her grandniece, Nona. When the year was up and Nona wouldn't go, the board tried to end Anna's lease, claiming an illegal sublet. The court said nonsense. The sublease wasn't illegal, it was expired. And under the Roommate Law, Nona could live in the apartment even though Anna wasn't there and had no plans to return.[25]

This ruling struck terror in the hearts of co-op boards because it threatened to strip them of the power to regulate who resides in their buildings and to allow subtenants in through the back door of the Roommate Law without the need for *any* board approval.

Return to Power

But the cold sweat lasted only about a year. Then a higher judicial authority said the first judge was wrong. Nona's tenancy was, after all, an illegal sublet and the Roommate Law didn't help because it required that the occupant (Nona) live in the apartment *with* the shareholder (Anna), who had to occupy the place as her primary residence. In other words, it's okay to share but you can't have a disguised sublet under the Roommate Law. Still that didn't stop shareholders from trying—at least for a while.

One apartment owner, who primarily lived elsewhere, figured he'd let out his apartment during the week to someone else and stay there himself on weekends. Occasionally they both hung out together in the apartment and divvied up expenses. (Each had another residence.) The board said it was an illegal sublet and sued the owner. The owner said he had a "roommate" protected under the law. Score another for the board. As long as the owner doesn't call the apartment home (*and* actually live there), his boarder doesn't get help from the Roommate Law. The law is intended to let shareholders share their places, not save for a second one.[26]

Another shareholder couple who moved out of their apartment and let their niece move in took a different tack. They argued she was a roommate allowed to live alone in the apartment because there was no lease and no money had changed hands. That's not what matters, the court said when the board sued. The Roommate Law will help only if the owner stays put in the apartment together with the other person.[27]

Shareholders in my own building have given it a try. One owner who seemed unnaturally law-abiding approached the board and asked if he needed sublet permission to have a friend share his apartment. (He'd be out of town on occasion.) We told him "No problem," until we saw his furniture being hauled out and his "friend's" being moved in. The board saw to it that this informal (and illicit) arrangement was turned into a formal sublet—documentation and all. Another shareholder recently told us his roommate would move in with him and, by the way, please put him on the lease and stock certificate. But the Roommate Law doesn't give you the right to transfer ownership without board approval.

End result: The Roommate Law (which initially held such promise for the antiauthoritarian in us all) has been declawed as a shareholder weapon. It cannot be used as an end run to sneak in a subtenant and avoid board approval.

Taking Legal Advantage

But, the Roommate Law can be used (legally and profitably) if you want to share your apartment with someone who is not on the lease. Who is up to you. The relationship can be friend, companion, or strictly business. As long as you're the individual named on the proprietary lease, you can take in *one additional person* without board approval (in addition to your immediate family, of which more later). One board fined a shareholder $500 for refusing to have his roommate come to a board meeting for an interview and submit to financial screening and a credit check. Give it back, the court said. All you can ask for under the law is the occupant's name.[28] Since you have to live with this person, you'd better be able to tolerate him or her.

Things get a little tricky under the Roommate Law when there are two or more of you on the lease—let's say, a husband and wife or a brother and sister. I guess the lawmakers figured since you're already living with someone you don't need a companion. If that's the situation, then you can bring in another occupant (in addition to your immediate family) *only if* the total number of tenants and occupants doesn't exceed the number specified on the lease. In other words, if one of you isn't staying in the apartment, the other can bring in a replacement without board approval. Otherwise, no dice. (Maybe not a formula for marital bliss, but okay as far as the law is concerned.)

Here are a few examples to set you straight:

1. Other than your Siamese it's only you at home and on the lease. You figure it's time for some human companionship and decide to let your officemate move in and share expenses, hoping both romance and riches will strike. Answer: No problem and no board approval necessary.
2. You and your sister (both named as tenants on the proprietary lease) occupy a spacious prewar with your brother. He knows he's got a

> good thing going and lets his girlfriend join the party. Answer: Maybe you don't object, but the board could. Since there are only two of you on the lease and you're both in residence, the girlfriend (occupant) goes, although the brother (family member) can stay.[29]

Although usually it's shareholders who take advantage of the Roommate Law, in my building the board called upon its help. Two financially fit brothers sought to buy an apartment to be occupied by the son of one—and his "friend." Rather than engage in futile battle (since we have only a right of first refusal), but unwilling to set a precedent for unauthorized occupancy, we said, Make the son an owner, which also rendered him a "tenant" under the law, and with that status the right to have a roommate.

Assuming it's not love but money that motivates your decision to take in a roommate, how much can you charge? Not long ago the law was changed to prevent rent-stabilized tenants from charging roommates more than their proportionate share. That didn't stop one renter from charging her live-in $2,200 a month even though the monthly rent for the *entire* apartment was only $1,850, until the court stepped in and said no.[30] The idea is that rental tenants shouldn't be allowed to benefit at the expense of their landlord, but this rationale isn't necessarily transferable because *you* are the co-op owner. For now, at least, unless and until some case is decided otherwise, you're probably safe charging your roommate whatever you want.

Is It a Family Member?

So maybe you can't have strangers move in (when you're not around) and get away with it by calling them roommates. But surely you can have family members come and go as you (and they) see fit. Not if the board has anything to say about it. Most co-ops have what are called restrictive use clauses. A typical one might say something like this:

> The Lessee [you] shall not, without the written consent of the Lessor [the co-op] on such conditions as Lessor may prescribe, occupy or use the apartment or permit the same or any part thereof to be occupied or used for any purpose other than as a private dwelling for the Lessee and Lessee's spouse, their children, grandchildren, parents, grandparents, brothers, sisters and domestic employees, and in no event shall more than one married couple occupy the apartment without the written consent of the Lessor.

If you're thinking like a lawyer, the first thing you're probably asking is, How can the board restrict use of your apartment to you and your family when the Roommate Law says you can share an apartment with anyone you want without board approval? You'd be right (and are sure to get a stellar score on your LSATs if you choose to join the fold). These use provisions exist in one form or another in virtually all co-ops. To the extent they try to limit occupancy of your apartment to you and your immediate family members and prevent you from having a roommate of your choosing, the Roommate Law declares them void as against public policy. You can ignore what they have to say and go ahead and get that roommate without going to the board.

But you can't ignore these provisions when it comes to dealing with family members. On their face, they exempt at least certain family members from the need to get board consent to stay in your apartment. What most of you really want to know, though, is not whether that relative can come and live *with* you but whether she can come and live *without* you. In other words, can you turn these provisions into a consent-free route for subletting to family members?

More than a few shareholders have given it a shot. For those of you looking for a shortcut to hassle-free subleasing, the results aren't encouraging. One grandmother, who moved to Puerto Rico, let her grandson stay in her co-op without telling the board. When the board went after her for an illegal sublet, she argued that no board approval was necessary because under the use provision "grandchildren" were permitted to occupy the apartment. That's true, but only half the story, the judge said. Since the lease talked about the lessee *and* her grandchildren, that meant Grandma had to live together *with* her grandson for the arrangement to be legal.[31] The same thing happened when a mom moved into her son's co-op (after he had moved out) without letting the board in on their secret. Once again the judicial word came down that Mom could live in the apartment without board consent only if her grown darling lived with her.[32] And a shareholder who bought a studio, intending for it to be occupied only by her child's nanny, had a rude awakening and sleepless nights (plus an extra apartment on her hands) when she was told that the nanny (a domestic employee) couldn't live there without board approval unless the rest of the family did, too.[33]

It's not all bad news for shareholders. A few courts have ruled that "and" really means "or," thereby effectively letting your relative sublet. One judge found that an owner who moved out of his apartment didn't need board permission for his brother to move in.[34] Another said a shareholder's stepdaughter could stay in his apartment without board consent even though he had gone.[35] To make matters more complicated, though, one court recently ruled the opposite: that "or" means "and," thereby mandating that an adult child could live with (but not without) her shareholder parent.[36]

Anyway, don't get your hopes up because several higher judicial authorities have dashed the prospect. In one case, the co-op board demanded

$25,000 in sublet fees from a shareholder who, it claimed, had let his mother-in-law reside solo in his apartment in violation of the lease. Maybe it's not a permitted occupancy, but allowing a family member to stay in your place isn't a sublet, the court ruled, rescuing Mr. Violator from paying tribute.[37] Likewise, another court told the board, in a building where the shareholder let his daughter and her fiancé move in while he lived elsewhere, that it's not clear under the lease if this type of family arrangement is a sublet requiring consent.[38]

The bottom line, however, is that while you might escape paying a sublet fee, violation of the restriction on occupancy could subject you to worse punishment, including termination of your lease.

One final note: There are two possible ways you can win. First, if the board knows that your relative is living in your apartment and you're not—and nevertheless continues to accept maintenance checks, it may have waived its right to complain later. One East Side building tried to evict the shareholder and her son, who had been living there by himself for eleven years with the board's apparent knowledge and consent. Too late and too bad, the court said. You've lost that right.[39]

Second, if your building has one of those kitchen-sink occupancy provisions that covers all bases and says the lessee *and/or* family members may reside in the apartment, you should be home free.

Even if you've resigned yourself to the fact that you can't turn your place over to a family member and leave, the board still may not be out of your bedroom. That's because it may want a say in *which members* of your family can stay with you. Suppose your building's bylaws limit occupancy to "immediate family" without saying who that includes. Chances are you will win if you come up with a logical definition of your own (even if it's not strictly traditional). With the courts' help, shareholders have pushed boards to define *immediate family* to include nieces, stepdaughters, and daughters-in-law. And the trend is in shareholders' favor for stretching the meaning still further beyond conventional bounds.

Given this fact, even when the lease specifically spells out which family members can live with you, that doesn't mean you'll have to abide. If you're so fond of some relative (unnamed in the lease) that you want him or her at your side and the board is foolish enough to say no, take it on. You stand a good chance of winning and in the process breaking new ground for all shareholderkind.

Is It a Guest?

When you get beyond the orbit of kith and kin to mere guests, the rules on use of your apartment tend to get even tougher. Most co-op leases have something like the following to say on the subject:

> The apartment may be occupied from time to time by guests of the Lessee [you] for a period of time not exceeding one month unless a longer period is approved by the Lessor [the co-op], but no guests may occupy the apartment unless one or more of the permitted adult residents are then in occupancy or unless consented to in writing by the Lessor.

What this means is that no guests can stay in your place without board approval unless you're also there, and even if you are, the guest can't stay for more than a month. How this translates into real-world practice depends on how aggressive an enforcer your board is. In my building, we do not send out the boarder patrol if a shareholder goes away for a few weeks and allows a guest to stay in his or her apartment (as long as everything on the home front remains quiet). But there are those boards that mean business and impose rules to let shareholders know who's in control of the guest list. In some buildings guests have to sign in hotel-style so that Big Brother can keep an eye on their comings and goings—and come after them if they don't check out on time. I've heard of boards imposing fines (up to $1,000) for guests overstaying their welcome, or banning entry to violators of the policy. One shareholder who repeatedly breached her co-op's guest policy was ordered by the court to restrict visitors, and when she violated the order she was forced to pay the building $33,000 in attorneys' fees it incurred in having her judged in contempt.[40]

Using the label *guest* as cover for an illegal subtenant is generally not a winning strategy. After all, most guests do not come with a truckload of exercise equipment in tow. That's what did in the Dakota shareholder who told building management that actress Michelle Pfeiffer was to be his guest. (Whether he was delusional or just in need of cold cash, you decide.) He entered into a "Guest Agreement" with Pfeiffer to rent her his place for four months at a then-whopping $11,000 a month, $33,000 of which was prepaid. But he failed to tell her that the apartment was set to be sold at foreclosure the following week. When Pfeiffer's movers showed up, exercise equipment and all, the board smelled trouble and said no entry. Pfeiffer sued Mr. Dreamer for return of her money. He blamed the movers for mischaracterizing their relationship. The court called a spade a spade and ordered the Dakotan to pay up for his illegal sublet—thereby dashing his fantasies for good.[41]

So if you're planning on having guests, save yourself, and them, the embarrassment and possible expense of trying to convert their authorized stay into illegal status.

No, It's a Bed-and-Breakfast

A few shareholders have a way of pushing the envelope still further, attempting to turn their apartments into hotel rooms for fee-paying "guests."

One shareholder transformed his Upper East Side co-op into a bed-and-breakfast, inviting boarders to stay overnight for a fee, a practice he defended as necessary to defray the costs of his maintenance, mortgage, and upkeep. His status as part-time hotelier went undetected for more than three years, until one of his "guests" asked the doorman for a bellhop, and the board denied his guest access. Mr. Hotelier went to court to stop the board from interfering, but the court said the definition of *guests* did not include commercial boarders.[42]

It took the board of an Upper West Side co-op more than a decade to figure out that a rent-controlled tenant there for almost forty years had been using her apartment as a bed-and-breakfast, renting two extra bedrooms for $100 a night, or $6,000 a month (plus tax, no less), when she was paying only $2,750. You'd better put an end to it, the board told the owner, who had bought the occupied apartment (probably for a pittance) and now was at risk of losing his $1.5 million worth of shares. Undoubtedly overjoyed at the prospect of finally gaining access to his prize, he terminated her lease and, when she wouldn't go, took her to court. They're only my roommates, she said with a straight face, just a few artists and scholars who came to visit me—except they were all referred by a hospitality service that handed out welcome flyers and told them to check out by 11 A.M. Who do you think you're kidding? the judges said.[43]

Another couple took the guest ruse a step further, claiming that since they had bought their two apartments from the sponsor they inherited the status of holders of unsold shares and could do whatever they wanted. They never moved into the apartments but rented them out by the night, coming by only to deliver mail to their "guests," make nice with the doormen, and be sure the accommodations were comfy. Their hotel service was likewise terminated by the court.[44]

In my own building it took us a few months to realize we had a similarly enterprising lawbreaker in our midst. There was no trace of her, only guest forms, which she left with the doormen. It wasn't till the list of names got longer, and the stays shorter, that we got suspicious and hired a private eye to pose as an out-of-towner in search of a room. Even though our detective didn't turn up any intelligence, we let Ms. Violator know we were on to her, and she put her place up for sale—at a fat profit.

So as we leave the boarder wars just remember, it's not always the board that's the enemy. You have to give the board its due for occasionally rescuing you from shareholders gone haywire.

16

High Crimes and Misdemeanors

ROOTING OUT TRAITORS

Feuding between the board and its constituents is in the natural order of things, given their different status on the food chain. The powers that be and the would-be empowered just don't see things the same way all the time. But you and your compatriots in apartments (whether condo or co-op) should stand shoulder to shoulder, united as one. That's why offenses by shareholders or unit owners directed at one another—whether it's not paying your way, misusing your apartment, or impinging on your neighbor's quality of life—prevent the rank and file from staying in their best form. For that reason the perpetrators of such crimes and misdemeanors cannot be left unchecked. Rehabilitation, punishment (proportionate to the offense), or, if all else fails, involuntary separation are called for. And ironically, it's the board that may have to intercede on your side to save the body politic.

FINANCIAL TREASON

No offense is more unpardonable than not paying. An integral part of your compact with fellow owners is the commitment to carry your fair share and keep those monthly checks rolling in. Emergencies can happen to us all, and I'm sympathetic to a point. Beyond that I have no tolerance for deadbeat shareholders. I figure if I have to pay every month on time, even if it means forgoing other more immediate pleasures, they should suffer similar deprivation. Even worse are those who don't pay at all, sometimes for months on end, leaving their comrades to cover for them. But it's not only defaulting on those monthly charges that can get you into trouble. In most co-ops and condos, assessments (and other charges) are considered to be additional rent and are subject to the same nonpayment penalties[1]—from a slap on the wrist to a kick out the door.

Reproached

Assuming your check doesn't arrive by the tenth of the month (or whatever date your building has designated), you'll likely get a computer-generated note from the agent reminding you to pay up. Included could be a request for late fees (see below) or a demand for payment by certified check (so the agent knows the money's really there). If the agent doesn't get results, the board may call in a lawyer to do some written arm twisting. Most buildings have collection counsel on hand ready to snap into action when a shareholder defaults.

Fined

If a little saber rattling doesn't get you to pay up, then maybe hitting you where it hurts will. With that in mind, many buildings make you do financial penance for the sin of slothful payment. Assuming the proprietary lease (or, in condos, the bylaws) specifically gives it the power, the board can charge you late fees if you don't pay up by the designated due day. The general power of the board to oversee the co-op's cash requirements doesn't give it power to impose late fees. Condo boards have more leeway because the Condo Act authorizes them not only to charge late fees for owners delinquent in paying common charges but, where the violation is repeated, to demand security for future compliance.[2] Despite this proviso, one court held unenforceable a $75 late fee imposed by a condo board when not supported by the bylaws.[3]

Late fees often take the form of interest charges at the maximum legal rate. At least one court has said that a board operating under such a provision can charge up to 25 percent a year, even though the board there gave its Park Avenue shareholder a break, charging only 1.5 percent a month or 18 percent annually. It may not sound like a lot, but if your lease has the added kicker that unpaid interest is treated as additional rent (as many do and this one did), those dollars can really start piling up, especially if you withhold for a long time. An I'll-show-you lawyer-shareholder at the building decided to withhold payments for a variety of perceived ills (from a wine cellar that was too hot to an apartment that was too cold). What started out as a small-scale sum mushroomed years later when Judgment Day arrived and the court told him to pay an award of nearly $400,000 in arrears and interest in favor of the co-op.[4]

One Size Fits All

Some buildings take the easy way and charge you a flat fee for late maintenance payments, usually $50 or $100, though they can only impose it if they have power. One board found that out when it decided to adopt a House Rule setting a flat-rate late fee of $30 a month despite the fact that the lease provided for payment of interest at the maximum legal rate on late maintenance. Its power play backfired because the court told the board it couldn't unilaterally change the interest penalty in the lease without shareholder consent.[5] Even if the fee is legal, that doesn't mean shareholders pay it. Some do; plenty don't. But whether you realize it or not, your past will catch up with you. When you try to sell or do anything major requiring board consent (like renovating), you'll find the answer is no until you say yes to making good on your debts.

Grounded

Some things in life are more important than money—and more calculated to get a rise. Just think back to your adolescent days. All your parents had to do was threaten to take away your driving privileges and you could be persuaded to see things their way. Nothing has changed. Only now it's co-op and condo boards in their capacity in loco parentis that mete out punishment when you've been naughty. Assuming the board is authorized, it may temporarily suspend parking or other house privileges as long as those monthly charges remain outstanding. Although making you pay a $50 fee may not be sufficient to get you on the straight, removing your Beamer from its safe, warm spot onto the mean streets is sure to help you see the virtues of prompt payment.

Disenfranchised

A central precept of any democracy is the right to cast your ballot. But if you're a deadbeat you may be denied the vote, though the board's power to strip you of your franchise is strictly limited.

Since co-ops are corporations, they have to follow the state's Business Corporation Law, which says that every shareholder can vote unless the certificate of incorporation says otherwise. There's the rub—for unsuspecting boards. In commercial corporations the powers that be pay attention to the certificate because it's a working document with real meat. In co-ops, the certificate is sort of like your appendix, a remnant that reminds you of your origins but doesn't serve any useful daily function. That's why lots of co-op boards that want to deprive shareholders of the vote make the mistake of putting the provision in the bylaws instead of the certificate. If the board's gotten it wrong, you can ignore it and vote even if you haven't paid.

A Soho board engaged in a larger dispute with an unfriendly shareholder and told him he couldn't vote because he hadn't paid. It went on to elect a friendly slate. But the election was overturned and a new one was ordered in which he could vote. Since the ban was only in the bylaws, it didn't count.[6] Of course, if the board gets it right and puts the provision in the certificate it will be given effect. An insurgent faction in Clinton tried to oust the board but came up short because one of its adherents was two months delinquent in maintenance and thus banned from the ballot.[7] Either way you can see how not being current can have political consequences.

Condo boards can disenfranchise their owners with greater dispatch. Since condos are what's called unincorporated associations, they go by the

Condo Act, not the Corporation Law. You can forget that, but you should remember the resulting difference: Condos, unlike co-ops, can use their bylaws to ban the ballot for delinquents. For those of a theoretical turn of mind, the rationale is that condo owners' voting rights are protected in the bylaws because it takes their two-thirds vote to change them, whereas in most co-ops the board can change them (and thus shareholder voting rights) on its own.[8] It follows logically that if you can't vote for directors because you're delinquent you shouldn't be able to become one. And some buildings disqualify you from taking on that higher calling if you're not paid up.

Betrayed

Rather than run after you for the money (especially if your pockets are empty), the board may rat on you and get your lender to pay. By now you know that if you took out a mortgage to buy your apartment you signed a recognition agreement, which spells out the rights and duties among you, the co-op, and the bank, and includes the co-op's recognition of the lender's security interest in your lease and shares. It's standard that the co-op has to tell the bank if you don't pay your maintenance (or other charges) and give it a chance to dig into its deeper pockets to come up with the cash. Since your apartment is its security for the loan, it usually will send in a check because it doesn't want the board to terminate you or your lease (or do anything to jeopardize its collateral).

That doesn't mean you get to stay rent free. It only means the bank, not the board, will be the one coming after you—and that could wind up costing you more, at least in the short run. The bank doesn't know (or care) about your battles with the board. It just wants to protect its interest. To do that it will likely pay up in full and then charge you (for good measure, adding any attorneys' or other fees it spent in getting you out of the jam). If you have a bone to pick with the board that you claim entitled you to a maintenance offset, you'll probably have to go back to the board and fight on your own for a refund.

Lenders to condo owners are not so generous. Under the law (see below), the way things work out is that they get first crack at any cash that results if your apartment is foreclosed, *before* the condo gets paid any outstanding common charges. So paying your arrears is like taking money out of its own pocket—not something any self-respecting banker would do.

Sued

Assuming you still haven't reformed your nonrent-paying ways despite deprivation of basic rights and house privileges, the board may finally remove its kid gloves and set the litigation machine in motion. Which machine and where depends on whether you live in a co-op or a condo. If the building is run commando-style, the agent is programmed to attack automatically by setting those collection attorneys on you (without the board even knowing).

In co-ops, before the board lets slip the dogs of war, it will serve you with notice demanding payment. If that doesn't trigger action, it will haul you into Housing Court by serving you with a petition for nonpayment. Don't make the mistake of ignoring it, thinking the whole thing will go away. It will only get worse. In your absence, the co-op may get a default judgment against you and then have a marshal apply for a warrant to evict you.

Answering the board's petition gives you a chance to get even. You have a right to defend against and counterattack the board in its summary nonpayment action against you. Maybe you have a beef with the board for not stemming the gusher that burst from the pipes (turning your living room into a permanent sauna), or for refusing to silence the menagerie below or to repair some other condition that you claim rendered your place uninhabitable. That Warranty of Habitability (see chapter 8) can be a powerful defense.

Keep in mind that generally it's a shareholder-friendly system and even then you can get a reprieve. As long as you pay the amount due (which by now probably has grown to include late and lawyers' fees) at any time up to and including ten days *after* a judgment, you're in the clear and the slate is wiped clean. Resist the urge to revert to your errant ways and start paying. For some, delinquency is a matter of principle: the later you wait to pay the longer you can use the float. For others, it's congenital: no matter whether going to the movies or paying maintenance, you're never on time. The truth is that if you're so disposed there's not much the board can do to rein in your aberrant social conduct. You're safe if you come clean even after being adjudged a delinquent, though the added costs of holding back and then paying several months late should make you rethink your self-defeating strategy.

One of the benefits of living in a condo if you're a white-collar deadbeat is that the board can't collect so fast from you. In a co-op, the board can drag you into Housing Court, where justice is swift and payment is assured (provided you have no excuse) because even though you're an owner of shares you're also a tenant living under a proprietary lease. In a condo, you're lord of the manor, owner outright of your apartment, so you get treated with the kid gloves, not the iron fist, of the law. Since there's no landlord-tenant relationship, the board can't use the summary nonpayment route to get you to pay. When one Yonkers condo board tried to collect quickly this way from an owner in arrears, the court kicked it out and told it to go the long way around.[9] The board can still sue you for the amount of your unpaid common charges in a so-called court of general jurisdiction, where the calendar is clogged with cases of every stripe, but there's no rush to judgment in most of those places.

Billed

Not only will the co-op sue you, it also will make you pay for the suit. Most proprietary leases and many condo bylaws have provisions requiring you to pick up the tab for attorneys' fees the building had to pay to collect what you owed.[10] Usually these provisions say the board can only recover fees *after* bringing an action for your default. Courts read these fee clauses narrowly. Lawyers tell boards to make them broad enough so they can charge you legal fees from the moment of default—even *before* any lawsuit is begun. I'm telling you so you can keep your eyes open for this difference in case you find yourself in a default dispute. The board can bill you for legal fees only as far back in time as the lease (or bylaws) say.

Sometimes boards overreach. One board tried to use the standard co-op provision to make a shareholder reimburse it for legal fees it had paid in defending a suit she brought complaining about the co-op's business conduct. When she refused, the board said she was in default and tried to cancel her lease, that is, until the court put a halt to it all.[11] And even if the board is entitled to collect attorneys' fees because it had to sue you for unpaid maintenance, watch out that the lawyers don't get too greedy. On the complaint of an irate owner, one condo board had its claim for legal fees cut down to routine collection size by the court;[12] another had it limited to its foreclosure action, and not its other claims against the owner.[13]

Although the lease is a one-way street (making you responsible for the co-op's legal fees), the law is not. There's a law on the books that evens the score for tenants (of which shareholders are a subspecies).[14] It says that if the lease lets the landlord collect attorneys' fees from you, the law will let you recover legal fees from the landlord (the board) if: (1) it violated the lease, or (2) you successfully defended a suit brought by it. The board sues you for not paying your maintenance. You claim you were justified because your place was rendered unlivable by an invasion of killer roaches that it did nothing to root out. If the court sees things your way, not only do you get off maintenance free (till the army retreats) but you can seek recompense for your legal headache. You don't even have to win by a knockout punch. You just have to *substantially prevail* to take advantage of this quid pro quo.

Terminated

Most co-op leases contain a provision giving the board the right to terminate your lease if you don't pay your maintenance for a certain period of time, usually a month or two. (For would-be lawyers out there, it's called a *conditional limitation.*) In theory, if your lease has expired you have no right to remain, so the board (as landlord) can order you out of hearth and home. Such rough justice might make some sense for renters whose legal welcome lasts only as long as their leases (which, after all, are their only claims to their apartments). But as an owner, your lease is attached to some pricey shares in a co-op in which you have an interest and hopefully a pile of equity. Making you forfeit all that for not paying a month (or even a few months) of maintenance seems like overkill. Don't get nervous. Just because some lawyer dreamed up these draconian measures doesn't mean courts will enforce them. Most won't, because forfeiture is against public policy. Courts have held that boards can't use a conditional limitation in proprietary leases to terminate a tenancy where you claim nonpayment of maintenance because of that Warranty of Habitability or other reason.

As we just saw, if the board sues you for not paying you can counterattack, claiming the right to a maintenance offset in the amount of any damage caused by its wrongs against you. And assuming you make good, your lease remains intact and you return to the fold as a shareholder in good standing. But if the board is allowed to invoke these imperial prerogatives given by the lawyers (not the law) and to terminate your lease for nonpayment, the game's over before it's begun. You don't get the same rights to defend, to deduct, or to cure. That hasn't stopped hard-nosed boards from giving it a shot.

One East Side board canceled the lease and then brought an action to evict a habitually delinquent shareholder, claiming he was beyond redemption. But the court said termination went against public policy.[15] Another West Side board tried a similar maneuver. Although unsuccessful in booting its own deadbeat, it got the court to recognize that really chronic nonpayers don't rate policy relief.[16] Again, recently, the court reaffirmed the rule, telling the board it couldn't automatically terminate a shareholder's lease for nonpayment because she had a right to assert her defenses first.[17]

Beware of boards that try to circumvent the landlord/tenant system to collect unpaid maintenance (and cut off your rights) quickly. One West Side board claimed its co-op had a lien on owners' shares (pursuant to the bylaws) to secure payment of maintenance. On that basis, it tried to terminate the lease and cancel the shares of a shareholder who owed $14,000 in maintenance fees. But the court said the shareholder had a right to present her dampness defense, in which she claimed that a leak had rendered her place uninhabitable, before the board could terminate her. The court then sent the parties packing to fight it out in Housing Court.[18]

Another board tried a similar end run under a different legal theory (the Uniform Commercial Code, for those lawyers among you) to sell a shareholder's shares to pay outstanding maintenance—without giving her a chance to defend before a judge. It had no better luck.[19]

The most important thing to remember is: Don't get uptight if you find yourself in a dispute with the board over maintenance it claims you owe. Just because the proprietary lease says the board can, *on its own*, automatically terminate your lease for nonpayment doesn't make it so. You have a right to your day in court and your defenses before the board can get you out.

Liened On

Under law, in addition to going to court and suing you for the money, condo boards can put a lien on your apartment for any arrears (together with interest).[20] That prevents you from selling without first paying what you owe, but it doesn't put any instant cash in the building's pocket (or take it out of yours). In theory (and in law), it can foreclose to get the money, but as you'll see most often the bank beats it out.

Dishonorable Discharge

The free ride doesn't last forever. If you're truly incorrigible and a traitor to the common charge cause despite all the outs you've been offered, you will be drummed out of the co-op or condo corps. Assuming you refuse to comply even after the board gets a judgment against you for nonpayment, the court will grant the board legal possession and you'll eventually be ousted from the building. Once the board is in control, it gets to choose how to squeeze out the most cash from its newly acquired asset in order to save the co-op from your financial contempt.

One option is to sublet. Most proprietary leases let the co-op (when it's regained possession) lease out your former home sweet home and apply the rent it collects toward the amount you owe. Or it can foreclose and sell the shares (and the apartment attached to them) at auction. If the only bidder is the co-op, it winds up the owner but has to hand over to you any surplus it makes (above what you owe) from a subsequent resale. If others step up to the plate and the winner bids more than the amount of the co-op's judgment, the excess gets returned to the once (and maybe future) member of the corps.

Usually it's the bank, not the board, that sends you packing in cases of unreformed default. Since the bank has the right to cure, it figures it's safer to pay and then pursue. As shareholders, you are sworn to uphold the currency commandment (number ten on the list). But if you realize that for reasons beyond your control default is inevitable, you might as well do it right. When marshaling scarce resources, it's in your best interest to pay the mortgage bill before the maintenance man. The bank will make good your maintenance but the building sure won't pay your mortgage. We had a financially strapped shareholder who got it wrong. For months he paid us but not the bank—an error that hastened his demise and left him with less cash when the day of foreclosure finally arrived.

In co-ops (under the recognition agreement), the bank has to pay back any outstanding maintenance arrears off the top of its resale proceeds. As a result, whether or not the bank comes out whole, your ex-co-op comrades who've had to put up with your financial treachery usually will. A good thing, too, because it's not like most lenders go out of their way to maximize profits, though now with prices through the roof they're trying harder. Their object is to get back their money and get out. To achieve that goal they'll often bid the amount of the judgment against you (plus any expenses). If somebody tops them by a hair's breadth the bankers generally are happy to let the speculators brave the vagaries of the real estate market and return to the gentleman's art of making money. Although they have to pay you any excess they receive above what you owe, more often than not there is none. The only time the bank foreclosed and auctioned a shareholder's apartment in our building, the board acquired the apartment for $90,000—only to turn around and resell it for a tidy profit.

In condos, things work out better for the bank than the building in cases of default by unrepentant owners. As we've seen, there's no quick fix against nonpaying condo owners. The board can file a lien and wait till the holdout sells to recover the arrears. Or it can foreclose, bid for, and acquire the apartment to do with as it will to raise cash. Sounds good in theory, but in practice it doesn't usually work out that way. That's because owners who stiff the building usually also stiff the bank. So there's one potential cash-producing asset and at least two parties fighting over the prize. In co-ops, the building is the clear winner. It gets back all maintenance charges due before the bank sees a dime of the proceeds from the foreclosure sale. But given the way the law[21] has been interpreted, in condos, banks are the victors of the spoils. Generally, if it forecloses and sells your apartment it first takes all that it's owed, and only then does the building get its chance to pocket any change left over.[22]

What's the fallout from all this? For the condo, a pile of unpaid common charges that probably never will be recouped. For those unit owners left behind, a sense of betrayal by one of their own. And for the offender, dishonorable discharge—plus relentless pursuit by bank and board, each trying in whatever way it can to collect some cash.

OCCUPATIONAL OFFENSES

Apart from not paying, one of the worst offenses you can commit toward your fellow owners is turning your apartment into something it wasn't meant to be—a tattoo parlor, a belly-dancing studio, a yoga classroom. The uses shareholders try to make of their spaces is a cause for never-ending wonder. Years back, we had our own Madam X, who conducted a thriving call girl operation from her rented studio. The sponsor did its best to put her out of business, but each time she showed up in court with a Mona Lisa smile and a Talbot's suit, a ruse that caused the judge to send her home and back to work. Finally, as word of her prowess spread, increasing her customer base (and shareholder ire), the sponsor brought in a hulk of a security guard who kept track of every John, Joe, and Dave who visited, the list so long that when she was confronted with it, she capitulated.

Most owners aren't interested in converting their apartments into brothels, but with the world only a computer screen away, the line between home and work is becoming increasingly blurred. The question many of you may be asking is, What can I do with my apartment besides live in it?

Old Guard

The first thing you have to figure out is whether your building is a member of the old or new guard. If the former, your proprietary lease (or bylaws in condos) will say something like this:

> Lessee [that's you] shall not occupy or use the apartment for any purpose other than as a private dwelling.

On its face, the answer seems a slam dunk, like those weapons of mass destruction: if you can use your place only for dwelling, then by definition, you can't use it for working. Only, like those WMDs, nothing is so straightforward. Because thus far not many of these legal battles have been waged in the co-op and condo context, we have to look at what courts have said in rental regimes. The answer comes down to whether limiting use of one's apartment to residential occupancy is a *substantial obligation* of the lease. Assuming it is, is the violation a minor indiscretion or a major transgression?

Awhile back, this state's highest court was faced with an angry landlord who wanted to oust a psychotherapist-tenant, who had reconfigured her apartment into an office where she saw twenty patients a week, conducted her entire counseling practice, and earned all her professional income. The court told her she had to go because her use of the apartment as a shrink's office was a big-time violation of her substantial obligation under the lease only to reside there.[23]

Although maybe you can't turn your apartment into a psychotherapy practice, under the old guard rule there is no one-size-fits-all answer to what you can or can't do. Faced with a similar lease, one court said you *can* use your apartment as an artist's studio just like Chagall and Picasso (even if you don't sleep or cook there).[24] Another said you *can't* outfit your bedrooms with grand pianos and rent them out as practice rooms, as one Upper West Sider did.[25] But you *can* use it to give voice lessons for fixed hours, accompanied by piano playing, as another West Sider did to the dismay of his upstairs neighbor.[26] And if all you want to do is use the computer and send and receive faxes and phone calls, you don't really need a court to say that's okay, though one has done so.[27]

To figure out if your planned enterprise is prohibited or permitted, you need to ask several questions: Will it disturb your fellow owners? Will what you want to do significantly affect the character of the building? Will it burden the building staff and facilities? If the answer to one or more questions is yes, you are looking for trouble. So if you're living under an old-guard regime, it might be okay to tutor a few students a day for the MCATs, maybe even engage in talk therapy with a couple of patients, or provide personal training on a quiet and limited basis. But if you add throbbing music to get your client's heart rate pumping (and give your fellow shareholders a headache) or have a steady stream, not a mere trickle, of invitees who tax the physical plant and pose a security risk, the board can probably put a stop to it. The truth is it could take even less to brand you a violator as an owner than a renter, because co-ops and condos are more like private clubs where the board has greater say over what you do than a landlord does over a mere tenant.

Sometime the law overrides the lease. Want to use your apartment as a day care center for children? One court told the owners of a condo that they could even though the building's declaration said they could use their unit for residential occupancy only. They won because the court said both the law and public policy were intended to expand the limited availability of day care, and these considerations preempted what the condo's documents said.[28]

New Guard

Maybe you live under a new-guard regime where, in addition to residing in the apartment, the governing documents permit you to use it for a *home occupation*. That doesn't meant you can do what you want. The law tells you what you can do—sort of.[29] For starters, you have to meet certain threshold conditions: the use can be only incidental to your residential occupancy; can't take more than 25 percent of total floor area, and in no event more than 500 square feet; and can't cause any loud noise or objectionable effects. Then it tells you what you *can't* do, but not all of what you *can*.

So, for example, you can't have an interior decorator's workshop, but you can have a professional office (though nowhere is it specified how many clients can come a-calling, and they certainly can't use the lobby as a waiting room). You can have a fine arts studio but not a pharmacy. You can teach up to four pupils at a time except if it's musical instruction (only one), but you can't have a beauty parlor (something I guess the haircutter I went to for years didn't know, not that it would have stopped me). Can my wife use the apartment for her electrolysis business? one shareholder recently asked me with a straight face. My instinctive no was confirmed by the law, which also says, if you can believe it, that you can't use your apartment for a stable (as if we all have enough extra space for a few palominos). And even though the law says nothing about recording studios, a court recently said that's not a home occupation.[30]

Under the new guard, if you're crazy enough to try to house horses in your home or engage in any of the other proscribed activities from stockbroker's office to veterinary medicine, you'll run afoul of the law and lease. Engage in one of the few specifically permitted uses and you should have a safe harbor. If what you want to do falls in the unspoken gray middle ground—neither expressly allowed nor banned—things get trickier, but if you ask yourself the questions old guarders must regularly confront, you should come up with the right answer.

Even if you're conducting a permitted home occupation, that doesn't mean you're home free. Can the board set any restrictions? Suppose you use your place to give shrink sessions. Can the board limit the number of patients you see, or the times during which you can see them, or impose a fee for the extra wear and tear your visitors cause?[31] The answer comes down to what's reasonable, balancing your right to legally use your apartment against those of your fellow shareholders to live undisturbed. So a rule that said no patients late at night or set a surcharge to offset the real cost of increased traffic might be okay. But a restriction designed to put the shareholder-shrink out of business would not.

Affirmative Guard

Regardless of the system, if the board says okay to your proposed use, its word is binding (just as it was with renovations). Having agreed to let a shareholder use her co-op loft both as a residence and dance studio (God help the owner below), the board couldn't renege but had to pay damages when she was forced to move due to the resulting defect in her commercial use of the space.[32]

It works both ways; if *you* agree to bounds on your business, you can't change your mind either, so that the court told a doctor who had permission to use his Gramercy Park apartment as an office *only* for himself that the board was within its rights in refusing to let him add other practitioners without its consent.[33]

Sometimes actions speak louder than words. Even if the board doesn't *say* yes, if it *acts* like it means yes by not doing anything to stop what you shouldn't be doing, if it acquiesces long enough, it may give up its rights to later complain. (In the law, it's called a *waiver.*)

Endgame

As you know if you've read this far, I don't preach blind obedience: with some things you can skirt the letter of the law. Running an unauthorized business from your apartment isn't one of them. You will have shareholders up in arms and the board on your back. Once the directors are on to you, if they're smart, they'll act with dispatch. If it's a co-op, the board will serve you with a warning to clean up your act (a.k.a. a notice to cure); in a condo, the board will try to enjoin your misguided activities. Either way, the next step is a full-fledged legal battle—and the board will win, so give it up before you start.

CONDUCT UNBECOMING

More often the offenses committed by one owner against the next do not rise to the level of such high crimes but are relative misdemeanors—minor infractions that threaten inner peace and sanity but not the building's well-being. Indeed, few of us who've called a high-rise home for long have escaped unscathed from some minor scuffle with our fellow owners.

Has your upstairs neighbor decided in midlife to fulfill her Ruby Keeler fantasy by taking up tap dancing—on the bare wood floors? Are those newlyweds next door hanging a Rembrandt or a Rauschenberg using a superindustrial-strength drill against your wall? Or is the couple downstairs acting—or worse, screaming—out its divorce Hollywood-style, complete with crashing vases? Making up can be worse than breaking up—from your neighbors' perspective, anyway. A friend of mine lived in a Christopher Street co-op next door to a couple that was into S & M in a big way, and had to contend with heavy doses of whips and chains. Another pal has learned the Kama Sutra from an amorous couple in the adjacent apartment, built without benefit of a soundproof dividing wall. When he whispers sweet nothings into his partner's ear, they resound more like a bang than a whimper on my friend's aural senses.

The latest battleground is secondhand smoke, with diehard puffers fighting to preserve their private pleasure against the onslaught of unaddicted neighbors determined to keep their apartments smoke free. As any of us with firsthand experience know, these kinds of attacks, although not fatal, can undermine one's sanity and goodwill toward fellow shareholders.

What you can do, and whether the board can or should intervene on your side in these kinds of internecine struggles, depends on the nature and severity of the offense. If you're the princess who slept on the pea type, for whom every indignity is perceived as an imagined affront, then get some more mattresses—or, since you live in a co-op, not a castle, maybe added wall insulation will help. Assuming the infraction is anything of consequence (and even if it's not), it's probably covered by House Rules, in place from the start or imposed by director resolution, or by the lease and bylaws, which the board has the power (though not necessarily the will) to enforce.

Most buildings have codes regulating everything from decibel levels to laundry carts, holiday decorations to animal behavior—and some have even more. Sometimes the conduct, whether caused by two-legged or four-legged creatures, is so extreme that it independently violates your real-world legal rights, in which case the board (as surrogate landlord) is duty-bound to come to your defense. For things to reach this point, generally you have to be able to show that your health, safety, or well-being is in jeopardy. If you get to that point there are different legal theories that can be used, from nuisance to constructive eviction, but the one most commonly called on is that now-familiar breach of Warranty of Habitability. Before you prepare to do battle, why not try the path to peaceful coexistence?

Twelve Steps to Peaceful Coexistence

Given their subjective and evanescent character, these offenses are difficult to combat, so I won't hold out any false hope of a quick fix. What I do offer is a stepped path to dispute resolution with your fellow owners and the board. Unlike those other programs that require you to complete all twelve steps before you can claim victory, the object of this one is to achieve maximum results with minimum steps.

1. Diplomatic Communiqué

A civil note left under the door asking your neighbor to cease and desist from the offending conduct, whether it's noisy kids, scratching cats, or permeating odors, is a good first step. If the neighbor is guilty of the deed but innocent of your resulting discomfort, this should be enough to restore the peace. In my building, it is the method of choice for conveying pet peeves, which for the most part have been peaceably resolved with the addition of area rugs, the subtraction of offending toys, and an exercise regime designed to calm master and mutt.

2. Civil Confrontation

I prefer the direct approach, talking face-to-face with the perpetrator. A note can be discarded, and once it's out of sight it's out of mind. But your visible presence is not so easily ignored, and the offender may prefer reform to accusation (even if done with a smile). When I told my neighbor my tastes tended to Handel, not his hard rock, which I was receiving as background interference, he got the message and I got back my music unmixed.

3. Undercover Investigation

If that doesn't work, a little hard evidence (where appropriate and available) sometimes makes the difference. That did the trick when I was having a problem with one of my neighbors who, though able-bodied, seemed unable to throw down his trash, preferring instead to let the bags sit on the floor until someone else did the dirty work. Several polite notes did no good. I considered returning the bags from whence they came, branding their owner as the compactor criminal for all to see. Instead, when I next spied those telltale sacks, I donned a single glove (Michael Jackson–style), put my hand in, and plucked out an envelope bearing the suspect's name, which I presented to the target of my investigation at the elevator. Case closed: The compactor room floor has remained clear forevermore.

4. Inside Intermediary

Sometimes it's useful to bring in a neutral party to run interference between you and your offending neighbor. Doormen are perfectly suited to the task. They have access to all and allegiance to none. And since they aren't emotionally involved in the dispute, they can dispassionately (and anonymously) pass on your complaint via intercom. That way a modus vivendi can be reached without either accuser or accused losing face. In my building it's taken as a given that these guardians of the gate are on-call aides integral to the dispute-resolution process. They have quieted overexuberant merrymakers and silenced squawking parrots. I have used their services myself to convey unidentified shutoff requests for my neighbor's CD player. And when several anonymous attempts proved less than successful, our resourceful intermediary had the good sense to arrange a three-way intercom conference, thereby resolving the problem and setting himself on a new career path as mediator.

5. Next Step Up the Command Chain

If keeping the dirty laundry in the family has gotten you nowhere, it may be time to go outside and bring in the managing agent to try to make the recalcitrant shareholder see reason. Although the agent shouldn't identify you as the complainant, he may ask you to put your complaint in writing just for the record (and to protect himself from false accusations). An official-looking letter from the managing agent often ups the ante in the shareholder stakes—all the more so if the agent adds legal heft to your charges by quoting chapter and verse from the House Rules or a lease provision that has supposedly been violated. If the problem is that stiletto-heeled insomniac upstairs, the answer may be a managerial missive informing her that carpeting is required and remedial (and that a few sleeping pills wouldn't hurt). If it's the jackhammer sound of home improvement that's keeping you from getting your forty winks, the answer may be a reminder of the rules limiting renovation to normal waking hours. And if the agent's law-and-order pitch doesn't produce results, he usually can assume the role of house detective and inspect the premises of the presumed offender to see if the breach of the peace is also a breach of the lease.

6. Bringing In the Big Guns

Still no solution? It may be time to go to the top and get the board to intervene. Although that's my sequential advice, most shareholders take this one out of order and put it (and me) on top and in the middle of their disputes, not a badge of honor I appreciate. I've received requests to silence barking dogs, remove seeping smoke, stop surging power, and discipline misbehaving toddlers. It's not that I want to shirk my responsibilities. But it only seems fair that the two combatants try to go it alone before widening the conflagration and assuring that all three of us will ride down the elevator with looks that could kill. If you want to maintain your credibility when asking for board action, don't cry wolf; exhaust self-help remedies first.

Talk Is Cheap:

Assuming you've done that, what can the board do? In buildings where genteel is the style, the board or committee members might invite the parties in for talk and tea, hoping their demeanor will comport with the drink and the whole problem will come to a civilized end. That's not my style or my taste. I need that caffeine jolt from my morning java. Thus revved up and ready for action, my building's board is more likely to bring in our hired gun and let her fire off a written missile to the misbehaving shareholder. (Fortunately, this is something we've had to do only rarely.)

Fines Are Not:

If talk doesn't work, money may solve the problem. Some buildings impose fines for violating the rules. First thing you should ask if the board socks it to you is whether it has proper authority. As fines are getting steeper, owners are fighting back and courts are helping by demanding that bylaws and leases contain specific authority before boards can make you pay. No court has yet opined on exactly what they have to say to be enforceable, but here are some guidelines:

Silence: If you search through your proprietary lease and find it says nothing about penalties or liabilities for rule violations, odds are that the board has no power to impose a fine.[34]

Implied Promise: Some bylaws say the board can terminate or void your lease for rule violations though, trust me, no court in its right mind is going to evict you for leaving your bike in the corridor. The real question is whether a fine would be considered a sort of lesser-included offense subsumed within this more drastic remedy. At least one court has said yes in connection with enforcing a fine for a rule violation in a leased condo unit,[35] but the board there had the benefit of the Condo Act, which specifically says that failure to comply with rules is grounds for an action for sums due or damage.[36] There's no comparable statute for co-ops, leaving it unclear whether a provision, such as my building has, that says a rule violation is a default under the lease, would allow the board to hit you up with fines.

Express Promise: There are no magic words, but if your building's documents say that a violation of the rules is considered a violation of the proprietary lease, for which the board may impose such conditions as it sees fit, including monetary fines, the provision would probably pass judicial muster.

The point is: Don't assume the fine is valid just because the board demands payment.

Since most fines are relative peanuts, fifty or a hundred dollars a pop, owners figure they're not worth fighting over. They pay—or ignore them till they're forced to come clean (before selling or renovating). So there haven't been loads of legal challenges. An angry unit owner took on his condo board—and won—when it assessed him the cost to repair the parking lot's card reader without having authority in the bylaws or providing him an opportunity to be heard.[37] Another court said it was okay for the board to fine disruptive residents.[38] One court told a co-op board that the twenty-five dollars it fined a shareholder for driving too fast wasn't enforceable because nothing in the bylaws gave it the right.[39] Another court let stand a twenty-five-dollar fee a condo board fixed for parking violations.[40] Go figure.

Even assuming your board has the power to make you pay for engaging in antisocial behavior, it's not without limits. The amount should bear a rational relationship to the wrong, enough to undo the damage but not so much as to send you running for therapy. Your dog leaves his calling card on the mail room carpet. A fee sufficient to cover the cost of cleanup may be okay, but not one so steep that it could pay to replace that Karastan with an antique Kashan.

Passing fines is one thing; collecting another. In co-ops, the board can deduct them from the offender's monthly maintenance—which means the fine is paid but your neighbor is now in arrears—and can get hit with a nonpayment action if he doesn't come up with the cash. Condo boards have a harder time collecting. They can slap a lien on the perpetrator's unit, but he probably won't feel any pain till he goes to sell.

7. Seek Outside Reinforcement

You may want to try going the governmental route and make some of its bureaucrats your private attorneys general. The sleeping giants of state and local agencies usually have better things to do than go after petty co-op criminals whose offenses don't impinge on the general welfare of the outside world. But if you make a specific complaint, they'll come to investigate, which may result in enforcement action against your neighbor.

If it's smoke that gets in your eyes, call on the Fire Department, whose inspectors can check to see if your neighbor's barbecuing is legal or not—and issue a fine to ensure future compliance. If it's sound or smell that's the problem, the Department of Environmental Protection is your agency. One of its team can come have a listen or a whiff and, if a violation is found, fine the perpetrator. The problem is that arrival of the investigator may not correspond with commission of these transitory crimes. But patience is a virtue, and your friendly inspector will, if necessary, do nighttime surveillance.

Outside assistance can also come from the bank that holds the offending shareholder's mortgage. In case the board doesn't think of this one, help it (and yourself) out with a cost-free and effective solution. If the board tells the bank it's planning to terminate the shareholder's lease, the bank may threaten to foreclose—a tactic sure to bring your neighbor to his knees.

8. Go for Legal Therapy

Before things deteriorate to the point where you're not on speaking terms, you might give mediation a chance. The idea is to force the disputants to lay down their arms and give talk a chance to achieve a lasting peace. You can go the informal (and usually free) route and ask a board member to act as peacemaker. Some buildings even have quality-of-life committees, members of which are available on demand. Or you can hire a professional mediator (at upwards of $200 an hour) to do the job. Recently New York Law School inaugurated a project to promote the use of mediation by co-op residents.[41]

You have nothing to lose—and maybe your sanity to regain—so why not give it a shot? The idea is voluntary agreement, not mutual capitulation, so both sides can save face. If it doesn't work, there's nothing to stop you from dragging that nuisance down the hall to court. And if it does, and you and your former nemesis enter into a written peace treaty, it's enforceable in court—so both parties have an interest in maintaining the truce.

Since few, if any, co-ops and condos have mediation clauses, neither side can force the other to partake of the process. But if your own run-in with a fellow owner has convinced you it's an idea whose time has come (to co-ops and condos), why not spearhead the movement and suggest an amendment to your bylaws that would make mediation mandatory as a first resort to resolving disputes, whether between fellow constituents or comrades and their board commanders.

9. Uniform Persuasion

Sometimes a show of force is enough to bring the problem to an end. Having been on both the receiving and the giving end of this strategy, I know it can be effective. When I was a kid growing up, my family lived above a lady who never saw the light of day but heard every pin drop. No sooner did we turn on the stereo at party time than a policeman was at our door communicating her complaint, which was enough to silence us (for a while). Upon her demise we rejoiced at our freedom, only to find that a male alter ego, possessed of even greater aural sensitivity and lunacy, had taken up residence in her apartment. This time we took the offensive and prevailed on a friend at the metro desk at one of the dailies to have his pal, a sergeant with a Schwarzenegger physique, pay a call. It worked like a charm. In today's climate of police cutbacks and civil liberties, it's harder to get the men and women in blue to make these kinds of house calls except in matters extreme. But a simple visit can do wonders to restore peace and tranquillity. And now there's even a quality-of-life division to deal with noise from your neighbors.

10. Call On the Enforcer

If you're a law-and-order type you may want to put your knowledge to real-life use and file a criminal complaint against your offending neighbor for creating a nuisance. It's not a legally winning strategy and it won't in itself result in his eviction, but it may give him sufficient agita to make him cease whatever he's doing.

Just don't get so bent out of shape over your neighbor's noise that the enforcer winds up coming after you. That's what happened to an elderly man in a Manhattan co-op. When he could no longer endure the sounds he claimed poured forth from the gal above, he turned vigilante, allegedly leaving ungentlemanly messages on her machine—even etching choice words on her apartment door. He got arrested for aggravated harassment and criminal mischief, no less. And though his co-op Cochran got him off (his advanced age and her boyfriend's questionable conduct helped), the shaken shareholder doubtless learned his lesson. So unless you're willing to risk trading in your co-op for a cell, don't resort to such dangerous self-help.

11. Go for Broke

Assuming things have really gone beyond the point of no return, there's the lawsuit option. Let me state at the outset that suing in these cases is a no-win situation. The only thing you have going for you is that the legal trend is to make the board the problem solver. Since your neighbor's nuisance is probably a breach of a House Rule or the lease or even that Warranty of Habitability, it's the board's job to act as enforcer and get rid of it.

If rough-and-tumble justice is its style, the board can haul the offender into Housing Court. But it's a tenant-friendly forum, so odds are against the judge's throwing the troublemaker out on the street over violating a House Rule. It's got to be something bigger— something that threatens the health or safety of the populace.

The results here are relatively quick and dirty, but not forever conclusive. The court can order the offender to reform or face eviction, but even if the board (and thus you) wins, the miscreant has ten days to shape up before eviction goes into effect. As long as he has stopped the misdeed—whether beating the drums softly or banging the pipes loudly—for ten days, he has complied. If he starts breaking the rule again after that, you have to go through the whole process anew.

Justice is slower and more expensive—but also more enduring—if the board goes into the state's Supreme Court. Here the board's object is not to get possession of the apartment but to get the judge to order the offender to cease and desist from carrying on the conduct that plagued you. That way if the troublemaker acts up again, the judge can haul him back for contempt. And once the board gets such a judgment, it can use it against other violators.

Don't count on the board to go charging into battle on your behalf. Since it costs plenty to fight these feuds, most boards are reluctant to take on causes that are strictly individual, preferring to reserve its firepower (and dollars) for antisocial behavior that has a more widespread impact. One East Side board rose to defend its constituents from attacks by a shareholder who banged the pipes, pounded the ceiling, screamed the day (and night) away, and then threatened to burn down the building after the lawsuit began. The court agreed that the board had to fight fire with fire. It enjoined the harasser from further verbal inflammation, directed that she stay with someone who would restrain her incendiary tendencies, and ordered her out if she didn't comply.[42] (And now, as you know, boards have the power to remove shareholders for objectionable conduct.)[43]

Whatever battlefield is chosen (and whoever takes the lead), be forewarned that the results in these kinds of cases are erratic unless the conduct is totally off the wall. One tenant leasing from a condo owner got off rent free for breach of the warranty because the board (and the owner) failed to silence excessively noisy neighbors above.[44] Another shareholder who sued his noisy neighbors and the board for its failure to silence them was told there was no breach of the warranty (but the board might be liable anyway).[45] One condo owner was awarded more than $70,000 for the board's failure to abate noise and vibrations from the building's cooling system and the supermarket below.[46] Another co-op owner was told he had to suffer in silence from the garage's noise and light because it was there first and he had agreed to buy "as is."[47] One tenant sued for a cool $6 million for the smell of java coming from the coffee bar below and got relief in the form of a vapor barrier (to seal off the fumes) before she and the aroma offender both called it quits and left the building.[48] Another co-op owner sought to end the third degree he claimed he was getting from the bright awning light shining in his window, only to be chastised for hypersensitivity and told to get drapes.[49]

I hope you get the message and realize that legal combat is not the way to go.

12. Join the Resistance

If you are convinced that right is on your side and you are willing to gamble on the courage of your convictions, one final gambit is to withhold maintenance payments. I know this violates the Tenth Commandment (against currency), but where necessity calls divine forgiveness follows. We've seen that the Warranty of Habitability can be a potent weapon in getting the board to do repair duty. It can also help rescue you from your neighbor's misdemeanors. The rationale for this self-imposed relief is that the problem—whether an affront to the auditory, olfactory, or some other sense—is so out of control that it makes your apartment uninhabitable—and the board has done nothing about it. (In condos, where owners don't have this warranty protection, and thus no corresponding offset right, this strategy is not available.)

You're sure to get the board's attention. The question is how will it respond? It may see the light and set forth into battle on your behalf. Or it may remain unmoved and haul you into court for not paying. If the court agrees with you, you're home free (or at least you'll be allowed to deduct part of your monthly charges). One long-suffering shareholder was granted a 50 percent maintenance cut because the board failed to take action to put an end to the endless noise emanating from her neighbor's apartment while the rest of the city slept.[50] Another got 20 percent off for months because the board had done nothing to silence an all-night supermarket (which the court partially shut down).[51] Others have not fared so well.

The risk you take is that the court will side with the board, in which case you will not only have to pay the maintenance but maybe late charges and attorneys' fees, too. Depending on how long you've been on strike, the board may even try to terminate your lease (though, as we've seen, courts rarely grant such drastic relief). So if you want to get even without getting shafted, it's safer to deposit those monthly checks into escrow until your dispute with the board (and your fellow shareholder) is resolved.

17

Joining the Ruling Ranks

POWER TRIP

Hopefully you have learned your lessons well enough to go on your own power trip, to join the ruling ranks and put your knowledge to work for the service of your fellow owners. In your new capacity you will have the benefit of the Rule that allows you to make decisions virtually unchallenged, which can foster tranquillity or foment dissent, and doubtless will have an enduring effect on the well-being—or demise—of the building.

Other perks come with the territory. As a director you have an *absolute* right to examine the corporation's books and records at any time, not the *limited* access available to those regular shareholder Joes. The idea is that you have to run the enterprise, so you need to know what's going on. And there's no surer way than to follow the money trail—who's being paid, how much, for what—and to keep your eyes on what your fellow officers are doing. I've had calls from skeptical shareholders at other buildings asking why they're being assessed with nothing to show for their money, and who want to get elected so they can see the books. But the right of access may also be manipulated as a strategic weapon by divided board members, who demand review of everything and get nothing done.

RISK EXPOSURE

Before you embark on your journey, be forewarned that the grass isn't always greener on the other side. With power comes responsibility—and potential liability. A prospective purchaser complains you shouldn't have turned down his application and takes you to court, the roof contractor says you didn't pay him what's due, a shareholder claims you didn't fix the leak and now he's living in a floodplain. The possibilities are as creative as those overeaters suing McDonald's for making them fat. If you've been paying attention, you're probably already asking, What is the extent of my exposure, and am I fully protected? As a director, so long as you're acting in your official capacity, you cast aside your individual identity and become part of the board, which, for legal purposes, is a kind of self-contained, living entity. Like it or not, your legal fate is tied to your fellow board members, so for your *own* sake you'd better watch out that they know what they're doing and do what they're supposed to. Unless you independently do something wrong, the board as a whole may be held liable, but *you* cannot be held personally liable,[1] which should let you sleep a little better at night. As a director of a co-op or condo doing good without getting paid, you benefit from courts trying hard not to make you pay out of your own pocket. None of this means that you (collectively or individually) won't be sued, so before you begin your new life as a director—indeed, before you even run—you should take a look at the relevant documents, advice I admit I didn't follow till much later on, though, fortunately, our board and building have remained litigation free.

Protection Begins at Home . . .

The place to begin is the bylaws, which usually contain indemnification provisions. In broad outline, here's what you want to find:

- A requirement that the co-op or condo indemnify any board member or officer who, by reason of carrying out his responsibilities, is named a party to any action or proceeding, civil or criminal.
- The indemnification should cover any judgments, settlement amounts, fines, and expenses, including attorneys' fees, incurred as a result of such action or proceeding, provided the board member didn't act in bad faith or obtain any personal benefit.

You have to understand that indemnification is like the morning-after pill; it affords relief only after the fact. Before it kicks in you have to foot the bill yourself, which could amount to serious money, and then wait to get reimbursed. Much better would be a requirement that your co-op or condo will pay the sums up front. If that's not what your bylaws say, your directors probably can—and should—amend them, a change that has to be communicated to shareholders usually by the next annual meeting.

. . . And Extends Beyond . . .

It's not just what the bylaws say that matters. As a director, you want to be sure that your building has Directors and Officers (D & O) liability insurance to protect you. Don't wait till you've been served with a complaint: it's too late. I'd ask to see the policy *before* I agreed to come on board. Until recently Chubb was the market leader for co-ops and condos, but it has largely pulled the plug: too many nickel-and-dime lawsuits slapped on client buildings that weren't worth the cost it took to defend them. Its place has been taken by CNA and Travelers, whose policies are identical in most, but not all, respects to those previously available. These are the key items to look for:

Defend and Indemnify

Ideally, you want a policy that does both, that pays for the cost of counsel to defend you in any covered action and indemnifies you for any judgment or other sums that may be incurred, otherwise you—or your co-op or condo (depending on what the bylaws say)—may have to shell out substantial amounts that could put your cash flow in the red. The quid pro quo for this up front protection money may be that the insurer gets to pick the attorney, who may or may not be someone you want tableside.

Individual and Collective

You also want to know *who* is covered: Is it the board as a whole, individual directors, or both? Contrary to what you may think, this is a distinction with a difference. Odds are that the board will be named in any lawsuit involving the building. But sometimes the wronged party makes a mistake and goes after the president, as the most visible symbol; or adds a specific director who he thinks did him in; or hopes by naming multiple parties to drive a wedge between board members so they'll settle. Unless you directors are covered individually *and* collectively, you may be in trouble, as one board found out the hard way when a shareholder sued it, claiming she was allowed to sublet without consent. Because the policy limited recovery to claims against individual officers or directors, none of whom was named, the court said the co-op wasn't entitled to defense or indemnification.[2]

Covered and Uncovered

Most policies cover a wide variety of claims from shareholder actions to third-party claims. And usually if any part of a lawsuit is covered, so is the entire suit. Just as important is to take a look at the exclusions, which are not necessarily either clear or logical. You might expect that directors *wouldn't* be covered for deliberate dishonest acts or illegal personal profiteering or fraudulent conduct, and they're not. But also among the typical exclusions are any actions on a contract, which intuitively you might think *would* be included. That's why there's no substitute for reading and trying to understand what the policy says.

How Much

The typical co-op or condo D & O policy has liability limits of $1 million a year (payable after a deductible, usually $2,500), which sounds like a lot, but with today's runaway verdicts isn't that much, especially if the limit includes defense costs, which can mount quickly. You still should be okay because beyond these limits, your building's umbrella policy should take over, which generally has to provide coverage for the excess amount on the same terms as the primary D & O policy.

. . . But Comes Back to You

Even the most comprehensive bylaws and D & O policy don't—and can't—provide you with absolute protection because the law says you're on your *own* in certain circumstances.

Cash Punishment

If you do something really outrageous, you can get hit with so-called punitive damages. How bad do you have to be? In legalese, your conduct must be "egregious" and directed not only at the person complaining but at the public generally. Unlike regular (or compensatory) damages, which are meant just to reimburse the injured party for any loss, punitive damages are designed to punish the wrongdoer, so they're usually for an amount that really hurts. Because it's so hard to meet this standard, directors aren't subject to payment of punitive damages for garden-variety disputes, not that shareholders haven't tried to get them. When a co-op board didn't approve the sale of an apartment because it said the price was too low, the court refused to award the disappointed shareholder punitive damages for breach of contract.[3] A condo owner who complained that the board failed to take necessary steps to reduce the noise in her apartment got the same answer: The board wasn't bad enough.[4]

The result is different if the board knows a problem needs fixing, but it sits back and does nothing. For six years the board refused to repair water leaks in a shareholders' apartment, threatening their health and safety and all their possessions. That's conduct outrageous enough to make it pay punitive damages, the court said.[5] Other shareholders complained their board took so long to repair the leak in their apartment that they had to sell rather than get soaked. Their claim for punitive damages was allowed to stand, though they didn't show that the co-op was responsible for the problem to begin with.[6] It's not just for sloth that directors can get hit with these damages. One Soho board that tried to shake down a shareholder for all sorts of unauthorized fees as a condition of approving his sublease got slapped with $100,000 in punitive damages.[7] Another board was forced to defend against a claim for punitive damages in a case for alleged breach of fiduciary duty involving a financial dispute between minority shareholders and the co-op.[8]

But by far the most painful punitive damage sting was felt by the president and director of a Beekman Place co-op where the board rejected the sublet application of a financially capable couple on racial grounds and then retaliated against the subletting shareholder when she objected to the denial. The court said Mr. President had acted in bad faith in violating the civil rights laws and individually assessed punitive damages against him that ultimately totaled $125,000.[9]

I was only doing my job, Mr. President said, and he sued the co-op to make it pay for him under its bylaws. What are you talking about? the judges said. You intentionally denied the application and exposed the co-op to liability. That's not acting in good faith, so it's against public policy for the building to indemnify you because you wouldn't feel the pain if someone else pays the price. Anyway, the Business Corporation Law[10] bars the co-op from picking up the tab when you've been found to have acted in bad faith.

Okay, you may be thinking, won't the D & O policy kick in to save his skin? The answer is no. On the same theory, in New York, it's against the law for insurance to indemnify a director against punitive damages. (The insurer still has to *defend* against lawsuits seeking both regular and punitive damages because its duty to defend is broader than its duty to pay.)[11] The result of the mess that Mr. President got himself into is that *he* had to pay out of his own pocket, which he did by selling his apartment.

And who do you think wound up paying the punitive damages assessed against the board in Mr. President's Beekman Place co-op? The owners, of course. Remember you're one of them even if you're *also* on the board, though after the assessments are imposed on your fellow shareholders for your wrongdoing, you may not be for long.

Thanks to Mr. President, the law is now clear that a director of a co-op or condo must pay his own punitive damages, something you should think about before you, or any of your fellow board members, use their power to exact revenge, or wait till hell freezes over to fix a shareholder problem. Neither insurance nor the bylaws can save you from your own self-inflicted fate. After Mr. President's rude awakening, boards demanded that the law be changed to allow directors and officers to be indemnified under their co-op's or condo's bylaws, but it's unlikely that those legislators are going to save you from your own ill-advised folly.

House Arrest

The thought of being socked with monetary punishment is bad enough, but as a board member you could also find yourself a convicted criminal. That's what almost happened when a Brooklyn co-op and three of its directors were charged with violating the City's Health Code after a child fell to his death and inspection revealed that nine apartments had faulty window guards. The board members moved to dismiss the indictment, claiming they couldn't be held personally liable for criminal violations by the co-op, but the court said the corporation acts only through individuals so that officers can't escape criminal liability, even though the co-op was also named as a defendant.[12]

Although the case was finally settled without criminal liability for board members, the decision still stands, allowing for the future possibility that a co-op or condo director could be held criminally responsible, even if he didn't intend to violate the law and didn't know the law had been broken. Lots of laws that apply to the maintenance of buildings—everything from elevators to window guards—allow for criminal sanctions (though they're rarely enforced).

To make matters worse (or at least more nerve-racking) it's not clear whether the D & O policy would have to provide defense coverage if you were charged with a criminal violation in your capacity as an individual board member. Most policies provide for defense in a civil, criminal, or administrative adjudicatory proceeding, so it's possible, but not certain, that your defense costs would be covered until a finding of guilt. What *is* certain is that insurance would *not* indemnify you as an individual board member, or the co-op, for any fines or penalties resulting from a criminal proceeding. And given what the court said to Mr. President about punitive damages, it's unlikely that the co-op's bylaws would help, leaving *you* to pay on your own. Laws have been proposed to exempt volunteer board members from criminal liability if they had no intent to violate the law or knowledge that it had been broken. But as a matter of policy, it cuts against the grain to excuse criminal wrongs, so I wouldn't count on legal aid.

Self-Help

Ultimately, *you* are your own best insurance policy. Don't do anything you'll regret, and you won't find yourself out on a financial or criminal limb. You shouldn't need me to tell you that discrimination is against the law—and if you're caught in the act, you'll pay. If a shareholder has a leak or complains of persistent loud noise from the restaurant below or suffers damage to her apartment as a result of renovations the building did, ignore the problem at your peril even if she is your sworn enemy. Otherwise she may have sweet revenge—and the last laugh—on the legal front. And if you don't want to risk criminal sanctions, you and your fellow directors had better be sure that your co-op or condo is in compliance with all relevant laws.

It's not enough to act right; you also need to accurately record your actions. If the issue is a recurrent leak and you've brought in professionals to fix the problem, a written report of their efforts to date will help show you're being diligent, if not yet successful, in finding a solution. If the problem is of building-wide scope, the best way to maintain the peace is to keep shareholders regularly informed of your progress. Maybe most important are board minutes: For owners and prospective purchasers they are a way to find out what's going on; for *you*, as a director, they are presumptively valid evidence of what you did or didn't do and can be used in a lawsuit to help or hurt your co-op's cause. In a recent dispute over a financial transaction, the minutes recorded that the complaining shareholders had consented to the very action they sought to challenge, and got the board off the hook.[13] So take the time to read them and be sure they're right, because what they say is presumed to be true.

THICK SKIN

You can, and should, control what's said about your official acts in the board minutes to be sure it's correct, but you have no control over what shareholders say about you. As a board member, you are a lightning rod for any building-related wrong, whether real or imagined, individual or collective. And shareholders figure that they'll get more action, and attention, if they communicate their discontent to fellow owners—sometimes in tabloid-like prose.

I speak from personal experience. My particular nemesis was a longtime resident, not even an owner, who decided he'd show me because the board had fired a doorman who spent his day talking with Mr. Malcontent rather than tending to his duties. He embarked on a disinformation campaign against me, circulating leaflets accusing me of unjust firings and assorted wrongs, taking his case door to door to shareholders. I admit I contemplated possible countermaneuvers, but I decided any response would only give credence to his fictional claims. Sure enough, in short order the populace figured out *I* wasn't the crazy one—a good thing, too, because the reality is there is no legal recourse.

Remember Mr. Pullman, the shareholder who was evicted by his board for objectionable conduct? Among his misdeeds were creatively offensive memos he circulated to shareholders, claiming the board president had undisclosed conflicts, had breached his duties to the co-op, had a Napoleonic complex, and was married to a woman who was having a relationship with the professor's wife upstairs. After the shareholder from hell had been kicked out, the president (yes, a lawyer) sued him for defamation. Sorry, the court told him. Your fellow shareholders have to be able to communicate with each other about what's going on in the building, including your actions as a director, and the law gives them what's called a "common interest privilege," so they can. Even if they've defamed you, there's nothing you can do unless they acted with malice, which is practically impossible to prove.[14]

Another board member, at a Mitchell-Lama co-op, took a shot with the same result. A ninety-year-old shareholder, who was on the opposite side of the privatization fence from one of the directors, wrote a letter (that was distributed to the board) saying that she had filed a police complaint because Mr. Opposition had physically blocked her passage down the stairway and attacked her with oral slurs. He sued for defamation, arguing that her allegations sullied his professional reputation and his standing with the other directors. Doesn't matter, came back the judicial answer. She's protected by the privilege.[15]

Likewise, the law allows board members to sling verbal mud at each other, so you'd better get used to it. After the treasurer of a co-op was removed, he wrote a letter to two other directors, which he also circulated to shareholders, saying it was all their fault. He said they wrote checks without invoices for work supposedly done and submitted false financial information to obtain a loan for the building, though he'd never seen the application. The two sued him, demanding $250,000 in damages for ruining their reputations, but without a finding that he had acted out of spite, the same privilege protected the ex-treasurer.[16]

The moral of these stories is that if you can't stand the heat, stay out of the kitchen—or, at least, develop a thick skin because you won't get any help from the law for what shareholders or fellow directors say about you.

18
Filing Out

GETTING AN HONORABLE DISCHARGE

Whether you're coming or going, the powers that be have you on their radar scope. Coming in, you have to pass inspection. Going out, you have to make it through the rear guard without tripping any land mines that might kill your sale, if not you. The one most likely to inflict pain (at least of the financial sort) is the honorable discharge fee, better known as the flip tax (or waiver fee)—a form of involuntary tribute that requires you to turn over a portion of your sale proceeds to your former comrades and commanders. You also may have to fend off board attempts to set the price at which you sell your apartment or to impose other conditions for granting you a discharge. You may even have to fight over who your successor will be. And as any of you who've been through the drill know, it's not uncommon for a few skirmishes along the way between you and your battalion replacement (a.k.a. your buyer). This chapter offers you step-by-step passage to safe (though not necessarily cheap) separation from the ranks.

DEPARTING DOLLARS

In many buildings you have to pay through the nose in the form of transfer taxes before you go. These tithes are a way of life in co-ops but have made few inroads thus far in condos. In theory they're supposed to discourage speculation, defray maintenance, and underwrite capital improvements—not a rationale likely to impress any but the truly altruistic, because your dollars don't benefit you, only those fellow owners (friend or foe) you left behind. The only way to avoid seeing red when you write the check is to view your contribution as a payback for all the fat fees forked over by previously departing owners that helped keep costs in check, paid for enhancements, and thereby increased the value of your apartment. The true beneficiaries of such enforced largesse—those who stay in the building—don't pay anything. Not exactly a model of equality before the law. (But if you think you can mount a case that it's unfair for departing shareholders to foot the bill for their remaining brethren, forget it. That battle has been tried and lost, so don't waste your time.)

Personally, I prefer the pay-as-you-go approach to the onetime payback. If I'm smart (or lucky) enough to buy low and sell high, it cuts against my capitalist grain to share the wealth with fellow shareholders I'm leaving behind. Moreover, relying on maintenance forces the board to sharpen its pencil and figure out how to keep the building's cash flowing and its reserves sound using only those monthly checks (or any assessments) and not to depend on cash infusions contingent on sales. By definition, these are most needed when least available—in tough markets.

Transfer taxes come in all sizes and shapes but are of two basic varieties. The most common (and dreaded) is the *flip tax*, which assesses you a fee (how much depends on what your building's tax code says) when you sell your apartment to an outsider. Then there's what's called a *waiver fee*, which you pay in some buildings for the privilege of being allowed to sell your shares to a third party rather than having them redeemed by the co-op. Whatever their names and however they work, these fees can set you back plenty, though both their calculation and their cost vary widely from building to building.

The time to focus on them is *before* you buy. Then you can soberly do a few hypothetical calculations (based on how the building charges and how much you hope to sell for) and figure out your tax bill in dollars and cents. If too many zeros for your entrepreneurial comfort flash before your eyes, you still have time to change your mind and buy in a building where you won't have to pay to go. If you wait till it's time to sell to figure out the damage, you will suffer sticker shock with no recourse.

TO TAX OR NOT TO TAX

Home of the Brave

It's clear that co-ops can charge shareholders transfer fees. The only real legal bone of contention was whether boards could take it upon the royal we to tax shareholders themselves or whether they had to be given this power by the people. That battle was waged (in the courts and legislature) and came out on the side of democracy. This is the result:

Rule Number One

Directorial status does not confer dictatorial tax prerogatives. This means the board can't by itself pass a resolution and impose a tax on you whenever it runs short of cash. Its power to manage doesn't give it the power to tax. Its right to raise revenue for the building doesn't give it the right to impose a levy. It must be given power to tax. Exactly what magic words need to be incanted before it can legally put its hands in your pocket, we'll see a little later. But the point is that its power derives from the people.

Rule Number Two

This second rule flows ineluctably from the first. Shareholders have their say in setting tax policy. That's true in theory and in law, but not necessarily in real-world practice, where a majority of one—the sponsor—can vote in the tax code by which shareholders must then live and die.

These taxes usually are established at the dawning of the co-op republic, often with the blessing of insiders who figure it's better to buy low while they can and (maybe) pay later. So as a quid pro quo for getting the sponsor to reduce prices they agree to a tax that is payable *only if* and *when* they sell. The sponsor is willing to oblige because he'll have to pay less into the building's cash reserve coffers. And since the sponsor is also the sole shareholder, he can unilaterally vote to impose a tax on would-be owners (and all those to come) while exempting himself. It may not be equitable, but as we've seen, it's perfectly legal for the sponsor to exclude himself from the rules he makes. Lest you be contemplating corrective action, know that other outraged shareholders already have put the issue to the judicial test, only to be told that they can't make the sponsor pay tax. So like it or not, that's the way it is.

Even though as an insider you had nothing to do with setting the tax wheels in motion, as long as the mechanism is laid out (in the offering plan, proprietary lease, or occupancy agreement), you're on notice and you're bound if you buy. Shareholders who come afterward have less to gain. They still have to pay, although they don't get the benefit of those rock-bottom insider prices. Their only choice is to vote with their feet and walk away from a building that charges too hefty a sales tax—not an unreasonable decision.

Assuming this money machine is put in place at the outset, odds are the board will let it be and keep those dollars rolling in. It's just easier to keep the cash flowing than to turn off the spigot and dream up some other revenue-raising device.

However, if your co-op started its life as a tax-free refuge, it's difficult (though not impossible) thereafter to transform it into a tax-collecting state because shareholders then have to vote to tax *themselves*—not a winning platform. The prospect is further dimmed by the fact that most co-ops require not just a majority but a two-thirds shareholder vote to make the transition. During the conversion of my building, our lawyer told us soon-to-be board members that it was now or never. If we wanted to have a flip tax code, the only sure way was for the sponsor to be the heavy and vote to tax the shareholders before they could vote themselves. As with sublease fees, we decided to forgo our power to tax and have remained tax free and financially sound ever since.

Land of the Free

In condos, transfer taxes are the exception. First, there's the practical reason. Condos appeal to the antiauthoritarian among us who want to live free or die. Any attempt to stifle self-determination by saddling owners with taxes could lead to desertion in the buying ranks. Then there's the legal angle. Remember back to that old rule against perpetuities (just think Kathleen Turner) and how it prohibits unreasonable restraints in selling real estate (which is what your condo is). Some among the legal set say that flip taxes are illegal restrictions on your ability to sell. On the flip side, there's the Condo Act, which says it's okay for condo bylaws to have provisions governing the sale or lease of your units.[1] The battle lines have been drawn, but the legal fight has never been waged definitively in the courts.

One condo seller tried to get back the $700 in processing fees he had been charged to transfer his apartment, claiming they were an unauthorized and illegal flip tax. But the court said the flat fee was an administrative expense, not a flip tax.[2] In the past few years the trend has been to allow condo boards to impose more restrictions. One court said they could ban subleases.[3] Another said they could charge owners fines for violating subletting rules.[4] We can only wait and see if judicial approval for condo flip taxes is next.

For now, the result is this critical difference: In co-ops, it's clear the board can charge you a flip tax if it's properly empowered. In condos, before you even get to the issue of board authority, there's the more basic question of whether it's legal for condos to charge owners *any* sales tax. The most likely to be upheld would be one approved by owners themselves. Some condos ignore the whole mess and include flip taxes in their bylaws, hoping that unsuspecting owners won't know any better and pay (a mistake you will not make).

DECIPHERING THE CODE

Assuming your building can charge you a transfer fee, you have to look at its tax code to see *what* is said by way of a power grant to the board, *where* it's said, and sometimes even *when*. A word of caution: Since courts have not yet spoken for sure on the basic issue of whether condos can charge you a sales tax, they haven't yet been confronted with the more mundane tax details we'll be discussing below. But condo owners can take guidance from the co-op rules (established after hard fighting) to see what you may be in for if flip taxes rear their ugly heads in your building.

What Power Is Given

So how do you know if your directors have been deputized to serve as agents of financial terror? Look to see what kind of power fix they've been given. The scope of their authority depends on whether they've been granted the right: (1) to collect set-rate taxes, (2) to fix the amount themselves, or (3) to charge only specific, limited fees.

Fixed-Rate Certainty

Many co-ops give boards power to assess a set-rate tax. It may be 5 percent of profits, 2 percent of your resale price, or $50 per share. With these kinds of taxes (usually in your lease), you know where you stand even if you may not like the view from there. In addition to certainty, this fixed rate usually gives you the benefit of control. If the board claims a cash crunch and wants to increase the tax from 5 to 10 percent of profits, it can't do it on its own but has to come to you for approval, which generally means convincing two-thirds of you that the ends justify the means.

Dictatorial Discretion

Even more to be feared are blank check power grants, sometimes given at the outset (and urged upon us by our lawyer), which authorize the directors at their discretion to fix the amount of any transfer fee when you sell. These are the most dangerous because you don't know when the board will decide to flex its taxing muscles or how much it'll squeeze you for. And since it's been preauthorized to set the fees as it sees fit it doesn't have to ask your permission. So before you buy into a building you should check to see that even if there's no current sales tax in effect, there's none lying in wait to entrap you later on.

Limited Authority

On the other hand, if the taxing power is too specific it can cut the board's power down to pint size. One co-op authorized its board to fix a reasonable fee to cover actual expenses, attorneys' fees, a service fee, and such other conditions as it might determine in connection with sales. Although the provision gave the board an inch, it took a mile and decided it could make shareholders pay a many-thousand-dollared flip tax. Not so, said the court (New York's highest). If the board is given authority to set only specific fees and other conditions on resale, that's all it can do. It can't use that limited grant as a pretext to charge you a flip tax when you go to sell.[5]

Where It's Imparted

Assuming you've mastered the art of tax substance, you're ready to move on to the issue of site. If the tax provision is not in the right place, the board may not be able to make you pay anything.

In Bounds

Since lots of these taxes are put in place at the co-op's creation, it's not uncommon to find them right in the offering plan. But usually they're also included in the proprietary lease, which generally requires a two-thirds vote of shareholders for amendment, and thus assures that you really have a say in how much you're taxed—or at least in any changes made to fixed amounts. If the board wants to increase the sales tax in your lease from 2 percent to 5 percent of your resale price, it has to get your approval.

And it may give you sweet satisfaction to know that even if the board comes to you hat in hand for a hike, if it doesn't go about it the right way, you may end up with a tax holiday. That was the happy (albeit temporary) ending for shareholders in one building where the board sought to impose a new flip tax without continuing the old one till passage was sure. It made the mistake of getting its constituents to vote for an amendment to the wrong document—with the result that shareholders got nine months of tax amnesty and the board sought to recover from the managing agent for the $150,000 snafu.[6]

Out of Bounds

You may be able to avoid paying the piper altogether if the sole source of the board's taxing power is in the co-op's bylaws because a transfer tax that *only* appears there generally is not enforceable. The rationale is to prevent directors, who in many co-ops may change the bylaws on their own, from setting tax policy for the shareholder masses, leaving you out in the cold except to foot the bill. One board tried this, but a shareholder who knew his rights called the board's bluff and got back his $12,000. Since the bylaws were the sole source of the flip tax, it was invalid.

In contrast, assuming condos can have flip taxes, bylaws would be the place to find them. As the main governing documents in condos, bylaws can be changed only by the approval of two-thirds of the owners, preventing board usurpation of tax policy.

When Board Power Attaches

Timing also can count in determining if you pay as you go or if you pass go without paying. What's critical is whether an enforceable tax is in effect before the sale to your purchaser is *substantially complete*. If the answer is yes, you pay. If it's no, you're off the hook.

Seems like a simple enough question, but it's gotten different answers. One shareholder found out the meaning of bad timing. He bought as an insider (from an offering plan that authorized the board to impose a flip tax), only to turn around and contract to sell soon after—in October. In a race for dollars, the new board passed a $50-per-share fee in November, effective immediately—and then interviewed the prospective purchaser, who was later approved. At the closing, which took place in December, the board said pay. The seller balked, saying the deal was done before the tax was passed. Not so, ruled that judicial higher authority. Since the buyer was interviewed and approved *after* the tax was set, the sale had not been substantially completed, so the shareholder had to hand over the cash.[7]

Those of you not happy with this answer can take some comfort in the fact that other lower courts have said that for flip tax purposes the date that counts is when your sales contract is signed[8]—in which case our friend would have gotten off tax free. Of course, if you live in a building like mine, where the board only has a right of first refusal, you have a stronger argument that the tax deadline may be the contract date. The point of all this: If you hear even a whiff of flip tax talk while you are in the process of selling, better get cracking and get your buyer signed, sealed, delivered, and approved before the tax comes down the pike so you can take (all) the money and run.

TOTING UP YOUR BILL

Now that you know the tax code basics, it's time to look at some of the creative techniques devised to effect the levy: how the fees are calculated, how much they can cost you, and whether you can expect the board to cut you any more slack than the IRS.

Flipping Out

Like it or not, flip taxes are here to stay (at least in co-ops), so you may as well understand how they work. Co-ops have a complete arsenal of flip taxes—varying in kind and degree—from which to choose. (Condos, to the extent they have sales fees, borrow from among co-ops' caches.) The particular tax weapon in effect should help you figure out not only the amount of the tithe you'll pay but also something of the financial and philosophical character of the building.

Equality for All

Some buildings calculate flip taxes based on a flat fee per share. Theoretically, what could be fairer? Since everyone is paying the same amount per share, the financial pain is proportional to your ownership interest. The only problem is, you can proportionally all lose money. That's because under this method you pay whether or not you make a profit. Let's say you own an apartment having 400 shares that you bought for $500,000. You get lucky and sell for $600,000, netting a $100,000 profit. Even after forking over the flip tax, which we'll assume here is $50 per share—or $20,000 ($50 × 400 shares), you're still $80,000 ahead of the game. But what if the market takes a dive and that $500,000 apartment now fetches only $400,000? In addition to taking a $100,000 bath you still have to pay the same $20,000, so all told you've dug yourself into a $120,000 hole.

Disproportionate but Equal

Then there are flip taxes tied to profits: If you make money on the sale of your apartment, the co-op gets a percentage of your gain. If you don't, the co-op gets nothing.

Let's return to our $500,000 apartment to see how it works. Only this time we'll assume that the co-op imposes a flip tax of 10 percent of profit on resale. Under this scenario, if you sell for $600,000 you realize a gain of $100,000 and have to hand over $10,000 to the co-op (10% × $100,000). If you lose on the deal and pocket only $400,000 you don't have to spill any more red ink by paying a fee.

Now let's look at the fate of another selling shareholder—that neighbor down the hall who owns the mirror image of your apartment, which, like yours, also has 400 shares. He bought as an insider and paid only $300,000. But the real estate gods smiled upon him and he, too, sold for $600,000, making a $300,000 profit. Using a flat fee per share he would pay the same amount as you because both of you own 400 shares. But under the profit percentage formula, he pays $30,000 (10% × $300,000) to your $10,000—or three times as much per share.

Assuming you've been paying attention to all that's come before, you may be asking how can a fee that *unequally* impacts shareholders be legal? Since New York's Corporation Law, which applies to co-ops, requires that each share must be equal to every other share of the same class,[9] the courts have said, as we've seen, that sublet fees must be equal based on the number of shares you own.

Flip taxes are the exception. Years back at the height of the conversion craze, several shareholders, who had bought as insiders and stood to make a killing when they went to sell, objected to the $40,000 profit-based tax they were charged, saying it was illegal because it wasn't in proportion to the number of shares they owned. This state's highest court agreed and tossed out the fees,[10] only to be overturned by the legislators, who were convinced by boards that the decision would deprive co-ops of cash needed for capital improvements. Since then the law has expressly allowed co-ops to set transfer fees that are *not* equal per share, including those tied to profits or sales.[11] You may as well become attuned to the finer points of profit terminology because the differences in definition can mean differences in dollars.

Gross

In some buildings the flip tax you pay is based on a percentage of your gross profit—the difference between the price you paid when you bought and the price you will receive when you sell. If you bought for $500,000 and sell for $600,000, your gross profit is $100,000. Assuming a 10 percent transfer tax, you pay the co-op $10,000.

Net

The calculation can be more complicated (though less costly) if it's based on your net profit. Even though you bought for $500,000 and sold for $600,000, that's only the beginning of the story. Under this scenario, before you can figure your tax you have to deduct the cost of capital improvements and your sales-related expenses. Let's say you fulfilled your Nigella Lawson fantasy and redid your kitchen as a paean to good taste at a cost of $40,000. This may not have improved your culinary skills, but it should help your bottom line. The process of selling your apartment also can set you back a pretty penny. The real estate broker gets his commission, usually 6 percent of the sales price—here, $36,000. The lawyer gets his due for handling the closing—say, $2,000. All these items ($40,000 + $36,000 + $2,000 = $78,000) can be added to your initial cost ($500,000 + $78,000 = $578,000) (in accounting lingo, used to increase your cost basis) and thereby reduce your profit ($600,000 – $578,000 = $22,000). Whereas your gross profit on the transaction was $100,000, your net profit is a mere $22,000. Assuming the same 10 percent transfer tax, you pay only $2,200 instead of $10,000.

A word of caution: Since boards don't go by the honor system you'd better keep records of all that you have spent on these items and any others you can use in calculating your net profit. I hope you've been hoarding all those renovation receipts for your day of reckoning with Uncle Sam. But, if not, it's better late than never to start creating a proper paper trail.

Confused

Expect confusion or more serious trouble if your building's tax code doesn't spell out what it means by *net* profit. Although accountants are bound by convention, co-ops can be more creative in their definition so long as they say what they mean. Some allow you to include the cost of renovations; others figure it's too easy a way to pad your purchase price and reduce your profit (and their cut). Some say you can take closing costs into account; others say no. When there's no definition, there may be a dispute, which is what happened when a co-op demanded from a selling shareholder a flip tax of 15 percent of net profit without specifying what that meant. The shareholder claimed she had a right to deduct costs for capital improvements and brokerage and legal fees, which reduced her taxable sale amount from $74,000 to $36,000. Since the co-op had neglected to define its terms, the court got to figure out what its tax code meant and how much she owed.[12]

From Profit to Sales

What's good for profit is good for sales—and a lot easier to figure out, which is one reason why flip taxes based on your selling price are probably the most common. If you sell for $600,000 and the transfer tax is 3 percent, you turn over $18,000 regardless of what you paid originally or whether you see a profit. Win, lose, or draw, you have to pay. Where properly implemented, courts have upheld these sales-based taxes even if they preclude you from earning a profit on resale. So before you buy, you'd better decide if you're willing to give the first cut off the top to the co-op when you sell.

Hobson's Choice

In some buildings you get to pick your poison because the flip tax is a choice between the lesser of two evils: a set percent of your profit or a fixed (but usually lower) percent of the total resale price. On the upside, this choice cushions the pain of sharing too much of your gain. On the downside, it softens the blow of a bad deal or a down market by limiting your loss.

The hybrid tax implemented at my friend's building at the time of conversion shows you how this system works. Selling shareholders there have the choice of handing over 10 percent of their profit or 5 percent of the selling price, whichever is less. If you bought at the bottom as an insider for $300,000 and then hit pay dirt when you sell several years after into a rising market for $500,000, you have the choice of paying 5 percent of the resale price ($25,000) or 10 percent of the $200,000 profit ($20,000). If you're lucky enough to reap a profit bonanza, the price-based option limits how much of the windfall you have to share.

On the other hand, if you bought at a peak for $600,000, only to have to sell into a downdraft for $500,000, the profit-pegged option assures that you won't be out any more than your market-inflicted $100,000 loss. In calculating your flip tax here you have the option of paying the lesser of 5 percent of the sales price ($25,000) or 10 percent of a $100,000 loss, which gets you into negative territory (–$10,000). If life were fair and there were a quid pro quo, the co-op would pay you $10,000 to help make up the shortfall. Although such a state of equilibrium has not yet been achieved, at least you don't have to hand over anything to the co-op if you sell at a loss.

Time Travelers

Then there are fees that vary over time, which are largely a relic of those heady conversion days.[13] These can be based on a percentage of profit or sales price or can be a flat fee per share. But the way they usually work, the longer you hold the less you pay. The goal of these time-based taxes was to stick it to those get-rich-quick speculators who bought as insiders and wanted to flip fast, and to ease the pain for the stabilizing shareholders willing to stay put over the long haul. Since the days of conversion fever are past, time-sensitive taxes are no longer a big factor.

Fee for All

Finally, some buildings impose a flat fee per transfer, say $2,000, $3,000, or some other fixed number. (One condo I know of has a sales tax equal to two months' common charges.) Not based on profit or sales price or shares held, these fees are equal for all and arguably fair to none. But as long as they're relatively modest, they have the benefit of letting you know before you buy exactly what your total tax bill will be when you sell.

Fee for One

What boards *can't* do is set flip taxes that are meant to single out individual shareholders. As you'll remember, the board of a Greenwich Village co-op passed a fee that applied *only* to one recently departed owner, figuring she had gone on to a place where she couldn't complain, but the court got it overturned for her.[14]

Waiving Good-Bye

Another less common, but potentially more costly way to go, is paying the co-op a so-called waiver of option fee. Unlike flip taxes, which are predicated on your going straight to market for a buyer, the premise of a waiver fee is that you *first* have to offer your shares for sale to the co-op corporation, usually at book value or some other below-market price. In lieu of exercising its option, the co-op can release you and give you the green light to sell to a third party at market price, making you pay a waiver fee for the privilege.[15] Still, the way most of these fees are set up, you'll wind up ahead of the game because the price at which you'd have to sell to the co-op is so low that even after it extracts its pound of flesh, you'll end up with more.

Equality is no more necessary in waiving good-bye than it is in flipping out. The price of your handshake need not be based on the number of shares you own. It can be a percentage of your profits or a portion of your sales price. But like flip taxes, option fees have to be properly enacted. On that basis, the children of a deceased shareholder objected to the $39,600 waiver of option fee they paid on the sale of their mother's apartment for $86,000. Because the fee was passed only by a board resolution, the court said it was no good, but it didn't make the co-op return the amount the thwarted sellers already had paid.[16]

Testing the Limits

Is there any limit on the cost of bidding your building adieu? Since in theory these taxes are a compact between the co-op and its constituents as long as the assent is mutual (no matter that the sponsor in reality may have been the sole assenting shareholder), the price of departure can be whatever you've supposedly agreed upon.

And indeed there are cases on the books upholding sizable going-away fees. One shareholder complained that a waiver fee of 60 percent of her sales price was unconscionable only to be told that contract, not conscience, is what counts.[17] Another who sought relief from a 40 percent waiver fee on the sale of her shares fared no better.[18] Ditto for the seller forced to pay a waiver fee of 25 percent of her profit on the difference between purchase and sale.[19] One poor shareholder even had to pay a fee that was more than the price for which he sold.[20] Flip taxes of 10 percent and 15 percent of profit (and more) have received the judicial stamp of approval.[21]

But, to a large extent, the market has corrected what the law had decreed. As apartment prices have skyrocketed, the percentage of sales price (or profit) demanded by way of flip tax has declined so that nowadays a typical tax would be around 3 percent of your sales price, which is still not pocket change. If you live in one of those buildings that hasn't yet adjusted its flip tax for inflation, it may be time for you to get together your fellow shareholders to vote for tax relief (usually by amending the proprietary lease). The task is sure to be easier once insiders (who got cheap prices in return for paying future flip taxes) are outnumbered by newcomers (who paid relative top dollar and are less willing to share their more limited gains).

Pay Now, Fight Later

Assuming there's a sales tax in place when you go to sell, the board has you over a barrel. It can hold you financial hostage by refusing to transfer shares to your intended (and approved) purchaser unless you cough up the cash. If you refuse to pay and it refuses to close, you'll all end up in a standoff. Even if some court later declares you the winner and invalidates the tax, in the real world you probably still lose. By the time the court makes a decision your buyer will have walked and you may wind up selling for less (to say nothing of the fact that he may have a claim against you for breaking the deal).

Although it may be unpalatable, your best option is still to pay the tax under protest so you can close the deal, and then seek a refund in court. To preserve your rights and leave no room for doubt, send a letter to the board protesting its authority to impose the fee. (Or better, have your attorney do the dirty work, since he or she should know the right legal lingo.) For added good measure, inscribe your protest on the face of the check for all the world (and the directors) to see.

Knowing how popular flip taxes are, boards have come up with their own counterdevices to insulate themselves and their fees from attack. Don't be surprised if, as a condition of closing, your building's board makes you sign a general release absolving it of all claims or a waiver acknowledging the fee is valid.[22] Since you don't have any choice but to sign if you want to close (and thus are not exercising your free will) these disclaimers probably have more psychological than legal impact. They have not prevented shareholders from getting refunds when a court finds the flip tax invalid.

Fight Fire with Fire

If you want to give the board a taste of its own tactics, you may try the approach taken by one enterprising shareholder and his lawyer, assuming you have a better claim than he did. He signed a waiver and paid the flip tax under protest (with his lawyer's escrow check). The lawyer then turned around and stopped payment on the check right after the closing. Though possession is nine-tenths of the law, in this case the other tenth prevailed. The co-op sued (lawyer and client) for the $5,400 due plus interest—and won, because the tax was legitimate. But at least the shareholder had the satisfaction of making the board work hard for the money.[23]

Although this strategy has a certain street fighter appeal, it's not one I'd necessarily advise because if you lose you could wind up paying extras, such as interest and even attorneys' fees. Anyway, it's not usually an available option because most co-ops, fearing shareholder self-help, make you pay with cash-equivalent certified checks.

GETTING OUT WITHOUT A FIGHT

If you're selling, that means you've bought and know the drill, so the process should be less anxiety producing the second time around, especially because it's not *your* credit or credibility that's on the line. Also working in your favor is the fact that as you're a shareholder the board owes you duties it didn't when you were just a buyer hoping to get past the gates. Still, even as a seller, the board holds the balance of power. As you know by now, as long as the board is acting within its authority and in good faith, it can reject your would-be replacement with impunity.

And don't expect any help from the courts for your board's hard-hearted rejection. One shareholder on a crusade for us all tried to recover damages for his board's refusal to approve a prospective purchaser, only to be met with a stone wall and a reminder that judges won't second-guess those directors' decisions.[24]

In condos, where the right of first refusal is the standard, the board can't reject your buyer, only buy the apartment itself (which, as we've seen, isn't a realistic option). Just remain patient and persistent and your discharge (and sale) will come through.

Self-Help Techniques

All this doesn't mean it's a totally one-way street. There are things you can do (or not do) to improve the odds that your purchaser will get approved without a problem.

Advance Financial Scouting

It's easy (and fashionable) to complain that the board unfairly rejected your buyer, the most common (though usually unannounced) reason being money. But from my experience, sellers don't generally have a clue about their buyers' financial status or whether it complies with the building's requirements. Truth is, the moment shareholders become sellers, they part company with the board and their fellow owners. Sellers want to get the highest price and pocket as much cash as they can, and don't usually give a thought as to whether the buyer is financially fit. That's human nature; I'd probably do the same thing. But the board is obligated to protect the shareholders you left behind by seeing to it that newcomers can pay their own way. Knowing what the board is up against, and remembering that it holds the cards, you'd do yourself a favor to find out the state of your buyer's finances (through your broker) as early in the process as possible, but in any event *before* the application is submitted. That way you have a pretty good idea in advance if there's a problem and can make a realistic assessment whether to risk rejection and go for the last dollar or opt for a surer, if slightly lower, bidder.

Patience is a Virtue

Not infrequently, I get calls from selling shareholders inquiring about the status of their buyer's application *before* the board has even received it. Assuming financing is involved, it can easily take two months from the time the contract was signed till the board actually gets the package. On top of that, the board usually has thirty days to act from when a completed application is submitted (and most require additional information). I'm not saying you should sit by endlessly in passive silence, but knowing the timetable should help you to communicate with the board in a way that facilitates, rather than frustrates, the deal. And if there is some special circumstance (other than normal seller angst) requiring expedited treatment—you need the cash to close on another property, your job is taking you out of the country—the best way is to submit a letter with the application letting the board know up front.

Standard of Review

Although there's not much you can do about it, knowing what level of scrutiny your buyer (and thus you) is up against may at least help you to understand a seemingly incomprehensible process. Most buyers and sellers assume the application is determined by an all-knowing, all-powerful board, when, in fact, it may be assigned to a managing agent, who's usually less emotionally attached and may be more flexible. Even if the board assumes responsibility, only one or two directors may be doing the reviewing. Ferreting out this information should give you some sense of by whom and how thoroughly the application will be scrutinized—and an indication of whether your new recruit will be approved.

Legal Aid

In addition to taking action on your own, sometimes the law is on your side when it comes to selling.

Price Fixing is Banned

We've just seen that the board can get a piece of the action by taxing your sales proceeds. Some have even tried to set the price—-high or low—at which you can sell, a form of market manipulation that's been challenged by shareholders acting as antitrust police.

The Lower Depths

Faced with sagging prices caused by a declining market, one board decided to play God and prop them up. First it had an appraisal done of 2 out of 160 apartments. Then it adopted a resolution authorizing itself to withhold approval of any sale in which the contract price was more than 10 percent below the value of the appraised apartments. One unhappy shareholder caught in the downdraft contracted to sell his one-bedroom for $37,500 only to have the board say no because the floor price it had fixed was $49,000.

But the court overruled the board, and the owner got to sell. Since the coming of a turnaround is no more predictable than that of the Messiah, setting prices effectively prevents shareholders from selling. It's okay to make you share the proceeds of a sale (via flip taxes or waiver fees), but the board can't destroy the market altogether.[25] Just remember the result may not be the same if a prospective purchaser challenges his rejection on the ground that the price was too low because the board owes no special duty to outsiders.

The Sky's the Limit

On the other hand, if your board is more civic-minded than value conscious, it can't force you to sacrifice profits in the name of its cause by setting the *maximum* price at which you can sell. That's what happened at one Lower

East Side building. The residents there bought out the owner for a relative song and converted to co-op status, thereby transforming themselves in body, but not in mind, from tenants to landlords. Determined to stay true to their working-class roots and to help purchasers find affordable housing, the board set out to suppress prices at which shareholders could sell. It passed a provision requiring shareholders first to offer their apartments for sale to the co-op. If the co-op passed, then the shareholder could sell on his own (assuming the board approved the purchase)—but only at a predetermined below-market price calculated by using a base value of $2,500 and adding 20 percent a year.

Based on this formula, when the lone capitalist in this collectivist den went to sell, he could charge only $21,500 for two apartments valued at $40,000—not a result likely to convert him to the fold. You'll be happy to know that his pursuit of the American dream prevailed. The board can subject shareholders to a right of first refusal, but it can't deprive them of a free-market option.[26] So if perchance you find yourself among a band of unrepentant do-gooders (who haven't succumbed to the lesson that greed is good), take comfort in knowing that the profit motive is alive and well in co-ops.

But what the board can't do out in the open it may do under cover of silence. Since most boards can turn down your buyer without giving a reason, there's nothing (except conscience) to stop a board from just saying no if it doesn't like the price. (You'll probably never be the wiser unless it establishes a pattern.) But if the board's ill-advised (or honest) enough to tell you it's turning down your buyer because the price is not right, as a shareholder you've got good grounds to challenge it.

Petty Holdups

Although the board can't tell you how much to sell for, it can hold you up if you owe the co-op any money. Many buildings have proprietary leases that don't allow transfer of shares if you have outstanding debts. If that's the case, the board can refuse the transfer if you owe even a pittance. A couple of would-be owners who bought a bunch of apartments from a sponsor tried defiance to their regret. Rather than pay the $3,000 in late fees, they sued for $3 million, claiming they couldn't market the apartments because the co-op refused to issue them new stock certificates. They got nowhere, except adding the cost of the lawsuit to the amount they already owed the co-op. Since the lease there had a pay-or-stay provision, the court said the board was within its rights.[27]

No Overreaching

In addition to price fixing, if the board acts in bad faith or imposes unreasonable transfer barriers, you've got a shot. One shareholder prevailed when the board tried to hold him and the sale up unless he paid attorneys' fees it claimed were due.[28] Another victory for the good guys took place at a posh Park Avenue prewar where the estate of a shareholder who had a lawsuit pending against the building (for damages from a leaking roof) sought to sell. The board figured it'd show her and pushed through an amendment that said you have to settle before you sell. But the court said nothing doing. The board can't absolve itself and then deny shareholders their day in court. Shareholders can sell and sue.[29]

Although such shareholder victories offer sweet revenge, they are few and far between. Don't count on them.

Avoiding the Board Altogether

You may stand a better chance avoiding the courts and enlisting the aid of fellow owners to make an end run round the board. Many co-op leases have provisions that offer alternative approval routes—*either* consent by a majority of the board *or* by a specified percentage of shareholders.

Taking the self-help route worked for one shareholder whose psychiatrist-purchaser had been nixed by the board because it thought he intended to use the apartment for seeing patients, not sleeping in. Although the board challenged shareholder approval, saying some joint owners had not signed the consent, it was overruled by the court and the shrink got to stay.[30]

So if you think the board's rejection is not a reflection of shareholder sentiment (and live in a smaller building where the whole process is manageable), go directly to the people. If you get enough of them to approve your purchaser the deal should go through—no matter what the board said.

SUCCESSION WITHOUT INSPECTION

Death, divorce, and force of law may offer other routes to free you from board bondage and allow you to transfer your rank and apartment to your chosen successor on your own.

The Hereafter

You may have to take leave of this earth, but eventually you will triumph over the board. Assuming you hold your apartment together with someone else (what the law calls *joint tenants*), ownership should be promptly transferred to your survivor. The board vetted you both back when you initially acquired, and it has no right to do so again. If there's a preexisting occupancy agreement between the owners and the co-op or condo, setting out who will live and own the apartment after their deaths, the current board has to abide by it, like it or not. Thus, even though a daughter had never lived in her parents' co-op, the court ordered the board to transfer the shares and lease, and let her move in, based on an agreement between the parents and the co-op that said she could own and occupy the unit upon their deaths.[31] A good thing they had thought about it in advance because as parents get older and potentially more troublesome, boards often are less likely voluntarily to allow such transfers. And with trusts becoming a more common form of ownership, occupancy agreements are sure to increase in kind and complexity.

In addition, most proprietary leases (and condo bylaws) have a spousal exception that allows the owner to transfer (whether by gift, bequest, or inheritance), and the surviving spouse to acquire, the apartment's shares and lease without board approval. In some buildings, transfer without board consent has been extended to adult children; and in others, especially those with a right of first refusal, parents, siblings, and grandparents are also exempt from board interference in such transfers. The theory is that your family home should be protected against eviction hardship following the death of the owning spouse. Also, if your partner has departed, he (or she) has probably left you with the cash so you can pay for the apartment.

Domestic (but unmarried) partners generally have the same rights to automatic succession in these circumstances. This state's highest court established succession rights for renters a decade ago when it blocked the eviction of the gay life partner of a tenant in a rent-controlled apartment who had died of AIDS.[32] Thanks to an intransigent board at a Sutton Place co-op, that right was extended to domestic partners in co-ops as well. The board there twice refused to approve transfer of a studio apartment whose deceased owner had bequeathed it to his longtime gay companion, though it allowed such transfers for married couples. He filed a complaint with the Human Rights Commission alleging discrimination based on sexual orientation and marital status. When the co-op denied him access to the apartment, he got an order preventing the board from interfering until the complaint was resolved. The Commission ruled that the co-op's lease had to be equally applied, and to make sure that it was, the board agreed to amend the building's lease to specify that domestic partners have the same right to transfer their apartments upon their deaths as do married spouses.[33] And since that right exists under the terms of the lease itself, at least one court has said that even if the shareholder died without leaving a will bequeathing the apartment, his domestic partner should be able to succeed to it.[34]

Since these developments, boards have been advised to amend their leases to reflect such legal and practical realities and to provide the same succession rights to gay life partners and married couples. Take a look at what your building's lease or bylaws has to say on the subject. If by chance its documents are back in the Ozzie and Harriet days, you should still prevail, but I'd want to know why the building's documents haven't been amended in order to avoid a battle from the beyond.

Things get trickier if the person to whom you want to transfer ownership of your apartment is not a member of your immediate domestic orbit. But it should give you some solace to know that the balance of power shifts in your favor when you're gone. Some co-ops have provisions in their leases that say if you die, the board can't *unreasonably* withhold consent to transfer your apartment to a "financially responsible relative." That was enough to turn the tide in favor of a deceased shareholder who had left his apartment to his brother, a doctor with a net worth in excess of $1 million. Although the board purported to come up with reasons for denying the transfer, the court said that under that objective standard none of them was sufficient.[35]

Absent such reasonableness requirement, the person to whom you bequeath your apartment may inherit and own the shares, but won't necessarily be able to live there. In one case, Mom made an inter vivos gift of her apartment to her two children by transferring her shares and proprietary lease. But the co-op had a typical provision requiring board approval for any transfer. Although the board couldn't prevent the owner from making a gift, it could prevent the brother and sister from taking occupancy. Result: Title passes to the kids and they get the rights to the financial interest in the apartment, but if they want to move in they'll need board approval.[36] So if you want to be sure the person to whom you leave your apartment actually gets to live there, you'd better pick someone you not only care about but who has the cash to carry your gift.

Finances aside, some co-ops don't even allow immediate family members to inherit in peace. In one Queens co-op, a son lost not only his father but the apartment he had inherited from him, as well. The board said too bad—it wanted to purchase the place and get possession. And since the co-op's bylaws said *all* shareholders had to first offer their shares to the co-op, it prevailed—even in the face of death.[37]

While, as we've seen, death may protect you from the board's bounds if you want to transfer to family members, it's back to the standard rules if your estate wants to sell the apartment to some third party. The board's otherworldly power was reaffirmed when an executor tried to sell her deceased husband's co-op. She claimed that the board was preventing her from carrying out her obligation to settle the estate by rejecting all her potential buyers—and asked for an order that she didn't need consent. Instead, the court told her that executors and estates are not exempt from the sale restrictions that apply to flesh-and-blood shareholders. In life and in death the board controls, since the lease said there could be no transfer without co-op consent.[38]

Although an estate has to get board consent to sell, any family members or other permitted occupants probably can remain in an apartment (without approval) after the shareholder has gone on to his or her home in the sky.

How long can they stick around? That's the $64,000 question. Usually the lease (and thus their stay) terminates when the estate sells the apartment, but most leases don't specify a time limit. If the estate isn't selling and they're staying, it's possible that their occupancy can turn into a de facto assignment. If you find yourself in this situation and want to strengthen your position (and your claim that the board consented), pay those monthly checks in your own (as opposed to the estate's) name. The longer all this goes on, the better your chances are.

Here and Now, but Nevermore

If it's divorce, not death, that separates you from your mate, ordinarily the apartment is transferred from one to the other as part of the separation agreement without need of board approval. But if the divorce is contested and thus husband and wife are no longer spouses but only exes (or the building doesn't have the standard spouse-to-spouse exemption), then things could get messy. In that case the board may have its say. If the spouse without the money gets to keep the apartment, the board may refuse to release the one with the money from liability for maintenance and assessments. In some co-ops, the board can demand financial proof (including income and net worth information) from the spouse who is staying. And if the board doesn't think the spouse is up to snuff, it can deny transfer of the apartment.

That's what the board of an Upper East Side co-op tried after the owner, as part of a divorce settlement, assigned the shares and lease to his wife. Even though the transaction didn't need approval, the board refused to transfer the apartment because it said she had submitted the wrong forms. Instead, once the couple was divorced, the board tried to evict her as a nuisance, claiming she was not a wife, but an ex no longer entitled to the exemption, leaving it to the judges to cut through the catch-22 and declare what mattered was that they were still married when the transfer was first made.[39]

Whether or not the board gets involved, the bank surely will (assuming there's a mortgage on the apartment). Although you may be happy to see your mate go, the bank may not let her (or him) off the hook. Releasing your worse half means it will have one less pile of assets to go against in case of default. In order to protect itself (and make some cash in the process), it likely will require you to refinance the loan or at least qualify on your own.

If either the board or the bank refuses the transfer, you may be stuck together—on the lease (and stock certificate), even if not in life. But the two of you can have your own private pact. The departing spouse relinquishes all right, title, and interest in the apartment (and you), usually in return for some monetary distribution. The remaining member of the team agrees to pay the monthly mortgage, maintenance, and assessment charges—and to indemnify the ex for any failure to make such payments. You remain united (on paper) until the transfer is finally completed when the apartment gets sold (no dispensation from board approval here) and the stock certificate and proprietary lease are turned over to the new (let us hope, more happily married) couple.

The Hand of Justice

If it's the law at work, the board can't prevent the transfer (though you may wish it could). In the category of don't let it happen to you, take the case of the East Side shareholder who owned an apartment worth $200,000 (back in the days when that was real apartment money). After refusing to pay $350 she owed for secretarial services, a default judgment was obtained against her in Small Claims Court. When she wouldn't pay it, the angry creditor turned the matter over to the sheriff who, in order to satisfy the judgment, eventually sold her apartment for a mere $15,000. The creditor got her $350, the buyer got a bargain apartment—and the original owner did more than cry over spilled milk; she tried in vain to void the sale.

When Ms. Original wouldn't turn over the shares and lease to the apartment, the buyer went to court to make the board transfer ownership to her. The sale was valid, three courts said. And besides, it's against the state's policy for a co-op board to use its rules to let an individual get away judgment free. The shares and the lease were transferred to the buyer. But, alas, our tale ends without knowing if our buyer's luck continued or ran out, because the court left it up to the board to decide if she was financially fit to actually reside in her bargain digs.[40]

Just remember, the law is a higher authority than the board. Whether it's execution on a judgment or inheritance (as we saw above) if the law says transfer, the board can't say no, but it can prevent the new owner from becoming an occupier.

PUTTING OUT BUYER BRUSHFIRES

Sometimes the battle is not with the board but with the buyer. In this arena you are, or should be, in control and can dictate whether and on what terms you want to sell—all of which should be spelled out in a contract. Leave the minutia to the legal technocrats. But you'd better stay tuned to the big picture and know what you're getting into—or disaster may ensue. I offer the following cautionary tale to sellers as a reminder to think before you contract because you will be bound by your word.

Back before the dawning of the co-op age, actress Diahann Carroll was in search of an apartment. An attorney (savior or snake, you decide) who lived in a Riverside rental had acquired a lease to a second unit in the building and was amenable. Since the actress wanted to lease directly from the landlord and the attorney wanted the right to use the place after she left, they struck a bargain. If the building went co-op, Carroll would buy the apartment, and if (and when) she decided to sell she would offer it to the attorney—at the price she had originally paid.

Over time this marriage made in heaven turned into a pact with the devil. When the building converted in 1968, Carroll bought the apartment for $32,000. By the time she was ready to unload it in 1993 its value had soared to $1.5 million and the attorney—who had defied Father Time and the gods—was there to collect. Too late, Carroll realized the error of her ways and tried every way out. But there was no exit, only enforcement. Aside from letting her deduct the costs of improvements and assessments over the years, the court told her she had to sell for the price formula they had agreed on.[41]

Hopefully, having been forewarned, you will not let such (greater or lesser) riches slip from your fingers.

Collecting on Broken Promises

Even assuming you're dealing with a more standard contract for selling your apartment in the here and now, not the hereafter, one of the parties may have a change of heart. If your buyer cancels for some reason contemplated by the contract, those are the breaks. As we've seen, if there's a standard mortgage contingency clause and he can't get a loan despite trying, he's off the hook and you have to hunt down another buyer. (Remember, this provision is only for the benefit of the buyer; as the seller, you can't use it to cancel.)

But what if after the contract has been signed, sealed and delivered (and received board approval) the buyer backs out for some unjustifiable reason—he decides his heart is where his (current) home is, he found a better deal—do you have any recourse? As we've seen, most condo and co-op sales contracts have a provision that says the seller gets to keep the 10 percent deposit as liquidated damages. Just because that's what the contract says doesn't necessarily mean that's what you'll get. When it comes to real property (of which condos are a subspecies) the law says a seller can keep a 10 percent down payment if the buyer defaults.[42] But the courts have said that for purposes of deciding whether to enforce these provisions, co-op shares are personal property.[43] So they're governed by the law for selling goods (called the Uniform Commercial Code), and under the Code[44] you may not automatically get to pocket your buyer's deposit but have to show that the amount is reasonable in relation either to the harm that the parties anticipated when they entered the contract or the damages you actually incurred when the buyer walked.

What exactly this means is for the judges to rule and you to find out. One jilted seller got to pocket the $29,000 deposit when his buyer defaulted but he sold for $33,000 less the second time around, leaving him several thousand dollars poorer.[45] Another got to keep the $63,000 down payment after his initial purchaser backed out of their $630,000 deal and he then sold for $5,000 less seven months later.[46]

More recently, as the numbers have gotten more eye-popping, the answers have become more complicated. When a Sutton Place seller sought to keep his buyer's $105,000 deposit (10 percent of the $1,050,000 purchase price) the court said, not so fast. It made the seller come back and prove his losses (lawyers' fees, moving expenses, rent, and the like) were enough to justify keeping the stash.[47]

The decision got the attention of co-op buyers and sellers alike, who wanted to know what would happen to those megasized deposits if the deal collapsed, and to find out, engaged in legal sparring. After the purchaser of a $1,150,000 co-op terminated the contract and demanded return of her $115,000 deposit, the seller refused—only to resell for more. Although he didn't have any *actual* loss, the court let him keep the money because the amount was a reasonable estimate of the harm they anticipated when they entered the contract and, anyway, even if the Code applies to co-ops, they're like real property.[48] Another court also allowed the seller to keep the deposit, saying only that the amount wasn't so unreasonable as to be a penalty.[49] Then came a breakthrough. The buyers of a co-op on the East Side backed out of a $1,050,000 contract without any valid excuse and wanted their $105,000 deposit back. This time when the court let the seller keep the cash, it didn't make her *prove* the amount was reasonable but just *presumed* it was, effectively saying the same rule applies to co-ops and condos.[50]

So if your co-op buyer leaves you without consummating the deal, can you automatically retain the 10 percent deposit? You're not entirely out of the judicial woods, and no higher court has yet officially ruled that the distinction between co-ops and condos is dead. But the trend is toward applying the traditional real estate rule to either, letting the stood-up seller automatically hold on to the money.

Still, having provided emotional succor to friends who went through three signed contracts before they actually closed a sale, I assure you it's better to get what you asked for the first time round and get out with a smile than having to hassle over who gets the deposit.

On the other hand, if *you're* the one that wants out, your would-be buyer may seek blood, not money—or at least your residential body and soul. The law says if you breach a contract to sell real estate, the buyer may be able to make you go through with the sale anyway (what the law calls *specific performance*). The idea is that the unit is unique so only possession (not cash) will make the purchaser whole. And though, as we've just seen, for some purposes co-op shares are personal, courts have said that for these purposes they're real (property, that is). So if you refuse to go through with your sale without reason, theoretically the buyer could get an order requiring you to close on the deal. But in real life it's hard to do. One buyer who tried was told the seller didn't have to convey the apartment because she had never lived up to *her* side of the bargain, having failed to supply all the documents requested by the board.[51] Another, who was unwilling to close on the terms provided in the contract, got the same answer.[52]

Chances are by the time the dispute gets to court, you will have sold to someone else, and the buyer will have to settle for money—a result you also want to be careful to avoid. Take the case of the elderly seller who, without bothering to find out the value of his apartment (in which he never lived), contracted to sell it to a buyer for $225,000. Mr. Buyer, wiser in the ways of real estate, then turned around and assigned his rights to someone else—for $390,000. The seller, claiming he'd been duped, refused to go through with the deal, so the buyers got together and sued to make him close the sale. Trying to outmaneuver the buyer, who had outsmarted him, the seller agreed to sell to Mr. Assignee for $225,000, only to have the buyer demand—and get—the $165,000 difference ($390,000 – $225,000) in cash: a reminder that if you breach as a seller, you'll pay the consequences.[53]

Assuming you and your buyer want to proceed, you're ready for separation. Although I hope now that you have learned all you need to know to assume your own co-op or condo command, you are not wasting your talents and deserting the shareholder ranks for the life of a go-it-alone home owner. To be sure there are no surprises and you know what it will cost, take the quiz at chapter's end. If you pass, you'll be discharged with distinction.

WILL YOU GET AN HONORABLE DISCHARGE?

Who Decides Your Separation Status?

Is it the Old Guard?	They can prevent your departure (and sale) by rejecting your buyer for no (or any) reason.
Is it the Moderates?	They can prevent your departure (and sale) but only by giving an objectively reasonable explanation for rejection.

Is it the Libertarians?	Your separation (and asking price) are assured. The only issue is whether your replacement is your chosen buyer (or theirs).
Is it the condo Freedom Fighters?	Same result as for the Libertarians.

Is There Any Reprieve from Rejection?

- Do the bylaws allow you to go directly to the shareholders for approval of your sale?
- Was the rejection based on a floor price set by the board?
- Was it based on a ceiling price?
- Was it because the board president wanted the apartment for his own love nest?
- Was it because the directors wanted to resell the apartment for a personal profit?
- Was it because you refused to settle litigation against the building?
- Was it a case of illegal discrimination?
- Did the board act in bad faith?

If the answer to any of the above is "Yes," you may have recourse. If not, lick your wounds then go back to market.

HOW MUCH WILL SEPARATION SET YOU BACK?

(Assuming you're selling a $600,000 co-op)

	Estimated Range	Assumed Cost
• Flip tax:	(typically 1–3% of sales price, if applicable)	$12,000 (2% of $600,000)
• Managing agent closing fee:	$450–$800	$500
• Stock transfer stamps:	($.05 per share)	________
• N.Y.C. transfer tax:	(1% of sales price if $500,000 or less; 1.425% of sales price if more than $500,000)	$8,550

	Estimated Range	Assumed Cost
• N.Y.S. transfer tax:	(.4% of sales price)	$2,400
• UCC-3 filing fee:	$50	$50
• Move-out fee: (may be a *refundable deposit* of up to $1,000)	$250–$500	$300
• Your attorney:	$1,500 and up	$1,750
• Broker's commission:	(6% of sales price)	$36,000
• Payoff fee to bank (if applicable)	$300–$400	$350
TOTAL		$61,900

(Assuming sale of $600,000 condo)

	Estimated Range	Assumed Cost
• Managing agent closing fee:	$450–$800	$500
• N.Y.C. transfer tax:	(1% of sales price if $500,000 or less; 1.425% of sales price if more than $500,000)	$8,550
• N.Y.S. transfer tax:	(.4% of sales price)	$2,400
• Move-out fee: (may be a *refundable deposit* of up to $1,000)	$250–$500	$300
• Your attorney	$1,500 and up	$1,750
• Broker's commission	(6% of sales price)	$36,000
• Payoff fee to bank (if applicable)	$300– $400	$350
TOTAL		$49,850

19

Conclusion: Reform or Revolution?

I hope I have converted you to the cause and gotten you to think about your co-op or condo not just as a place to call home but also as a business enterprise of which you are a member. It's easy to blame the board for everything that goes wrong—but it wouldn't be fair. Like you, your co-op and condo commanders are both victims and enablers of a system that needs fixing.

Think about it: Where else do you have multimillion-dollar businesses run by unpaid volunteers? Every company I know, at least in theory, has a paid chief executive officer hired for her particular expertise (assisted by an in-house management team), a professional board to whom she reports, and shareholders (with financial interests) looking over their shoulders to be sure they're doing the right thing. They even have outside directors to lend an objective voice and help oversee the selection and performance of management. There are also established standards, such as maximization of shareholder value, at least in the profit-making corporate context, to measure how well officers and directors stack up against their peers.

And even with all those built-in checks and balances, there have been scandals galore over the past few years, from Enron on down, triggering stricter requirements for companies to improve their reporting and governance practices, including the need—now more than ever—for directors to be fully informed and on the case.

Few of these controls exist in co-ops and condos, which are also substantial ventures with significant cash flows and expenditures. It's a sui generis system that puts the burden of management on the shoulders of unschooled residents and gives them legal authority to carry out that role, but it doesn't require them to know what they're doing or give them the depth of management that does. Even though board members aren't required to have any business expertise, as we've seen (chapter 9), they get the benefit of the Rule, just like those professional directors of public companies, which insulates virtually all their decisions from challenge. But a little bit of knowledge and a lot of power can be a potentially dangerous thing, especially in a system where much of that power is parceled out to third parties.

As you probably know, but never really focused on, the day-to-day task of running co-ops and condos is assigned by the board to a management company, whose name you can find on the brass plaque affixed to the facade.

By definition, outsourcing has its problems, as you're doubtless aware if you've ever tried to get a question answered by your credit card company and found yourself on the phone with someone halfway around the world who didn't know what you were talking about. Only co-ops and condos don't just parcel out the complaint department, but almost *all* management functions.

That's the problem. Because there are so many tasks to perform, and so few set boundaries, it's often hard to tell where the board's role ends and the managing agent's begins, leaving the building caught in the middle. You may not realize it. The floors get mopped, the staff paid, the garbage collected. It's the bigger stuff where things break down. If there's a major project afoot—an elevator modernization, a roof replacement, a lobby renovation—who's responsible for what? Bet you don't know. Plenty of times it's not clear to *me*.

Boards figure they can count on the managing agent's superior industry knowledge to ferret out the right pros and filter the proposals through their personal information bank. Except, in reality, agents sometimes function more as conduits than as processors of information, so that *neither* party has negotiated the best deal for the building they *both* serve. This scenario is repeated many times over: whether the issue is handling sublets or apartment sales or building investments or real estate taxes, the way the system is set up, too many things can fall through the cracks.

Apart from this structural deficit, agents and boards necessarily see the same building differently. A good board should aim to run its building with corporate efficiency: maximizing revenues, controlling expenses, negotiating to best advantage, resolving shareholder problems with dispatch. But under the present system, carrying out that mandate takes more time and skill than most outside agents have: They have to tend to the nitty-gritty details for multiple buildings, making it virtually impossible for them to do what's best for any one building (which is precisely what your board should be doing), instead doing what's good enough for all.

The same kinds of problems exist with other outside co-op and condo pros. Although many buildings, especially larger ones, have general counsel, as we've seen (chapter 13), unlike their corporate brethren, they aren't usually viewed as part of the management team but used on an ad hoc basis, preventing either party from making the most of the relationship. Unless they're legally savvy, boards don't always know when to call in counsel, and even if they do, given the knowledge vacuum that sometimes exists, they may utilize them more as decision makers than legal advisors.

Maybe your building is lucky enough to have a financial whiz kid acting as treasurer to interface between management and the building's outside auditors. But most co-ops and condos have only nominal treasurers and have to rely on independent accountants to audit the building's financial operations who, in turn, depend on whatever controls may (or may not) exist in their outsourced managing agents.

As you may have figured out by now, "the buck stops here," a notion central to successful corporate governance, is not one that is built into the co-op and condo model. There is no guarantee that anyone is really in charge as each party—managing agent, lawyer, architect, contractor, accountant—operates more or less independently of one another and often of any meaningful central authority. Boards want to do what's best, but aren't always trained to know what's right, and members may not have the time to spare from their day jobs to figure it out. The result is that the outside agents, not the board, may wind up in de facto control of the building, a role reversal that can have potentially troublesome consequences. And as the demands of shareholders and challenges of running buildings mount, the strains in this makeshift system are becoming more apparent.

What then can be done? You've already taken the first step by having your consciousness raised in these pages so that at least now you're tuned in to the problem. How to correct it is more difficult.

Knowledge is power—that was my parting advice to you in the first edition of *The Co-op Bible*, and it remains rock solid. Now, more than ever, you need to be an informed citizen of your co-op or condo. That means asking questions, attending annual meetings, going on record when necessary to help cure a building problem, reading (not tossing away) financial statements. Those documents alerted someone I know to $100,000 in unexplained legal fees, which proved the tip of the iceberg, and prompted him to get on the board. Being an active investor (as opposed to a passive head-in-the-sand shareholder) is the only way to have a sense if the board is doing its job.

Just as with any company, there needs to be a fully engaged chief executive who knows what she's doing and bears ultimate responsibility for running the corporation (or condo) and overseeing all outside agents. Taking into account the realities of co-op and condo governance, it doesn't have to be a single person, but can be a composite of two or three directors who together have the necessary set of skills. If your building is run with corporate efficiency—or anything like it—give those directors a round of applause and reelect them for another term. But from all that I've seen and heard, I suspect that such a state of nirvana is more the exception than the norm.

One way to upgrade the system is to make the board president a paid position, requiring competence in exchange for a check. (Yes, you could say it's a self-interested solution, but I've been serving gratis for more than a decade.) Anyway, realistically it's not likely to happen anytime soon because co-op and condo bylaws prohibit directors and officers from getting compensation.

Another option is to establish a new role—let's call it a Coordinator: an objective and skilled professional, knowledgeable in co-op and condo governance but unaffiliated with either the inside building directors or the managing agent—to serve as a kind of functional CEO or COO. The Coordinator, accountable to the board, would be able to implement its goals by delegating appropriate responsibilities to agents and other third parties, and overseeing their performance.

By tailoring governance to suit the characteristics of the particular co-op or condo, the Coordinator could help the building take a giant leap forward in rationalizing its business practices: establishing a workable organizational setup specific to the building's needs and the board's abilities; delineating lines of authority and responsibility, both among board members and between the board and managing agent (and other professionals); and then identifying and addressing any tasks that otherwise might be left to happenstance. This synergistic whole would function more efficiently than its constituent parts because each entity—board, agent, and Coordinator—would be acting within its capacity and performing those jobs for which each is best suited. And by bringing internal accountability to buildings, the proposed model also would begin to alter the landscape of how business is done by outsiders with the co-op and condo community as a whole.

As an added benefit, the Coordinator could serve as an in-house instructor, offering on-the-job training to board members in need, helping them understand the scope of their power as well as the restraints imposed by their duties—a grounding that will allow them not only to run the business of their co-op or condominium more efficiently, but also to govern with more impartial consistency toward owners. Moreover, the presence of such a credible and objective outside professional would serve as a buffer between board and shareholders (who often view empowered directors with instinctive suspicion), diffusing conflicts before they become costly legal wars.

Given that buildings are minirepublics with individual personalities, in addition to business ventures, no one-size solution is right for all. But there is near universal need to professionalize and regularize how co-ops and condos are run so that they may begin to approach the standards demanded for the rest of corporate America. Whether you choose to remain a member of the rank and file or opt to join the ruling class, I urge you to use the knowledge you have gained here to advocate for reform.

Hot Links

Half the problem in resolving problems is figuring out where to go for help. The following list tells you. Tear it out and tack it to the refrigerator. That way when you get angry you can act instead of eat, thereby getting double rewards for your trouble. (It's easier than ever to navigate the system now that you can reach most city agencies 24/7 with a single call to 311.)

Problem	Solution
Got a problem with noise or smells from some commercial establishment: the ever-present aroma of that greasy spoon, the all-night pounding of its ventilation system?	Department of Environmental Protection: Dial 311 or, for more info, log onto www.nyc.gov/html/dep/html/helpcenter.html
If it's your next-door neighbor who's making the racket, then it's an issue of residential quality of life.	Police Department, Community Affairs: Dial 311 or, for more details, log onto www.nyc.gov/html/nypd/home.html
Want to put an end to your neighbor's over-zealous barbecuing?	
Are they using an illegal propane tank or violating the Fire Code?	New York City Fire Department, Fire Prevention Bureau: www.nyc.gov/html/fdny/html/units/Fire_Prevention
Or maybe they're not disposing of those ashes as they should in metal containers?	Sanitation Department Complaints: Dial 311 or log onto www.nyc.gov/html/dos/home.html
Getting asphyxiated from that chain smoker who lives beneath you?	Some things have no good answer; it's not illegal to smoke in the privacy of your own place.
Got a garden-variety complaint against the board: insufficient heat or hot water, leaky ceilings, lack of window guards, unwanted mouseketeers?	Department of Housing Preservation and Development, Central Complaints: Dial 311 or log onto www.nyc.gov/html/hpd/home.html

Got a question about your building's real estate taxes: how they're calculated, why they're so much, and if there's a way to get them reduced?	Department of Finance: www.ci.nyc.ny.us/html/dof/home/html/
Want to give peace a chance and try to mediate away those disputes with your fellow owners for little cost?	New York Law School, Co-ops and Condos Mediation Project: (212) 431–2318 or try http://www.nyls.edu/pages/705.asp
Have things gone beyond mediation to litigation: Is your co-op board suing you for nonpayment or do you want to sue for correction of some violation?	Housing Court: (212) 791-6070 (Now there's a special part for co-ops and condos.)
Planning to make more than cosmetic changes to your co-op or condo and think Buildings Department permission may be required? It's easy to find out on their Web site and print out the forms you need. For your sanity—get a registered architect and let him deal with it.	New York City Department of Buildings: www.ci.nyc.ny.us/html/dob/home.html
Do your renovations involve remaking history? Better check with the Preservationists. Their Web site will answer many of your questions, and if it turns out you need a permit or other forms, you can download applications.	New York City Landmarks Preservation Commission: (212) 669-7700; or log onto www.ci.nyc.ny.us/html/lpc/html/permit
Want to seek reimbursement from the board for repairs ($3,000 or less) you had to make because it did nothing?	Small Claims Court: (212) 791-6000
Think you're a victim of illegal discrimination in buying or subleasing?	
Try the City	New York City Commission on Human Rights: Call for info, (212) 306-7500, or better yet, click on the Web site, which takes you through the process from filing the complaint to final order; www.nyc.gov/html/cchr/home/html
Or the State	New York State Division of Human Rights: Same drill, different numbers. (212) 480-2522; or log onto www.nysdhr.com

Or get your own lawyer.

The choice is yours.

Need info on co-op and condo rules and regulations? Have a problem with the building's sponsor who won't go when he should? Here's the place to get help, even download complaint forms.

New York State Attorney General's Office: www.oag.state.ny.us

Want to learn more about how your co-op should function and what issues are on the horizon? Classes are offered (at a fee) for you and your board.

Council of New York Cooperatives and Condominiums: (212) 496-7400; or log onto www.cnyc.org

Looking for legal news and events related to co-ops and condos? You can even submit questions about the operation of your building.

Federation of New York Housing Cooperatives & Condominiums: (718) 760-7540; or log onto www.fnyhc.org

Want to find out if your building is a paid-up member of the Realty Advisory Board (which provides it with counsel in staff arbitrations)?

Realty Advisory Board for Labor Relations: (212) 889-4100; or log onto www.rabolr.com

Want to know what policies the real estate pros seek to promote and how they can affect you? Much of the info is for "members only," but there's enough for you to get an idea of their agenda.

Real Estate Board of New York: www.rebny.com

Endnotes: Legal Ammunition

Before you take aim, you need to know how to find the right ammunition. For you non-lawyers, set forth below is a key to the citations that follow:

COURTS AND COMMISSIONS

Civ. Ct. N.Y. Co. Civil Court (of the State of New York), New York County (each borough is a different county, e.g., Civ. Ct. Kings Co. for Brooklyn, as are areas in other parts of the state)

Crim. Ct. N.Y. Co. Criminal Court (of the State of New York), New York County (each borough is a different county, as are areas in other parts of the state)

Sup. Ct. N.Y. Co. Supreme Court (of the State of New York), New York County (each borough is a different county, as are areas in other parts of the state)

App. Tm. Appellate Term of New York State Supreme Court

1st Dept., 2d Dept., etc. New York State Supreme Court, Appellate Division, 1st Department, which includes Manhattan and Bronx; 2d Dept., includes Brooklyn, Queens and Richmond; 3d and 4th Depts., include other areas throughout the state

NYCCHR New York City Commission on Human Rights

S.D.N.Y. Southern District of New York (Federal District Court)

E.D.N.Y. Eastern District of New York (Federal District Court)

2d Cir. Second Circuit (Federal Court of Appeals: reviews decisions from federal district courts in New York and several other states)

CASE REPORTERS

Misc.2d/3d Miscellaneous Reports, Second/Third Series: official reports of decisions from New York State's lower courts, including civil, criminal, and supreme

N.Y.S.2d New York State Reports, Second Series: unofficial reports of decisions from New York State's lower courts

A.D.2d/3d Appellate Division Reports, Second/Third Series: official reports of decisions from the Appellate Division of New York State Supreme Court

N.Y.2d New York Reports, Second Series: official reports of decisions from the New York State Court of Appeals

NYLJ New York Law Journal: daily journal that publishes many newly issued decisions of New York State courts

Slip Op Slip Opinion: Newly issued decisions not yet recorded in bound reporters, can be found online (LEXIS/NEXIS) using date that precedes and reference number that follows.

Index No. 12345/99 Unreported New York State court decisions are identified by their assigned court index number/date of commencement of lawsuit, and may be found on file at the relevant court.

QDS:12345 Quick Decision Service: Some unreported decisions of New York State courts may be obtained (for a fee) via this service by reference to their designated number.

F.Supp./F.Supp.2d Federal Supplement/Federal Supplement, Second Series: reports decisions of federal district courts

F.2d or 3d Federal Reporter, Second or Third Series: reports decisions of federal courts of appeals

B.R. Bankruptcy Reporter: reports decisions of federal bankruptcy courts

So.2d Southern Reporter, Second Series: regional reporter of decisions from southern states, including Florida

Note: The numbers preceding each reporter refer to the volume; those following denote the page on which the case begins.

DISPOSITION

AFF'D Case affirmed on appeal

REV'D Case reversed on appeal

STATUTES AND CODES

N.Y. Bus. Corp. Law New York State Business Corporation Law

N.Y. Gen. Bus. Law New York State General Business Law

N.Y. Real Prop. Law New York State Real Property Law

N.Y. U.C.C. New York State Uniform Commercial Code

N.Y.C.R.R. New York Code of Rules and Regulations

U.S.C. United States Code

C.F.R. Code of Federal Regulations

F.C.C.R. Federal Communications Commission Records

Note: New York State statutes are codified in volumes cited as "McKinney"; the date indicating the year of publication of the last bound volume; McKinney Supp. refers to annually updated supplements to such volumes. (The statutes also may be found online using services such as LEXIS/NEXIS.)

Chapter 1—Which Regime Is Right for You?

1. N.Y. Real Prop. Law, Article 9-B, §§ 339-d to 339-kk (McKinney 1989).
2. N.Y. Real Prop. Law §§ 339-u,v (McKinney 1989).
3. See, N.Y. Bus. Corp. Law §§ 701, 706 (McKinney 2003).
4. N.Y. Real Prop. Law § 339-v(1)(j) (McKinney 1989).

5. N.Y. Real Prop. Law § 339-j (McKinney 1989).
6. N.Y. Real Prop. Law § 339-r (McKinney 1989).
7. See chapter 16, pp.317 to 318.
8. Ira Pekelnaya, as Guardian Ad Litem for Michael Taratuta v. Jerri Allyn, Index No. 116732/01, January 8, 2004, Sup. Ct. N.Y. Co. (consolidated with Index No. 115288/01).
9. N.Y. Real Prop. Law § 339-g (McKinney 1989).
10. N.Y.C. Administrative Code § 27-2009.1; See chapter 14, pp.260 to 266.
11. N.Y. Real Prop. Law § 235-f (McKinney 1989); See chapter 15, pp.302 to 305.
12. N.Y. Real Prop. Law § 235-b (McKinney supp. 2005); See chapter 8, pp.154 to 157.
13. See, N.Y. Real Prop. Law § 339-e(10) (McKinney 1989).
14. Internal Revenue Code, 26 U.S.C. § 216(b)(2).
15. Condominium and Cooperative Protection and Abuse Relief Act of 1980, 15 U.S.C. §§ 3601 et seq.
16. See, e.g., Darnet Realty Associates LLC v. 136 East 56th Street Owners, Inc., 214 F.3d 79 (2d Cir. 2000); Penny Lane Owners Corp. v. Conthur Development Co., NYLJ, Feb. 25, 2000, p.36, col.5 (S.D.N.Y.).
17. Uzan v. 845 UN Limited Partnership, NYLJ, June 21, 2004, p.18, col.1 (1st Dept.).
18. See, e.g., Bd. of Managers of the Alfred Condominium v. Carol Management, 214 A.D.2d 380 (1st Dept. 1995).
19. See, e.g., Regatta Condominium Ass'n. v. Village of Mamaroneck, 303 A.D.2d 739 (2d Dept. 2003); Bd. of Managers of the Alexandria Condominium v. Broadway/72nd Associates, 285 A.D.2d 422 (1st Dept. 2001); The Residential Bd. of Managers of the 99 Jane Street Condominium v. Rockrose Development Corp., NYLJ, Oct. 17, 2001, p.13 (Sup. Ct. N.Y. Co.).
20. Northeast Restoration Corp. v. K & J Construction Co., NYLJ, May 19, 2004, p.18, col.1 (Sup. Ct. N.Y. Co.).

Chapter 2—Preparing for the Hunt

1. See, e.g., Cooperative/Condominium Directory for New York City, Yale Robbins, Inc., available (for a fee) online at www.yrinc.com
2. See, Weisz v. 233 East 69th Street Owners Corp., NYLJ, April 19, 1995, p.25, col.2 (Sup. Ct. N.Y. Co.).
3. Purches v. Carroll, NYLJ, Dec. 3, 2003, p.22 (Sup. Ct. N.Y. Co.).
4. Alper v. Seavy, 780 N.Y.S.2d 564 (1st Dept. 2004).
5. See, e.g., Finkelstein v. Tainiter, NYLJ, Sept. 20, 1999, p.26, col.4 (1st Dept.); Ittleson v. Lombardi, 193 A.D.2d 374 (1st Dept. 1993).
6. Robb v. 423 Broome Street Corp., Index No. 123034/97, June 19, 1998, Sup. Ct. N.Y. Co.

Chapter 3—Arming Yourself with the Financial Facts

1. N.Y. Bus. Corp. Law § 624 (McKinney 2003); N.Y. Real Prop. Law § 339-w (McKinney 1989).
2. N.Y.C. Local Law No.70, § 26–703.
3. 89th Street Tenants Ass'n. v. Dwelling Managers, Inc., Index No. 28332/90, Feb. 19, 1992, Sup. Ct. N.Y. Co., aff'd, 191 A.D.2d 403 (1st Dept. 1993).

4. American Institute of Certified Public Accountants (AICPA), Audits of Common Interest Realty Associations, 1991; For discussion see, www.nysscpa.org/cpajournal/old/12106213.htm.
5. McHam v. Wintney 540 N.Y.S.2d 416 (Sup. Ct. N.Y. Co. 1989).
6. Citipark II Associates, Ltd. v. Lincoln Plaza Tenants Corp., Index No. 605769/99, December 2003, Sup. Ct. N.Y. Co.
7. Ittleson v. Lombardi, 193 A.D.2d 374 (1st Dept. 1993); See also, Savasta v. Duffy, 257 A.D.2d 435 (1st Dept. 1999) (seller's failure to disclose $4,400 in assessments not material relative to contract price in excess of $1 million).
8. Finkelstein v. Tainiter, NYLJ, Sept. 20, 1999, p.26, col.4 (1st Dept.).
9. N.Y. Real Prop. Law § 339-jj (McKinney 1989).
10. N.Y. Real Prop. Law § 339-r (McKinney 1989).
11. See, Attorney General's Regulations, 13 N.Y.C.R.R. § 18.5(c)(3).
12. 511 West 232nd Owners Corp. v. Jennifer Realty Co., 98 N.Y.2d 144 (2002).
13. West Gate House v. 860-870 Realty, 2004 NY Slip Op 04086, May 20, 2004, 1st Dept.
14. See, www.oag.state.ny.us/real estate/documents/proposed.
15. See, N.Y. Gen. Bus. Law §§ 352-eeee[1](d) and [1](e) (McKinney 1996).
16. Paikoff v. Harris, 178 Misc.2d 366 (Civ. Ct. Kings Co. 1998), modified, 185 Misc.2d 372 (App. Tm. 2d Dept. 1999); See also, Geiser v. Maran, 189 Misc.2d 442 (App. Tm. 2d Dept. 2001) (upholding protection of postconversion renters, but finding that protection doesn't apply to a tenant in a building that was converted *after* the effective date of Martin Act); 100 Apt. Associates, Inc. v. Estavillo, NYLJ, Jan 15, 2004, p.19 (Village Ct. Briarcliff Manor) (questioning whether tenant rented from co-op sponsor so as to be protected by the law).
17. See, Park West Village Associates v. Nishoika, 187 Misc.2d 243 (App. Tm. 1st Dept. 2000); Pembroke Square Associates v. Coppola, NYLJ, May 5, 1999, p.32, col.6 (Civ. Ct. Queens Co.); Parkchester Preservation Co. L.P. v. Hanks, NYLJ, Aug. 23, 2000, p.23, col.5 (Civ. Ct. Bronx Co.) (condo).

Chapter 4—Penetrating the Front Lines

1. N.Y. Real Prop. Law § 339-v(2)(a) (McKinney 1989).
2. Anderson v. 50 East 72nd Street Condominium, 119 A.D.2d 73 (1st Dept. 1986).
3. David v. Trujillo, Index No. 120556/97, June 18, 1998, Sup. Ct. N.Y. Co. (self-employed artist breached contract by refusing to furnish asset and income verification information).
4. Extract v. Residential Board of Beaumont Condominium, 261 A.D.2d 130 (1st Dept. 1999).
5. Ng v. Baybridge at Bayside Condominium III, 161 A.D.2d 688 (2d Dept. 1990).
6. Board of Managers, Kingsley Condominium v. Villinvestment, NYLJ, Aug. 27, 2003, p.18, col.6 (Sup. Ct. N.Y. Co.).
7. Cohen v. Olmstead Condominium, Index No. 602764/98 (1st Dept. 1998).
8. Internal Revenue Code, 26 U.S.C. § 216(b)(2).
9. Moustakas v. Noble, 259 A.D.2d 602 (2d Dept. 1999).
10. Pierre Properties v. Marcus, NYLJ, May 3, 2000, p.27, col.4 (Sup. St. N.Y. Co.).
11. Alpert & Kimmel v. Herman, QDS: 22235889, Sept. 1999, Sup. Ct. N.Y. Co.; See

also, Moss v. Brower, 213 A.D.2d 215 (1st Dept. 1995); Meyer v. Nelson, 83 A.D.2d 422 (1st Dept. 1981).

12. Shulkin v. Dealy, NYLJ, July 18, 1990, p.18, col.2 (Sup. Ct. N.Y. Co.).
13. Gutowski v. Louie, NYLJ, Nov. 20, 2002, p.23, col. 3 (Sup. Ct. N.Y. Co.).
14. Glazer v. Jack Seid–Sylvia Seid Revocable Trust, NYLJ, March 7, 2001, p.17 (Dist. Ct. Nassau Co.).
15. See, e.g., Wheeler v. Grieg, 224 A.D.2d 209 (1st Dept. 1996).
16. Capati v. Dolorico, 2004 NY Slip Op 50898U, Aug. 4, 2004 (App. Tm. 1st Dept.).

Chapter 5—Preparing for the Final Assault

1. See, e.g., 142 East 49th Street Owners Corp. v. BRT Realty Trust, NYLJ, July 2, 1997, p. 26, col.2 (Sup. Ct. N.Y. Co.).
2. Woo v. 215 Tenants Corp., NYLJ, May 8, 1996, p.29, col.2 (Sup. Ct. N.Y. Co.); See also, Bankers Trust Co. of California v. West Shore Apt. Corp., 281 A.D.2d 351 (1st Dept. 2001).
3. Melsten v. Board of Managers 178–84 East Second Street Condominium, NYLJ, May 2, 1994, p.28, col.2 (Sup. Ct. N.Y. Co.).

Chapter 6—Dealing with Rejection

1. Weisner v. 791 Park Avenue Corp., 6 N.Y.2d 426 (1959).
2. In re Folic, 139 A.D.2d 456 (1st Dept. 1988).
3. Hitter v. Rubin, 208 A.D.2d 480 (1st Dept. 1994).
4. Murphy v. 253 Garth Tenants Corp., 579 F. Supp. 1150 (S.D.N.Y. 1983).
5. Moustakas v. Noble, 259 A.D.2d 602 (2d Dept. 1999).
6. Samuel Maull, "Carly Simon Sues to Force Return of $99,000 Apartment Down Payment," Associated Press wire report, Sept. 26, 2003.
7. See, e.g., Weiner v. 150 West End Owners Corp., 298 A.D.2d 385 (2d Dept. 2002).
8. Park Tower Holding Corp. v. Bd. of Managers of 500 Park, NYLJ, Aug. 5, 1999, p.26, col.5 (Sup. Ct. N.Y. Co.).
9. Murphy, note 4 at p.1156.
10. Miller v. Swingle, 143 A.D.2d 984 (2d Dept. 1988).
11. See Murphy, note 4.
12. Smolinsky v. 46 Rampasture Owners, Inc., 230 A.D.2d 620 (1st Dept. 1996).
13. Boisson v. 4 East Housing Corp., 129 A.D.2d 523 (1st Dept. 1989).
14. Barbour v. Knecht, 296 A.D.2d 218 (1st Dept. 2002); See also, Bernheim v. 136 East 64th Street Corp., 128 A.D.2d 434 (1st Dept. 1987) (board members can't reject purchaser to buy apartment and resell for a personal profit).
15. Louise Laskin Trust v. 775 Park Avenue, Inc., 299 A.D.2d 264 (1st Dept. 2002).
16. N.Y.C. Admin. Code Title 8; See, § 8–107(5).
17. N.Y. Executive Law § 296(5) (McKinney 2001).
18. N.Y. Civil Rights Law § 19-a (McKinney 2001); See also, N.Y. Real Property Law § 236 (McKinney 2001) (prohibiting discrimination against children).
19. 42 U.S.C. § 2000 et seq. (1994).
20. 42 U.S.C. § 3601 et seq. (1994).
21. 610 F.2d 1032 (2d Cir 1979).

22. Steele v. 400 East 77th Street Corp., NYLJ, Jan. 30, 2002, p.18, col.1 (Sup. Ct. N.Y. Co.); See also, Rives v. 164 23rd St. Jackson Heights, Inc., Complaint No. H-92-0115, Recommended Dec. & Order, July 31, 1995, adopted as modified, Dec. & Order, NYCCHR Sept. 28, 1995 (upholding discrimination claim by a single man of Latin American descent against board rejection without an interview, allegedly based on financial unsuitability); But see, Tufano v. One Toms Point Lane Corp., 64 F. Supp.2d 119 (E.D.N.Y. 1999), aff'd, 229 F.3d 1136 (2d Cir. 2000) (dismissing purchaser's claim of discrimination and civil rights violation in connection with rejection of his application where no credible showing was made that he was a member of a protected minority class).
23. Broome v. Biondi, 17 F. Supp.2d 211 (S.D.N.Y. 1997).
24. Axelrod v. 400 Owners Corp., 189 Misc.2d 461 (Sup. Ct. N.Y. Co. 2001).
25. Bachman v. State Div. of Human Rights, 104 A.D.2d 111 (1st Dept. 1984).
26. Scarozza v. Tudor Plaza, Inc., 306 A.D.2d 927 (4th Dept. 2003).
27. See, e.g., Axelrod (see note 24).
28. Laurenti v. Water's Edge Habitat, Inc., 837 F. Supp. 507 (E.D.N.Y. 1993); See also, Sirianni v. Rafaloff, 284 A.D.2d 447 (2d Dept. 2001) (shareholders' claim for racially motivated termination of proprietary lease was dismissed where facts established the real reason was their use of the apartment for business purposes).
29. Shoyinke v. 120 25th Street Jackson Heights, Inc., Complaint No. FH-139061687-DH, Recommended Dec. & Order, Sept. 22, 1989, adopted Dec. & Order, NYCCHR, Dec. 21, 1989.
30. Irizarry v. 120 West 70th Owners Corp., 1986 U.S. Dist. LEXIS 22849 (S.D.N.Y.).

Chapter 7—Decor and Decorum

1. See, e.g., Rosenthal v. One Hudson Park, Inc., 269 A.D.2d 144 (1st Dept. 2000); Seven Park Avenue Corp. v. Green, 277 A.D.2d 123 (1st Dept 2000).
2. N.Y. Real Prop. Law § 339-v(1)(i) (McKinney 1989).
3. See, e.g., Bongiasca v. 775 Park Avenue, NYLJ, Aug. 26, 1980, p.9, col.3 (Sup. Ct. N.Y. Co.).
4. Whalen v. 50 Sutton Place South Owners, Inc., 276 A.D.2d 356 (1st Dept. 2000).
5. Babeli v. 7–11 East 13th Street Tenant Corp., NYLJ, Dec. 3, 2003, p.22 (Civ. Ct. N.Y. Co.).
6. Residential Bd. of Managers of Columbia Condominium v. Alden, 178 A.D.2d 121 (1st Dept. 1991).
7. Levandusky v. One Fifth Avenue Apartment Corp., 75 N.Y.2d 530 (1990).
8. Korelitz v. 975 Park Avenue Corp., NYLJ, Jan. 7, 1987, p.13, col.3 (Sup. Ct. N.Y. Co.).
9. Odell v. 704 Broadway Condominium, 284 A.D.2d 52 (1st Dept. 2001).
10. 259 West 72nd Street Owners Corp. v. Benson, NYLJ, April 15, 1991, p.27, col.4 (Sup. Ct. N.Y. Co.).
11. N.Y. Real Prop. Law § 339-k (McKinney 1989).
12. Odell (see note 9), See also, Fried v. 20 Sutton Place South, Inc., 2 A.D. 3d 351 (1st Dept. 2003) (condominium board did not unreasonably withhold approval of owner's plans to erect a greenhouse by conditioning approval on consent of an adversely affected neighbor); But see, Demas v. 325 West End Avenue Corp., 127 A.D.2d 476

(1st Dept. 1987) (board's written approval to shareholder's penthouse addition plans couldn't be rescinded based on objection of fellow rooftop owners).

13. Farnsworth v. Wells, NYLJ, Nov. 28, 2001, p.27, col.4 (Sup. Ct. Kings Co.).
14. Cohen v. Board of Managers of the 22 Perry Street Condominium, 278 A.D.2d 147 (1st Dept. 2000).
15. Gramercy Park Residence Corp. v. Ellman, Index No. 603071/02, Sept. 25, 2002, Sup. Ct. N.Y. Co.
16. Rudey v. Landmark Preservation Commission, 82 N.Y.2d 832 (1993).
17. Soho International Arts Condominium v. City of New York, NYLJ, Sept. 14, 2004, p.20, col.1 (S.D.N.Y.).
18. Behler v. Ten-Eighty Apartment Corp., NYLJ, April 11, 2002, p.18, col.4 (Sup. Ct. N.Y. Co.).
19. 179 East 70th Street Corp. v. Steindl, NYLJ, May 14, 2003, p.21, col.3 (Civ. Ct. N.Y. Co.).
20. See, e.g., In re Application of Pace Plumbing Corp., NYLJ, Feb. 6, 1991, p.22, col.1 (Sup. Ct. N.Y. Co.); Dash v. Slater, NYLJ, Jan. 25, 1989, p.22, col.3 (Sup. Ct. N.Y. Co).
21. N.Y. Real Prop. Law § 339-l (McKinney 1989); See, Matter of City of Albany Industrial Development Agency v. DeGraff-Moffly, 164 A.D.2d 20 (3d Dept. 1990).
22. Glen Oaks Village Owners, Inc. v. Balwani, 115 Misc.2d 948 (Civ. Ct. Queens Co. 1982).
23. Bayview Gardens Ltd. v. Sperazza, NYLJ, Sept. 10, 1997, p.29, col.1 (Civ. Ct. Kings Co.).
24. Clearview Gardens Fifth Corp. v. Rabinowitz, NYLJ, March 1, 1989, p.26, col.2 (Sup. Ct. Queens Co.).
25. Bd. of Managers of the 77 Park Avenue Condominium v. Silver, NYLJ, July 10, 1985, p.7, col. 3 (Sup. Ct. N.Y. Co.).
26. Andrew Jackson Condominium v. Gomez, NYLJ, June 28, 1988, p.25, col.2 (Sup. Ct. Queens Co.).
27. Edgewater Apts. Inc. v. Freeman, NYLJ, Aug. 1, 1986, p.7, col.5 (Sup. Ct. N.Y. Co.).
28. Barnard v. Nash, NYLJ, June 3, 1992, p.22, col.3 (Sup. Ct. N.Y. Co.).
29. Roter v. Wexler, 195 A.D.2d 323 (1st Dept. 1993).
30. N.Y. Labor Law § 240 (McKinney 2002).
31. See, e.g., Brown v. Christopher Street Owners Corp., 211 A.D.2d 441 (1st Dept. 1995), aff'd, 87 N.Y.2d 938 (1996); Tumminello v. Hamlet Development Co., 174 Misc.2d 239 (Sup. Ct. Nassau Co. 1997).
32. DeNota v. 45 East 85th Street Corp., 163 Misc.2d 734 (Sup. Ct. N.Y. Co. 1995); See also, Pineda v. 79 Barrow Street Owners Corp., 297 A.D.2d 634 (2d Dept. 2002) (co-operative is absolutely liable under the law to worker injured while painting in a shareholder's apartment).
33. Bowers v. Riverdale Tenants Corp., NYLJ, March 25, 1994, p.23, col.4 (Sup. Ct. N.Y. Co.).

Chapter 8—The Rules of Repair

1. But if it's a restricted common element, like the land or concrete slab beneath your unit, you're responsible, as one unhappy condo owner found out to the tune of

$6,500. See, Teitelbaum v. Woodbury Village Condominium II, NYLJ, June 5, 2002, p.26, col.3 (Sup. Ct. Nassau Co.).

2. See, Linden Hill No. 3 Cooperative Corp. v. Berkman, 61 Misc.2d 275 (Sup. Ct. Queens Co. 1969).
3. Levine v. Linden Towers Corp., 405 N.Y.S.2d 407 (Civ. Ct. Queens Co. 1982).
4. Moskowitz v. Bd. of Managers of the St. Tropez Condominium, Index No. 017962/92, Sup. Ct. N.Y. Co.
5. Hauptman v. 222 East 80th Street Corp., 100 Misc.2d 153 (Civ. Ct. N.Y. Co. 1979).
6. Susskind v. 1136 Tenants Corp., 43 Misc.2d 588 (Civ. Ct. N.Y. Co. 1964).
7. Hauptman (see note 5).
8. Smith v. Parkchester North Condominium, NYLJ, Nov. 23, 1994, p.28, col.1 (Civ. Ct. Bronx Co.).
9. N.Y. Real Prop. Law § 235-b (McKinney Supp. 2005).
10. Suarez v. Rivercross Tenants Corp., 107 Misc. 135 (App. Tm. 1st Dept. 1981).
11. Frisch v. Bellmarc Management, Inc., 190 A.D.2d 383 (1st Dept. 1993).
12. Park West Management Corp. v. Mitchell, 47 N.Y.2d 316 (1979).
13. Solow v. Wellner, 86 N.Y.2d 582 (1995).
14. 29-45 Tenants Corp. v. Rowe, NYLJ, Jan. 8, 1992, p.23, col.4 (Civ. Ct. N.Y. Co.).
15. Delulio v. 320-57 Corp., 99 A.D.2d 253 (1st Dept. 1984).
16. Witherbee Court Associates v. Greene, 7 A.D.3d 699 (2d Dept. 2004).
17. Kaniklidis v. 235 Lincoln Plaza Housing Corp., 305 A.D.2d 546 (2d Dept. 2003).
18. Protano v. 16 North Chatsworth Avenue Corp., 272 A.D.2d 597 (2d Dept. 2000).
19. Jacobs v. 200 East 36th Owners Corp., 281 A.D.2d 281 (1st Dept. 2001).
20. Verbitsky v. Lamborn, 269 A.D.2d 314 (1st Dept. 2000).
21. See, e.g., Leventritt v. 520 East 86th Street, Inc., 266 A.D.2d 45 (1st Dept. 1999), leave to appeal denied, 94 N.Y.2d 760 (2000).
22. River Terrace Apartments, Inc. v. Robinson, NYLJ, May 27, 1998, p.27, col.3 (Civ. Ct. Bronx Co.).
23. Mosesson v. 288/98 West End Tenants Corp., 294 A.D.2d 283 (1st Dept. 2002).
24. Ogust v. 451 Broome Street Corp., 285 A.D.2d 412 (1st Dept. 2001).
25. See, e.g., Bunny Realty v. Miller, 180 A.D.2d 460 (1st Dept. 1992).
26. See, e.g., 142 East 16 Cooperative Owners Inc. v. Jacobson, NYLJ, June 5, 1998, p.29, col. 3 (App. Tm. 1st Dept.); Verrazano Residents, Inc. v. Kuppler, NYLJ, July 14, 1993, p.28, col.1 (Civ. Ct. Kings Co.); Halkedis v. Two East End Avenue Apartment Corp., 161 A.D.2d 281 (1st Dept. 1990).
27. 87-37 Bay Owners Corp. v. D'Angelo, 183 Misc.2d 558 (Civ. Ct. Kings Co. 2000).
28. Frisch (see note 11).
29. Linden v. Lloyd's Planning Service, Inc., 299 A.D.2d 217 (1st Dept. 2000); leave to appeal denied, 99 N.Y.2d 509 (2003).
30. Residential Bd. of Managers of the Century Condominium v. Berman, NYLJ, Dec. 15, 1993, p.22, col.3 (Sup. Ct. N.Y. Co.), aff'd, 213 A.D.2d 206 (1st Dept. 1995).
31. Pershad v. Parkchester South Condominium, 174 Misc.2d 92 (Civ. Ct. N.Y. Co. 1997).
32. Board of Managers of the Hayden on the Hudson Condominium v. Rubens, NYLJ, Dec. 14, 2000, p.30, col.1 (Civ. Ct. Bronx Co.).

33. See, e.g. Bd. of Managers of the Mews at North Hills Condominium v. Farajzadeh, NYLJ, June 20, 2000, p.21 (Dist. Ct. Nassau Co.) (unit owner ordered to repay $23,000 in common charges, late fees, and interest improperly withheld for board's failure to fix leaking roof).
34. O'Brien v. Edgewater Apts., Inc, NYLJ, March 14, 1988, p.16, col.2 (Sup. Ct. N.Y. Co.).
35. Grinnell Housing Development Fund Corp. v. McClain-James, 240 A.D.2d 203 (1st Dept. 1997).
36. 27 Victoria Owners Corp. v. Colbert, NYLJ, Nov. 3, 1993, p. 22, col.3 (Sup. Ct. N.Y. Co.).
37. 78th & Park Corp. v. Hochfelder, 262 A.D.2d 204 (1st Dept. 1999).
38. Wiener v. State Farm Fire and Casualty Co., Index No. NYLJ, June 17,1998, p.31, col.1 (Civ. Ct. N.Y. Co.).
39. McMunn v. Steppingstone Management Corp., 131 Misc.2d 340 (Civ. Ct. N.Y. Co 1986).
40. Gazdo Properties Corp. v. Lava, 149 Misc.2d 828 (Civ. Ct. Kings Co. 1991).
41. See, Motoko Rich, "Nightmares On Mold Street," The New York Times, Dec. 11, 2003, Sec. F, p.1.
42. 157 East 57th Street LLC v. Birrenbach, NYLJ, May 15, 2003, p.22, col.6 (Civ. Ct. N.Y. Co.).

Chapter 9—The Ruling Class

1. N.Y. Bus. Corp. Law § 701 (McKinney 2003).
2. See, e.g., N.Y. Real Prop. Law § 339-v (McKinney 1989) (ability to acquire, lease, or convey units on behalf of owners); § 339-w (duty to keep records of account); § 339-dd (ability to institute legal proceedings); § 339-jj (power to borrow under certain circumstances).
3. Johar v. 82-02 Lefferts Tenants Corp., NYLJ, Jan. 3, 1996, p.28, col.2 (Sup. Ct. Queens Co.).
4. Feld v. 710 Park Avenue Corp., NYLJ, Jan. 15, 2003, p.19, col.1 (Sup. Ct. N.Y. Co.).
5. N.Y. Bus. Corp. Law § 702(a) (McKinney 2003).
6. N.Y. Bus Corp. Law § 702(b)(2) (McKinney 2003).
7. N.Y. Bus Corp. Law § 705 (McKinney 2003).
8. N.Y. Bus. Corp. Law §§ 707, 709 (McKinney 2003).
9. N.Y. Bus. Corp. Law § 708(c) (McKinney 2003).
10. N.Y. Bus. Corp. Law § 708(b) (McKinney 2003).
11. See, Attorney General's Regulations, 13 N.Y.C.R.R. §18.3(v)(i)(co-ops); § 23.3 (w)(1) (condos).
12. See, Attorney General's Regulations, 13 N.Y.C.R.R. §21.3(s)(1)(xii)(a) (co-ops); § 20.3(u)(1) (condos).
13. See, e.g., Park Briar Associates v. Park Briar Owners, Inc., 182 A.D.2d 685 (2d Dept. 1992); Rego Park Garden Associates v. Rego Park Garden Owners, Inc., 174 A.D.2d 337 (1st Dept. 1991), appeal denied, 78 N.Y.2d 859 (1991).
14. Matter of Calas v. Vastola, NYLJ, Aug. 6, 1997, p.22, col.5 (Sup. Ct. N.Y. Co.).
15. Visutton Associates v. Anita Terrace Owners, Inc., 254 A.D.2d 295 (2d Dept. 1998).

16. Mundiya v. Beattie, 2 A.D.3d 317 (1st Dept. 2003); But see, Mishkin v. 155 Condominium, 2 Misc.3d 1001A (Sup. Ct. N.Y. Co. 2004) (allowing sponsor to elect four directors despite bylaws that limited it to voting for only three).
17. Wright v. Board of Managers of the 188 East 70th Street Condominium Ass'n., Index No. 105139/98, Apr. 20, 1998, Sup. Ct. N.Y. Co.
18. N.Y. Bus. Corp. Law § 703 (McKinney 2003).
19. N.Y. Real Prop. Law § 339-v(1)(a) (McKinney 1989).
20. 75 N.Y.2d 530(1990).
21. Canon Point North, Inc. v. Abeles, 160 Misc.2d 30 (1st Dept. 1993).
22. Martino v. Board of Managers of Heron Pointe Condominium, 6 A.D.3d 505 (2d Dept. 2004).
23. Nuzzo v. Bd. of Managers of Jefferson Village Condominium, 228 A.D.2d 568 (2d Dept. 1996).
24. Lawrence Park Condominium v. Karabachi, NYLJ, March 15, 2000, p.30, col.1 (Sup. Ct. Rockland Co.).
25. Caruso v. Bd. of Managers of Murray Hill Terrace Condominium, 146 Misc.2d 405 (Sup. Ct. N.Y. Co. 1990).
26. See cases cited in notes to chapter 14, pp.272 to 280.
27. See cases cited in notes to chapter 6, pp.108 to 109; chapter 18, pp.355 to 358.
28. See cases cited in notes to chapter 15, pp.283 to 302.
29. See, e.g., Schultz v. 400 Cooperative Corp., 292 A.D.2d 16 (1st Dept. 2002) (board acted within its business judgment in refusing to reduce the number of shares allocated to a professional apartment pursuant to a long-standing agreement that had been negotiated with shareholders); Cohn v. 120 Owners Corp., 205 A.D.2d 394 (1st Dept. 1994).
30. See cases cited in notes to chapter 8.
31. Untergleider v. One Fifth Avenue Apartment Corp., NYLJ, March 8, 1995, p.25 (Sup. Ct. N.Y. Co.).
32. Michaelson v. Albora, 196 Misc.2d 517 (Sup. Ct. Suffolk Co. 2003); See also, Van Camp v. Sherman, 132 A.D.2d 453 (1st Dept. 1987) (board member who used her position to stake out building rights on the roof above her penthouse forced to back down for engaging in self-dealing).
33. Bd. of Managers of the Fairway at North Hills Condominium v. Fairway at North Hills, 193 A.D.2d 322 (2d Dept. 1993).
34. Id.
35. State of New York v. Metz, NYLJ, March 10, 1994, p.24, col.6 (Sup. Ct. N.Y. Co.).
36. N.Y. Bus. Corp. Law § 713 (McKinney 2003).
37. Excelsior 57th Street Corp. v. Lerner, 160 A.D.2d 407 (1st Dept. 1990).
38. Bd. of Managers of General Apartment Corp. Condominium v. Abramowitz, 155 Misc.2d 828 (Civ. Ct. Queens Co. 1992).
39. Residential Bd. of Managers of the Columbia Condominium v. Alden, 178 A.D.2d 121 (1st Dept. 1991).
40. Boisson v. 4 East Housing Corp, 129 A.D.2d 533 (1st Dept. 1987).
41. Bernheim v. 136 East 64th Street Corp., 128 A.D.2d 434 (1st Dept. 1987).
42. Allen v. Murray House Owners Corp., 174 A.D.2d 400 (1st Dept. 1991).

43. Kratsov v. Thwaites Terrace House Owners, NYLJ, Dec. 23, 1999, p.28, col.1 (1st Dept.).
44. See Feld (note 4).
45. Self v. Horatio Street Owners Corp., NYLJ, Feb. 6, 2002, p.18, col. 5 (Sup. Ct. N.Y. Co.).
46. Louis and Anne Abrams Foundation, Inc. v. 29 East 64th Street Corp., 297 A.D.2d 258 (1st Dept. 2002).
47. Salmansohn v. Fourth Avenue Owners Corp., NYLJ, Sept. 11, 1996, p.21, col.4 (Sup. Ct. N.Y. Co.).
48. Baker v. 16 Sutton Place Apartment Corp., 2 A.D.3d 119 (1st Dept. 2003); See also, Aronson v. Crane, 145 A.D.2d 455 (2d Dept. 1988) (court took part of selling shareholder who claimed unequal treatment because board coached buyer, also a shareholder, how to get out of deal).
49. Milliken v. Hatfield, NYLJ, July 19, 1993, p.23, col.6 (Sup. Ct. N.Y. Co.).
50. Uhr v. 2330 Voorheis Terrace Owners Corp., Index No. 13426/90, Oct. 30, 1990, Sup. Ct. N.Y. Co.
51. Ludwig v. 25 Plaza Tenants Corp., 184 A.D.2d 623 (2d Dept. 1992).

Chapter 10—Widening the Gap

1. 40 West 67th Street Corp. v. Pullman, 100 N.Y.2d 147 (2003).
2. 40 West 12 Tenants Corp. v. Seidenberg, 6 A.D.3d 243 (2004).
3. West Gate House, Inc. v. 860-870 Realty LLC, 7 A.D.3d 412 (1st Dept. 2004).
4. Woodrow Court Inc. v. Levine, NYLJ, Nov. 15, 2002, p.22, col.4 (Civ. Ct. N.Y. Co.).
5. 13315 Owners Corp. v. Kennedy, NYLJ, July 28, 2004, p.18, col.3 (Civ. Ct. N.Y. Co.); See also, London Terrace Towers, Inc. v. Davis, 2004 NY Slip Op 24497, Dec. 6, 2004, Civ. Ct. N.Y. Co. (finding board acted properly in terminating shareholder's tenancy for objectionable conduct).
6. Sirianni v. Rafaloff, 284 A.D.2d 447 (2d Dept. 2001).
7. Jones v. Surrey Coop Apts. Inc., 263 A.D.2d 33 (1st Dept 1999).
8. Cooper v. Greenbriar Owners Corp., Index No. 11648/91, Sup. Ct. Queens Co., aff'd 239 A.D.2d 311 (2d Dept. 1997).
9. Woo v. Irving Tenants Corp., NYLJ, Aug. 18, 1999, p.23, col.2 (Sup. Ct. N.Y. Co.), aff'd, 276 A.D.2d 380 (1st Dept. 2000).
10. Cooper v. 6 West 20th Street Tenants Corp., 258 A.D.2d 362 (1st Dept. 1999).
11. Park Tower Holding Corp. v. Bd. of Managers of 500 Park, NYLJ, Aug. 5, 1999, p.26, col.5 (Sup. Ct. N.Y. Co.).
12. Captain's Walk Homeowner's Association v. Czeczil, NYLJ, Nov. 19, 2000, p.22, col.1 (Sup. Ct. Suffolk Co.).
13. Jacobs v. 200 East 36th Owners Corp., 281 A.D.2d 281 (1st Dept. 2001).
14. Lawrence Park Condominium v. Karabachi, NYLJ, March 15, 2000, p.30, col.6 (Sup. Ct. Rockland Co.).
15. Hidden Ridge at Kutsher's Country Club Homeowner's Ass'n., Inc. v. Chasin, 289 A.D.2d 652 (3d Dept. 2001).
16. Braun v. 941 Park Avenue, Inc., Index No. 117589/00, May 13, 2003, Sup. Ct. N.Y. Co.
17. Horowitz v. 1025 Fifth Avenue, Inc., 7 A.D.3d 461 (1st Dept. 2004).

18. Merolo v. Bd. of Managers of the Hills at Grasmere Condominium II, 3 A.D.3d 520 (2d Dept. 2004).
19. 10 East 70th Street, Inc. v. Gimbel, 309 A.D.2d 644 (1st Dept. 2003).
20. Kleinman v. Point Seal Restoration Corp., 267 A.D.2d 430 (2d Dept. 1999).

Chapter 11—Restoring the Balance

1. N.Y. Bus. Corp. Law § 706 (McKinney 2003).
2. N.Y. Bus. Corp. Law § 716 (McKinney 2003).
3. N.Y. Real Prop. Law § 339-v(1)(j) (McKinney 1989).
4. N.Y. Bus. Corp. Law § 601 (McKinney 2003).
5. N.Y. Bus. Corp. Law §§ 909, 1001 (McKinney 2003).
6. N.Y. Bus. Corp. Law § 602 (McKinney 2003).
7. N.Y. Bus. Corp. Law § 624(e) (McKinney 2003).
8. N.Y. Bus. Corp. Law § 624(b) (McKinney 2003).
9. N.Y. Real Prop. Law § 339-w (McKinney 1989).
10. Tessler v. Mayer, NYLJ, Dec. 21, 1988, p.22, col.2 (Sup. Ct. N.Y. Co.).
11. N.Y. Bus. Corp. Law § 602 (McKinney 2003).
12. N.Y. Bus. Corp Law § 624(a)(b) (McKinney 2003).
13. Id.
14. A&A Properties NY Ltd. v. Soundings Condominium, 177 Misc.2d 200 (Sup. Ct. N.Y. Co. 1998).
15. Mishkin v. 155 Condominium, 2 Misc.3d 1001A (Sup. Ct. N.Y. Co. 2004).
16. N.Y. Bus. Corp. Law § 624(a) (McKinney 2003).
17. Brodsky v. Bd of Managers of Dag Hammarskjold Tower Condominium, (Sup. Ct. N.Y. Co. 1 Misc. 3d591/2003).
18. N.Y. Bus. Corp. Law § 605 (McKinney 2003).
19. See, e.g., 4260 Broadway Realty Co. v. Assimakopoulos, 264 A.D.2d 626 (1st Dept. 1999).
20. N.Y. Bus. Corp. Law § 609 (McKinney 2003).
21. N.Y. Bus. Corp. Law § 618 (McKinney 2003).
22. Liberty Court Condominium Residential Unit Owners Coalition v. Bd. of Managers of Liberty Court Condominium, NYLJ, Jan. 29, 2004, p.26, col.4 (1st Dept.).
23. N.Y. Bus. Corp. Law § 701 (McKinney 2003).
24. N.Y. Bus. Corp. Law § 712 (McKinney 2003).
25. Timmerman v. Bd. of Managers of the Anchorage Condominium, 212 A.D.2d 523 (2d Dept. 1995).

Chapter 12—Taking the Offensive

1. N.Y. Bus. Corp. Law § 602 (McKinney 2003).
2. Breezy Point Cooperative, Inc. v. Young, 123 A.D.2d 354 (2d Dept. 1986).
3. N.Y. Bus. Corp. Law § 615 (McKinney 2003).
4. N.Y. Bus. Corp. Law § 603 (McKinney 2003).
5. See, e.g., Brodsky v. Bd. of Managers of Dag Hammarskjold Tower Condominium, 1 Misc.3d 591 (Sup. Ct. N.Y. Co. 2003).
6. N.Y. Bus. Corp. Law § 601 (McKinney 2003).

7. N.Y. Real Prop. Law § 339-v(1)(j) (McKinney 1989).
8. N.Y. Bus. Corp. Law § 706 (McKinney 2003).
9. Bd. of Managers of the Townhomes of Eastbrooke Condominiums One, Two and Three v. Padgett, 185 A.D.2d 650 (4th Dept. 1992).
10. N.Y. Bus. Corp. Law § 706(d) (McKinney 2003).

Chapter 13—Government in Action

1. The Internal Revenue Service no longer seeks to apply Section 277 of the Internal Revenue Code to co-ops. See, e.g., Cooperative Housing Bulletin, National Association of Housing Cooperatives, Vol. XXV, No.2 (March/April/May 1999).
2. 360 Owners Corp. v. Diacou & Arensberg, NYLJ, Feb. 23, 1994, p.22, col.3 (Sup. Ct. N.Y. Co.).
3. 815 Park Avenue Owners, Inc. v. Lapidus, Index No. 30618/91, Nov. 2, 1995, Sup. Ct. N.Y. Co., aff'd, 227 A.D.2d 353 (1st Dept. 1996).
4. AICPA, Statement on Auditing Standards No. 99 (2002); For discussion see, www.aicpa.org/antifraud/detection/understanding_new_sas/homepage.htm.
5. Fazzino v. Ridgefield Towers Tenants Corp., NYLJ, Dec. 3, 1997, p.33, col.3 (Sup. Co. Kings Co.).

Chapter 14—Everyday Skirmishes

1. Jacobs v. 200 East 36th Owners Corp., 281 A.D.2d 281 (1st Dept. 2001).
2. N.Y.C. Admin. Code § 27-2009.1.
3. Bd. of Managers of Parkchester North Condominium v. Quiles, 234 A.D.2d 130 (1st Dept. 1996).
4. Bd. of Managers v. Lamontanero, 206 A.D.2d 340 (2d Dept. 1994).
5. 111 East 88th Partners v. Reich, NY Slip Op 50007U, Jan. 8, 2002, App. Tm. 1st Dept.
6. Hudson View Associates v. Andrews, NYLJ, Dec. 27, 1995, p.34, col.1 (City Ct. Yonkers); See also, Palmer House Owners Corp. v. Brennan, NYLJ, Nov. 15, 1995, p.38, col.1 (City Ct. New Rochelle).
7. Trump Village Section 3, Inc. v. Sinrod, 219 A.D.2d 590 (2d Dept. 1995).
8. Waterford Association, Inc. v. Hoody, NYLJ, April 23, 1997, p.25, col.5 (Sup. Ct. N.Y. Co.).
9. Robinson v. City of N.Y., 152 Misc.2d 1007 (Sup. Ct. N.Y. Co. 1991).
10. Adee Tower Apartments, Inc. v. Levy, NYLJ, May 27, 1998, p.27, col.1 (Civ. Ct. Bronx Co.).
11. Seward Park Housing Corp. v. Cohen, 287 A.D.2d 157 (1st Dept. 2001), leave to appeal denied, 2002 N.Y. App. Div. LEXIS 3751, April 11, 2002.
12. 930 Fifth Corp. v. Miller, NYLJ, Aug. 14, 2002, p.18, col.3 (Sup. Ct. N.Y. Co.).
13. Olympic Tower Condominium v. Cocoziello, 306 A.D.2d 159 (1st Dept. 2003).
14. Riverdale Park Corp. v. McDermott, NYLJ, May 8, 2002, p.22, col.1 (Civ. Ct. Bronx Co.).
15. Matter of Kaufman v. Tudor Realty Services Corp., 2004 NY Slip Op 01133, Feb. 19, 2004, 1st Dept.
16. Seward Park (see note 11).
17. Park Holding Co. v. Emicke, 168 Misc.2d 133 (App. Tm. 1st Dept. 1996).

18. Winnie Hu, "Sorry, No Pets . . . Unless Yours Just Died," The New York Times, June 24, 2004, Sec. B, p.3.
19. Bell Apt. Owners Corp. v. Melamed, NYLJ, Nov. 1, 1995, p.34, col.5 (Civ. Ct. N.Y. Co.).
20. 445 East 86 Owners Corp. v. Kayatt, NYLJ, June 25, 1986 (Civ. Ct. N.Y. Co.).
21. Canon Point North Inc. v. Abeles, 160 Misc.2d 30 (App. Tm. 1st Dept. 2003).
22. 255 Fieldston Buyers Corp. v. Michaels, 196 Misc.2d 105 (App. Tm. 1st Dept. 2003).
23. 3530 Owners Corp. v. Wilamowski, NYLJ, April 17, 1996, p.26, col.4 (Civ. Ct. Bronx Co.).
24. Crystal Apartments Group v. Cook, 147 Misc.2d 676 (Civ. Ct. Queens Co. 1990).
25. 47 C.F.R. § 1.4000 et seq., 11 F.C.C.R. 19276.
26. See, Matter of Implementation of Section 207 of the Telecommunications Act of 1996, 13 F.C.C.R. 23874 (1998).
27. Fawn Ridge Condominium v. NASR, NYLJ, Nov. 8, 2000, p.25, col.1 (Sup. Ct. Richmond Co.).
28. 2682 Kingsbridge Associates, LLC v. Martinez, NYLJ, Jan. 22, 2003, p.20, col.6 (Civ. Ct. Bronx Co.).
29. Sherwood Complex LLC v. Vouzan, 4 Misc. 3d 73 (App. Tm. 2d Dept. 2004).
30. Lemle Realty Corp. v. Desjardin, 3 Misc.3d 1104A (Civ. Ct. Bronx Co. 2004).
31. Urban Horizons Tax Credit Fund v. Zarick, 195 Misc.2d 779 (Civ. Ct. 2004 Bronx Co. 2003).
32. Greenberg v. Board of Managers of Parkridge Condominium, NYLJ, Sept. 19, 2000, p.31, col. 6 (Sup. Ct. Queens Co.), aff'd, 294 A.D.2d 467 (2d Dept. 2002).
33. Vacca v. Board of Managers of Primrose Lane Condominium, NYLJ, Dec. 13, 1996, p.25, (Sup. Ct. Suffolk Co.).
34. Kevin Kraus, "Condo Says No Menorah: Jewish Residents Want Their Decorations, Too," Sun-Sentinel, Dec. 14, 1996, p. 1B.
35. Neuman v. Grandview at Emerald Hills, Inc., 861 So.2d 494 (Fla. Ct. of App. 4th Dist. 2003).
36. "Hanukah Bows Go Up At Entrance After Court Order," The Florida Times Union, Dec. 24, 2000, p. B5.
37. Staffin v. Scarsdale Manor Owners, Inc., QDS: 92413722, April 28, 1999, Sup. Ct. Westchester Co.
38. See, Dennis Hevesi, "Co-op Board Bans Smoking in Apartment for New Owners," The New York Times, April 30, 2002, Sec. B, p.1.
39. Washburn v. 166 East 96th Street Owners Corp., 166 A.D.2d 272 (1st Dept. 1990).
40. Figlia v. Sutton Manor Apartments, Inc., NYLJ, June 3, 1992, p.22, col.4 (Sup. Ct. N.Y. Co.).
41. O'Neill v. 225 East 73rd Owners Corp., NYLJ, Nov. 1, 2000, p.26, col.2 (Sup. Ct. N.Y. Co.).
42. Rubinstein v. 242 Apartment Corp., 189 A.D.2d 685 (1st Dept. 1993).
43. Katz v. 215 West 91st Street Corp., 215 A.D.2d 265 (1st Dept. 1995).
44. Benasuli v. 1010 Tenants Corp., NYLJ, Jan. 16, 1985, p.12, col.2 (Sup. Ct. N.Y. Co.).
45. Rutherford Tenants Corp. v. Kaufman, 212 A.D.2d 416 (1st Dept. 1995).
46. 123 Apartment Corp. v. Hayman-Chaffey, NYLJ, April 22, 1985, p.6, col.2 (Sup. Ct. N.Y. Co.).

47. Carr v. 77 Bleeker Street Corp., NYLJ, Oct. 30, 1991, p.21, col.2 (Sup. Ct. N.Y. Co.).
48. Mariaux v. Turtle Bay Towers Corp., 301 A.D.2d 460 (1st Dept. 2003).
49. 360 East 72nd Street Owners, Inc. v. Rutter, Index No. 603850/02, March 11, 2004, Sup. Ct. N.Y. Co.
50. See, e.g., 29-45 Tenants Corp v. Rowe, NYLJ, Jan. 8, 1992, p.23, col. 4 (Civ. Ct. N.Y. Co.); 77 E 12 Owners, Inc. v. Yager, 137 Misc.2d 138 (Sup. Ct. N.Y. Co. 1987).
51. 29-45 Tenants Corp (see note 50); See also, 2 Sutton Place Tenants Corp. v. Kaniclides, NYLJ, July 29, 1992, p.23, col.4 (Civ. Ct. N.Y. Co.).

Chapter 15—Boarder Wars

1. See cases cited in notes to chapter 9, p.184.
2. Deering v. 860 Fifth Avenue Corp., 220 A.D.2d 303 (1st Dept. 1995).
3. Uhr v. 2330 Voorheis Terrace Owners Corp., Index No. 13426/90, Oct. 30, 1990, Sup. Ct. N.Y. Co.; See also, Sporn v. 86-88 Owners Corp., NYLJ, May 27, 1993, p.29, col.3 (Sup. Ct. Kings Co.) (board's right under proprietary lease to determine whether or not to approve apartment subleasing doesn't permit it to completely refuse to allow any subletting).
4. Ludwig v. 25 Plaza Tenants Corp., 184 A.D.2d 623 (2d Dept. 1992).
5. Curto v. Edgemont Apartments Inc., Index No. 7843/96, Nov. 4, 1996, Sup. Ct. Westchester Co.; But see, Rosenberg v. Riverwood Owners, Inc., 304 A.D.2d 547 (2d Dept. 2003) (after allowing shareholder to sublet her apartment various times, board not acting unreasonably in denying a subsequent sublet application based on financial information).
6. Bd. of Managers of Village House v. Frazier, 81 A.D.2d 760 (1st Dept. 1981), app. dismissed, 54 N.Y.2d 604 (1981).
7. Four Brothers Homes at Heartland Condominium II v. Gerbino, 262 A.D.2d 279 (2d Dept. 1999).
8. Bd. of Managers of Plymouth Village Condominium v. Mahaney, 272 A.D.2d 283 (2d Dept. 2000).
9. Rakowsky v. Excelsior 57th Corp., 167 Misc.2d 476 (Civ. Ct. N.Y. Co. 1995).
10. Yochim v. McGrath, 165 Misc.2d 10 (City Ct. Yonkers 1995).
11. Warner v. West 90th Owners Corp., 170 A.D.2d 315 (1st Dept. 1991).
12. Zimiles v. Hotel des Artistes, NYLJ, March 15, 1994, p.21, col.3 (Sup. Ct. N.Y. Co.), aff'd as modified, 216 A.D.2d 45 (1st Dept. 1995).
13. See, e.g., McCabe v. Hoffman, 138 A.D.2d 287 (1st Dept. 1988) (court upheld imposition of a monthly surcharge of 5 percent of the rent collected from subletting shareholders, provided the rent was more than the maintenance).
14. N.Y. Bus. Corp. Law § 501(c) (McKinney 2003).
15. Wapnick v. Seven Park Avenue Corp., 240 A.D.2d 245 (1st Dept. 1997).
16. Susser v. 200 East 36th Street Owners Corp., 262 A.D.2d 197 (1st Dept. 1999).
17. Spiegel v. 1065 Park Avenue Corp., 305 A.D.2d 204 (1st Dept. 2003).
18. Peckolick v. 135 West 17th Street Tenants Corp., NYLJ, July 15, 1998, p.21, col.3 (Sup. Ct. N.Y. Co.).
19. Bailey v. 600 Grand Concourse Owners, Inc. 199 A.D.2d 1 (1st Dept. 1993).
20. Susser (see note 16).

21. Sherry Associates v. The Sherry-Netherland, Inc., NYLJ, June 13, 1996, p.30, col.4 (Sup. Ct. N.Y. Co.).
22. N.Y. Real Prop. Law § 235-f (McKinney 1989).
23. See, e.g., Southridge Cooperative Section No. 3, Inc. v. Menendez, 141 Misc.2d 823 (Civ. Ct. Queens Co. 1988).
24. See, e.g., Smith v. Bd. of Managers Leland Gardens Condominium, NYLJ, Nov. 16, 1993, p.28, col.6 (Sup. Ct. Bronx Co.).
25. Lincoln Guild Housing Corp. v. Stuckelman, NYLJ, April 9, 1992, p.24, col.4 (Civ. Ct. N.Y. Co.), rev'd, June 30, 1993, p.21, col.1 (App. Tm. 1st Dept.).
26. Mill Rock Owners Corp. v. McEvoy, NYLJ, April 14, 1993, p.25, col.5 (Civ. Ct. N.Y. Co.)
27. W.P. Owners Corp. v. Caramihi, NYLJ, April 15, 1993, p.21, col.2 (Sup. Ct. Queens Co.).
28. Board of Directors of the Old Yorktown Village Corp. v. Hitt, 2003 Slip Op 51228U, July 18, 2003, App. Tm. 1st Dept.
29. 425 Realty Co. v. Herrera, 146 Misc.2d 790 (App. Tm. 1st Dept 1990).
30. Ram 1 LLC v. Mazzola, 2001 NY Slip Op 50073U, Dec. 28, 2001, App. Tm. 1st Dept.
31. Thwaites Terrace House Owners Corp. v. Vega, NYLJ, April 29, 1994, p.30, col.2 (Civ. Ct. Bronx Co.).
32. Bell Apt. Owners Corp. v. Melamed, NYLJ, Nov. 1, 1995, p.34, col.5 (Civ. Ct. Queens Co.).
33. Weisz v. 233 East 69th Street Owners Corp., NYLJ, April 19, 1995, p.25, col.2 (Sup. Ct. N.Y. Co.).
34. Barbizon Owners Corp. v. Chudick, 159 Misc.2d 1023 (Civ. Ct. Queens Co. 1996).
35. Mitchell Gardens No. 1 Cooperative Corp. v. Cataldo, 169 A.D.2d 983 (Civ. Ct. Queens Co. 1996).
36. Bikoff v. 198 East Tenants Co., Index No. 101483/04, March 8, 2004, Sup. Ct. N.Y. Co.
37. Owners Corp. v. Haydon, NYLJ, Dec. 16, 2002, p.18, col.6 (1st Dept. 1992).
38. Wilson v. Valley Park Estates Owners Corp., 301 A.D.2d 589 (2d Dept. 2003).
39. 201 East 37 Owners Corp. v. Cass, 2004 NY Slip Op 50339, April 23, 2004, Civ. Ct. N.Y. Co.
40. 178 East 80th Street Owners, Inc. v. Jenkins, NYLJ, Dec. 30, 2003, p.24, col.3 (S.D.N.Y.).
41. Pfeiffer v. Baldwin, NYLJ, June 24, 1993, p.26, col.1 (Sup. Ct. N.Y. Co.).
42. Hoffman v. 345 East 73rd Street Owners Corp., 186 A.D.2d 507 (1st Dept. 1992).
43. Peck v. Lodge, NYLJ, Nov. 12, 2003, p.18 (Sup. Ct. N.Y. Co.).
44. Merioz v. Addison Hall Owners Corp., QDS: 22220079, March 2, 1999, Sup. Ct. N.Y. Co.

Chapter 16—High Crimes and Misdemeanors

1. See, e.g., Board of Managers of 140 East 56th Street Condominium v. Hausner, 245 A.D.2d 209 (1st Dept. 1997); 1050 Tenants Corp. v. Labow, NYLJ, June 15, 1994, p.31, col.1 (Civ. Ct. N.Y. Co.).

2. N.Y. Real Prop. Law § 339-j (McKinney 1989).
3. Board of Managers of Executive Plaza Condominium v. Jones, 251 A.D.2d 89 (1st Dept. 1998).
4. 815 Park Avenue Owners, Inc. v. Lapidus, 227 A.D.2d 353 (1st Dept. 1996).
5. North Broadway Estates, Ltd. v. Schmoldt, 147 Misc.2d 1098 (City Ct. Yonkers 1990).
6. Milliken v. 96-100 Prince Street Inc., NYLJ, Jan. 11, 1993, p.25, col.1 (Sup. Ct. N.Y. Co.).
7. Bell v. Allen, NYLJ, Sept. 18, 1991, p.22, col.4 (Sup. Ct. N.Y. Co.).
8. See, e.g., Ronald Smith v. Heron Park Condominium, Index No. 1273/94 (Sup. Ct. Richmond Co. 1995).
9. Board of Managers of Hillcroft Townhouse Condominium v. Anderson, NYLJ, Sept. 13, 1993, p.25, col.5 (City Ct. Yonkers); See also, Prosnitz v. Augustus, NYLJ, Jan. 28, 1998, p.25 (Civ. Ct. Bronx Co.).
10. See, e.g., Bd. of Managers of 55 Walker Street Condominium v. Walker Street LLC, 6 A.D.3d 279 (1st Dept. 2004); Isaacs v. Jefferson Tenants Corp., 270 A.D.2d 95 (1st Dept. 2000).
11. Dunn v. Prospect Owners Corp., NYLJ, Oct. 17, 1997, p.28, col.5 (Sup. Ct. N.Y. Co.)
12. Granada Condominium I v. Morris, 225 A.D.2d 520 (2d Dept. 1996).
13. Board of Managers of Dickerson Pond Condominium I v. Jagwani, 276 A.D.2d 517 (2d Dept. 2000).
14. N.Y. Real Prop. Law § 234 (McKinney 1989).
15. 61 East 72nd Street Corp. v. Zimberg, 161 A.D.2d 542 (1st Dept. 1990).
16. 205 West End Avenue Owners Corp. v. Adler, NYLJ, Nov. 2, 1990, p.21, col.4 (App. Tm. 1st Dept.).
17. Castle Apartment Corp. v. Mesrie, NYLJ, March 15, 2000, p. 29, col.2 (Civ. Ct. Kings Co.).
18. Berman v. 300 West 108 Owners Corp., NYLJ, March 19, 1997, p.25, col.2 (Sup. Ct. N.Y. Co.).
19. Saada v. Master Apts. Inc., 152 Misc.2d 861 (Sup. Ct. N.Y. Co. 1991); See also, McMillan v. Park Towers Owners Corp., 225 A.D.2d 742 (2d Dept. 1996).
20. N.Y. Real Prop. Law § 339-aa (McKinney 1989).
21. N.Y. Real Prop. Law § 339-z (McKinney 1989).
22. See, e.g., Bankers Trust Co. v. Board of Managers of the Park 900 Condominium, 81 N.Y.2d 1033 (1993); Citibank, N.A., v. Park 100 Condominium Board of Managers, 292 A.D.2d 269 (1st Dept. 2002); Fleet Mortgage Corp. v. Nieves, 272 A.D.2d 435 (2d Dept. 2000).
23. Park West Village v. Lewis, 62 N.Y.2d 431 (1984).
24. Haberman v. Gotbaum, NYLJ, Aug. 18, 1999, p.24, col.6 (Civ. Ct. N.Y. Co.).
25. Ansonia Associates v. Bozza, 180 Misc.2d 702 (App. Tm. 1st Dept. 1999).
26. Besser v. Beckett, 253 A.D.2d 648 (1st Dept. 1998).
27. Nissen v. Wang, 105 Misc.2d 251 (Civ. Ct. N.Y. Co. 1980).
28. Quinones v. Board of Managers of Regalwalk Condominium I, 242 A.D.2d 52 (2d Dept. 1998).
29. N.Y.C. Zoning Resolution § 12-10(a).
30. Mason v. Department of Buildings, 307 A.D.2d 94 (1st Dept. 2003).

31. See, Zeitz v. Evans Tower Board of Managers, 1990 N.Y. Misc. LEXIS 729, May 10, 1990 (Sup. Ct. N.Y. Co.) (court questioned ability of board to limit number of patients seen by psychologist unit owner where bylaws allowed professional use of apartment).
32. Dinicu v. Groff Studios Corp., 257 A.D.2d 218 (1st Dept. 1999).
33. 24 Gramercy Park Tenants Corp. v. Weiss, NYLJ, Oct. 14, 1998, p.25 (Civ. Ct. N.Y. Co.).
34. Sead Realty Co. v. Walkly, NYLJ, Dec. 17, 1986, p.14, col.4 (Sup. Ct. Bronx Co.).
35. Sweetman v. Bd. of Managers of Plymouth Village Condominium, 1998 WL 1112655 (Sup. Ct. App. Tm.).
36. N.Y. Real Prop. Law § 339-j (McKinney 1989).
37. Cohn v. Brodsky, 138 Misc.2d 1020 (City Ct. Nassau Co. 1988).
38. Kloppenburg v. Loftus, NYLJ, Nov. 13, 1996, p.35, col.3 (Sup. Ct. Suffolk Co.).
39. Matter of Maloney, NYLJ, Dec. 8, 1975, p.11, col.1 (Sup. Ct. Queens Co.).
40. Gillman v. Pebble Cove Home Owners Ass'n., Inc., 154 A.D.2d 508 (2d Dept. 1989).
41. See, Lawrence M. Grosberg, "Dispute Resolution: Using Mediation to Resolve Residential Co-op Disputes," 22 N.Y.L. Sch. J. Int'l. & Comp. L. (2003), p.129.
42. Phoenix Owners Corp. v. Weitzner, 231 A.D.2d 427 (1st Dept. 1996).
43. 40 West 67th Street Corp. v. Pullman, 100 N.Y.2d 147 (2003).
44. Brodsky v. Gaulke, NYLJ, Jan. 12, 1989, p.28, col.15 (Civ. Ct Kings Co.).
45. Bush v. 785 Park Avenue Owners Corp., NYLJ, Nov. 30, 1988, p.22, col.4 (Sup. Ct. N.Y. Co.).
46. Hohenberg v. 77 West 55th Street Associates, 118 A.D.2d 418 (1st Dept. 1986).
47. Root v. 650 Park Avenue Corp., NYLJ, March 20, 1997, p.27, col.4 (Sup. Ct. N.Y. Co.).
48. Anthony Ramirez, "Eating, vs. Living With, Doughnuts," The New York Times, March 9, 1997, Sec. 13, p.6.
49. 169 East 69th Street Corp. v. Leland, 156 Misc.2d 669 (Civ. Ct. N.Y. Co. 1992).
50. Nostrand Gardens Co-op v. Howard, 221 A.D.2d 637 (2d Dept. 1995).
51. Stroh v. Shopwell, NYLJ, July 28, 1988, p.17, col.4 (Sup. Ct. N.Y. Co.).

Chapter 17—Joining the Ruling Ranks

1. See, e.g., Jackson v. Trapp, 3 Misc.3d 139A (Sup. Ct. N.Y. Co. App. Tm. 2004); Bd. of Managers of Lido Beach Towers Condominium v. Gamiel, NYLJ, Sept. 20, 2004, p.19 (City Ct. Long Beach).
2. 85–10 34th Avenue Apartment Corp. v. Nationwide Mutual Insurance Co., 283 A.D.2d 604 (2d Dept. 2001).
3. Oakley v. Longview Owners, Inc., 165 Misc.2d 192 (Sup. Ct. Westchester Co. 1995).
4. In re West 56th Street Associates, 181 B.R. 720 (S.D.N.Y. 1995).
5. Minjak Co. v. Randolph, 140 A.D.2d 245 (1st Dept. 1988).
6. Schimmel v. The Ritz Tower, Inc., NYLJ, Feb. 9, 2000, p.28, col.6 (Sup. Ct. N.Y. Co.).
7. Milliken v. Hatfield, NYLJ, July 19, 1993, p.23, col.4 (Sup. Ct. N.Y. Co.).
8. Sherry Associates v. The Sherry-Netherland, Inc., 273 A.D.2d 14 (1st Dept. 2000).
9. Biondi v. Beekman Hill House Apartment Corp., 257 A.D.2d 76 (1st Dept. 1999), aff'd, 94 N.Y.2d 659 (2000).
10. N.Y. Bus. Corp. Law § 721 (McKinney 2003).
11. See, e.g., Hatfield v. 96-100 Prince Street, Inc., 1997 U.S. Dist. LEXIS 3804 (S.D.N.Y.).

12. People v. Premier House, Inc., 174 Misc.2d 163 (Crim. Ct. Kings Co. 1997).
13. Sherry Associates v. The Sherry-Netherland, Inc., Index No. 124479/95, July 6, 1998, Sup. Ct. N.Y. Co.
14. Pusch v. Pullman, NYLJ, Nov. 5, 2003, p.18, col.1 (Sup. Ct. N.Y. Co.).
15. Cooper v. Lipschutz, NYLJ, March 23, 2004, p.18 (Civ. Ct. N.Y. Co.).
16. Yates v. Ramos, NYLJ, June 18, 2003, p.19, col.2 (Civ. Ct. N.Y. Co.); See also, Golub v. Tang, NYLJ, Oct. 1, 2004, p.18 (Sup. Ct. N.Y. Co.) (defeated board member unsuccessfully sued incumbent director, claiming she had distributed a letter to shareholders calling him "bitter and resentful" and stating that he had a "hunger for power").

Chapter 18—Filing Out

1. N.Y. Real Prop. Law § 339-v(2)(a) (McKinney 1989).
2. Vasilou v. The 203 Condominium, NYLJ, Oct. 19, 1990, p.23, col.1 (Civ. Ct. N.Y. Co.).
3. Four Brothers Homes at Heartland Condominium II v. Gerbino, 262 A.D.2d 279 (2d Dept. 2000).
4. Bd. of Managers of Plymouth Village Condominium v. Mahaney, 272 A.D.2d 283 (2d Dept. 2000).
5. Fe Bland v. Two Trees Management Co., 66 N.Y.2d 556 (1985).
6. 79th Street Tenants Corp. v. Brown, Harris, Stevens, Inc., 227 A.D.2d 149 (1st Dept. 1996).
7. Holt v. 45 East 66 Street Owners Corp., 161 A.D.2d 410 (1st Dept. 1990).
8. Ray v. 169 Spring Owners Corp., NYLJ, March 2, 1988, p.14, col.3 (Civ. Ct. N.Y. Co.).
9. N.Y. Bus. Corp. Law, § 501(c) (McKinney 2003).
10. Fe Bland (see note 5).
11. The amendment provided that "shares of the same class shall not be considered unequal because of variations in fees or charges payable to the corporation upon sale or transfer of shares and appurtenant proprietary leases that are provided for in proprietary leases, occupancy agreements or offering plans or properly approved amendments to the foregoing instruments." (L 1986, ch. 598, § 1).
12. Thomas v. 81-87 Owners Corp., 142 Misc.2d 237 (Civ. Ct. N.Y. Co. 1989).
13. See, e.g. Mogelescu v. 255 West 98th Street Owners Corp., 135 A.D.2d 32 (1st Dept 1988); 305 East 24th Owners Corp. v. Ruskin, NYLJ, Feb. 18, 1987, p.12, col.6 (Sup. Ct. N.Y. Co.).
14. Self v. Horatio Street Owners Corp., NYLJ, Feb. 6, 2002, p.18, col.5 (Sup. Ct. N.Y. Co.).
15. See, e.g., Badowski v. Roosevelt Terrace Cooperative, 148 A.D.2d 406 (2d Dept. 1989); Meichsner v. Valentine Gardens Cooperative, Inc. 137 A.D.2d 797 (2d Dept. 1988).
16. Zilberfein v. Palmer Terrace Cooperative, Inc., NYLJ, Nov. 12, 2003, p.21, col.1 (Sup. Ct. Westchester Co.).
17. Pomerantz v. Clearview Gardens, 77 A.D.2d 651 (2d Dept. 1980).
18. Amer v. Bay Terrace Cooperative Section II, Inc., 142 A.D.2d 704 (2d Dept. 1988).
19. See Meichsner (note 15).
20. Jamil v. Southridge Cooperative Section 4, Inc., 102 Misc.2d 404 (App. Tm. 1979), aff'd, 77 A.D.2d 822 (2d Dept. 1980).
21. See, e.g., Mogelescu (note 13); Vaughn v. Manor Towers Owners Corp., 135 A.D.2d 380 (1st Dept. 1987).

22. See, e.g., Quirin v. 123 Apartments Corp., 128 A.D.2d 360 (1st Dept.), appeal dismissed, 70 N.Y.2d 796 (1987).
23. 1326 Apartments Corp. v. Barbosa, 147 Misc.2d 264 (Civ. Ct. N.Y. Co. 1990).
24. Cooper v. Greenbriar Owners Corp., 239 A.D.2d 311 (2d Dept. 1997).
25. Oakley v. Longview Owners, Inc., 165 Misc.2d 192 (Sup. Ct. Westchester Co. 1995); See also, Marine Midland v. White Oak Cooperative Housing Corp., NYLJ, March 19, 1997, p.31, col.5 (Sup. Ct. Westchester Co. 1997) (co-op can impose waiver-of-option fee but can't restrict price at which shareholder can sell to third party).
26. 534 East Tenants Corp. v. Preheim, NYLJ, Dec. 4, 1991, p. 22, col.2 (Sup. Ct. N.Y. Co.).
27. Allen v. Murray House Owners Corp., 174 A.D.2d 400 (1st Dept. 1991).
28. Black v. Alexander House Residences, 226 A.D.2d 186 (1st Dept. 1996).
29. Chemical Bank v. 635 Park Avenue Corp., 155 Misc.2d 433 (Sup. Ct. N.Y. Co. 1992).
30. Ebner v. 91st Street Tenants Corp., 126 Misc.2d 108 (Sup. Ct. N.Y. Co. 1984).
31. Nagdimon v. Mainstay Cooperative Section Two, Inc., 158 A.D.2d 452 (2d Dept. 1990).
32. Braschi v. Stahl Associates Co., 74 N.Y.2d 201 (1989).
33. Kirkpatrick v. 60 Sutton Corp., N.Y.C. Comm. on Human Rights Complaint No. FH164032991DN, Recommended Dec. & Order (Oct. 30, 1992), aff'd as modified, Dec. & Order (Dec. 21, 1992).
34. 170 West 85 Street HDFC v. Jones, 176 Misc.2d 262 (Civ. Ct. N.Y. Co. 1998).
35. Stowe v. 19 East 88th Street, Inc., 257 A.D.2d 355 (1st Dept. 1999).
36. In re Estate of Katz, 142 Misc.2d 1073 (Surrogate's Ct. N.Y. Co. 1989).
37. Joint Queensview Housing Enterprise, Inc. v. Baloghi, 174 A.D.2d 605 (2d Dept. 1991).
38. Cavanagh v. 133-22nd St. Jackson Heights, Inc., 245 A.D.2d 481 (2d Dept. 1997).
39. Arlov v. 519 East 86th Street Tenants Corp., NYLJ, Dec. 16, 1998, p.22, col.2 (Sup. Ct. N.Y. Co.).
40. House v. Lalor, 119 Misc.2d 193 (Sup. Ct. N.Y. Co. 1983).
41. Carroll v. Eno, NYLJ, Aug. 30, 1994, p.21, col.4 (Sup. Ct. N.Y. Co.), aff'd, 237 A.D.2d 102 (1st Dept. 1997).
42. See, e.g., Maxton Builders, Inc. v. LoGalbo, 68 N.Y.2d 373 (1986).
43. Silverman v. Alcoa Plaza Associates, 37 A.D.2d 166 (1st Dept. 1971).
44. N.Y. U.C.C. § 2-718 (McKinney 2002).
45. Shulkin v. Dealy, 132 Misc.2d 371 (Sup. Ct. N.Y. Co. 1986).
46. Wojciechowski v. Birnbaum, 191 A.D.2d 247 (1st Dept. 1993).
47. Savasta v. Duffy, NYLJ, March 20, 1998, p.26, col.1 (Sup. Ct. N.Y. Co.).
48. Fleck v. Daniel, NYLJ, Sept. 5, 2000, p.26, col.5 (Sup. Ct. N.Y. Co.).
49. Blackmun v. Genova, 268 A.D.2d 547 (2d Dept. 2000).
50. Amato v. Hird, NYLJ, Sept. 11, 2002, p.18, col.3 (Sup. Ct. N.Y. Co.).
51. D'Anthony v. Lender, 262 A.D.2d 247 (1st Dept. 1999).
52. Stadtmauer v. Brel Associates IV, L.P., NYLJ, March 13, 2000, p.23 (1st Dept.); See also, Keles v. Morningside Heights Housing Corp., 8 A.D.3d 160 (1st Dept. 2004).
53. DiGiulio v. Robin, NYLJ, May 13, 2003, p.23, col.5 (S.D.N.Y.).

Index